Paper, Scissors, Rock-n-Roll

This memoir has at once all the joy and all the fears of discovering teenage freedom while learning about the reality of the world one is living in. Bill Thames's moving stories of the effect Duane and Gregg Allman had on his life in the 1960s are revealing of himself and the two brothers on many levels. We all owe Thames a warm "Thank You" for taking the time to share these stories. I will stop here and hope that you enjoy this warmly inspired work as you would an old friend!

—Tommy Talton, musician, composer,
and cofounder of the band, Cowboy

I am very enthusiastic about this new memoir written by Bill Thames! Here he shares many interesting stories that even I have never heard. Throughout this book, it is evident that Thames knows how to tell a compelling tale—with all the push and pull tension of a well-crafted song. Enjoy reading, as he takes you on the beginnings of a wild and fertile time in Southern musical history!

—Joe Bell, *Hittin' the Note Magazine*
and *Merchandise*

Bill Thames is a Renaissance man—and he truly loves music. He has a unique perspective on the beginnings of a cosmic shift in Southern American music and was there in Daytona Beach when Gregg and Duane Allman started playing in their early cover bands—and recognized their explosive talent. Thames's passion for their sound and the story of its evolution shines bright in *Paper, Scissors, Rock-n-Roll* and reminds us how extraordinary those times were for us all.

—Randall Bramblett, singer-songwriter
and multi-instrumentalist

We all have heard "the rest of the story" about famous musicians who made their mark in Southern Rock at Capricorn Studio in Macon, Georgia, but no one, to my knowledge has written about the early environment that fostered those musicians. At least not until this book. Bill Thames takes you back to when everything was a youthful adventure and there was music to be made. He knew the people, he played with them, and they were his friends. This is a story only he could tell and I'm very glad he did.

—Anathalee G. Sandlin, author, editor, publisher,
music writer, musician, and co-owner
at Duck Tape Recording Studio

In my opinion, there can never be too many books about the Allman Brothers. It seems that every new book uncovers stories I had never heard before. This book is filled with great memories of the early bands that the Allman brothers played in. It is a welcome addition to the chronicled history of Southern music. Excellent!

—Michael Buffalo Smith†, author of *The Road Goes on Forever: Fifty Years of The Allman Brothers Band Music (1969–2019)*

Take a musical trip back in time to the late 1960s, to the old bars of Daytona Beach and the campus of Clemson University, when a young man was finding his footing on the stage and in life, with the help of two young brothers who would go on to become Rock-n-Roll royalty. Bill Thames's warm prose invites you into this world and takes you along on this ride, part *Blues Brothers* mixed with some *American Graffiti*, as the times they were a-changin'. With many personal anecdotes and conversations with Duane and Gregg and comprehensive knowledge of their careers as only someone who knew them could have, this is an indispensable book for any fan of the Allmans and American musical history. It is indeed a pleasure to read.

—Benjamin J. Johnson, author and editor

MUSIC AND THE AMERICAN SOUTH

For a list of titles in the series, see the back of this book.

Paper, Scissors, Rock-n-Roll

Ringo, Duane, & Me

BILL THAMES

MERCER UNIVERSITY PRESS
Macon, Georgia

MUP/ P644

Published by Mercer University Press
1501 Mercer University Drive
Macon, Georgia 31207

26 25 24 23 22 5 4 3 2 1

Books published by Mercer University Press are printed on acid-free paper that meets the requirements of the American National Standard for Information Sciences—Permanence of Paper for Printed Library Materials.

Printed and bound in the UNITED STATES.

This book is set in ADOBE CASLON PRO.

Cover/jacket design by BURT&BURT.

ISBN 978-0-88146-846-5
Cataloging-in-Publication Data is available from the Library of Congress

Dedicated to the memory of

Nena Louise Thames and

Robert Ervin Thames,

my two siblings who left this earth too soon.

Each encouraged me to write in their own way.

MERCER UNIVERSITY PRESS

Endowed by

TOM WATSON BROWN
and
THE WATSON-BROWN FOUNDATION, INC.

Contents

Preface

Totally enthralled by my first computer back in 1995, I began to chronicle memories and interesting anecdotes with no particular objective in mind. In the beginning, my computer was simply a distraction to pass the time when business was slow, but before long it became much more. As life would have it, I lost several close friends during that same time, and out of a sense of grief, I began writing stories about one of them, my longtime friend and Rotary brother, Norm Miller. Those initial stories were written for Norm's unborn granddaughter so that she would know the fiber of the man she would never have the opportunity to meet. While working on the "Norm Miller" stories, I found writing and sharing life stories extremely gratifying.

I also began exploring the internet and eventually reached out to some of my musical heroes in an attempt to convey how much their music had meant to me over the years. During this time, I discovered that there were many thousands of like-minded people in cyberspace, especially those enthralled and enamored with The Allman Brothers Band and all of their affiliated musical entities. Included in this large group of devotees was an interesting brotherhood of Allman Brothers fans who gathered yearly in Macon, Georgia, called GABBA (Georgia Allman Brothers Band Association). Plans were made, and my wife, Patti, and I decided, in 2003, to attend one of their gatherings: that weekend was life changing!

On our last morning in Macon, Patti and I journeyed out to Rose Hill Cemetery to visit my old friend Duane Allman's gravesite. Reading Duane's grave marker was an epiphany, and I knew right on the spot exactly which direction my writing was taking me...but I never dreamed how much fun and how exciting that journey would become.

I wrote a few articles for GABBA and *Hittin' the Web*, The Allman Brothers online magazine, and it was there that I found my voice. While working full time at my own business I wrote magazine articles as well as music and CD reviews, mostly about Allman Brothers-related musicians, and I also added photography and graphics to my talents. In the meantime, I continued working on my stories about Duane Allman; Betty Jean Pendleton, better known as Ringo; and the vibrant 1960s Daytona Beach music scene. I wrote from up-close, personal experience just how riveting and important Duane and his musicianship was to the world. My band was front and center to witness much of the developmental years of Duane and

Gregg Allman, dating back to 1964, a time when I believe Duane already sensed that he was on a supercharged trajectory to stardom. Duane knew early on that he was going to prevail, but he also knew that it would surely take years of continuous struggle. Still, if he followed his dream, and the music in those dreams, he could only succeed where so many others fell by the wayside.

As the '60s rolled on, my high school band followed closely behind Duane and Gregg and played many of the same teen dance halls and nightclubs in Daytona Beach and the surrounding area. We stayed in closer contact with the Allman Joys than most of the other local bands because of our common connection to the Martinique and to Ringo, the club's perennial manager. Ringo was always our common thread. After the Allman Joys morphed into the Hour Glass, we opened for them when they came back to town. When my band, the Soul Patrol, became the house band at the Martinique, Duane and Gregg would often simply stop by to jam with us. However, if truth be known, the real attraction for Duane and Gregg was always Ringo. Ringo was a second mother to every musician worth his salt to ever set foot in the Martinique, and she was always at the club when we were there.

Acknowledgments

First and foremost, I thank my wife, Patti Thames, who persisted with me unwaveringly during this long process and never allowed me to throw in the towel regardless of how often I felt compelled to do so. Patti somehow found the strength to reread these chapters when even I couldn't. A huge thank you to Ann Sandlin, who kept me moving by reminding me that I was the one who started the "P.A.D." club and who kept my nose to the grindstone. Thanks especially to Professor Reggie Williams who gave me the P.A.D. idea and made it sound so simple.

A very special heartfelt thank you to my proofreading army during this process: Katy Wilkes, Lee Phillips, Mark Mangum, Joe Bell, and Ann Sandlin. A special thank you to Lee Phillips, Russell Atwell, Kip Marshall, and Marcia Cassel Ford, who so generously chronicled our journey with photographs. There are so many who pushed and prodded me to complete this project that it is impossible for me to begin to thank them all, and I know I'm leaving someone out: Liz Parsons, Reuben Morgan, Danny Randolph, Jim Jacobs, Danny Ramsey, John Howard, Renee Littlewood, Skoots Lyndon, Barb Hilke, and Dave Pierson, who never tired of hearing my stories and kept on me to finish my book. And finally, to my original bandmates and musician friends, who truly understand that a book like this comes from a place in my heart that most who never played will ever fully understand: Ralph Bundy, Kip Marshall, Carl Persis, Charlie Simpson, Tim O'Brien, Ross Yost, Scott Stanley, Mike Wilson, Cecil Johnston, and Jay Laing. A special thanks to Tommy Talton, who inspired me by his words and actions to be the best I could be, and to Steve Conn for teaching me that "gut wrenching" is a good thing. And also to Randall Bramblett for the music that allowed my mind to wander and these words to flow.

Author's Note

Of Perspective, Point of View, and Memoir

Perspective and point of view—two terms commonly misconstrued and confused. Point of view is the vantage point from which a story is told. The events of the story are told by a character or outside observer. The focus here is who is telling the story. Perspective is a narrator's attitudes or beliefs about an event, person, or place based on their own personal experiences. Perspective focuses on how the story is told. Perspective is most often personal while point of view is how we presume others should react to, or relate to, certain situations.

The higher one rises, the more one's frame of reference expands, and the more that becomes included within one's point of view. Perspective embraces tone, awareness, and attitude. Awareness of one's own perspective is the lamp that lights the pathway to point of view. Long resting in Rose Hill Cemetery, Duane Allman inspired the chorus of words and personal point of view that follows. They include my personal memoir and are part and parcel of my own memories, related directly to my own unique perspective.

A memoir is an intimate, penetrating form in this age of digital information. It is a curiously human-paced experience, demonstrating the way one's mind works and how ideas develop and unfold throughout a particular time. History volumes are linear in form and, more often than not, barren of empathy and emotion. The diary of a person's heart, blindly struggling through his or her awkwardness and personal history, is jarringly different. Prolonged engagement in another's spirit begs empathy, and empathy is a commodity that has become extraordinarily rare.

Paper, Scissors, Rock-n-Roll

Prologue

Music at the Speed of Life

As a young teenager, my closest friends were bandmates and other musicians who watched as a local hotshot guitar player, Duane Allman, danced on the edge of a cliff, blindfolded, while wearing Satan's bowling shoes. Duane's younger brother, Gregg, danced near that edge too, but he danced with Beatle boots, and his blindfold peeled back just a bit. We could feel that Duane and Gregg were on the brink of launching themselves into stardom, and it became more apparent every time they walked out on a local stage. With a mix of great adolescent interest and nervous trepidation, we continued watching as Duane danced closer to the precipice. Like race fans at the Daytona 500, apprehensive of a Fireball Roberts-style ending, we knew full well that Duane possessed a temperament that provoked drifting ever closer to the cliff's edge and the rocky chasm below.

If here, Duane would tell you not to postpone anything. He would tell you that you should embrace life because you are only allotted a certain amount of time, and the stage lights can flicker and dim at any moment...as they did for Duane and so many other heroes and idols from my youth.

We will never stop missing Duane Allman. Never again will I wake up and queue the newest recording by Duane, as I did so many times in my teens and early twenties. There will never be a new musical genre envisioned by Duane, and pushed into fruition by his bandmates, whomever they might have been. There won't be another new generation of albums made sweeter, or given guidance by his delicate touch and crystalline vision. There won't be new stories, just the old stories, and the inevitable question to which there is no answer: "What if?"

Duane Allman cannot be replaced, though many have made it their life's ambition to duplicate the unmatchable. Occasionally, I'll overhear a young guitar buck with a touch so soft and a tone so clear that it jerks my head around...but it's never really Duane...not really. This has happened to me a dozen times, and each time, there is a glimmer there, but somehow it's just not quite the same. There is an unfillable void on the stage where Duane once stood. His impact on me and my friends was monumental. Duane was there for us when music began to take root in our hearts, and we watched as he picked up speed and became more and more famous, and more and more reckless. Fame was, to Duane, just a state of mind. He imagined us all as just humans traveling the same path as equals. Some had more jingle in their pockets, some had more musical ability. Some could afford to buy better equipment, and some had more experience. Others were Black, Brown, long-haired, or preppy, but to Duane, we were all the same as far as his outlook and acceptance was concerned.

Duane promoted and fostered this life philosophy. On the other hand, he also believed that life made little or no sense. A person can organize his life and force it to make sense in his own personal timeline, believing achievement is everything. But the best-laid plans are so often thwarted by time. Duane knew that everything is fleeting, that you can draw a map of the future that you are happy with, but it can all go up in flames in an instant if you dance too close to the edge.

Duane never postponed anything. He was a man in constant motion, drawing, revising, and navigating his own map. Duane Allman lived his life on the edge, the same way that he played guitar—music at the speed of life.

Chapter 1

Sweeping Out the Ashes (My Bio)

Some adventures never end, and in some cases, the road actually does go on forever. My musical adventure began at the ripe old age of six, while exploring the magnificent mountains and deserts behind my home on the army base at the government's ballistics proving ground at Fort Huachuca, Arizona. In 1958, my friends and I neutralized deadly rattlesnakes with sticks and Wham-O Slingshots, picked up and collected spent ammunition and artillery shells, and threw rocks (from a distance) at live hand grenades and mortars. Fort Huachuca was bordered on one side by the Huachuca mountain range and on the other by a vast desert wasteland which served the army as a proving ground for the precursors to today's stealth drones and incredibly accurate and deadly Tomahawk missiles. Saturday mornings at the off-base skating rink, I learned early lessons about racial bias, bigotry, and self-defense when the local Apache Indian kids did their best to relieve me of my equilibrium with their elbows. Other than dealing with my own personal "Custer's Last Stand" and being sprayed by a skunk on my screen porch while "sleeping out" with my guard dog, I experienced a relatively uneventful but adventuresome first grade. My family had placed me into a habitat that revealed everything an intrepid six- or seven-year-old boy who loved the outdoors could possibly want. I could hunt, fish, target shoot, collect rocks and cactus, explore, watch rockets and missiles lift off, and view the massive monthly military parades that filed directly in front of my home. I even had my very own pet crow that lived above the orderlies' quarters behind our adobe brick home that sat directly facing the parade field. There was more than enough benign trouble to get involved in, and my particular group of army brat friends were keen on finding trouble where they could, and especially keen about not being caught by the MPs.

My perception of the world tightened instantly from childish to serious one afternoon when I passed by my older sister's bedroom and heard the peerless voice of Elvis Presley crooning "I Can't Help Falling In Love With You" coming from her portable 45-rpm record player. My sister, Nena, was eleven years my senior, and she was a full-tilt, incoming high school senior when we moved to Arizona. Nena was a normal, well-adjusted high school teenager in most respects with the exception that she made straight As all the time, every time; worked as a writer and editor on the school paper; and was a regular contributor for *The Tombstone Epitaph* in Tombstone, Arizona, a few miles away. Because she used the family car to get back and forth to her job in Tombstone, the car radio vacillated between her favorite local rock and roll station and my father's favorite Patsy Cline-tinged country station. The night of my Elvis epiphany, I scanned the available stations with my pocket transistor radio for something I liked. When happy with what I had found, I slid that radio beneath my pillow so I could listen to the music until the wee hours while pretending to sleep. I was never caught.

In Arizona, my love for music developed and simmered for the next three years while I took both violin and piano lessons and listened to as much Elvis and Buddy Holly as I could find. Unfortunately, Arizona proved not to be the hotbed of music that I was yearning for, but we weren't stationed there but for three more years. We moved in the middle of my third-grade year back to our original home in Arlington, Virginia, where my father had permanent offices in the Pentagon as well as in the Army Combat Surveillance Agency.

The move back to Virginia from Arizona was fortuitous since shortly after I moved, my gang of friends set fire to the mountain behind our houses and burned the entire face of the mountain from the service road up to the firebreak that ran along the mountain ridge. It was a huge mountain, and the photographs I saw of the resulting blaze, all black and charred, were hard to look at. If my family had not moved at the exact time that we did, I surely would have been a willing participant, if not the one holding the matches.

After only two years back in Virginia, we moved to Fort Monmouth, New Jersey, for another short time. Fort Monmouth is located just south of New York City but close enough to Philadelphia that I learned to dance the twist and the pony to Chubby Checker, and slow danced breathlessly with Kathy Sabo, the daughter of a throaty master sergeant on base. It was also there that I settled on piano lessons for a time. And it was at Fort Monmouth where my father retired from the army as a highly decorated brigadier general in the Signal Corps. Seeming like a family of nomads, we eventually moved back to our home base in Arlington, Virginia, just long enough to sell the house there and for me to take up reed instruments in the band at Swanson Junior High in Arlington.

One evening at dinner my father announced that he had been offered two jobs to consider in order to continue his career. One job was as a manager in Minnesota, working for Westinghouse Electric Corporation, and the other was as a consultant for General Electric's Apollo Support Division in Daytona Beach, Florida. My father asked the family what we thought, and after much discussion, I told everyone that it didn't matter to me where the family decided to move but to forward my mail to Daytona Beach. The discussion ended for me with the word "Beach." Soon we were packing our furniture and belongings for what would be my family's final move together.

My music appreciation finally exploded into full bloom with our resettlement to Daytona Beach in 1962. I had been a surfer, like most kids in my beachside neighborhood, until the afternoon in 1964 I heard a band called the Escorts play, after which nothing was ever quite the same for me again. To say the least, watching and hearing a young Duane and Gregg Allman perform that day, when the Escorts played both before and after a showing of Bruce Brown's *The Endless Summer* surf movie, was nothing short of life changing. After hearing Duane and Gregg's band that afternoon, I left my surfboard virtually untouched in a friend's garage, turned in my Seabreeze High School football uniform after my junior varsity season, and rode my skateboard down our steep driveway one last time, all before Thanksgiving became Christmas.

My musical hayride through the '60s was a journey of such righteousness that showing up and simply occupying a space in time was not an option. The '60s unfolded before me like fruit from an abandoned orange grove; sweet and free for the picking. From the instant that the first rabid teenager waved a bare-skinned farewell to their past, everything after entered a shadowy, nebulous zone, replete with incomparable music.

The music scene in and around Daytona Beach has always been a bottomless cocktail of equal parts joy and chaos, as fertile a mixture of capability and inventiveness as was any other region in the American South. Duane and Gregg Allman, Pete Carr, Johnny Sandlin, Paul Hornsby, Tommy Talton, Scott Boyer, Lenny Leblanc, and a host of other visionary musicians pushed and stretched local boundaries until there was nowhere for this boundless musical pressure to vent. Until, that is, the formation of The Allman Brothers Band.

Duane's guitar screamed like a hellish banshee in the middle of the night one minute and then cried real tears, as pure and soft as any from a baby, the next. Gregg's voice could sooth you and lull a person into indifference one minute, and then in a moment of sublime change, he could growl and scream with a backwoods, gravel-road dialect that would command immediate attention to him, and only him. Even as the Hour Glass was challenging Liberty Records for the authority to write and record their own brand of music, the march down the road toward The Allman Brothers was already well on its way and utterly unstoppable. The members of the Hour Glass became, for us, administration and faculty in our musical microcosm for the next seven years.

The mid- to late '60s was an incredible time to be a young musician in Daytona Beach. The local Central Florida music scene was beyond anything I could have ever imagined, and it was only going to get better. A parade of talented musicians exploded out of Daytona Beach from the four local high schools. Talented musicians and singers were finding one another and developing bands as diverse as the neighborhoods from which they came. With a few notable exceptions, nobody was better than anyone else, and nobody was trying to one-up anyone else. These talented musicians turned out on a level playing field that was nurtured by sun, surf, and the brothers Allman.

The beach sand that blew onto Main Street could blister bare feet in the noonday sun. By late afternoon, that same beach sand cooled to a comfortable level, aided by the evening breeze that rolled in faithfully off the Atlantic waves. Coming of age in a time and place circumscribed by surf, sand, waves, and music was as wondrous an experience as can possibly be imagined.

With the Beatles leading the British Invasion of radios all across America, many high school musicians took up arms in defense of their turf in the form of guitars, keyboards, and percussion. My friends from school, who always met at the beach on Friday nights, guitars in hand, for a sing-along hootenanny, were no different. All learning, playing, and singing the favorite hits of the day, we evolved slowly into a band that went from neophyte to professional as we wove our way conscientiously through the minefield that was our high school years.

While most of the musicians in my band graduated with honors, during our senior year in high school we created music on stages across the states of Florida and Georgia for more than two hundred unforgettable nights. Then, like shutting off the closing-time lights in a nightclub for good, we all went our separate ways in August of 1968 to colleges all across the South. However, we each took something important and deep-seated with us in our hearts when we left town. We had succeeded beyond our wildest imaginations and had done what only a handful of musicians ever do: we made it into the spotlight and then left everything but a burning memory behind.

There's a tendency in life to remember the last meal or the last movie as the best one ever, but that's rarely true with music. Our experiences were spread smoothly and evenly over a five-year period. I still remember our first concert at Peabody Auditorium in front of a sold-out audience, as well as our last night playing together as a band at the Martinique Club on Wild Olive Avenue in Daytona Beach.

Fast-forward thirty years, and my musical journey would find me sitting behind my first computer screen in a quiet corner in my business that sustained my family for forty years. At that time, in 1995, I had not played professionally but a handful of times since putting away my drum kit in 1972, but my interest in and devotion to music and the music community never wavered. It was there, in front of my first computer, that my journey took a curious dogleg to the left as two previously unexplored worlds suddenly became available to me: writing and digital photography.

A notoriously miserable speller, but decent typist, the significance of a typewriting machine pointing out and actually correcting my misspellings as I typed a word was earthshaking. Along with writing becoming a much simpler task, a longtime hobby and art form, photography, reblossomed before me. For years I had shot film, and as computers enveloped the photography industry, an interesting niche appeared to me. Before computers and digital photography, a photographer had to change an entire roll of film in order to move easily from one light source or brightness to another. With the advent of digital photography, simple changes only needed to be made on the camera itself to cover a myriad of light sources as well as brightness and colors. This in itself rendered music photography simpler and less invasive. No more glaring strobe light exploding in a musician's face in order to get a great photograph, never mind the fact that correcting and printing a photograph now took only minutes instead of hours or days like before.

In time, my love for music and writing melded as I began writing music articles and regular album reviews, supplementing my writing with photographs and graphics. With these changes in artistic mindset also came a yearning to chronicle my life's experiences, coupled with the extraordinary musical paths my life had crossed over the years, complete with stories and anecdotes. So, I dug in and my new musical direction proved luminous, cathartic, and redemptive, everything that fried chicken, mashed potatoes, and gravy promised to be. My memoirs became a labor of love, but then seemed to drag on forever.

As I drifted ever closer to the terminus of this project, I came to the realization that the central reason it had taken me so long to complete this book is that I really enjoy immersing into that extraordinary time. I so enjoyed returning to a time in my life so full of fun and friends and music that I found myself lingering there more and more often. I dawdled longer each time I crossed into that magical realm. Eventually, I found myself becoming concerned that when I finished writing these pages it might not be as easy and convenient to simply return to that time and place again.

Then I began to muse, what if one day my wife comes into my office to discover my computer on, with a steaming cup of coffee next to the keyboard, and I have vanished to the past...I will have finally discovered that one magical keystroke that unlocks all the doors, and I will have transported myself back to 1964, or '65, or '66, or '67, or '68, or '69, permanently. I'm not so sure that if I could return to that time I would ever find my way back home again. That's the way that we each become truly lost.

It is my sincere ambition that these pages transport you, too, back to those times, and that you can relive some of those stories with me, or that you can at least ride along in the car next to me and gaze through the window of my life. Possibly, we will run into each other sitting on a blanket, back in the shade of a pecan tree, at the Atlanta Pop Festival over the Fourth of July weekend of 1970. Or maybe we will find ourselves sitting in with the same small band in some smoky nightclub, playing our hearts out for an appreciative audience, after which we will become friends for life.

If not for this book, one day this will all become an insignificant speck on the surface of my rearview mirror, and then it will disappear behind me forever, as the next owner of my car cleans the glass. I want—actually, I need—to make certain that these memories continue to roll down the highway forever. If not, we will both become lost.

Thankfully, one Monday morning, sitting at my living room coffee table while a Buffalo Springfield recording was playing some of my favorite music, and the next-door neighbor was chipping merrily away at resurfacing his swimming pool, I completed the final pages of *Paper, Scissors, Rock and Roll: Ringo, Duane, and Me*. We'll sweep out the ashes later...

Chapter 2

Ringo, Duane, and Me

Until my family's move to Daytona Beach, Florida, in 1962, my musical education consisted of hour after hour of lifeless music lessons and what seemed like decades of repetitious practicing. Moving to Florida happened between my seventh and eighth grade years of junior high school, at a time when the magic of music had only just begun to empower young people. Music permeated our culture in a way it had never done before. Music was central to our lives, and the music groups of our day led us to new lands, opening our minds to new ways of living. Our entertainers showed us that we didn't have to walk in our parents' shoes anymore.

1962 was the year my music education and my appreciation for music began to interfuse. The junior high band lost my attention, and I saved lawn-mowing money and bought a reasonably priced Harmony guitar that I could take to beach parties and strum with classmates. My family and I had moved from Virginia to Florida's middle child. Daytona Beach was neither the introverted upper peninsula of the Sunshine State nor the extroverted southern coastline. My parents had dropped my family onto the Goldilocks of the Florida coast...it was just right. Daytona Beach is where I eventually swapped years of music lessons (and one slightly used Harmony archtop guitar) for a set of blue sparkle Ludwig drums, purchased at Manny's Music Store in New York City in 1965.

The fledgling band that I had been a part of for many months began to flourish in the midpoint of that decade. My ever-tightening group of musical friends had grandiose aspirations but little or no equipment to this point. During 1965 we made a concerted effort to upgrade our ragtag equipment roster, and as a result of those upgrades, the band began to develop aggressively. The harder we practiced, the more work we got, and the more work we had, the more apt we were to spend some of that green on new equipment. It was no coincidence that our band's explosive growth sandwiched itself neatly between the releases of the first two movies by the Beatles: *A Hard Day's Night*, released on July 4th of 1964, and *Help*, which was released on August 25th of 1965. The release of those two movies empowered literally thousands of teenage garage bands across the US. Our enthusiastic group of local wannabe musicians was riding high on the crest of that wave.

Looking back on those years, I consider my musical journey through the '60s a voyage of high-minded spirituality. Along with my bandmates, I was thrust into a musical world vastly different from that of other teenage musicians across the United States. To regularly rub elbows with the likes of Duane and Gregg Allman, Johnny Sandlin, Paul Hornsby, Pete Carr, Lee Hazen, Jim Matherly, Tommy Ruger, Sylvan Wells, and Ted Conners kindled a spark and ignited a yearning to replicate what we were hearing from our mentors. Daytona Beach during the mid- to late 1960s was a prodigious place to practice one's craft, and for a young musician, the music scene in Daytona Beach was just about as good as it got.

In those days, the music scene in and around Daytona Beach was an extraordinary combination of competence and inventiveness. The blossoming of music in my hometown was unlike any other location in the South. Along with Duane and Gregg Allman, Jim Matherly, Pete Carr, and Lenny LeBlanc seemingly appeared out of thin air, pushing and stretching Daytona's musicality nightly, combining a rich mixture of rock, blues, and sweet country music. Still developing musically during his formative years, Duane's guitar screamed one minute and wept like a wounded bird the next. He easily coaxed ecstasy or agony from his guitar, transitioning on the downbeat. Duane's brother, Gregg, could yield similar melodic extremes from his voice and showed an early knack for penning words in a fashion consonant to his brother's guitar work.

Coming of age as a high school senior and musician in Daytona Beach, shadowed by those musical greats, was an experience equaled by only a few. My bandmates, who became my closest friends, were, to the man, fully aware of the gumbo that simmered around us. We all realized that we would be hard-pressed to develop near their talent, but just being in the presence of Duane and Gregg Allman made us strive to be the best that we could be. Duane was quick to offer encouragement, and we were happy to gather around him to drink in his advice and to file away his gems with our other life lessons.

High school graduation sent my bandmates in different directions, but whether in our dorm rooms at college or from various jobs, we all followed, to some degree, the careers of Duane and Gregg, Jim Matherly, Pete Carr, Lenny LeBlanc, and that whole group of local standouts as they continued to distance themselves from the rank and file. Some of us stopped in the coming years to visit or gain summer employment at the

Martinique, where the Soul Patrol finished its last months as the house band in August of 1968.

It was at the Martinique that Ringo, the perennial manager, would catch me up on the latest comings and goings of the local musicians, as well as those who were on a rocket trajectory toward the stars. Visiting Ringo in Daytona Beach was a much-anticipated diversion from the lackluster existence I had been enduring in the music-bare foothills of rural Clemson, South Carolina, during my freshman year.

Many students at Clemson University were suspicious, if not downright frightened, of the '60s. With my years in nightclubs, involved with musicians and witnessing as much drug usage as I had in my high school, I welcomed the hippie counterculture that spilled over to backcountry Clemson from Atlanta with open arms. My old boss and friend Ringo was my bridge from South Carolina to Haight-Ashbury, and she also kept me in touch with my musical heroes from afar.

Ringo was an engaging, resourceful, and fashionably clad young woman in her late twenties when we first became friends. Two opposing forces continually burned within her mind—one, through the circumstances of her employment, pulled her gently back; the other, through the influence of the music she had heard and the acquaintances she had made, pushed her forward. Those opposing forces were apparent in her speech and manner, which were degraded somewhat by her environment but improved significantly by her understanding of music and people. Ringo was fidgety and nervous, terribly talkative, and had a habit of picking up things within easy reach and fiddling with them while she was speaking.

Ringo's heart was ablaze with curiosity and music fueled that blaze. A musician could not come into or leave the Martinique without it becoming her knowledge. She attired herself almost entirely in tight-fitting, hip-hugger, bell-bottom blue jeans in those days. Halter tops, cinched in the front with a knot, accented her gentle curves, and beach-ready flip flops slapped loudly as she walked with intention through the club. Ringo's shining russet hair parted neatly in the center and fell gently and evenly, barely reaching her shoulders, accentuating the eagerness in her smile and the fearless wonder in her eyes. Ringo's voice bore the gentle dust of Southern backroads. But when she clamored to explain the latest music from Duane and Gregg Allman, as she often did, her voice took on the characteristics of a NASCAR radio announcer describing the finishing-line confusion of a three-abreast finish. Ringo sometimes got so excited it appeared she could carry both sides of the conversation without drawing air.

Ringo taught those who would learn from her much about valuing friendships, fairness, and emotional devotion. Along with universal people skills, Ringo taught me the proper and improper way to mop a floor...a talent lost on most males. Ringo's teetering relationship with club owner Bill Cook gave her reason to spill her guts to close friends, and I was lucky enough to be a shoulder to cry on and the occasional "Rum-ing" buddy.

When Ringo had endured enough of Cook's chauvinistic male nonsense, and I was simultaneously having problems of the heart, Ringo and I would, on occasion, go "Rum-ing." Ringo coined the term, which simply meant we would buy a bottle of Bacardi Rum, a few mixers and snacks, and stay awake all night long at a friend's apartment, commiserating with each other until the sun came up and the bottle of rum was empty. We chose to never return with a half-empty bottle of Bacardi. These Rum-ing sessions were cathartic and purely platonic in nature. A better friend could not be had.

Ringo lived her life well with no regrets, but circumstances dictated that she never had children of her own to raise. I often wondered if that was why she watched over all of us like the mother hen she never was. Certainly, though, she loved and nurtured all of her musician children and looked after us with a keen mother's eye and loving heart.

All of the musicians who played at the Martinique over the years will attest that we each owe Ringo an enormous debt of gratitude for the way she treated us with warmth, kindness, and understanding. She loved all of her bands and musicians, but Duane and Gregg were her two favorite children. And it was obvious to us all that Ringo had her favorites; she had a very special place in her heart for those two brothers, and she still does.

Duane was like the prodigal child to Ringo, always in some kind of trouble, but with a talent she couldn't quantify. Ringo sat back and watched Duane grow like an aggressive vine, taking over stage after stage and filling the air with his uniqueness.

Gregg was Ringo's handsome problem child who constantly dodged trouble with his good looks and savoir faire. Gregg's predisposition for enjoying dessert before dinner also worried and perplexed Ringo. Much of her time was centered on keeping Gregg clean and somewhat sober.

Both boys were drawn to the Martinique because of their love for

Ringo and the music scene there. Duane was also drawn by the acoustics of that grand old wooden building. For Gregg, the tug was the barmaids. It was always the barmaids.

Ringo grew up in Daytona Beach as Betty Jean Pendleton, the daughter of a Daytona Speedway security officer, but she was undeniably and unquestionably Ringo. Her name was not derived from the stage name of the famous Beatles drummer, Ringo Starr, but from her love of the shiny baubles that she sported on every finger (and most toes). "Ringo" served her as first, middle, and surname. To myself and the few who really knew her well she was, and is, referred to lovingly as "Rings." She was six years my senior when we met, but as we both matured, those six years felt less and less divisional. We were both driven by a burgeoning love for music, and, unlike most, our flames never burned out. Ringo and I lived to hear notes played pure and easy.

I can't remember a time during the eight or ten years that I worked at the Martinique, which became the Wreck Bar during my tenure, when Ringo did not work somewhere in that stately old building. She collected admission at the front door, tended bar, mopped the floors, did maintenance, cleaned urinals, and she even replaced toilets. Her plumbing expertise was necessitated by annual New Year's Eve tomfoolery that traditionally included the flushing of M-80s and cherry bombs into the antique plumbing system. However, Ringo's primary job was to spread unity and love through the power of music. She did that flawlessly while simultaneously earning money for the club.

Only eleven days after Ringo's twenty-sixth birthday, on October 29, 1971, Duane Allman's death became the grim new reality. Ringo and I both still loved music after that day, but it was never quite the same for either of us. I would never drive up to the back parking lot of the Martinique and be pleasantly surprised to see Duane and Gregg's gray Delta 88 parked there ever again. I knew that I would never walk through the back door of the Martinique to be met by those sublime throwaway licks that Duane would coax from his fretboard while warming up. Not ever again. Just like that, it was all over.

For me, dealing with Duane's death was like watching a huge oak sprout from a seedling into a mighty tree in one's front yard, and then opening the door to discover that the once-magnificent tree had been savagely hacked down and removed overnight, without a sound. The only things left to prove it had been there were the leaves and chips, like the sessions and recordings that Duane left us. My first reaction was, "How much taller and stronger would that tree have grown, and how many more devotees would that tree have drawn under its shade?"

As soon as I heard about Duane's death, I tried through the night to call Rings, but nobody at the Martinique picked up the telephone, which was beyond the pale. When I finally got Ringo on the phone the next afternoon, she recounted the way she had heard the terrible news. Not even able to give her a consolatory hug, what had been a gut-wrenching night for both of us began to unfold from her perspective, 450 miles from my apartment in South Carolina.

Ringo began explaining, "Someone in the band that was playing that night, I don't remember who it was, had heard the news somehow and announced from the stage that Duane Allman was dead. I ran full tilt from the front of the club to the stage and snatched the microphone away from him and told him I wouldn't have that in my club, and if he wanted to know anything about Duane or Gregg to ask *me* or Bill Cook."

Ringo continued, "I couldn't believe that he'd say anything like that from my stage. It wasn't long, though, before I learned from others that he was right. My heart sank and my knees just got all numb and weak and I just couldn't stop crying, couldn't stop sobbing. It was awful, it was just the worst night of my life. That night we closed the club early, and Bill put me in the car and drove me around all night and let me cry myself out. It was the only time he ever did that. In all those years, he never closed the club for any reason. Bill really respected Duane."

Then I recounted to Ringo how I had heard the news: "I was driving from Simpsonville, South Carolina, toward the town of Clemson that afternoon on I-85 after picking up Laurel Blackwell, my date for the weekend. We were driving along listening to my radio play 'Layla,' and I told Laurel that she would probably not believe me but that I knew the musician playing guitar on that song. In fact, I knew him real well. I was right, she didn't believe me...but why should she? When 'Layla's' piano coda and Duane's dazzling slide guitar trailed off there was an unusually long, unnatural silence on the radio. The deejay finally spoke, and as he cleared his throat, he starkly announced that Duane Allman, the man who had played that beautiful slide guitar on Eric Clapton's song 'Layla,' had died earlier that afternoon in a motorcycle accident in Macon, Georgia. I carefully pulled my car to the side of the highway and put the transmission into park, wordlessly. After a few minutes of me staring blankly at the barren countryside around us, it was then that Laurel began to understand that I did indeed know that man who was playing that guitar. I tried to soldier on but I wasn't much company that night or for the rest of the weekend, for that matter."

Some years later, when I told Ringo about Stacey, Gregg's wife, and how she looked after Gregg and helped keep him clean, Ringo confided, "I used to hate it when Gregg would come into town and stop by the club. Everyone wanted to give him drugs. They were all trying to buy his friendship. I used to lock him up in the apartment over the club to keep them away from him."

Over the years, I've thought a lot about the night I learned about Duane's accident, the way I reacted to the grief and the depression like no other, which wrapped around me tightly. I've even thought about how sad and lifeless the trees in South Carolina looked that day, as they cried their brown tears of fall. Duane was my first peer to be taken in an accident. Making matters worse, I always felt he held more promise than anyone I had passed in my orbit. I thought I knew how to handle his passing but I was wrong. It was not like losing an aunt or uncle who had grown old. Duane's death left an empty spot that begged questions with no answers.

Not long ago I reread an interview with Duane that included a conversation between him and his bandmates after a concert at Littlejohn Coliseum at Clemson University. I had attended that concert just weeks before Duane's death, and I had kept a copy of the student newspaper, *The Tiger*, as a keepsake all these years. The article contained some ominously haunting quotes from Duane and Dickey. That article caused me to immediately flash back to growing up in Daytona, and moved my mind slowly forward from there. I came full circle, joining my own story and Ringo's, who was equally hard hit by Duane's passing. Rereading that article reminded me once more how savagely Ringo had gotten the news. I can only imagine how difficult it was for her to get past the longest day in her life. Duane's death rattled every one of my music friends and everyone on Main Street in Daytona. We were all affected deeply and took Duane's death to heart. Not one of my musical cohorts ever listened to music quite the same way again after that night, not one.

There was always the one looming question going forward from which all the rest sprang forth..."What If?" The endless mental queries with no answers were all that inevitably followed:

What if...Duane had taken his bike in to have the throttle repaired, as Dickey recommended the night of the Clemson University concert?

What if...Duane had left the birthday party ten seconds earlier, or ten seconds later?

What if...a single traffic light had kept him from meeting that truck in that intersection on that day?

What if...it had rained that day and Duane had not been on his bike in that intersection at all?

And what if...after all the questions, Duane's accident was predestined, and there would simply be another day, another time, or another truck in some other intersection?

And certainly there would follow a hundred other questions, so glaring but with no better answers:

How would the next Allman Brothers albums be different if Duane had been playing on them?

Where would Duane's ghost lead The Allman Brothers sound into the future?

Would the band's music become more jazzy and horn-infused, as Duane intended, or would the band become more country-oriented or delve deeper into the blues?

So many questions thrown against the wall, and only time will tell what sticks and what does not. After fifty years of endless discussion and debate, most of the questions that have been posed in relation to the "what ifs" remain unanswerable, but not all. The music that came after Duane's death speaks for itself.

I hesitate going forward because I will regret sounding like my father, like everyone's father, and also an awful lot like Duane might if he were here. This is where I am reminded that Duane would insist not to postpone anything. He would insist we devour life because we are here for such a short time and it can end at any moment, as it did for him.

Duane Allman will never be forgotten. He simply cannot be replaced for me or for those of my close friends who understand his music and what it took for him to get to the place where he was when he died. There is a huge chasm where Duane's life played out, not only for me but for so many others...so many who were not even born when he died.

Duane had an effect on all of us; he was there for me and my friends, providing us direction as we developed musically. In those formative years, fame was only a far-distant concept, a condition of possibilities. We were all musicians working the same stage, trying not to trip over the guitar chords and cables, equal in so many respects. We all shared a common outlook. Still, Duane had so much more of himself to give.

The one and only truth, as my friend Steve Conn wrote, is that you will never see a hearse with a luggage rack. You can do your best to organize life and to make it linear. Most lifetimes are spent believing achievement is everything, but the best-laid plans can be dashed by something as simple as a faulty throttle cable. Everything is temporary. You can chart a map to the future, but those plans can easily blow out the window of an eastbound truck entering the intersection of Hillcrest Avenue and Bartlett in Macon, Georgia.

For Ringo and Duane, whose gentle kindness, fierce resolve, and undying love for their compatriots have touched more people in more ways than they could ever know.

Chapter 3

Main Street Dreams

For more than fifty-five years, Daytona Beach and its legendary Main Street neighborhood existed within me essentially as a magnificent, romantic dream. I left early one August morning in 1968 bound for college and only sporadically visited that boulevard thereafter. As the months and years turned gradually into decades, my visits to Main Street became less and less routine, and my memories chronologically less vivid. If during my waking hours I became aware of Gregg Allman crooning through a set of stereo speakers, or saw a young, long-haired hippie seemingly lost in a faraway city, or encountered some thoughtlessly exaggerated photograph of Duane Allman playing guitar, I would instantly be transported back to the community and the era that changed my life permanently.

In my reoccurring Main Street dream, I am always eighteen, my wavy brown hair is beginning to trail down to my shoulders, my body is still lean, and I am a drummer in one of the finest rock and soul bands in Central Florida. In my dream, it is always midsummer along Main Street, where warm breezes paint the town nightly with heavy wetness, fanned in from the cresting Atlantic waves. My bell-bottom jeans, flowered shirts, and Beatles boots define me as a late-teen hippie and musician. I assume the knowing, streetwise persona of a California-style musician and surfer kid, far from Huntington Beach. The truth of the matter is that I know almost nothing of the world beyond the military bases that I grew up on and the beach town where I now live.

In fragments of that dream, the Vietnam War rages vaguely somewhere in far-off Southeast Asia. The *Daytona Beach Morning News Journal* tells us that American support for the war in Vietnam took a huge hit after the Tet Offensive. There will never again be even the slightest glimpse of American strategic success on that loathsome peninsula in the confusing years to come. In the meantime, I while away summer nights as the drummer in a band called the Soul Patrol. We work every Sunday afternoon hosting a jam session at the Blind Pig on Mason Avenue in Daytona Beach. The other six nights we work as the house band in a mammoth nightclub nestled on the southeast corner of Main Street and Wild Olive Avenue known for decades as the Martinique.

In my Main Street dream, I am in a constant state of excitement. At eighteen, I resist the discipline of my soon-to-be-former high school; I loathe its racism and the unspoken tradition that forces so many Blacks to serve only as athletes, cooks, or janitors. As our senior year nears its end, teachers are on strike and most students are sympathetic to the teachers, and some, like myself, help stage student walkouts. However, most classmates and younger students simply grow weary of the tedium brought about by perpetually being told to "just take out any book and read." Our high school education concludes abruptly as we make our way across the stage at Peabody Auditorium, picking up our diplomas from our principal, William Cuddy. I am driven to exasperation by the often arbitrary actions of adults and the condescending tone of nightclub owners who subsidize my college fund. Simultaneously, I am overflowing with wonder. It's the morning tide of my life. Everything seems possible, and even the slightest trickle appears to lead to the sea.

Vignettes of that dream wash over me from time to time as I drive from the Atlantic Ocean west on Main Street toward the Halifax River, a drive of barely twelve blocks. I occasionally need to find myself among those buildings again. I need to consult maps and experience the subtle evening glow as the sun withdraws and streetlights begin to illuminate that world in their extraordinary incandescence. My mind searches for the doors of barely remembered businesses and second-floor apartments. Personal monuments are vaguely enshrined by those ruins.

In many ways, everything along Main Street is different now. In my youth, Main Street was like another country, its food, music, language, and second-story-apartment architecture far removed from my life in upper-middle-class Ormond Beach. Today, much of the Main Street architecture of my youth has been overpowered by the dominant franchisers, Burger King, McDonald's, Wendy's, Holiday Inn, and Hilton. Cable TV networks regulate the entertainment and news. Once highly regarded local radio stations now carry the same computerized Top 40 music list that I hear no matter where I drive on the Interstate Highway System.

Just the same, I am struck by how much remains of the lost snippets of my dream. Nobody could despoil the glorious Atlantic itself: flat, placid, and blue-green on a Sunday morning. Still capable of rising into twenty-foot walls of water by noon, driven by the freight train intensity of an Atlantic hurricane. Fishermen still populate the Main Street Pier and the Main Street Bridge, bookending that community where, in the past, sun-parched fishermen often handed hungry hippies fresh-caught fish and walked away to their cars without a word. That dilapidated old Main Street, where by ten minutes I narrowly avoided arrest with my two best friends for ignoring the open-container law at 3:00 A.M. The two other friends I left behind that night were not so lucky. Much of old Main Street is still there to find, for the judicious eye.

In my years on Main Street, we merged together from every corner of the country. We were conjoined by the music and the camaraderie and the excitement of Daytona nightlife. Sometimes we traveled in pairs, other times we would be seven or eight in a car, disguised as crazed hippies, roaring to the next adventure and always learning something new along the way.

I remember being in a Black nightclub at the base of the Main Street Pier. Race was a plague on the South in those years. Now, as I drive down Main Street, I am encouraged to pass a Black man taking his wife and children for a Sunday drive. I see Black Americans eating alongside White Americans in family restaurants. I notice Black couples walking casually on the snowy-white beaches in Daytona, all things that were unthinkable even in the mid-'60s. I remember that I was invited to the Surf Bar that night by a Black musician friend. It didn't really dawn on me at the time, but he couldn't comfortably go into White joints in those years, not even as a musician. He wasn't permitted to even visit some of our city and state parks. So, he took me to see his portion of America, teaching me about his music and the uncompromising spirit it embodied. I was riveted to my chair by a tight-fisted R & B band named the Untils confidently working their magic. Duane and Gregg Allman shared the stage with the band that night for a set, as was their habit, and they fit like the last two pieces to a magnificent puzzle.

That night, I realized that jazz and slow blues belong to all of us, Black and White. The remarkable music of Black America didn't come from the classroom. It sprung from within the heat and smoke and sweat of a thousand grueling Saturday nights in clubs just like the Surf Bar. The blues are about truth, justice, and emotions stripped bare to the bone. In meaningful glimpses, so like my Main Street dream, at least some portions of America's promise have been fulfilled in the past fifty-five years.

Chapter 4

Duane's Mountain of Green

Every unfamiliar experience or individual that a person encounters along their life road is analyzed psychologically through a uniquely personal collection of prior experiences. Like a computer, we compare the unfamiliar with the familiar. We make assessments and comparisons based on thousands of prior experiences and file the data away for future use—human nature on the most basic level. Try as we may to break away from the tendency toward stereotypical analyzing, it becomes a natural part of our psyche.

Only on those extraordinary occasions when we experience an event or meet people so utterly unique and innovative that they change our perspective and our lives forever, then and only then do we genuinely evolve. The first time I heard Duane and Gregg Allman, and watched them play, was one such occasion. I was stopped in my tracks, and my world changed from top to bottom from that time on.

With an extended family of lightning-fast lunatics and a microcosm of five unbalanced brothers, why would anyone expect Duane's story to result in anything other than tragedy? Clearly, enough disaster befell The Allman Brothers Band to fill volumes, but misfortune is not Duane's story. His story is the music—the excitement, the exhilaration, and the curiosity born of the genius to look beyond the bend in the road and to create his own new musical reality.

The story of Duane's music began scarcely ten years before the recording of the monumental live Fillmore East concert in a place far removed from New York City by time and distance. For me, the music began in earnest in Daytona Beach in the early '60s, where Duane and Gregg spent their teen years sending roots deep through the deep, rich layers of the soulful Florida music soil. In that stretch of scarcely ten years, their music evolved from mere pinpricks on the surface of genius to abruptly erupting into fame, fortune, and self-awareness.

An appropriate bookend to the epic Fillmore East concert of June 1971 is an obscure but equally important musical performance that took place in 1964, at Peabody Auditorium in Daytona Beach, by Duane and

Gregg's fledgling band, the Escorts. The Escorts were quickly gaining the reputation as a blistering band in a town teeming with fiery, young musicians. The Escorts were hired in the late summer of 1964 to play both before and after the presentation of the historic surfing movie *The Endless Summer*. It was that day that my musical perspective changed radically, forever.

My personal musical transformation began in earnest subsequent to my family's moving to Florida in 1962. At the age of twelve, though I had taken various music lessons for as far back as I can remember, my outlook and vision changed radically. Mine was a musical family. My mother played a bit of piano and she loved to lead family sing-alongs. My sister mastered the piano at an early age. I took piano and woodwind lessons, though I hated the monotony of practicing. My father and his siblings loved to sing spirituals and inspirational songs. Even my little brother itched to become a musician. My siblings and I were required to take music lessons as well as participate in team sports, either on the army bases where we mostly lived or in civilian schools. After living within the constraints and strict control of military bases most of my life, moving to Florida when my father retired from the Army Signal Corps was like giving sight to the blind. For once, I lived in a setting where chain-link fences were pleasant yard dividers, warm breezes blew in off the Atlantic, and barbed wire and military police were distant memories. Trading armed MPs for the smiling neighborhood postman, my family snuggled into paradise on the Atlantic.

Daytona Beach: race cars; Speed Weeks; palm trees; tropical foliage; twenty-eight miles of sandy, white beaches; the ocean; unlimited fishing; surfing; bikinis; and rumors of topless swimsuits on their way from Paris. What more could an adventurous adolescent with raging hormones possibly ask for?

Two local AM radio stations, WROD and WMFJ, kept teenagers intently listening for hidden sexual innuendo in songs like Chubby Checker's "Slow Twistin'" and Brian Highland's "Sealed with a Kiss." Local Boss-Jocks challenged us to out-vocalize groups like Jay and the Americans and the Everly Brothers as they played "She Cried" and "Cryin' in the Rain" while we showered before school. We sang these songs, or let them play in our heads, and life made sense. Just a hundred miles north on US-1, Jacksonville broadcast WAPE loud and clear and added a different flavor of music to the mix with the rich, cool sounds of groups such as Booker T and the M.G.'s, with their soulful "Green Onions," and Dion DiMucci's "The Wanderer."

Late in the evening, after the sun set behind Daytona's beach, the local stations wrapped up their broadcast days. As the local stations signed off, one by one, I could usually tune my transistor radio to clear-channel stations such as Nashville's WLAC and the far-away WOWO from Fort Wayne, Indiana. Late in the evening was when the real magic happened, when those stations bounced strong signals off the ionosphere, where the real R & B and blues were pulsing. Songs like "Can't Stop Lovin' You" by Ray Charles and King Curtis's "Soul Twist" somehow found their way to the transistor radio that I kept tucked neatly under my pillow. I had touched down in adolescent heaven, and music permeated our lives!

We moved to Florida from Arlington, Virginia, as soon as my seventh grade of junior high ended. Staying with my favorite aunt that summer, I spent my days working at our nearly completed house, so close to the beach that I could easily hear the waves breaking. My father began his job at the local General Electric office complex. GE was charged with communications as well as quality control for the Apollo moon program, and my father was hired as a consultant for that project. Every morning he would drop me off at our home building site to help wherever I could. This gave him the opportunity to check progress twice every day and make sure that there was a family member on-site while the house was being built. Not a great way to spend the summer, but I did learn much about construction and landscaping...mostly from the sweaty end of a shovel.

There were always ample break times to ride my bicycle down to the beach or to the corner drugstore for a soda and comic book. I met many similarly transplanted GE kids in the neighborhood, as our home site was on a major corner in our housing development. Having moved most of my life, I made friends quickly. There were touch football games and Friday-night beach parties complete with records, girls, and guitars. Along with new friends from all over the US came a wide variation of musical tastes to make life all the more interesting.

Like a tornado spinning out of control, picking up strength and growing with every new experience, I wanted to do it all, see it all, hear it all, and try it all. My new-found freedom was exhilarating beyond description. Naturally, the following summer of 1963, when my new friend a few doors down got the first surfboard on the block and asked if I'd like to try my hand at surfing, I grabbed his board and some Coppertone and fell in love with the sport immediately.

I spent that summer and the next winter cutting lawns, painting houses, installing sprinkler systems, helping builders, and doing anything else I could think of to earn enough money for my own board. Surfboards were pricey, even back in the early 1960s, with mass-produced boards, referred to as "pop-outs," starting around ninety dollars and custom-made boards beginning in the $150 range. The work was backbreaking, the heat oppressive, and the money minuscule. I was often paid six dollars biweekly to cut an acre-sized yard on the river. However, I kept working toward my own surfboard and borrowed a board here or there, when I could, from a generous friend.

At one point, when expenditures way outpaced income, I decided to try my hand at building my own surfboard. For a thirteen-year-old I had many talents, but surfboard building was certainly not at the top of that list. The edges, or rails, of my homemade board turned out practically square instead of gracefully rounded. Consequently, where my first-ever fiberglass job lapped from the top of the board to the bottom, there were hundreds of sharp, painful points where unintentional drops of resin and fiberglass cloth had dried like tiny, painful stalactites.

When my first surfboard made its beach debut, it was affectionately christened "the log" by my friends. It was heavy and an ugly brownish-gray color. "The log" was hard to maneuver, near impossible to paddle, and dangerous to everyone in the water, but overlooking those small stumbling blocks, it was my pride and joy. Amazingly, it rode the small East Coast swell relatively well, which was what mattered to me, and I didn't have to mooch boards any longer. Sadly, my handmade board was stolen from its resting place on the side of the house, on what must have surely been the darkest night of the year, by a thief who was obviously not a surfer and probably legally blind. I set my pride aside, and with the money that the insurance company paid my father for the theft, along with the remainder of my meager earnings, I was able to buy an entry-level pop-out from the local G. C. Murphy five-and-dime a few weeks later.

Those had been the hottest, hardest, dirtiest, most disappointing, and, in a way, greatest character-building two years of my young life. My reward was a brand-new nine-foot, eight-inch Ventura pop-out beginner board with wide red rails and a clear center showing off the smooth white Clark Foam blank and thin balsa wood stringer. It was a long way from the custom-shaped boards that many of my friends rode, but it didn't matter at all. Nothing in my entire world meant as much to me as that surfboard after what I had gone through to earn it. I immediately went to work building a "trailer" for the board because it was so long and wide it was nearly impossible to carry under my arm to the beach on my bicycle. As my fiberglassing skills improved, and the spring of 1964 became summer, I "concaved" the nose of that board for better stability and added a laminated walnut-and-maple tail block to the back, to give it the look of a custom-made board.

Along with the sport of surfing came all the trappings: surf shops; skateboards; white Levi's; wide, horizontally striped, and boldly colored Hang Ten T-shirts; surf movies; and the music that inspired thousands of surfers and became the soundtrack for a generation of sand junkies—surf music! So, for me, work continued in order to earn spending money for what had become my second love...music.

The Beach Boys, with their harmonies, were hot as summer sand, and their music told us what to do and where to go next. The Ventures never sang a word but their guitars vocalized the emotion of the waves and the ocean. Dick Dale and the Daletones, along with Jan and Dean, lived on "Dead Man's Curve" and put passion into our feet at parties and dances. One band, the Sandels, seemed to play their music with a distinctively different flare. They were an extraordinary instrumental group that seemed to convey the subtle energy of the ocean in their music, and they wrote and recorded the soundtrack for Bruce Brown's blockbuster surfing movie, *The Endless Summer*. These were all groups that predated the Beatles in the US and were, for the most part, "wiped out" later by the British Invasion.

In the days when the Bruce Browns of the world were breaking their backs shooting surf movies, the photographer, director, soundman, equipment man, driver, gofer, cook, promoter, beer runner, and projectionist were all one and the same. Early, primitive surf movies were shown to audiences mostly standing up in crowded surf shops heady with the smell of surf wax, foam dust, and resin; or in recreation centers, sitting on folding metal chairs; or in gymnasiums, school auditoriums, or, on a rare occasion, in a large setting like Peabody Auditorium.

The excitement before, and during, these primal movies was like the plastic-comb static that stands your hair on end—similar to the anticipation and exhilaration that came later during rock concerts. A surf shop or auditorium full of adolescent boys anticipating a surf movie was 100 percent pure testosterone on steroids.

Anticipation and expectation filled the house when Bruce Brown brought *The Endless Summer* to Daytona Beach's Peabody Auditorium. Just like the image of stepping up to the edge of the Grand Canyon at the age of seven, today I can close my eyes and I am transported there instantly. My mind immediately returns to the sounds of that day; the clamor of the crowd, the laughter, and the reverberation of good-natured pushing and shoving, the echo of an occasional hoot, the rat-a-tat-tat of a new class ring on the metal bottom of a seat, the clatter and scuffle of shoes with metal taps on a wooden floor, the sound of huarache sandals slapping bare feet, and hands slapping sunburned backs covered by T-shirts sticky with sweat. The sounds that filled Peabody Auditorium that afternoon were the sounds of an innocent beach-town summer.

The smells were the smells of the boardwalk: chili dogs, saltwater taffy, popcorn, Noxzema, Brute, Bay Rum, Coppertone, and English Leather, all muddled together with salt and sand and sweat. The sounds, smells, and anticipation of the crowd that day are all just a blink away, and with that blink my heart beats years younger.

My surf buddies and I showed up early to watch *The Endless Summer*. We were sitting in the fourth row of Peabody Auditorium that Saturday afternoon. All of us were too young to legally drive, but we were about to witness two significant historical events that afternoon.

Bruce Brown, dressed in trademark white Levi's and gold Hang Ten T-shirt, was at that time surfing's equivalent to John F. Kennedy. Brown sat between two tables that were set up near the middle of the auditorium. One table held two large reel-to-reel movie projectors and several film canisters. The other held a simple reel-to-reel tape recorder that was connected to the house public address system. Laying next to the tape player was a single hand-held microphone. Before the commercial success of *The Endless Summer* put the film in major theaters all over the United States, Brown would roll the movie, play the music, and kick back, barefooted with a cold beer, to narrate the film in person. So it was this summer afternoon.

Brown's lens documented and captured the meteoric rise of a fledgling cult sport with early titles like *Surf Crazy*, *Bear Foot Adventures*, *Waterlogged*, and *Slippery When Wet*. *The Endless Summer* was Brown's sixth surf movie and the one that would make his name recognizable to not only the surf crowd but to average Americans who lived miles from the ocean.

Before Bruce flipped the magic switch, however, we were going to be treated to some homegrown surf music by a local band called "The Escorts." The band was set up to the right of the projection screen. Their equipment consisted of three gray Sears Silvertone amplifiers, which were the cheapest that money could buy but available in just about any town large enough to support a Sears and Roebuck. Two of the amps were set up to the right of the drums, and the third amplifier was set up just to the left of the set of red sparkle Slingerland drums. Three microphones stood a few feet in front of the amplifiers and were wired to the house PA system.

By the time the Escorts were slated to start playing, Peabody was chaotic and overrun with keyed-up, animated surfers, and the grand old auditorium was buzzing wildly. Hoots and hollers punctuated the static air. Brown was confident that his film would become a hit if he just kept working at it, but I wonder if he ever realized that his opening band would become something larger, and much more impressive, to a generation of music-loving Americans. The second hand of my Timex agonizingly ticked the minutes away before starting time. It was hard to imagine the crowd sitting still for much local music when Bruce Brown was in the house. The crowd had come to see a historic surfing movie, but what the audience didn't realize was that they were about to experience a piece of musical history.

The Escorts walked out onstage, two boys with brownish hair and two with longish blond hair. All four boys were about sixteen. Their hair was long for 1964. The Beatles were still in England and we were still in the South. The blond boys actually had straight bangs long enough to comb down across their foreheads in a sweep and back up on the other side, surfer style...nearly touching their eyebrows. The band all wore dark English-style suits without collars and with darker piping along the edges, white shirts with skinny ties, and black, pointed, leather boots that zipped up on the sides that the surfers referred to—with a confidence in their ability to do so without blowback that now seems astonishing and positively shameful—as "Puerto Rican fence-climbers." Later, those same boots became famously known as "Beatle boots."

The Escorts didn't *take* the stage that afternoon, they *owned* the stage. The four walked from behind ruffled curtains without a word, confident and self-assured far beyond their ages. The drummer sat down and quietly picked up his sticks without a sound. Ready to play, he bent slightly forward to look under his cymbals at the front row for his cue, and smiled with lips pressed tight. The other three walked to their amplifiers, flipped them on, plugged in their guitars, stepped up to the microphones, adjusted their black guitar cables behind them, and paused for what seemed to be an eternity. Finally, when an eerie static hush fell over the entire auditorium, and they commanded the attention of the entire audience, almost unnoticed, the taller blond boy turned slightly to the drummer and counted off the first of four songs while snapping his fingers in time. With that, a symphony of musical magic filled every corner of Peabody Auditorium that incredible afternoon. Something extraordinary occurred as their music blanketed Peabody in mystical, salty benediction. There was a strange wonder in the eyes of the audience, and you could feel an eerie anticipation in the haunting silence between the songs. Something wonderful happened that day, and it happened in my own backyard! I was witness to the birth of a musical legacy that would last for another fifty-eight years and beyond.

Teenagers, whose entire universe had been surfing, were introduced to glimpses of a new spiritual-mindedness—and they listened to music, for the first time, in an entirely different way. The music didn't just go into their ears, it flowed into their minds. For me, it was all that and much more. All at once, surfing, surfboards, surf wax, baggies, bikinis, and everything else about the sport that I thought I would love forever drained out of me, and I knew that I wanted to do what they were doing. I wanted to be as inspiring as those four guys on the stage. I wanted to make other people feel what I was feeling right then watching them play. I wanted to make people envious, just like I was right then. I wanted to look out into the eyes of the crowd and see the same look that they were seeing, right then, in my eyes. I wanted to do what they were doing. No, I *had* to do what they were doing.

In the time it took for the Escorts to play a handful of songs, the entire focus of my life had changed, though I know now that I didn't fully understand how completely they would change me at the time. What I did know was that I had to be up on that stage one day, and somehow, I knew that it would happen.

The drummer with the pensive smile and shaggy brown hair and dark eyes was Maynard Portwood. His sullen look and pursed lips were owed to the fact that he was missing a couple of front teeth. Maynard rarely opened his mouth to laugh unless he was in the company of close friends. The bass guitar player was Van Harrison, whose father was a doctor in Daytona, and whose younger sister, Kane, was a close friend of mine all through high school and still is. After that afternoon, I would visit Kane more often, especially if I knew that her brother's band was out in the carport or in the living room rehearsing. Van never quite looked as if he fit in with the other Escorts. He was a bit more clean-cut than the others. His stiff stature slightly recalled a military background.

The two blond boys were brothers, though they looked about as alike as a flute and an oboe. The older brother was a bit taller and a bit thinner. His hair was a good bit longer than that of his brother, not nearly as blond, and unlike his brother's hair, his had a stringy wave, giving his locks a slightly unkept look. His eyes seemed to sink a bit into his long, expressionless face—that is, until he began to play guitar. When he played guitar, his face beamed and his eyes sparkled as if lighted by the music.

The younger and more handsome brother could have easily loaned his looks to the front of a Wheaties cereal box. His appearance was that of homecoming king, quarterback, and music star rolled into one person. There was an air of cool about his every move, and his eyes were always on the women in the audience. His hair was perfect, a black comb protruding from his back pocket, just in case. Both boys played guitar. The older brother played lead and the younger played rhythm. Their names were Duane and Gregg Allman.

When the movie was over and Brown was busy rewinding his film and his tape-recorded music, the Escorts came out on the stage and played a few more songs. This time, though, they played slower, more soulful, sweeter music, not the breakneck lightning guitar runs that were so popular in surf music. This time, the Escorts played rhythm and blues, and the younger Allman, Gregg, sang with an amazing richness in his voice, tinged with pain and desperation, so alien a sound coming from a blond-haired surfer boy of sixteen, or so it would seem.

This set was very different from the first and showed the promise of what was to be. Those who saw past the bend in the road stayed for that second set and traded soda fountain Coke for a tiny sip of Heineken.

Duane was playing real city slicker guitar, not garage band hacking, but indisputable, honest-to-goodness, professional, big-time guitar licks. He played well-defined leads and complex rhythm patterns. His searing lead guitar deftly blended the ghost of Robert Johnson with the simpler music that Duane's counterparts were relegated to play. Watching him that afternoon, it became apparent that Daytona Beach had been harboring the Mona Lisa. The faces in the band were sixteen, but their music was ageless.

I noticed, looking around, that most of the crowd had left the auditorium. The majority of my friends were headed for the sand, yelping and screaming, searching for Bruce Brown's perfect wave. In a flash, my surfing friends seemed immature and unsophisticated.

I stayed and listened until the last note echoed through Peabody. As they would come to do thousands of times in the next ten years, Gregg and Duane left the stage knowing they had nailed their audience to the wall. The march down the road toward The Allman Brothers Band was already well underway.

I stayed and intently watched while they carefully put their guitars away in their velvet cases, rolled up their cords, and patiently broke down the drum set. All that time, I inched a little closer to the stage to watch. From where I was sitting, it was obvious that Gregg was very happy with the show. Excitement overtook him as he corralled his brother, looking him squarely in the eyes with a Cheshire cat smile, and said, "Man! Ya know, Duane, it just doesn't get any better than this."

Duane, looking just past the bend in the road to a wall full of gold records, smiled and said, "Baby brother, just you wait."

I watched as they lugged every last piece of equipment out to the alley, where a station wagon was waiting. All this time, they laughed, giggled, cackled, and joked. They seemed to be having the time of their lives, and they were.

Then it happened. I watched as a broadly grinning Duane walked over to Bruce Brown, who was packing up his own gear. They shook hands, and then Duane held his left hand out and collected what looked to me like a mountain of green. Their laughter became uncontrollable.

A week or so after that Saturday in 1964, I took my surfboard to a friend's house who lived directly on the beach between the Neptune and Granada beach approaches to surf a fun break in front of his house. Something seemed different that day as I sat on the board that had cost me almost two years of work and sweat. The day was gray, but the smooth ocean reflected the clouds like mirror glass. I remember feeling the swells moving beneath me as I sat on my board that afternoon, but I don't think I paddled into the lineup once. After paddling in, with permission, I leaned my board against the wall in the corner of my friend's garage next to a half dozen other boards. All those surfboards belonged to neighborhood surfers who all gathered in front of that house in the afternoons to surf after school. His garage was a safe place to keep my board. I reasoned that it was convenient to leave my board there so I could use it without dragging it back and forth from my house.

As I pulled the garage door down, I glanced back toward my surfboard leaning in a line with all the other boards along the wall. In that instant, all the surfboards in the garage looked the same, and I couldn't tell one from the other. I never saw my board again after that day...and I never looked back.

Chapter 5

Dear God, What Is That Smell?

It is generally believed that luck is simply the natural result of a positive or negative outlook. Luck can be driven by an attitude that keeps a person open to fresh opportunities or random acts of chance. There is a definite correlation between good luck and the right attitudes and choices in life. Chance favors the prepared mind; conversely, bad luck snaps at the heels of a careless lifestyle.

I have always been blessed with an abundance of positive luck, or whatever it is...synchronicity, providence, chance, or being in the right place at the right time. Whatever you call it, luck has always snuggled close to my side. When a door would open, opportunity welcomed me in. Most of the decisions that I have made in my lifetime turned out to be dead on, down the line. Though there were times that it didn't seem so. Once, I wound up on the wrong side of the shamrock due to little fault of my own luck. Duane Allman taught me a lesson in innocent naivety. This once, the door opened, but misfortune jammed his muddy boot in my entryway rather than opportunity.

As far back as I can remember, my father would take me to Washington Redskins football practices and games near our home just outside of Washington, DC. Dad loved football, and he had played on a state-championship high school football team in Jacksonville, Florida, where he had grown up. After playing for Andrew Jackson's championship season, my father went on to play football at Clemson University, first under Coach Josh Cody, and later by the legendary Frank "Rock" Howard. My father's dream was that I would continue in his footsteps by becoming a high school and college football star. I pursued my father's dream as long as I could, but eventually my own dream followed a different fork in the road toward a different kind of stardom. Contrary to what most parents believe, dreams are the sole property and dominion of the dreamer.

During my junior high and high school years, I played football for Seabreeze. I worked at it and played hard, but I never attained anything close to star status. My football career screeched to a halt after my junior varsity season at Seabreeze High, but I didn't share my decision with my parents until almost the following fall. My father's plan was for me to continue the next year on the varsity team, but I was playing drums almost every weekend by the summer of 1966, and I knew that I had to decide between football and music. The choice was easier for me than it was for my father. But I hung up my cleats and played music almost every weekend for the next two years and beyond. In fact, during our senior year in high school, my band managed to play more than two hundred dates. Granted, almost ninety of them were in the grueling summer of '68 while we were the house band at the Martinique in Daytona Beach. At the Martinique we played six nights a week all summer. We were paid $125 per man for the week. A six-quart case of Pagan Pink Ripple wine was thrown in weekly to sweeten the deal. The Ripple was eagerly consumed and greatly appreciated.

As if six nights a week at the Martinique were not exhausting enough, on our only day off we hauled our equipment across town and hosted a Sunday-afternoon jam session. The Jam was a longtime Daytona tradition that was held weekly at a neighborhood dive bar on the corner of Madison Avenue and US-1 in Daytona, the Blind Pig. The Blind Pig was owned by an eccentric but benevolent character who went by the name of Cadillac Jack. "The Pig," as we called it, was known by local musicians for exceptional live music, and Cadillac Jack took great pride in keeping that tradition alive. When the summer of '68 came to an end and we were all preparing to play our last Sunday Jam, Cadillac Jack gave us each a Budweiser pitcher and a set of glasses for our dorm rooms. I still have my pitcher, and a few of the glasses remain. Jack and I stayed friends until his death some years later.

After Jack's death, the Pig fell into unsavory hands and eventually morphed into a notorious stripper bar and topless nightclub called the Shingle Shack. The Shingle Shack stood up to thirty or more years of vice raids, ownership changes, and arrests. Now known as Diamond Dolls, that wonderful old Daytona music venue traded live entertainment for pole dancers more than forty years ago. As the Pig became the Shingle Shack and finally Diamond Dolls, the building underwent drastic transformations. What started out as a tattered and worn but comfortable neighborhood bar is now a very large, modern, big-box-style, neon-crowned, Disneyland of adult entertainment.

The Blind Pig shared an interesting architectural feature with the Martinique that ensured both old buildings wonderful acoustics. Every great musician worth his salt will tell you that acoustics can make or break a nightclub. The great acoustics shared by the Pig and the Martinique were the result of their being built in the early 1900s using a very common and inexpensive byproduct of the cypress milling industry. The building material used in both buildings to panel the walls was called pecky cypress.

The pecky cypress effect is produced by a fungus and generally occurs in old-growth cypress trees, and then in only 10 percent of those trees. The fungus causes soft pockets or recesses in the wood that were once deemed undesirable. At that time, planks cut from the diseased trees were much less expensive than clear cypress. Pecky cypress was usually sold out of the back door of sawmills at a fraction of the cost of other woods. That is not the case today, however. Old-growth cypress is so rare today that a process to duplicate the look of pecky cypress paneling has been developed, but it is still extremely expensive and desirable. Both bars were paneled with beautifully marked, original pecky cypress planks because the material was the cheapest wood available at the time. Little did the builders know that the soft, sound-absorbing wood that required no finish would be so sought-after today, not only for its beauty but for its acoustic qualities.

Cadillac Jack paid the Soul Patrol thirty-five dollars a man to host Sunday afternoon jam sessions. Pitchers of frozen daiquiris and world-class meatball subs always appeared after our first set. Amazingly, through the haze of playing all those dates during our senior year, we all managed to maintain our grades. I only fell asleep while playing my drum set once that I can remember. Of the five members in my band, four of us—Carl Persis (vocals), Ralph Bundy (guitar), Scott Stanley (bass), and I—headed off to college in mid-August. Only Tim O'Brien (keyboards) remained to pursue music full time.

I continued to love the sport of football and followed my high school's team and my buddies from my playing days until graduation. I went to every game I could, as long as my band wasn't playing at a conflicting after-game dance at one of the local schools.

It was after one Friday-night Seabreeze football game during my junior year that Duane turned my lucky horseshoe upside down and drained every last drop of luck from it, and I paid dearly for my carelessness. I don't remember exactly which month it happened, but I do remember that it was very warm, as it is most of the early football season in Florida. After the game that night, my date and I headed over to the Seabreeze High campus for the customary Friday-night post-game dance in the school cafeteria.

Seabreeze High School is located just across State Road A1A from the beach. The school is so close to the beach, in fact, that it is still effortless for surfers to check out the surf from the second level of classrooms and disappear from campus after lunch, if the surf requires such. On the evenings when warm southeast breezes blew in over the sand dunes between the school and the Atlantic, it could be sultry and uncomfortable if a person left a car parked with the windows rolled up tight. More often than not, if the weather was clear we simply left our windows down when our cars were parked. Times were much simpler and less toxic then.

On that night in 1966, we drove into the main parking lot at the school, and the dance had been going on for an hour or so. The parking lot was crowded, but as luck would have it, I found a parking spot near the front line next to the sidewalk that led to the cafeteria. While opening my date's door, I could already hear the music coming from the cafeteria. I noticed Duane and Gregg's station wagon parked directly behind me in the next row of cars, deeper into the parking lot. Seeing their car parked outside a dance was always cause for excitement. It meant that the Allman Joys, the Escorts' new iteration, were the band of the evening. As a fledgling musician in Daytona Beach, watching the Allman Joys ply their craft was like watching the Beatles playing at the Cavern Club. We were front-row witnesses to a musical education second to none, and the Allman's were already conducting classes at graduate level.

As I remember, it was so warm that night that without thinking twice, we left the windows rolled down so the car would stay comfortable while we were inside the dance. We made our way to the center of the campus and walked up the steps to the cafeteria. I noticed that the music had stopped, and many of my friends were standing outside talking. As we neared the cafeteria door, Duane and Gregg walked out, followed quickly by Maynard Portwood and Bob Keller. They each had a Coke in hand and seemed to be intent on heading out to the parking lot on their break to do whatever it was that they were into doing at the time—beer, booze, or something equally illegal and stimulating. We said hello as we passed and I told them I'd see them after their break. They waved as they disappeared into the darkness of the parking lot toward Duane and Gregg's station wagon.

My date and I were both were anxious to hear the Allman Joys, and the break seemed to take forever. When the band came back to the makeshift stage in the cafeteria, the music was well worth waiting for. The crude, unsympathetic lighting and B-level sound system added to the realism and authenticity of hearing a band as good as the Allman Joys in a huge cafeteria with no acoustic quality whatsoever. As was the case back in the early 1960s when Seabreeze High School was built, the cavernous cafeteria was simply and institutionally built out of hard, cold glass, metal, and sound-reflecting brick. What we were treated to was steps above mid-'60s high school, garage band dance music.

Despite so much echo in that huge room, when the band began to play there was still an appreciable interplay between Gregg's vocals, his keyboard, and Duane's vibrato-driven guitar fills. Keller and Portwood added rhythm and grit to the mix, and before long the swell was head-swirling. From nowhere and everywhere came incredible guitar solos with notes being produced as if Duane felt each one, as they moved from his hands through the strings and finally pushed out through his amplifier. When Duane closed his eyes and contorted his mouth, he played music so soulfully that it made your heart ache. As the set moved along, we heard some Chuck Berry-style chicken pickin' out of Duane's Tele/Strat hybrid and some not-so-subtle Jimmy Smith-style organ keyboard from Gregg's Vox Continental.

Listening to them play was like a Sunday-afternoon jam where no one has to show off but everyone does. The band slid into the groove and obviously enjoyed playing music with each other. The notes were 1960s simple but played with an elegant sophistication beyond their time. The way Duane and the Allman Joys extracted notes from their instruments took your breath away, evoking pure emotion.

Walking outside at some point that night, I remember listening to the band and looking back at their magnified shadows, reflecting like musical giants against the floor-to-ceiling windows behind them. The band was harshly lit from the front by unflattering white floodlights that made the dancers seem to disappear and the band seem supernatural. Their shadows against the glass looked like an overexposed black-and-white Henry Diltz photograph. With all of that brightness and echo lifting the sound, it appeared from my perspective as if the Allman Joys were all alone in that huge room playing for themselves and to a future Phil Walden.

The Allman Joys ripped through set after set of well-chosen, well-rehearsed covers. The Beatles, the Rolling Stones, the Yardbirds, the Animals, and Paul Revere and the Raiders filled the air. Hard-driving rock and roll was augmented by plenty of slow-grinding R & B covers from the likes of Little Anthony and the Imperials and the Temptations.

Gregg even threw in some Andy Williams-inspired "Are You Sincere" to get everyone in the mood to get close.

Win, lose, or draw, the outcome of the football game didn't matter to me that night. There was nothing better than the Allman Joys playing at one of my high school dances. Duane and Gregg's stage presence was hard to quantify. The brothers and their band rarely moved much onstage. There were no Four Tops or Temptations-style dance moves coming from their boots. Mostly, they just stood, seemingly anchored by their instruments and amplifiers, and played with a professionalism that was lightyears beyond their eighteen or nineteen years.

Slow dancing to the Joys, especially to a baritone-driven Gregg Allman standard such as "Old Man River," and swaying to the music, holding tightly to your crush, was about as good as it got for a sixteen-year-old, testosterone-driven teenager in Daytona Beach back in 1966. Gregg's silky voice melted the girls then, as it still does. Duane was not a bad singer either, though he preferred to concentrate more on his guitar. Duane had a deep Bill Medley, Righteous Brothers kind of voice that wrapped its arms around the dance floor when he sang and gently pulled everyone close. He was also a master at harmonizing and singing duets with Gregg. The Gregg and Duane duo of "I've Been Trying," by the Impressions, was always one of my favorites that made it all the way from the Allman Joys set list right through to the last days of the Hour Glass. Gregg and Duane traded lyrics back and forth, with Duane somehow pulling off the high-end falsetto and the "Woooo,weeee,oooos" during the chorus. I can close my eyes and still hear the two brothers standing next to each other belting out those lyrics fifty-six years later. "I've Been Trying" was so wistful and so right.

The dance passed quickly, and soon it was time for Duane and Gregg to start their last set. I looked at my trusty Timex electric and was reminded by my date that it was nearing time for her to be home. She had an early curfew imposed by a stern ex-military father who always waited up by the door, so we had to leave before dances were over to get any privacy, and this night was no different. So, off we headed into the darkness of the parking lot so we could enjoy a quick make-out session in my mother's new car before we headed home.

I turned sixteen in March of 1966 and immediately traded in my learner's permit for a full street-legal driver's license and an overdose of high-octane testosterone. While I learned to drive, and after I earned my driver's license, I was resigned to using my mother's powder-blue Ford

Falcon with the three-speed stick shift on the column. The Falcon sported a marginal four-cylinder engine that could barely get out of its own way and no air conditioning. The interior was as plain and as spartan as the paint job. The cloth seats were worn thin, and the radio only worked occasionally, and when it worked at all it only received local AM stations. The flat floorboards in that entry-level Ford were covered with ugly rubber doormats designed to disguise the lack of carpeting.

The Falcon certainly wasn't much of a car, but it had four wheels and got me around as long as it was my turn to drive. Therein lay the biggest problem. I had to share that repulsive car with my mother, and she had first rights of refusal. Needless to say, even if I could wangle the keys to the Falcon, I didn't spend much time at the drive-in showing off my ride.

I've never been sure why, but a few months after I passed my driving test, my father relieved some of the building pressure on the family by coming home one day with a brand-new 1966 Plymouth Valiant Signet. The Valiant was a deep metal-flake blue color and equipped with a fully functioning radio that not only worked but also received FM radio stations. Late at night, that wonderful radio also captured WLAC from Nashville, a clear-channel station that bounced its signal off the ionosphere and somehow into the Valiant's dashboard. The Valiant was furnished with contrasting lighter blue plastic bucket seats in the front, automatic transmission, and its shifter located on the stylishly sporty console between the bucket seats. The floorboards were covered from stem to stern with a plush, fitted carpet.

The back seating area consisted of a comfortably wide bench seat. That area always seemed an appealing feature of the car to reveal to a perspective date. A date's initial response to the sheer roominess of that back seat could quickly signal positive or negative outcomes. That roomy back seat was handsomely embossed with the Plymouth logo, squarely in the center. It was a thing of comfort and beauty.

I was sure the Valiant was intended solely for my mother, but as mothers often do, she kept the Falcon, and the keys to the Valiant lived mostly in my pocket. The Valiant came with a 225-hp Chrysler slant-six engine, which had plenty of power for me, and it presented itself in a much better fashion than the Falcon. My mother and I often split time driving the Valiant, and I believe that she loved that car more than I did...that is, until that night of that dance in the fall of 1966.

Heading out to the Valiant that night, I knew my date and I would have at least a few minutes for a little romance in the back seat, and the excitement was almost impossible for me to contain. With a glint in my eye, I opened the back door for my date, very gentlemanly, and she started to step into the back seat, but, without warning, she reversed gears and backed out of the car as if she had seen a snake. With a deep-throated choking/coughing voice, she screeched, "Dear God, what *IS* that smell?"

By the time she had backed out of the doorway and stepped onto the parking lot, I could tell by the look on her face that my hopes for a romantic end to the evening were dashed. I also began to smell what she smelled. As a model car and airplane hobbyist in my preteen years, I knew in an instant the smell that was wafting through the air. We were both nearly overcome by the chemically laden stench of Testors Model Cement, and a lot of it!

When I got her calmed down a bit, I could see from the faint dome light that someone had thrown a brown paper sandwich bag into the back seat of the car through the open window. The bag was apparently well used, wrinkled, and turned down on itself from the top. When I moved the bag, I realized that glue was still seeping out of it onto the plastic seats, melting a hole in the Naugahyde fabric as if it was on fire. A thoroughly mashed tube of Testors Model Cement, covered with the horrible clear ooze, fell out of the bag as I moved it. The near-empty tube of glue landed squarely inside the ever-widening, dinner-plate-sized hole on the seat as I watched in horror while the disfigurement continued to expand in size.

Testors Model Cement doesn't act like most glue. Most glue and cement simply cure or harden, like superglue, forming a bond by filling microscopic holes and voids in the two materials to be joined together. Testors was formulated specifically as plastic model-building cement, and it melts the two pieces of a plastic model together, permanently joining them as if they were welded. Just a tiny bit was required for a permanent bond, and any more caused a nasty disfiguring mess, similar, but not nearly as huge, as what was happening on the back seat of my car. This was the hardest-learned secret of model building that took me many months to master. Too much glue was like lighting a match and holding it to the plastic. If a drop of Testors was carelessly dripped onto a model, that drop would simply ruin the project, just like the river of glue that was melting and ruining my mother's back seat.

I quickly found some newspaper and rags in the trunk to wrap the bag and empty tube of glue in, and then I turned my attention to wiping up as much of the glue off the seat as possible to minimize the damage...Nothing helped. It was a disaster of monumental proportions. To make matters worse, my stomach was beginning to writhe as I inhaled the stench, and I was becoming lightheaded. Wiping at the glue just spread it more, which melted more of the seat. There was nothing to do but to clean the mess as best as I could without spreading it more, and open the doors and turn on the AC to let the car air out. The fresh air allowed the cement to finish its process, melting the plastic seat and curing to a permanent, rock-hard consistency, totally obliterating the Plymouth logo. For as long as we could put off leaving, we both leaned on the hood of the Valiant, upwind of the mess, with all four doors open and the AC blasting, airing out the car. With the realization that I was in extremely deep trouble, my mind turned to identifying the culprit or culprits, and as I surveyed the parking lot, I immediately fixated on Duane and Gregg's car, parked directly behind mine and in a straight line to the dance where they were still playing.

In 1966, rumor had it that a few kids at Seabreeze High School were dabbling in glue sniffing, though I didn't personally know anyone who was doing it. Apparently, it was a cheap high, but what we had heard from adults and the media was that inhaling glue vapor caused brain damage. Most of my crowd was still reluctant to have a beer if the opportunity arose. Glue sniffing was still nothing more than another unsubstantiated rumor at my high school. In Duane and Gregg's circles, sniffing glue was a different matter entirely. Everyone knew that they were up for just about anything mind-numbing and that they were, in fact, glue sniffers from the get-go. And of course, Testors was the glue of choice among the glue-sniffing community.

The night was going south in a heartbeat. Not only was my make-out session dashed, but I had the feeling that I was about to go down for something I had absolutely no part in. Both my date and I were going home and would have to explain why we both smelled like we had been to a model airplane-building convention. It took me almost as long to explain to the retired captain what had happened as it did to explain the whole thing to my parents. It took my folks a long time to get over the dinner-plate-sized mass of melted plastic on the back seat of our new car, and I was made to drive the Falcon until they cooled down and eventually relented.

Possibly the worst upshot of the whole incident was that, of course, both sets of parents immediately became experts on different teen substance abuses, which just made things harder in the future for both myself and my date. I think that we were both followed by a shadow of doubt after the incident. I never sniffed glue, and I am positive that she never did either. I had no interest in glue sniffing and probably never worked on another plastic model ever again. To this day, the smell of any glue even remotely similar to Testors turns my stomach.

Circumstantial evidence? Oh, most definitely.

Bad luck? Well, hell yes, as bad as bad luck gets!

What could I do? I was already late getting my date home, and the reality was that I really had no proof it was Duane. At the time, I would have bet my Ludwig Speed King drum pedal that it was Duane who threw that glue bag in the back seat of my car on the way back to the dance from one of their breaks that night. I still would. Most likely he dumped his glue bag in the nearest receptacle, precipitated by panic and the fear of being caught when he noticed some adult heading to the parking lot from the dance; a well-meaning teacher or chaperone likely panicked Duane. Probably someone I knew.

A few years ago, I got together with Jim Matherly to have a chat. Matherly was the virtuoso guitarist for Sweet William and the Stereos whom Duane listened to at the Martinique and whose style Duane emulated. Matherly also spent several months playing with the Allman Joys when Duane played a host of dates with the Stereos in South Florida. Matherly confided to me that he was always at odds with Duane after he returned his band to him because Matherly contended that Duane had turned all of his old bandmates into glue heads. So, while the evidence is circumstantial, it is certainly conceivable as well as probable that he did it.

I never held the glue-bag incident against Duane. I learned several valuable life lessons from Duane that night, lessons that he would continue to augment in the years to come. One lesson was to not tempt providence and to roll up my windows and lock my car doors no matter how hot the night. I learned quickly that bad luck favors a careless lifestyle.

I also decided then and there to always separate myself a bit from Duane and his vices. I was lucky enough to be a few years younger than Duane and Gregg, so I luckily missed much of the mind-altering substances in which they indulged when I was beginning to play around town. I am sure that watching and learning from Duane at arm's length is why I have so many clear, unclouded memories from that era.

Chapter 6

The Combo Clash at the Ocean Pier and a Near Miss

Before delving into the meat of this chapter, some Daytona Beach history should be laid out to provide context for the atmosphere and climate of the times.

On January 30th of 1967, a nineteen-year-old local Daytona Beach teenager named Patricia (Patti) Ann Chandlee eloped to Jasper County, South Carolina, to marry twenty-year-old Duane Allman, much to her parents' chagrin. Their romance spanned several years but the marriage ended in divorce July 13th, 1970, according to Daytona Beach divorce records. Duane and Patti's relationship produced a daughter who was given up for adoption. Patti and Duane were a classic "Mutt and Jeff" couple; with Patti almost a foot shorter than the lanky Duane, she was cute as a button and often sported a handmade sweatshirt exclaiming "Allman's Joy!"

Between Duane's wedding and late March, the Allman Joys underwent a myriad of changes that kept the band and its members in a constant state of flux. Following close on the heels of Duane's elopement, Bill Connell, the Allman Joys' drummer, left the band when he received his draft notice. Connell's loss left the band with a key position to fill for the third time in a year. The resulting transitional ebb and flow eventually resulted in the Allman Joys combining forces with Johnny Sandlin's Minutes to form what would ultimately be dubbed the Hour Glass. Both the Minutes and the Allman Joys had worked tirelessly for years in order to create bands that would launch them into the brightest possible future. Both bands longed to be rescued from the wearisome Chitlin' Circuit, as well as from Top 40 nightclubs. Outside of the essential members, both bands made a point of replacing musicians as vacancies presented themselves, always with players of superior caliber, ability, and vision. When the Allman Joys and the Minutes ultimately joined forces in that spring of 1967, the resulting combination of remarkable musicians appeared to be the absolute crowning achievement for all involved. The subsequential musical shape-shift was, to each member of the resulting group, exciting, seamless, and, for all intents and purposes, permanent.

Fortunately for my high school band and for the Daytona Beach music community as a whole, the Allman Joys had solidified their union with the Minutes quickly. With only a few practices under their belts, the new configuration dashed off to St. Louis, Missouri, for a month-long stint at Pepe's A-Go Go. There, what would become the Hour Glass played from mid-March into April as the Allman Act or the Allman Joys, depending on which remaining member told the story. This musical marriage left bragging rights as to Daytona's "best band in town" up in the air. Had their newly formed band been in Daytona Beach, licking their wounds and planning their next move, my band would have had very little chance of winning what would become our ticket to a much better musical future..."The Greater Daytona Beach Combo Clash," co-hosted by the Ocean Pier and the "Good Guys" at local radio station WMFJ.

The Combo Clash ran April 13th to 15th, 1967. There were two preliminary heats, Thursday and Friday night, with four bands competing each night. Two bands would be selected from each preliminary heat, and the final four bands would compete on Saturday afternoon for $1,000 in cash and trophies. Eight of the finest bands that East Central Florida had to offer were selected to battle it out on the two stages in the huge, historic Ocean Pier and Casino Ballroom, positioned precariously out over the Atlantic Ocean waves at the east end of Daytona's Main Street. WMFJ's "Good Guys" disc jockeys were burning up the airwaves for weeks prior to the event pushing the bands, mentioning their names, and giving the Ocean Pier plenty of airtime.

WMFJ had deep roots in the Daytona Beach area and took to the air April 16, 1935, as Daytona Beach's first and only radio station. The original studios were located at 750 Root Street, just off Beach Street, near the core of old Daytona. In 1956, the studios moved to the basement of the Daytona Plaza Hotel at 600 N. Atlantic Ave. The Daytona Plaza studios ran adjacent to an extension of Seabreeze Boulevard that tunneled under the entire width of the hotel and led from A1A to the white-sand beach on the east end. The tradition for teenagers back in those days was to drive past the studio honking your car horn wildly while waving at the disc jockey through the plate glass windows. Concentration came hard to whoever was live on the air at the time, trying their best to ignore the obnoxious echoing of car horns.

In the 1980s, new offices and studios were built for WMFJ on

Beach Street across from the Daytona Beach Marina and Halifax River. The station's call letters were originally intended to be WMFB, to stand for "World's Most Famous Beach," but much to the station-owner's chagrin, "B" was not available at the time. The "J" in WMFJ didn't really stand for anything but was chosen because a fourth letter was needed for the call letter combination, and "J" seemed to fit better lyrically than "Z."

WMFJ was purchased in 1965 and became subsequently owned and operated by Walter-Weeks Broadcasting Company, a small Daytona Beach-based organization that later acquired AM-FM stations in Sarasota, West Palm Beach, and Tallahassee. After the station was purchased, Weeks went to work promoting his new venture, and two years later, in 1967, a natural choice for WMFJ was to sponsor an audience-grabbing "Combo Clash" at the historic, easily recognized Ocean Pier.

The Ocean Pier and Casino had historically been the most easily recognized and photographed landmark on Daytona Beach. Located at the east end of Main Street, the Ocean Pier anchors what had traditionally been considered the heart of Daytona's entertainment community. The original pier and casino was built primarily out of palm logs just before the turn of the 20th century. That original pier and casino were totally destroyed by fire in the early 1920s and subsequently rebuilt by new owners. Larger and longer, the newly rebuilt pier and casino opened to the public in 1925. Over the years, the pier has withstood the frequent pounding of Atlantic hurricanes, fires, and changes in ownership, but it still stands much as it was when it was rebuilt in 1925. During its lifetime, under different ownership, it has been called the Ocean Pier, the Keating Pier, the Pier Casino, the Main Street Pier, and now the Daytona Beach Pier. However, to most long-time Daytona Beach residents, it has been known simply as "the Pier."

My band, our classmates, and friends were no strangers to the nightly excitement offered by the Pier. During our high school years, my band and all of our friends enjoyed dances and concerts there as well as the helicopter rides and "Sky Rides" that the Pier and its current owner also offered. During the mid-'60s I attended a concert at the Pier headlined by Sam the Sham and the Pharaohs. While I can't swear to it, I believe that I remember Duane Allman and some of the other Allman Joys in the audience. Interestingly enough, five years later, Duane would add his singular slide guitar to Sam (the Sham) Samudio's 1970 solo album, "Sam, Hard and Heavy," playing tasty licks on "I'm Goin' Upstairs," which was written by John Lee Hooker.

They say that just showing up is half the battle, but simply showing up at the Pier to play was only the beginning. Getting all of our equipment out to the stage was more of a struggle than an actual battle. In order to play just one evening at the Pier, we were required to begin several hours earlier by trying to find an empty parking spot in the Pier's very small, sandy parking lot near Ocean Avenue, a half block south. If lucky enough to find a parking spot, it was time to start unloading our instruments and hauling our equipment several hundred feet over to the base of the Pier itself, where it would rest in a huge pile awaiting the next step. The next step in the hot, sweaty process was to climb the wide staircase that led up to pier level lugging heavy amplifiers, speaker cabinets, and drums, where they would rest in another great pile before we started the long trip out to the ballroom itself. All of that rigmarole was just the beginning. Dripping in sweat, we then had to schlep our gear across several hundred yards of scorching hot, uneven pier planks out to the ballroom. Once inside the huge un-air-conditioned building, past the fishing pier admission counter and bait-and-tackle counter, reeking of dead shrimp and chunk mullet, it was still another two hundred or so feet past the ballroom admissions booth, liquor bars, and storage rooms out to the main stage on the south end of the building. Quick learners that we were, those of us who couldn't carry our entire night's equipment easily in two hands quickly bought or made dollies to help save valuable energy for the evening's show. Eventually, even those who could carry their own equipment piggybacked on our dollies, and we ultimately furnished moving equipment for all.

During the mid-'60s, an ex-CIA pilot and all-around interesting character named Harry Doan operated the Pier. Harry wrung every dollar possible from the attraction. He built a helipad on the roof of the casino ballroom and flew helicopter rides up and down the beach during the day for courageous, foolhardy, or slightly over-served tourists. Visionary that he was, Harry also added a gondola-style "Sky Ride" that ran from the base of the Pier on the west end up over the ballroom and then out over the Atlantic Ocean and the south side of the Pier. The Sky Ride rode past where fishermen paid admission and bought bait so they could line up shoulder to shoulder, entangled in fishing line, in hope of catching the "big one." Once a gondola reached the end of the Pier, the Sky Ride would circle back and return along the north edge, ejecting riders back at the starting point.

One afternoon, after we set up our equipment and ran a quick sound check, Ralph, our band's guitar player and arranger, and I were outside at the Sky Ride admission booth shooting the breeze with our old friend and onetime bandmate Jay Laing, who had been given the responsibility of running the Sky Ride on the weekends. Business was slow that day and Jay offered us a free ride, so we quickly jumped at the offer. For Ralph and me, our first trip on the Sky Ride out over the Pier was exhilarating. In the meantime, Tim O'Brien, our keyboard player, who, like Harry Doan, motored down the road with one lug not securely tightened most of the time, had busied himself by catching up with Harry to talk about the night ahead. While we were sneaking our adventure on the Sky Ride hoping Harry had not seen us, Harry offered Tim and anyone else crazy enough to accompany them, a short, relaxing helicopter ride over the Atlantic that afternoon.

When we returned from our covert Sky Ride jaunt, Tim told Ralph and me about Harry's generous offer. I was game, as was Ralph, so we climbed the long set of stairs up to the heliport on the roof of the ballroom, where we joined Harry, already seated in his copter. Tim jumped into the front seat next to his buddy Harry, and Ralph and I took the two back seats; then we all buckled up for an exhilarating ride. Just exactly how exhilarating that ride was going to be none of us imagined, including and especially our pilot, Harry. I had hoped, out loud, and more as an adolescent joke than anything else, for a ride close to the blankets to check out the newest and smallest bikinis on the beach, not really expecting Harry to buzz a crowded beach full of tourists and cars. Undeniably, my idea had struck Harry as warranting further consideration, and to no one in particular, he suggested, sinisterly, "So, you guys want to get close to some girls, do you?" The tone of his response struck me as considerably more mischievous than my initial suggestion.

With us all strapped in and ready, Harry started the engines, did a cursory instrument pre-check, talked to someone on his two-way radio to get permission to lift off, and then we awaited the answer. Just before lifting off, Harry turned to his passengers and strongly suggested that we all check and tighten our seatbelts again. His final safety warning made me very uneasy, but by this time it was too late to exit the copter...Harry received permission to fly and began to rev his engines. Instantaneously, the cumbersome metal-and-glass enclosure began to take on an odd feeling of weightlessness and then lifted effortlessly off the roof of the ballroom.

Our liftoff was normal, smooth, and encouraging. Harry checked quickly for banner-plane traffic north and south, which was our only real competition for airspace over the beach. When he was confident there was no traffic impeding our flight in either direction, he pulled the stick back and put about twenty feet between the helicopter and the ballroom roof. So far, so good. Next, he rotated the craft slowly to the right, orienting the front of the helicopter toward the south, and then moved ever so gently out over the Atlantic waves. At this point, we were more than one hundred feet above the waves and enjoying our first glimpse of the Daytona beachfront skyline, with its afternoon shadows growing longer across the white-sand beach. When Harry was sure that he had moved far enough and gently enough south of the heliport so as to clear the edge of the building, he hovered there quietly for a moment, gaining our confidence. Then, in a millisecond, he chiseled the first and most likely last helicopter flight for three teenaged boys into their psyches forever.

Without warning, Harry dropped his helicopter straight down toward the water in a free fall that terrorized the living hell out of each one of us, catapulting our stomachs toward the ceiling of the copter and into our throats. In that instant, we essentially free-fell from one hundred feet in the air to a point where the struts actually touched the top edge of a cresting wave. Smirking back at us with that mischievous glint in his eye, the ride of a lifetime began to unfold before us, and it was altogether too late to jump off. Harry moved as near to the sand as possible and as close to the tops of the waves as he dared fly. His intention was to touch water as often as possible but steer just clear of disaster and startled tourists.

A normal pilot might worry that with his name and his business's name plastered all over the side of the helicopter, a terrorized tourist or stunned lifeguard might call the authorities. Harry wasn't worried one bit about getting into trouble in Daytona Beach...not even a little. He had CIA clearance and had flown guns, supplies, and cash to the CIA-backed Contra rebels in Nicaragua for the US government, dodging gunfire from angry Sandinistas during every single flight. Flying too low and fast over a beach packed with spring breakers was nothing more than child's play and folly to Harry.

So it continued that late afternoon, with Harry laughing maniacally in the captain's seat, glancing from time to time at the rest of us, who were white-knuckling whatever we could grab for security. We flew south for about six quick miles, skipping over the waves and dodging swimmers, surfers, and the occasional surprised porpoise on our way, on a joyride that can only be described as gut-wrenching. As we neared the much smaller Sunglow Fishing Pier in South Daytona Beach, Harry maintained his lack of altitude and aggressive forward speed and then lifted up and over that pier at the last possible second. This maneuver sent terrified fishermen on the pier scattering for safety and did little to reassure his passengers that he might be tiring of this recklessness. Once over and past the Sunglow Pier, Harry reversed course and continued the exhilarating six-mile, balls-to-the-wall ride back to his home base.

When we began to approach the Ocean Pier and Casino, Harry was still full throttle ahead and picking up speed. Still skipping across the waves, we were all sure that he intended to pull up at the last moment and fly over the Pier, just as he did at the Sunglow Pier, and we were right. Bracing ourselves in the slanting orange rays of the late afternoon sunlight for our last-minute lift over the Pier, Harry didn't disappoint. It was in that lipid moment, that flash in time that twinkles endlessly between now and the wink of an eye, that the day was distilled down to its essence in a scant millisecond. As the copter rose horizontally up and over the Pier while maintaining near-maximum forward speed, we all became conjoined in a Zen moment that very nearly entombed us in Daytona Beach history forever. As we crested over the ballroom, every eye in unison spotted the low-flying banner plane that was headed directly into our path from the north. In that Polaroid moment, our situation changed from featherbrained and flighty to life-or-death reality, as all four rectums constricted instantaneously, Harry's included.

In what was described later by witnesses as an incredible display of airmanship as well as spontaneous reflexes on behalf of both pilots, each craft peeled off to their respective right, avoiding a midair crash by mere yards. Amazingly enough, the seasoned pilot of the banner plane was able, in a split second of crystal clarity, to jettison his advertising banner, which gave him considerably more control and lift. Visibly shaken, flustered, and cussing like a drunk sailor on leave, Harry gained control over the copter and turned it back in a great wide arc toward the roof of the ballroom and settled the bird gently onto the helipad. Noticing the banner settling gently across the Sky Ride cables, we were reminded that we didn't want to be anywhere near the Pier when the pilot of that plane or the FAA came to retrieve that banner.

Without a word, Harry removed his headphones and hung them on a hook near the radio receiver to his left, and with a few committed flicks of his index finger, he switched off the main engine and then the tail engine. For a few moments, we simply sat there in the copter trying to breathe as normally as possible as the sound of the engines and rotors slowly gave way to the rhythmic crashing of waves on the beach far below us. When our heads became clearer, we all agreed that our first thoughts were how swiftly any one of a hundred fatal accidents could have ended our lives and our futures that afternoon. Really, it was astonishing that we were able to walk away from the helipad. In the moment, we were all shook to the core and trembling, but in reality, this episode had only augmented an already-sharpening sense of teenage invincibility.

When the feeling that we were still flying at breakneck speed began to slowly dissipate, and each of us checked that we had not soiled our pants or tossed our lunches, we finally felt comfortable loosening our safety belts. Tim began to reach for the door latch, shaking his head and collecting his thoughts, but truly, the rest of us fully expected some sort of apology or mitigation for our flat-rotor ride from hell. I was stunned when Harry turned around to all of us, but addressing Ralph and me in particular, barked, in a sibilate but oddly calm voice, with his teeth tightly clenched, "Okay, you little assholes," heavily accentuating the first syllable of *assholes*, "Let today be a lesson to you little shits! I want this to be the last time you or any of your friends ever try to con a free ride on MY Sky Ride from your pal Jay ever again!" Tim just looked at the two of us in disgust and mouthed, "What the HELL?!"

Harry exited his side of the copter while the rest of us quickly exited the other, with only an occasional glance back. He carefully tied the helicopter down and covered the engines and huge fishbowl windshield for the evening. While Harry secured the copter, we hastily made our escape down the stairs that led back to the pier level as the sun settled behind the boardwalk. On a different evening, we might have taken more time to appreciate the fading light of that day, as the lights from the arcades and the huge ferris wheel began to compete for prominence. But not tonight. On my way off of the Pier that evening, I stopped by the Sky Ride admission booth to let Jay know that I was sorry but he was about to share in our shitstorm, when Harry made his way off the helipad. Ralph and I both handed Jay two dollars, which was the Sky Ride admission, and pocketed our post-ride ticket stubs after we waved them to Harry.

I made a point from that day forward to be sure to respect Harry's money, as he did mine, and he never appeared to hold our transgression against us, allowing us a large chunk of playing time on his pier. We all learned a valuable life lesson that day, and that memory was a frequent reminder that I never wanted to get into another helicopter again. But anxiety and fear often spin off into the universe each time the earth revolves around the sun, melting worry and resolutions. Four years later, when I was home one summer for college break, Tim and I flew with Harry from the Pier to his South Daytona home landing pad in the near dark, making our way without lights on a perfectly nebulous starlit evening with only a few streetlights to guide Harry's craft home. Chalk it up to adolescent invincibility, but the terror and uneasiness that haunted me after my initial ride with Harry was nowhere to be found on that beautiful starry evening. I felt sure that Harry had pulled off a similar maneuver a time or two before, likely over Nicaragua, with the Sandinistas lighting his way with tracer bullets.

With a cursory Daytona Beach history lesson about Harry Doan, WMFJ, and the Ocean Pier swept into the hall closet, we can get back to what's really important...the music.

When the Consolidation played the Pier, the normal format during the busy summer months was for two bands to play each evening on facing stages. The purpose for two bands was to alternate sets seamlessly so the music would appear to "never end." In those enduring summer months of the mid-'60s, the long, wooden-planked pier leading out to the ballroom bustled with teenagers and young adults. The entire adjacent boardwalk area swarmed with teens and young tourists grasping for fun and excitement just beyond their parents' view after the prosaic arcade games grew tiring. An uninterrupted flow of rock and soul music floated softly on the easterly salt breeze, beckoning curious teens out to the Pier's ballroom with the promise of a titillating first dance, or maybe even a kiss.

Like the slow, steady flow of molasses on a summer afternoon, teenagers were drawn away from their family units, migrating from rides and games and moms and dads to the very real game of love and animal attraction. While Duane and Gregg Allman and their new band, the Allman Act/Allman Joys, were testing the waters in St. Louis, my band, the Consolidation, was back home in Daytona with most of us finishing our junior year in high school, preparing to compete in the Greater Daytona Beach Combo Clash at the Ocean Pier.

The Pier was the first, and one of the few, venues that I remember playing that had an actual "band room" for musicians to relax in during breaks. We enjoyed palatial comfort on three or four secondhand, discarded sofas and a couple of old ratty, overstuffed chairs. Ample space in the band room also gave us an out-of-sight place to store dollies and amplifier covers as well as guitar and drum cases. With the alternating band format, we found ourselves either enjoying quiet time with our girlfriends in the band room or listening and dancing to whatever band we were paired with for the evening. It made for as enjoyable and comfortable an evening as rocking and rolling over the waves could possibly provide.

Quite often, when we played the Pier, we found ourselves facing Little Abe and the Houserockers on the opposing stage because both bands were deeply steeped in very popular and danceable soul and R & B music. Abe was a talented and an astute showman who always filled his band with the best Black musicians that Daytona had to offer, including Floyd Miles on drums and Lindsey Morris on keyboards. Occasionally, Gregg and Duane Allman would sit in with the Houserockers, but Abe's core band didn't need much help to bring an audience to the dance floor.

Looking back now, it seems remarkable that none of Daytona's excellent bands composed of Black musicians were entered into the "Combo Clash." It was a different time, and Black musical groups in town had their place, but apparently a "Battle of the Bands" was not one of those places. The Combo Clash, like many other "band battles" during those years, was made up of primarily pop and soul bands that fit into the local AM-radio format. My band, the Consolidation, ordered 45-rpm records directly from Nashville's Ernie's (Ernest Tubb's) Record Mart, circumventing local record stores and radio stations and playing popular national hit songs, often months before they were heard in sleepy Daytona Beach. Clear-channel radio station WLAC in Nashville was our pathway to the newest music and our secret weapon. Having a reputation for playing new music first made us a quick selection for the "Combo Clash," and it didn't hurt, either, that WMFJ's programming manager, Don Skyler, was a personal friend of mine and many of my bandmates. The Consolidation would often stop by the WMFJ studios in the basement of the Daytona Plaza Hotel to help Don write and record advertising jingles and get a little live airtime for our trouble.

The format for the Greater Daytona Beach Combo Clash was decided weeks in advance of the event. The plan was that the Pier would rock with heats from great local bands competing Thursday and Friday night. Two bands would be selected by judges each night, culminating with the four finalists "clashing" Saturday afternoon for the grand prize. It was a win-win situation for the Ocean Pier and WMFJ, and one of

Daytona's great young groups would take home some cash and a trophy that stood nearly five feet tall, and they would also receive invaluable advertising and chatter for weeks before, during, and after the event. Even the losers won, and there were some amazing musicians among the "losers" who would eventually become national music names. Pete Carr, Lenny LeBlanc, Brad Yates, and Joe Hart were just a few of the stellar musicians who didn't win the event but went on to have extremely successful musical careers.

The Consolidation was selected to compete in the first heat on Thursday night, April 13th. We went head-to-head with the U-Main Society, the Original Sound, and the Movements—all great, up-and-coming bands who could hold their own on any stage. The Original Sound included standout musicians Brad Yates, Lenny LeBlanc, Dennis Culler, Mike Cameron, and Joe Hart, and they eventually proved our closest competition. Each band tried to amaze the judges by playing the best, newest, and most unique music that they knew. However, none were privilege to the music selections that we kept hidden under our hats that we had been playing for weeks and months. At the end of the first night, the judges voted, and from what we could discern, our uniqueness and tightness made the difference, and we were declared one of two winners, along with the Original Sound.

On Friday the 14th, the band that we had considered our biggest competition, the Mixed Emotions, played, and during their finale, they unleashed a praise-worthy version of "Eight Miles High" by the Birds. Shaken but not defeated, the One Way Generation, the In Sex, and the Lost Horizons all competed valiantly. The Lost Horizons, with a blues-tinged set, and the Mixed Emotions, with their pseudo-psychedelic guitars and close harmonies, won that heat. The Mixed Emotions leader, Mike Schneider, was a talented lead singer who left Daytona in his middle teens to become famous and was never heard of again.

The stage was set for Saturday afternoon's shootout. Numbers were drawn from a hat, and the order that each band was to play was set. The Lost Horizons kicked off the day with my band, the Consolidation, playing second. The Original Sound played third, and the Mixed Emotions played the coveted last slot.

There was quite a buzz Saturday afternoon as the bands began setting up on stages facing one another, tuning-up and checking sound levels. Most of the bands had played their best music during the heats and didn't have much variety left for the last day. We, on the other hand, played a new fresh set of never-before-heard music that only the WMFJ disc jockeys were even remotely familiar with, and I believe that is what astounded the audience and the judges. Imagine standing in front of a stage hearing for the first time "Gimmie Some Lovin'" by the Spencer Davis Group, "Baby I Need Your Lovin'" by Johnny Rivers, "I've Been Lonely Too Long" by the Young Rascals, "Devil with a Blue Dress On" by Mitch Ryder and the Detroit Wheels, "We Ain't Got Nothin' Yet" by the Blues Magoos, and "Mustang Sally" by Wilson Pickett. Then our set concluded with the never-before-heard ballad "Try a Little Tenderness" by Otis Redding, which got underway with a slow grind, building slowly, and finally exploding from the stage in a frenzy that ended our inspired set.

The Mixed Emotions, with their flamboyant lead singer, played a faithful version of "Winchester Cathedral" by the New Vaudeville Band that was amazingly good but fell flat on the judges as well as the audience. The Mixed Emotions took a stab at "I Had Too Much to Dream Last Night" by the Electric Prunes, but I think it was a bit too psychedelic for their guitar player's ability. "(I'm Not Your) Steppin' Stone" and "I'm a Believer" by the Monkees, played by the Lost Horizons, were both well received by a few of the judges but seemed a bit too light to impress. Among other superb national hits, the Original Sound played an interesting mix of music including what I considered a tremendous version of "Happenings" by the Yardbirds, "Let's Spend the Night Together" by the Rolling Stones, and "Little Black Egg" by the local band the Nightcrawlers.

When all was said and done and the judges' cards were tallied, all the bands were called up to stand together on the main stage, and the winner and runner-up were announced. The cards were tallied and retallied, and it seemed that the voting was close. Third place went to the Mixed Emotions. Hot on their heels was the inspired set played by the runner-up in the competition, the Original Sound. Relieved beyond words, my band had been hoping for the Original Sound to place second, because at that point we were confident for the first time in weeks that we might be the winners, but still, you never know. Declared the winners of the Greater Daytona Beach Combo Clash because of originality and musical finesse, the Consolidation took the grand prize.

Since then, I've wondered if some of the less-knowledgeable judges might have believed we had written some of the songs they really liked but didn't recognize, but regardless of that potential, I do know we were prepared when the time came to compete, and we played the hell out of our sets. Winning felt good. At the age of barely seventeen, it's hard to articulate what winning a competition like this meant to each one of us. We had started our musical journey scarcely two years earlier as a group of guitar-strumming, Friday-night beach-party-harmonizing classmates and friends who moved into the slot as Daytona's number-one band. We were able to avoid the usual teenage musician pitfalls and had huddled close, keeping our noses clean, and we worked hard and smart.

Tim O'Brien, our keyboardist, hordes the huge trophy that we intended to share equally. (Is it my turn yet?) As far as I know, only a single black-and-white Polaroid, "Tim's" trophy, and an event poster remain to mark what was certainly one of the highlights of my young life. We all shared in a prize much more meaningful and considerably more high-reaching than the towering trophy that we left with Tim that Saturday afternoon. The Consolidation shared in the ultimate satisfaction of becoming a single unit from a loosely scattered idea. We worked tirelessly toward a goal until we were declared the most outstanding among our peers. Even our parents, who never really liked the idea of any of us forming a band, took a certain sense of pride in what we had accomplished. That alone was worth the price of admission. It is said that nobody can go back and make a brand-new start, but anyone can start from now and make a brand-new ending...That's just exactly what the Consolidation did.

Chapter 7

Jimmy Burns and Haines City

(Back Roads and Orange Groves with the Soulsations Review)

At some point during the three-day Combo Clash, in April of '67, an older Black gentleman approached my band with an interesting proposition. He was forty-five-ish, stylishly dressed, and introduced himself by handing each one of us a business card that simply read: "Jimmy Burns...Promoter of musical events." Burns had been carefully evaluating all the bands that competed in the Combo Clash that weekend. He was listening for something special, and he found what he was listening for in the soulful selection and interesting arrangements of our music.

We were, undeniably, the best band entered in the competition that April but clearly not the best band in town. There were several Black groups from across the river that could dust us under any stage, but in those days, they weren't considered as worthy competitors by the organizers of the event. Also, it goes without saying that we never would have won any competition that included any incarnation of any one of Duane and Gregg Allman's bands. In April of '67, the Allman Joys had turned the page, becoming the Hour Glass, and they were on the road popping pills and trying to break out of the Chitlin' Circuit. The Allmans' dream progressed logically and analytically during the years I knew them: they evolved from the Escorts to the Allman Joys, which eventually became the Hour Glass, and then they finally exploded onto the world stage as The Allman Brothers Band. Meanwhile, back home in Daytona Beach, the Consolidation was playing our best card in what turned out to be a high-stakes game for our future in the Ocean Pier ballroom. At that point, we didn't really aspire to any grandiose expectations. We were simply hoping to win "$1,000 in Cash and Prizes" that April and maybe impress a few ladies along the way. In reality, winning the Combo Clash attracted the attention of Jimmy Burns, who ushered the Consolidation down the Chitlin' Circuit, awakening to us a world of realization—a world that we scarcely considered before that time.

After a bit of logistical and monetary discussion with our newly hired business manager, Lee Phillips, Jimmy Burns hired us to back up and accompany his all-Black soul review in nightclubs (most of which turned out to be roadhouses and dives) that he was actively booking all across the state of Florida. Burns's soul extravaganza, so we learned, was called the Soulsations. Most of the singers in Burns's stable were local rising stars or Bethune-Cookman College (now University) music majors. All the members were exemplary singers. Bethune-Cookman is a predominately Black university in Daytona Beach. It was and still is a harborage of explosive musical and vocal talent.

Our job was to lend musical accompaniment to the Soulsations in Black nightspots across the state of Florida for anyone who could afford the price of admission. Many of the clubs we played were on the outskirts of small towns and accessible only by dirt roads. Our fundamental job was providing energetic backup music and support for the singers Burns had under his management. We rarely stepped into the spotlights. We were the infrastructure, the foundation that supported everything and gave substance and drive to the review. Powerful, toe-tapping music was our greatest talent as a musical group whether onstage touring with the Soulsations or simply playing a high school prom or Sadie Hawkins Day dance back home. Subconsciously and quite unintentionally, we influenced hundreds of people from Central Florida to the southwest Florida coast because we were unafraid to take a stand, musically.

Our propensity to share love and unity through the music we played drew us close to our audiences. Many of the migrant farm workers for whom we performed were emotionally gutted. Their dismal lives consisted of following the fruit and vegetable growing seasons around the South, from town to town, and from one field or grove to another. Our challenge was to allow them a few hours to exalt in the healing power of music on weekend nights. Working our magic behind Burns's stable of entertainers, we performed a myriad of Temptations, Four Tops, Supremes, Stevie Wonder, and James Brown covers. When we joined with the Soulsations to form the "Southern Soul Review" on the road, the Consolidation spent many hours in our homes or at the Martinique practicing to perfect their individual acts. In time, we learned nearly the entire Stax and Motown catalogs, which prompted us to eventually change our name from the Consolidation to the Soul Patrol. Our time with Jimmy Burns and his singers was fascinating to say the least and at times marginally life-threatening. But those months exploring that uncharted netherworld forced us all to grow exponentially as musicians and as humans.

We were an all-White band of mostly seventeen-year-old high school juniors traveling the state, learning, and chasing down an unfamiliar road into the future. We played some of the roughest roadhouses anywhere in the South, many of which were packed with farm workers celebrating their time off from work with a pint of rotgut whiskey and a girlfriend who just might have been someone else's wife. We did our best, however, to bridge the color gap with our music and with our attitude. The responsibility of any artist is to spread unity and love, building an army much stronger than that of the opposition. Such is the power of music, the most compelling medium in the world. Anyone can raise awareness by vocally supporting an issue, but through our music we subconsciously propagated our message to thousands.

Once, one of our flirtatious band members became such a willing diplomat for integration that bogus rumors spread about the jealous boyfriend of one of the Supremes' impersonators threatening him with a gun. We all grew concerned that there was a slender chance these rumors were founded in fact, so for weeks we played our home gigs on high alert. One night, while the fictitious rumors continued to swirl around the stage, back home at the Martinique someone thought it would be funny to light a string of Black Cat firecrackers and throw them underneath the front of the stage.

A lightning bolt could not have caught any of my panic-stricken bandmates more unaware. After the first firecracker exploded, almost directly underneath the front of the stage, everyone stopped playing and jettisoned their instruments to ensure speedier departures. Before the fuse burned down on the third firecracker, several members of the band had materialized, crouching behind the large Coral bass speaker cabinet to my left. Then, in order to secure a safer haven, some others decided the safest place to hide was behind me on the drum riser two feet above and behind the band. Not at all interested in being in the line of fire, I personally did my best to bob and weave so as not to become a human shield. Fortunately for my heart attack-prone bandmates, nothing ever came of the "irate gun-wielding boyfriend" rumor, and we eventually got back to playing without nervously scrutinizing all the entrances and exits wherever we played. The name of the joker with the pocketful of firecrackers that night has been banished forever from my memory.

On our nervous first night out backing the Soulsations, we were directed to a Black nightclub called the Fox Lounge in Haines City, in the very center of Florida orange-growing country. The nightclub was located just inside of what was referred to as "the project" back in 1967. Haines City is located a few miles west and south of Orlando and east of Lakeland, a few miles south of I-4. In 1967, however, I-95, I-75, I-4, and even the Florida Turnpike were not completed through the state. The only reliable way to get to Haines City from Daytona Beach in those days was through miles of orange groves on backcountry roads. The most direct route in 1967, Highway 17-92, crossed the state and wound slowly from Daytona through Deland, DeBary, Sanford, Maitland, Kissimmee, and then finally to Haines City. There was a short section of I-4 open from Orlando to Lake City, and we completed our journey that way, exiting south toward Haines City through a dense patchwork of orange and grapefruit groves. What now takes an hour and fifteen minutes by interstate was, back then, generally a four-hour AM-radio-accompanied adventure through a twisted maze of cypress swamps and alligator glades, littered with broken-down pickup trucks.

My band left Daytona in Ralph's eight-passenger cargo van around noon that Saturday, and sometime around 4 P.M. we started loading our equipment into the club. There was the customary sound check and a quick run-through of two problematic songs, and then, as the time approached 5:30 P.M., we busied ourselves discussing culinary options, or rather, the lack thereof in Haines City. While we huddled in Ralph's van under the shade of a tree discussing our limited options, two fellows approached from across the dirt parking lot, suspiciously checking us out as they moved in our direction. When they approached the van, one finally asked, "Are you boys in the band?" Their faces told a questioning story of doubt, and it seemed that they might have been questioning our musical validity. They were most certainly not expecting a White band...and certainly not one so young. Proud to be playing anywhere, much less piloting a barge full of talent, Tim, our animated keyboardist, replied, "We sure are *in* the band! Hell, we *are* the band!"

We should have known by the twinkle in their eyes that these two fellows had likely spent their lives making a game of taking advantage of the kindhearted goodness of strangers, and they obviously saw an opportunity when it presented itself. Without wasting a moment, they made the best of this fortunate situation.

"Great, we've been looking forward to this show all week," one announced.

"We're really glad to meet you guys," the other man added, as they both slipped by us and helped themselves to the back seat of the van.

"You guys wanna give us a lift so we can all go and get a taste?"

As innocent young hayseeds, we all thought, "Now that's nice, our new friends want to take us somewhere special for a dinner." With visions of sowbelly and collard greens swirling in our heads, someone mentioned the Whataburger that we passed on the way to the club as a means of possibly demonstrating what kind of cuisine that we had in mind. We all piled into the van and started out across the parking lot, but when we got to the main road, instead of turning right to go back toward town, our two new friends insisted that we turn left. In an enormous leap of faith and absolute error in judgment, we followed their direction.

We drove further and further back into the project, and the neighborhood went from sketchy to doubtful in a hurry. Stray dogs and chickens began to populate the sparsely paved throughway, making navigation in Ralph's massive passenger van unsettling. When the road permanently swapped pavement for gravel, we began to surmise that we were no longer in search of Whataburger. Finally, just as we were all about to suggest turning the hell around, one of our newfound friends ordered Ralph, whose father owned the van, to pull into a dusty parking lot on the right. Surrounded by a slowly settling cloud of dust, we found ourselves surveying a whitewashed cinderblock building with peeling paint, no windows, and only one visible door. The neighborhood bar and liquor store sported a couch, bar-b-que grill, and a few chairs out front under its hand-painted business sign. The name of the business spoke volumes: Lester's Place: No Knives. The near-empty parking lot was a minefield of potholes so large that a compact car could easily vanish if its owner was foolish enough to venture there after dark. Ralph did a great job navigating the ruts and potholes as he found a level parking spot near the center of the lot, across from the front door. There was some space to park nearer the door, but this was obviously as close as Ralph wanted to be.

"I'll just stay here with the van," Ralph offered as the side doors opened and we all poured out into the dusty parking lot. Our new friends were already at the door motioning us to enter as we inched toward the building nervously. Nobody dared to say a word. Eight shoes dragged slowly though the dirt toward the open door as eight eyes kept glancing back to the van as if it were the only uncovered base and we were all hoping for a signal to steal home.

We passed through the door into what can only be described as a parallel universe, and we were initially rattled by the near-complete inkiness that presented itself. As our eyes began to slowly adjust to the darkness, a thick blue haze of smoke appeared first, as a surrounding dankness choked our senses. The smoke hung just at eye level in every direction and swirled around our heads as we walked slowly through the room. As our eyes further adjusted, we could barely discern an ancient bar before us fronted by a handful of decaying barstools, three of which were occupied by men who were either dead or resting their heads on the bar. Four or five shabby tables were arranged haphazardly to the left against one wall, and a pool table with scarcely more felt than slate showing was positioned to the right of the bar.

As we made our way deeper into the room, a man with his back to us was lining up a shot on the pool table. He drew his cue stick back and froze as he noticed us walking into his peripheral view. First he glanced at us and then at the other eyes around the pool table, squinting as if he sensed something dangerous was about to happen. Finally, the ragtag pool shark straightened up quickly, watching us with a suspicious curiosity, and rapped the butt of his cue stick on the floor with a *crack* and cocked his head back in order to better see through his bifocals. It appeared he was in sheer disbelief that we would enter his world, much less interrupt his pool shot. As our pool-playing friend tightened his grip on his cue stick, every soul in the room wondered silently what was going to happen next. An angry drunk with a tight grip on a pool cue was never a good sign. Conversations all throughout Lester's Place stopped, long drags of cigarettes were taken and expelled slowly in our direction, glasses were returned softly to tables, and breathing across the room nearly ceased. We were the center of attention but not in a good way.

Our tour guides were already leaning against the only empty spot at the bar, motioning for us to join them, seemingly obliviously insensitive to the tension that was slowly consuming the four of us. Our guides quickly turned their interest back to the liquor inventory against the back wall while discussing something with the bartender. The two deliberated the purchase that we were about to make with great interest, hand gestures, and finger pointing. One of them finally looked back at me and asked, "Ten High or Old Knotty Head?"

"Oh, Ten High's good," I replied nervously, not able to imagine what Old Knotty Head could possibly be.

"Pint good, or a fifth," he asked. This time he was starting to make sense. We were about to get our first serious taste of booze, but it was far removed from what I imagined my first drink of hard liquor would be like.

"What the hell, let's get the fifth," I replied, doing some quick arithmetic, remembering that we were five (one of whom was still in the van), and there were two of them, equaling seven drinkers.

As quickly as the tension in Lester's Place had turned south, smiles began to return to faces, breathing resumed, conversations continued, and drinking picked up where it left off. For some reason, the fact that we were probably the first White folks to ever set foot in that bar during business hours didn't matter anymore. As we discovered that night, and during many nights to come, White or Black, we were "the band," and just about everyone is at ease with "the band." We were unaware, but while we were busy scrutinizing every eye that pierced the darkness, we had been introduced to Lester, the bartender, and everyone else within earshot as the group on the poster taped to the back of the door and behind the bar. We learned that the Fox Lounge, where we were to play that evening, was the only Black nightclub/music venue within fifty miles. While they were indeed surprised that we were all White, they were all genuinely happy to see us in their neighborhood hangout. With the ice broken and tensions eased, our angst began to subside. So, Ten High it was. Not terribly bad bourbon, we learned, as we each pulled a couple of bucks out of our wallets and handed most of our dinner money to our tour guides. I should have become suspicious when I asked if we needed some Coke as a mixer and one of our new friends told us simply, "Nope, not necessary!"

Just about the time that everything seemed to be settling down inside, Ralph burst through the door and quickly found his way through the darkness to where we were standing. He was nervously mumbling something very emphatically under his breath from out of the side of his mouth, though none of us could figure out what he was saying…"They're millin'," he said.

"Wha?" I questioned softly, trying to conceal my own nervous mumble.

He just kept mumbling the same thing over and over with a tortured look on his face. None of us understood what he was saying, but Ralph kept saying it, "They're millin'!" Each time Ralph repeated it a little louder and a little more emphatically.

After the third or fourth time, I finally asked Ralph exactly what the hell he was talking about, and he elaborated a bit. "They're millin'," he said emphatically again, and then he said very clearly, "They are out in the parking lot milling around my f**king van!" There was a cold assurance in his eyes as if to say, "It's the only vehicle we have. And it's my father's pride and joy. If I lose it I may as well never go home again."

"Ohhhhh, I see," I said, sinking a bit and hoping not too many of the patrons had heard what Ralph was saying with his eyes. I winked at Ralph and turned to our tour guides and suggested that it was time for us to get back to the club for sound check. With everyone in agreement, they lead the way to the front door, paper sack containing our Ten High in hand. I told Ralph that I'd explain everything in the van as Lester cleared the curious crowd away from our partially obscured vehicle.

We settled into our seats for the trip back, I in the front seat next to Ralph, who was still visibly shaken. Tim, Carl, and Ross were in the middle seat, and our friends were cozily settled in the way-back. As if by magic, by the time we had driven the quarter mile or so back to the paved portion of the road toward our gig, the bottle of Ten High was opened, turned up, and emptied, with not a drop left for us. As soon as we got back to the club, the van doors blew open and our newfound friends boisterously removed themselves, stumbling and laughing, from the van. Smirking with a "We got ya" smile, they said they'd see us later and gave us a bit of a salute. With that, they vanished into the twilight, leaving the empty bottle, stench of bourbon, and brown paper bag in the back seat. Without a word, Tim picked up the bottle and emptied the remaining two or three drops of Ten High onto the dry dirt parking lot, watching dramatically as the liquid balled up and was quickly absorbed into the dust at his feet.

Convinced there was nothing left in the bottle, Tim hurled the glass projectile deep into the darkness of the woods. All we could do was stare at each other and silently wonder what the hell had just happened. Someone questioned out loud if we could have possibly been that gullible. There was a long silence, and then the laughter came...slowly and sparsely at first, but in a matter of minutes we were all belly laughing as if we had just cracked open a new George Carlin recording.

Lesson learned, we regrouped and soon found a place to grab a couple of cheap hamburgers, two orders of fries, and two Cokes to share between the band. We remained close to the club until it was time to tune up, laughing and licking our wounds. We pronounced ourselves damn lucky to be able to have dinner at all and fortunate to still have Ralph's van to drive around in. Things could have ended much differently that afternoon, we concluded. Then again, we were "the band" and everyone loves "the band." Still, none of us would burden our parents with the story attached to this gig, especially the part about what was to follow.

That evening we began our "Soulsations" show as we planned, playing an hour of our own music with our lead singer fronting the band to warm up the audience. After the initial warm-up, we normally plunged straight into the meat of the show without a break, transitioning seamlessly into a breakneck two hours with the Soulsations coming onstage one act at a time. After three hours of playing, we were afforded a merciful fifteen-minute break to recharge, after which we would run through another two-hour show with the "Review."

As we started the night, we normally played a warm-up song or two before the doors opened to get the crowd outside anticipating what was to come. Tonight, it sounded, from all the hoots and hollers that we heard, as if we were going to have a better-than-average crowd. Two very large Bethune-Cookman College football players always took the money at the door, stood guard, and kept the peace wherever we played. This evening, the doormen gave us a smiling thumbs-up sign as they peeked outside just before opening the doors to the public. It appeared as if it was going to be a good night after all.

When the bouncers opened the doors, we were already blazing through our second song and getting into the groove for the night. To our great surprise, the first two customers through the door were our "friends and tour guides" from our afternoon sortie to Lester's. We were absolutely astonished that they showed up at all after duping us earlier that afternoon. However, they appeared to still be under the influence of our benevolent investment as they stumbled through the door. Those two knuckleheads were the only people in Haines City that we knew, so as they stepped through the door, Carl began to tenuously wave his tambourine in their direction. The rest of us just smiled and nodded in acknowledgment as they continued walking toward us, waving excitedly at us as if we were long lost relatives. Their frantic waving directed the attention of the two football players away from the money box and toward the bandstand to gauge our reaction. What happened next seemed to occur in slow-motion.

While still grinning and waving clownishly at us with their left hands, our only two fans in all of Haines City sucker-punched the two doormen with their clenched right fists, knocking them to the ground. Undoubtedly fueled by our long-gone bottle of Ten High, they then grabbed the cashbox and vanished into the night, never to be seen again.

The air again began to vanish from our balloon as we looked at each other in total disbelief. Through all of the excitement, we still managed to continue to play, but the exhilaration was quickly being sucked out of the stage. I didn't even want to look over toward Jimmy Burns, who was guarding the door to the Soulsations' dressing room.

Ralph, our guitar player, turned around in the middle of the stage and just stared at me for a moment, making a feeble attempt to keep playing. Soon he folded his arms, resting them ergonomically on his Fender Stratocaster, and tucked his pick in his mouth between his front teeth. After what seemed like an eternity, Ralph finally took his eyes off me and raised them to the rafters, still clenching his pick between his teeth. Ralph's head bobbed slowly to the rhythm of my kick drum, as he rocked back and forth from heel to toe, staring blankly. Soon, though, a smile began to show itself and widened until it finally shone across his entire face. The comedy of it all was once again contagious, and in a few seconds we were all laughing and gesturing to each other unmercifully.

Somehow, we managed to recuperate enough from the confusion of the incident to perform a smattering of songs while those at the door regained their composure. The thieves didn't make off with much money, other than the hundred-dollar bank and change money that lived in the cash box that Jimmy Burns carried to each show. Later, we envisioned that our "tour guides" doubtlessly became local music promoters, legends, or liquor-store owners after getting their initial backing, compliments of our band that night.

As the night went on, we all performed harder than usual to make up for the nagging sense that we were somehow responsible for losing Burns's money box and petty cash, though nobody knew but us. The rest of the show was relatively uneventful.

We were still treated to our first *taste* that evening during our one and only concert break. Our taste came in the form of a noxious beverage called Colt 45 Malt Liquor, which has never crossed my lips since. After three hours of playing continuously at breakneck speed, we were offered a choice of Coca-Cola or malt liquor in the band room. I suppose it was to seem older than our seventeen years, but we all decided to reach for the Colt 45. The malt liquor doubtlessly explained how we had the energy to play two more hours with no additional breaks. It might also explain how we managed to get so horribly lost deep in one of Florida's largest orange groves while trying to navigate back to Highway 27, which was the one and only road back to the interstate. Finally, we found and settled for Highway 17-92, which eventually got us home, but which didn't connect to I-4 at that time. After hours of zigzagging through miles and miles of grapefruit and tangerine trees, we made it to the outskirts of Deland, still twenty miles from home, as the sun was beginning to peek above the horizon. We got to Ralph's home on North Wild Olive Avenue about an hour later.

I am reminded of many lessons learned that weekend in Haines City: unity, brotherhood, trust, and our influence on random people and theirs on us. Primarily, I am reminded that the older I get, the more I realize that none of us really has the slightest idea which way the road will lead. However, it mystifies that despite everything, race relations are barely treading water. Fifty-five years later, I carry a cell phone with a GPS in my pocket wherever I go. I don't often get lost in orange groves any longer, but from time to time I am reminded that there is no harm in asking for directions.

Chapter 8

Jimmy Burns and Baron at the Martinique

Things began moving faster for the Consolidation after we won the Combo Clash in April of '67. The competition had been cosponsored by the Ocean Pier and local AM radio station WMFJ. Before, during, and after the Combo Clash, WMFJ carried our name into every corner of the greater Daytona Beach area, and as far as Cocoa Beach to the south, Orlando to the west, and St. Augustine to the north. Inquiries and bookings rolled in more regularly, and finally it appeared that we were going to be able to repay our parents for some of our equipment purchases.

During roughly that same time, we agreed to back Jimmy Burns's Soulsations Review in shows around the state, and Bill Cook, the owner of the Martinique, hired us on a more regular basis. A more permanent slot at the Martinique represented financial security and a position of local musical prominence for the Consolidation. The Martinique's stage had been witness to some of the finest musicians to come through Daytona Beach during that era, such as the Stereos, a group that featured Jim Matherly, a guitar virtuoso, as well as Duane Allman's and Pete Carr's guitar mentor; Johnny Ford on organ; Bill Sauls on bass; Jimmy Stallsworth on drums; and soul singer extraordinaire, Tommy Knight. There were also the Houserockers, a virtual swinging door for local standout musicians, including Duane and Gregg Allman, Jim Shepley, Floyd Miles, and "Little Abe" Alexander. Of course, there were the Allman Joys: Duane and Gregg Allman, Van Harrison, Bob Keller, Mike Alexander, Maynard Portwood, and Bill Connell. Another local band, the Nightcrawlers, included: Chuck Conlin, Sylvan Wells, Tommy Ruger, Rob Rouse, and Pete Thomason. The Midnight Creepers included Bob Greenlee, who founded Kingsnake Records. December's Children included standout musicians such as Pete Carr, Don Bailey (who incidentally earlier auditioned for the slot in the Minutes that Gregg and Duane ultimately filled, becoming the Hour Glass), Winston Kelly, Tommy Ruger, Mike Wilson, John Rosselot, and Alan Johnston. Lest we forget the Hour Glass: Duane and Gregg Allman, Johnny Sandlin (engineer, executive producer, and head of AR at Capricorn Records), Paul Hornsby (engineer and producer at Capricorn Records), Pete Carr (highly regarded studio guitarist at Capricorn Records, and for the Muscle Shoals Rhythm Section for years), Bob Keller, and Mabron McKinney (Alabama bassists).

Countless amazing musicians did time on that dusty stage at the Martinique on their way to better things, and now it was our turn. Playing at the Martinique most weekends, we were usually paid the going nightly rate, but the real bonus was that we didn't have to haul our equipment to the far corners of the state for a one-night stand. As part of our agreement, Cook allowed us to practice and record with local recording legend Lee Hazen in the Martinique when it was convenient for everyone involved, when he was not napping. Soon the assumption was that we could easily kill two birds with one stone by inviting Jimmy Burns and different parts of the Soulsations Review to the Martinique after our usual practice sessions ended. On paper, it sounded like a solid business plan and good use of time. After a few closed practices, we jelled so well that some members of the Soulsations joined us onstage while we were working at the Martinique on weekends. We used their time sitting in with us to iron out future shows in front of a responsive, live audience. Looking back, our time backing the "Review" was magical and changed everyone involved musically, as well as spiritually. Still, there were a few unanticipated wrinkles to iron out.

Bill Cook and Ringo, who was his manager as well as chief cook and bottle-washer, lived in a small apartment behind his office in the Martinique with a hulking German shepherd police dog named Baron. In the Martinique there are two adjacent, facing doors in one corner of the enormous L-shaped nightclub. The door on the right led out into the small owner/employee/musicians parking lot. The other door led to Cook's business office and living accommodations. Once in Cook's office, there wasn't anything unexpected to see; a television was against one wall sitting on a bookcase that held mostly magazines and papers awaiting disposal. An unexpectedly luxurious desk faced several chairs filling the center of his office, and an overly plush leather sofa faced his desk just to the right as you entered the room. Behind Cook's desk, next to a large calendar thumbtacked to the wall, was a doorway that led to the small bedroom with a tiny bath attached. The office and bedroom were adorned with the stereotypical modern '60s look: green/gold shag carpet and dark faux wood-paneled walls. The only wall adornment in the complex was a small, self-serving plaque hanging above his king-sized bed that simply read: Workbench. This tiny apartment/office, with no kitchen in sight, was where Bill, Ringo, and Baron all cohabitated during most of my time working at the Martinique. A few years later, they would ultimately move into the much larger, more palatial apartment that was built onto the second floor of the Martinique.

As mentioned before, Ringo had a heart aflame with curiosity, and a fly could not slip in or out of the Martinique without her knowing. Her spirit was as pure as angel's breath, she harbored ill will to no person, and I only once heard her utter words in anger. Cook, on the other hand, was a turbulent, disordered, forty-five-year old who held himself in extremely high esteem. At one time he may have been an extraordinarily handsome, beach-lifeguard type. In 1967 his face had assumed that look which ultimately settles upon the faces of most athletes and laborers who have chosen too early a life of leisure.

Their only constant companion, Baron, was a dog of enormous proportions who took seriously his responsibility of protecting the Martinique and its owner. When Baron walked by, it seemed to take forever for the entire train to finally pass, nose to tail tip. He stood uncomfortably more than waist high, his neck was broad, and his thick chest considerable. Baron's beady eyes, slightly turned-up muzzle, lips, and mouth full of massive teeth made him always seem in a state of aggravated snarl.

As vicious-looking as Baron appeared, he was all puppy play and dog treats when Bill and Ringo piled into their Jeep for a ride to the beach. Cook would often leave the Martinique while bands like ours were practicing and go to the beach or cruise the strip to see what was shaking in town. Baron's massive tail wagged the rest of his body, making it clear that he loved to ride in the Jeep with Bill and Ringo. With his enormous head protruding from the side of the vehicle, and tongue waving wildly in the breeze, rivers of slobber dripped from his jowls, covering everything in the back seat.

One afternoon in late April, Bill, Ringo, and Baron were off in their Jeep leaving us alone to practice our music at the Martinique. After searching in vain for the air-conditioning controls for a bit, we surrendered to the reality that we were fated to sweat profusely on our instruments that warm afternoon. When our practice was finished, we were planning to rehearse with one of the male Soulsations groups, "The (faux) Temptations." Learning their music and getting used to their show was a pleasure and always as much fun as working on our own material. Backing up other performers without having to concentrate on background vocals and lead vocals allowed us to stretch out and let the music flow and slip into the pocket more effortlessly. Working with the

"Review" was a tremendous addition to our musical education.

Our guitarist, Ralph, was our undeniable musical leader. He was easily the most accomplished musician in the band from the very beginning. As such, his primary job was to chart the music and present it to us at practices in a way that we could all comprehend. We would each bring songs to the table, and Ralph would take the time to figure out chord progressions, solos, dynamics, and changes. It was something that Ralph enjoyed doing, and we all appreciated the amount of work he put into his task. This particular practice at the Martinique was no different, and there was always much to do.

Ralph had been working on our music and also "The Temptations" songs for some time, and this was the day it would all come together. That afternoon, by the time "The Temptations" and Burns joined us at practice, we had been playing and sweating for a couple of hours. "The Temptations" saw how hard we had been working, so, rolling up their sleeves, they made their way to the four steps on the side of the stage and waited for their signal to join us. We kicked things off with "My Girl," a song that was on their list and which we had played for years. Right on cue, they marched in unison up the stairs to the right of the stage, each stepping up to a microphone, and joined us in the stage lights for an hour of charismatic showmanship. Instantly, the combination of our music and their vocalizing and choreography turned the everyday into magic. The sensation of melding talents and passion with those five Black singers from another world with our band of White adolescents that day was, and still is, beyond description.

The music and dynamic interchange continued as we tore through "My Girl," "Don't Look Back," "Get Ready," "Ain't Too Proud to Beg," "Shaky Ground," and more. Many of the songs they sang were already in our set list. At this point, we only needed to get comfortable with the changes they required and showmanship they inserted into the songs to make them their own. As a unit, we had a tight grip on music dynamics, and "The Temptations" used the ebb and flow of our tempo to put an extra grind into their dance steps. Those guys loved the music, as did we, so in no time we became one entity—not a White band and five Black vocalists, but a well-oiled, soul-dripping, groove machine.

After almost two hours of hard-driving, kick-ass collaboration, we were pretty well all soaked in joyful sweat, laughing harmoniously and ready to take a much-deserved break to cool off. We huddled on metal chairs around small, round nightclub tables on the dance floor, just off the stage, fanning ourselves with extra pages from Ralph's music charts. The conversation, as it would, turned to getting to know each other as musical equals. We discussed important subjects that we all shared in common, like the upcoming first show, how our band got started, the power of the other singers in the "Review," and, naturally, college girls.

About this time, Cook came back from his ride to the beach with Ringo and Baron. Cook let Baron out of the Jeep just outside of the open back door to the club as he always did. That huge, lanky canine bounded into the room where we were relaxing like a puppy smelling for dropped hot dogs to see what was happening in his nightclub.

When Baron's eyes began to adjust and his other senses caught up with his vision, we discovered quickly that Cook's dog didn't share our newfound feeling of harmony and unity with our Black brothers in music. Unbeknownst to us, Baron was apparently vehemently discriminatory by nature. To say that Baron loathed Black people was much like saying that Adolph Hitler didn't care at all for Jews. The Consolidation also discovered that afternoon that Black people have a natural aversion to generously proportioned dogs, especially those that looked as if they could eat a husky five-year-old for lunch. The current feeling of harmony evaporated from the room in an instant and was replaced by an electric tension that crackled and snapped in the air. The atmosphere quickly returned to "us" and "them," and "us" realized that we were not in danger at all. Each member of the "The Temptations" along with Jimmy Burns nonchalantly but nervously began surveying the club for a safe evacuation route, but it was already too late for that.

When it happened, it happened in the blink of an eye and lasted less than a minute. And Baron's teeth blocked the only exit available to the singers and their manager. Baron's puppy-like demeanor completely changed as soon as he was able to focus on "The Temptations." As he puppy-ed across the dance floor, Baron locked down and froze in mid-bounding step, sinking forward as if his front paws had touched hot oil. His trembling head lowered and moved almost indiscernibly from side to side, as if taking inventory of victims. Every hair on his back bristled as his mouth broadened from front to back. Baron's teeth appeared to instantly double in size, still dripping with the innocent but worrisome slobber from his Jeep ride. Baron's appearance of salivating at the prospect of fresh meat only added to everyone's anxiety. From somewhere between those gnashing teeth, a guttural growl began to rise from the mysterious depths of that toothsome animal. That unholy growl quickly rose to an unbearable intensity. When it appeared that Baron was nothing more than a fur-covered ball of anger and resentment, he let out a bellowing wail that would have raised the hackles on the back of Lon Chaney's neck. At practically the same moment that Baron's anger exploded from behind me, from somewhere to my right came a bloodcurdling scream: "SSSSShhhhiiiitttt!!! Dog!!!"

Like somebody flipping the light switch on the doorjamb to hell, pandemonium broke out, and the Black singers who had been laughing and joking milliseconds earlier appeared to evaporate into thin air. They left only the spinning, crashing of metal chairs as proof that they had ever been there. Those five singers, Burns included, scattered instantly into different corners of the room as Baron, teeth gnashing, chased sweat-soaked Black apparitions through the darkness. The Consolidation could only watch in disbelief as Baron endeavored to fulfill his genealogical legacy.

One of the singers somehow made it safely back up to the stage from whence he came. He tried to conceal himself on the drum riser next to my drum kit and behind the bass amplifier. Soon he realized that he was unsafe and that he had basically cornered himself on the stage, making an easy target for Baron, who was bounding up the stairs close behind. At the sight of Baron on his trail, he somehow scratched and clawed himself up to a twelve-inch-wide decorative wooden trough that was connected to the wall about five feet above the drum riser. I watched with great trepidation as he lifted one leg into the trough and swung the other leg up, just as Baron ran across the riser snapping at his heel. Baron appeared to be deriving great joy out of running back and forth across the stage, barking wildly and snapping at the terrified singer.

Soon Baron tired of that folly and turned his fury to the two very athletic fellows who had somehow managed to jump onto the bar across from the stage while Baron was busy there. Insecure in their hiding place, the two then scrambled further up into the far reaches of the ceiling, to a balcony that was built just above the bar area. While they were clamoring to make their getaway, Baron caught a glimpse of their movement, took a running start, and bounded off the front of the stage, landing with a crash nearly halfway across the dance floor, plowing through tables and chairs as he worked at uprighting himself. With jaws snapping and barking wildly, he bounded onto the bar, barely missing their pant legs as they disappeared, screaming, into the rafters.

One more of the singers and Burns himself remained in the club, where they had cleverly barricaded themselves in the ladies' bathroom. With the door barely cracked, they surveyed the action, but Baron sensed their presence and tried his best to scratch and chew his way through the door. There is no telling what went on in the ladies' bathroom while Baron was gnawing and scratching at the door. By the screaming and pounding that we could hear from outside the door, we all assumed Jimmy and the other fellows were busying themselves by constructing a secondary exit from a room that never had one.

Baron seemed happy with his results thus far, though he hadn't caught anyone and there was no blood anywhere in the club. Breaking away from the bathroom door, he started taking victory laps around the perimeter of the club to be sure all the intruders had been scattered to the winds. After nearly completing his third lap, followed closely by Ringo with threatening leash in hand, Baron flew out the same door from which he had entered. A confused Bill Cook could only look on helplessly in disbelief as Baron bolted by. Unfortunately...the dog flew into the parking lot just in time to see the one remaining horrified singer scampering onto the top of one of the cars in the parking lot closest to the building. As Baron attempted to claw and scratch his way up onto the same car, the last of the singers was able to make his way up onto the low-hanging roof above Cook's office. This gave Baron's master and Ringo their only chance to stop the carnage and gain control over the situation.

All of this happened before Cook could figure out what the hell had happened to Baron's sunny disposition. He did realize that he was the only one able to stop what appeared to him as spontaneous madness. So, Cook pulled Baron away from the car that he appeared to be attacking, exasperated and bewildered, trying to settle the dog while Ringo snapped her leash onto his choke collar.

By this point, since nobody had been physically hurt, those not directly involved in the rout burst into uncontrollable laughter, pounding the tables where we sat, laughing as hard as we could. Still shaking our heads and laughing, we finally busied ourselves, helping the singers extricate themselves from their hiding places. Several of them required ladders to remove them from spaces that they were easily able to climb to when adrenaline fueled their escape. An extension ladder was borrowed from the sign painter next door to remove the man hiding in the ceiling crossties as well as the one on the roof of Cook's office. It really was pretty funny, at least to "us." Nobody was physically hurt, a little dirty maybe, and a few egos bruised, some heart-pounding moments certainly, but no one was physically harmed. As we all gained control of the situation, it became obvious that my band was much more tickled than the Soulsations. I am sure that this was not the first time that any of them had been chased by an angry watchdog. And I am also sure that this was our last rehearsal at the Martinique that included any of the Soulsations. After that, we would practice at Bethune-Cookman when we could and at some other neutral site otherwise. When the "Review" came to the club to sing on weekend nights, we made sure Baron was locked away securely in the office.

That was just one more episode in what became a bottomless well of quasi-educational experiences connected to Jimmy Burns and the Soulsations. There was much more to come, and so much more to be learned. They pulled us out of our single-minded selves and painted our band directly into the center of a bright new spiritual tapestry. Looking back, we all laughed and found great humor in the events of that day, but today I wonder if those events became commonplace occurrences to our friends as the years wore on. After all, the German police dog wasn't after "us" that day...He was never after "us."

Chapter 9

Jimmy Burns and Crescent City's Funland

(An Orange Picker's Saturday Night)

In late May of 1967, on what was to be our second outing with "The Soulsations Review," I introduced some of my band to a backcountry shortcut to the gig. Only a few weeks after winning "The Greater Daytona Combo Clash" at the Ocean Pier, and while Bill Russell was poised to become the first Black basketball coach in NBA history, we were about to make racial history of our own in the small Central Florida hamlet of Crescent City.

Located on a dust-covered marl road skirting around that sleepy Southern town, Jimmy Burns booked us to play at the Funland Club on a smoldering, ill-fated Friday night. Looking back, it's mind-boggling that the only time we ever felt even a momentary racial rub while working with "The Soulsations Review" happened with a well-intended and intimate family friend.

Crescent City had for years been a national largemouth bass fishing destination, straddling a once well-traveled tourist highway. Crescent City is located on the banks of picturesque Crescent Lake and firmly anchored in the post-World War II South. Beginning at the Florida/Georgia border, billboards all along Highway 17 touted the St. Johns River and Crescent Lake as "The Bass Capital of the World." For the most part, the town's residents made a rudimentary living commercial fishing and crabbing, cattle ranching, tree farming, collecting pine pitch for the turpentine industry, or growing and picking the miles and miles of citrus groves in and around Putnam County. By the time President Eisenhower's Interstate Highway System had finished subdividing the Sunshine State, "The Bass Capital of the World" had become an all but ignored Southern cracker cliché on a decaying strip of blacktop that led only away from town. But still, fishermen were drawn to the tannin-colored waters of Crescent Lake to fish.

Oaks and pines, heavy dripping with Spanish moss, lined the city's quiet streets, while coverall-clad retirees rocked and looked from well-used wooden porches crying for paint. Old-growth cypress trees and their protruding "knees" ringed Crescent Lake like a protecting army. Those same cypress trees also harbored huge bass for those who knew where to look, and the fishing remained outstanding. Crescent City might not have exactly been at the end of the earth, but you just might be able to see it from the Civil War-era square in the center of town.

From Ormond Beach, my shortcut to Crescent City included a fifteen-mile stretch of desolate, unpaved, dirt road that traversed one of the most unpopulated scrub pine forests anywhere in the state of Florida. For endless miles, there was nothing of interest to break the monotony for us as we drove on and on. There were only limitless strings of electric wires, widely isolated cattle ranches, and the hypnotic, row-upon-row sameness of Continental Can Corporation yellow pines standing neatly at attention. The occasional family truck farm and a random suicidal armadillo were the only other diversions on this section of the as-the-crow-flies country road. My family had driven this dust-choked shortcut hundreds of times over the years to quickly make our way to Crescent City for hunting and fishing trips on Crescent Lake, and we considered the shortcut to and from the lake the beginning and conclusion of our fishing/outdoors adventure. The desolate shortcut easily sliced a half hour off the two-hour drive from the Daytona area to Crescent Lake on primary roads.

Flowing north toward the St. Johns River near Palatka, this tannic, acid-stained lake was teeming with trophy bass, catfish, panfish, and huge blue crabs. Its shoreline concealed all types of wild game, large and small, to the delight of weary hunters. My father's good friend, army buddy, and the Honorable Constable of Putnam County, Les Pigue, owned and operated a fine old fishing camp on Crescent Lake along with his wife, Coreen.

At the age of twelve, Pigue's Fish Camp was my first experience at being immersed in an Old Florida, cracker-style "fishing camp," and it made a lifelong impression. At a deeply discounted rate, Les and Coreen rented my family cabins and fishing boats, where we spent many wonderful weekends and summer vacations fishing and hunting on Crescent Lake. Les and Coreen sold Missouri minnows (from Florida), red wigglers (from Georgia), and local wild shiners. The bait-and-tackle shop there carried the luckiest and fanciest bass lures from Heddon, Creek Chub, and Shakespeare. Coreen was able to augment even the most complete fishing tackle box with shiny lures designed as much to catch fishermen as fish. Coreen worked hard daily bailing out their fleet of slow-leaking plywood row boats, adjusting and repairing motors, and rousting water moccasins out of the tires tied to each dock piling that served as boat bumpers. Occasionally, Coreen would join my mother and my mother's sister, Vera Self, on the lake to prove that women were better fishermen than men. Les and Coreen were as close to family as was possible, and my father eventually became the unofficial godfather to Coreen's son, Stephen L. Boyles.

As the Consolidation caravanned its way to Crescent City that afternoon to play, bad luck struck early in the form of smoke and flames from a wildfire burning across the desolate area between Ormond Beach and the lake that rendered our shortcut intermittently closed. At one point, in the middle of nowhere, we found ourselves face-to-face with the county fire officials ordering us to turn around. The road closure posed a serious problem, because if they didn't let us through, we would have to backtrack to Daytona, making us late getting our equipment set up for the gig. Smoke from the controlled burn was posing a more serious problem than the minimal flames on the roadside. After some negotiation, the firemen on Rural Road #304 radioed ahead and gave us permission to drive through the one-mile section of road that had been closed due to fires and smoke. We were warned to make it a quick mile, and under no circumstances were we to stop for any reason.

Smoke completely obscured the road and trees burned sometimes perilously close to the road on both sides at several points. At times, the smoke seemed to soak up our car and the trees alongside the road like a giant sponge. We managed to stay conscious with windows tightly up, air conditioner groaning, and practicing shallow breathing. Frequent controlled burns were, and are, commonplace in Florida in order to remove undergrowth before allowing it to grow to the stage that it could seriously feed a wildfire. The controlled burns in and of themselves produce copious amounts of smoke but cause negligible damage to the woods and forests. Occasionally however, a controlled burn becomes out of control, as was the case this day. When this happens, fire, environmental, and wildlife officials work in symphony to wrestle the potentially life- and property-threatening disaster into submission.

I managed to keep my car in the center of the road, and we made it to our checkpoint with Ralph and the van close behind. There was a joint sigh of relief as windows came down when we emerged from the smoke and into a clearing sky. The rest of the drive to Crescent City was uneventful. We found our venue, loaded our equipment into the venue, did a quick sound check, and then I had one stop to make before we were to try and find dinner. I should have taken the missing "d" on the Funland sign as a harborage of disasters unseen. The venue's conspicuous sign over the doorway simply beckoned visitors to the Funlan, which became the butt of our jokes until it was no longer the strangest part of the experience. Still, there was no way I could be in Crescent City without at least trying to see Les and Coreen Pigue. So, I gathered Ralph and Ross with me and drove over to their house at the fish camp to say hello while Tim and Carl stayed at the "Funlan" with the equipment and waited for the singers to arrive.

Les and Coreen were members of an exclusive, card-members-only restaurant in Crescent City named "Franks" for the owner, Bud Franks, which, strangely enough, was the only restaurant in Crescent City. My family sometimes joined the Pigues at Franks and even borrowed Les's card a few times while staying at the fish camp to gain admittance to the place. The food at Franks was simple but good. It didn't strike me strange at the time that the only restaurant in town also required a membership card to enter. During my visit with the Pigues, I had hoped that I might get an invitation to use their card to take the band for dinner. What happened next was not at all what I expected.

I had called ahead from the spiderweb-covered pay phone outside of the Funland, so when we arrived at the fish camp, Coreen greeted us at the door of her house with a tray of ice tea, cookies, and a huge smile. Coreen and Les lived in a comfortable but small ranch-style home on the shores of the lake adjacent to the fish camp. It was only steps from the office and bait shop and just a few yards from the strip of motel-style cabins. All of the buildings were painted the same yellowish-brown color with green trim. I had spent at least one summer painting those buildings in turn for fishing and boating privileges.

Coreen was a rugged, leather-faced, pioneering woman who could fix a boat motor, cut the head off a water moccasin, filet a bass, or shoot the eye out of a squirrel before you could drink your morning coffee...and there was no side worse than Coreen's bad side. Marked forever by the sun, her face was a bundle of wrinkled Kraft paper. She was mid-fifties, and under the complex rows of wrinkles and furrows covering her face from ear to ear, the sparkle in her eyes told the history of the younger, more attractive young girl who still lived somewhere just below all those hard-earned crow's feet. Coreen never bothered herself with listless monotony or harassed anxiety, and she minced no words. Her expression was a strange blending of mechanical resistance and exuberant wonderment, and her face was invariably bejeweled with a toothsome grin. Her dress told the story of her diametrically opposing life. Coreen dressed always in comfortable slacks, neatly pressed, cheerfully colored blouses of matching gingham pastel, and harmonizing tennis shoes. She was simultaneously a Southern belle and an oar-wielding fisherwoman for anyone who bothered to notice.

After exchanging hugs and kisses, I introduced Ralph and Ross to Coreen. She explained to me that today being a migrant orange-picker's Friday, Les was pretty busy down at the constable's office. Unfortunately, he probably wouldn't be home until late, but he had asked Coreen to send his regards. However, they were both very excited and interested in where we were playing. Looking back, we were all such clean-cut, well-dressed, preppy young men that I'm sure she never imagined what I was about to tell her.

"Are you boys playing at the high school for a Sadie Hawkins Day dance?" she asked, smiling broadly as she slid the tray of tea on the coffee table in front of the sofa where we all had settled.

"No, Ma'am," I said, "Ah, well, ah, we are playing somewhere else in town. We're playing at a nightclub outside of town, actually," was all I could offer, and it took me a minute to finally blurt that out, while twisting and turning my napkin nervously.

Coreen's bright personality vanished and turned at once into a stone-cold glare. She knew full well that there was only one place to play on the outskirts of town, and it was unfathomable to her that a group of well-dressed White boys could be playing there tonight or any night. When I finally told Coreen that we were set up to play that night at the Funland, there was no denying that she was stunned.

To my dismay, her only verbal reaction was, "Oh, Really?!" It wasn't a surprised "Oh, Really," mind you...it was a "Not on your doggone life, not in a million years!" "Oh, Really."

Coreen quietly excused herself mysteriously into the kitchen and made a brief telephone call downtown. Returning scarcely a minute later, she told us to stay right where we were because Les was on his way home and he wanted to have "a word" with us. "A word" from Les Pigue had but one meaning, and I wasn't looking forward to whatever word or words he had to offer.

Les Pigue was part of a vanishing breed of backwoods cracker Southern lawmen that had built secure communities all across the rural

South after "the Big War." He was a rugged man, short in stature but long on integrity, intensity, and veracity. Les always wore a matching Southern sheriff-style khaki outfit: large, polished constable badge, gun belt complete with revolver, and gray Stetson hat. There was clearly little visual or ethical difference between his civic and civilian nature. When Les worked at the fish camp, he simply removed his badge and gun belt. Individuals intent on bending the law knew full well that Constable Pigue was hellbent on maintaining peace and order. Les was intelligent, straightforward, and rigidly honest. There was no man more esteemed or frightening in Crescent City or Putnam County, and he garnered the respect of all, particularly those foolish or unlucky enough to have spent time under his confinement.

Waiting for Les to arrive, Coreen's living room was silent as everyone stared at one another, uncomfortable and unsure what to do next. Nervously sipping my iced tea, the thought struck me that no good could come from dragging Les away from his office on a Friday afternoon. My stomach tumbled like a trampoline full of first graders as I became more and more anxious about the ensuing confrontation. Ralph and Ross were way ahead of me. From his corner position on the couch, Ralph was beginning to lean hard toward the window, scanning the weed-choked driveway for any glimpse of Les's arriving police car. Ross had gotten up and inched across the room closer to the front door, nervously fiddling with some figurines on one of Coreen's curio shelves that all appeared to be glaring at us. The three of us were wordlessly begging to leave, but we had no choice at that point, and we were hopelessly locked into the situation, grave as it was quickly becoming. I couldn't possibly leave before Les arrived home, and the Funland was simply too far for Ralph and Ross to hike back to.

In all the years that my family had spent with and around Les and Coreen, I had never seen Les upset, though I had heard stories when he and my father had gotten into the scotch that curled my toes. Les was rife with stories about late-night police raids on roadhouses, juke joints, and barely illegal whiskey bars on the wrong side of town. Accounts of well-oiled, hog-leg pistols, leather-clad bully clubs, and gangs of angry White men and mobs of drunken Blacks clashing on his streets and in back alleys instantly flooded back. I became privy to legendary stories from the '40s, '50s, and early '60s, when Putnam County was much less law-abiding than today...stories that a lawful man would prefer forgotten. I wondered quietly if some of those stories were about to be retold in the heat of argument. The thought of Les dressing me down in the presence of Coreen and two of my closest friends made me exceedingly uneasy. I could only hope that the ride from town would allow Les some time to reflect on his years of friendship with my father.

Our inner critics and negative mental chatter had whipped each one of us into a froth of trepidation, but looking back, our meeting with Les actually went much smoother than any of us could have anticipated. I would still rather it not had happened. To this day, I am reminded of that confrontation every time I see any member of Les and Coreen's family. That encounter on the banks of Crescent Lake is a bottomless family legend that remains forever as fodder for whitewash and smirks, even fifty-five years later.

With feathers flying in every direction, Les and Coreen's ever-present flock of guinea hens nervously preannounced Les's arrival. The good constable flew into the fish camp slinging dust, sand, and guinea hens in every direction as he wheeled unmercifully toward the house to where we were waiting. When he finally brought his patrol car to a stop, just inches from the house, a cloud of white marlstone dust settled over everything horizontal or vertical. His arrival shook all of us, Coreen included. The four of us watched from the windows as he slammed his police car door and hurried around from the carport. There was no happiness to be found anywhere in Les Pigue's face that afternoon. He threw the door open, slung his hat and sunglasses on an empty chair, and began by finger-pointing wildly at each of us, now standing in front of the sofa. Not a word was spoken, he just shook that crooked index finger, pointing alternately at each of us as he began collecting his thoughts and building steam while mentally planning his attack. His finger flailed the air uncontrollably and spoke volumes before Les breathed a solitary word, which gave us the awful impression that Les was so upset that he was unable to speak.

Les could not have emerged from a more shockingly different place and time than the three of us that afternoon if he had stumbled into a Beatles recording session in London. The migrant community was and had always been the sandspur under Les's saddle. Regardless of what we believed, that would likely never change. By that time, Les was under the conviction that life might have been different for him. Had his problem not been ongoing and lifelong, Les imagined a more "Andy of Mayberry" experience for him and Coreen. He might have been a full-time fishing-resort operator were it not for the people who inhabited the neighborhood where we were playing that night. Unfortunately, the only way that Les knew to keep the migrants under control was to keep a firm thumb on their community. While we understood the history from which Les came, my friends and I were from a more accepting generation. We knew full well where he was coming from, but to us, the Black singers we were working with represented a portal into a rich musical past and a foothold into the future.

Les had always been a man of few words, but when he spoke, his demeanor showed deliberation in both his thoughts and words. When the wild finger shaking subsided, Les's words began flowing, and, much as I expected, they were deliberate, considered, and unruffled. Les steadied himself against the mantle and waited patiently as Ross returned to the sofa with Ralph and me, staring him down all the way back. With us all settled in, Les began to hold court. He addressed me, but he looked across the couch at the three of us to make sure that there was no doubt from anyone as to his intentions...

Les kicked off the show sincerely but deliberately.

"Bill, forget for a minute that your father, my brother, and I all served closely during World War II together...Forget for a minute that I know and love your family like my own...Forget for a minute that your mother, your aunt Vera, and my wife are best of friends...Let's try to forget all of that."

A storm was building in Les Pigue's mind, but for the life of me he wasn't giving me any clues as to whether it was going to be a thunderstorm, tropical storm, hurricane, or just a summer shower. It's tough to fabricate a convincing defense when your opponent isn't willing to show his offensive cards. Les was winding up like a major league pitcher, and all that we could hope was that we didn't whistle while his fastball flew by home plate.

Les started again. This time his brow furrowed and his head cocked to one side menacingly. Les was intimidating, like a junkyard dog slowly backing his victim against a fence, getting ready to go in for the first taste of blood.

"I need to make myself absolutely clear, so that there is no chance at all for any confusion...Here it is...I need for you and your friends here to go back to that juke joint and get your stuff right now, pack it up, and drive back to Daytona. And! And this is a big 'And'...Don't you boys ever come back here to my town with the intention of doing anything like this ever again. Am I clear?"

His words fell over us like a blanket of soaking rain, and there was little to do but to let his words soak us to the bone. The three of us began to look at each other, trying to somehow find shelter from this storm, but even though his words subsided, the sting of the raindrops continued. Finally, I decided that there was nothing else to do.

"It was my fault, and Les was my friend," I thought, as we all sank deeper and deeper into the gully washer that was filling every inch of that room with an ethical uneasiness. No doubt, we needed a lifeboat, and I was going to have to be that lifeboat. I felt that we were reasonably safe playing at the Funland. The biggest dilemma here was not our personal safety but that we were crossing a line drawn across the Deep South more than a hundred years ago. Everyone, including Les, knew it. But we had a business arrangement, and a deal is a deal. Les was just going to have to understand that and put history aside for one night.

I don't have a clue where my words came from that afternoon, but they seemed to spill in Les's direction as if my mouth was moving but someone else was speaking. I dug my heels in and braced for a battle. Fortunately, the words I managed were precisely the words that Les needed to hear.

"Yes, Sir," I began, "I understand you, loud and clear, but it will be impossible for us to pack up and go home. We just can't do that. We have a contract with the promoter, an agreement with the singers that we work for, and there will be a very disappointed crowd at the club tonight if we don't show up. Our equipment and instruments are already set up. We've checked the sound levels, and we have our lights set up and ready to go. Everything is ready. Our two other musicians are waiting for us back at the club, and the singers will be arriving soon if they haven't already gotten there. Everyone is ready to play and expecting us to be there. All I wanted to do was to let you and Mrs. Pigue know where we'd be and to see if we could use your card to get into the restaurant downtown to get dinner before we played...I guess using your card for dinner is out of the question now?" I hoped that my final question might strip the bad air and some of the electricity from the room.

Les's stony glare began to soften somewhat as if something had tickled him deeply, but still he refused to allow a smile. He put his head to one side, nodding rapidly several times in succession like a bird pecking at a hard berry. A slight grin moved cautiously to the corners of his mouth, and for the first time since entering the house, his right hand moved cautiously away from the butt of the .45 caliber, police-issued revolver strapped to his hip. (I imagine now that he saw a bit of my father in me.)

Why I don't know, but as quickly as he had entered the room, Les turned on his heels, snatched up his hat and sunglasses, and started for the door. Waving his hand as if to say good-bye to no one in particular, Les managed only a few words on his way out. "Fine! You do what you have to do, and I'll do what I have to do!"

With that, he was gone, and Les took with him all the air from the room. To this day, it is still unclear why he backed off and began to consider allowing us to play at the Funland. More likely than not, Les began to look at our arrangement with the Black singers logically, more as a business agreement than a teenage folly. Still, there was a rub there that would not ever completely disappear. Race relations in Putnam County inched cautiously forward that weekend, but it was barely enough to move the needle.

With Les gone from the house, leaving us an unclear anointment, there was little left to do but to say our tenuous good-byes to a stunned Coreen and figure out something else to do for dinner. The ride back to the Funland turned from quiet to a nervous euphoria as the backwoods miles passed uneventfully. We pulled into the dirt parking lot next to Ralph's van to park, and I half expected to see Les's police cruiser there somewhere, but it was not. Still, there was a nagging feeling deep in my being that somehow Les hadn't totally let go of his prejudices that afternoon and that sometime, somewhere, there was going to be a reckoning.

That evening, after checking in with Les and Coreen, our night went pretty much as planned with one major exception. Very much to our surprise, when the music started and the doors were opened, two sheriff's deputies quickly stationed themselves on each side of the main doors, and two more deputies set up residence on either side of the stage where we were playing.

While this made us uneasy, and the club owner even more so, there was frankly nothing anyone could do. Legally speaking, this situation became Les's clause to our contract, thereby allowing us to work at the Funland for one, and only one, night. Going forward, Les could sleep well knowing that nothing would happen to this bunch of stupid White boys on his watch. I don't know if my father was involved, but Les certainly wasn't about to be complacent in any harm coming to me.

The following five hours went quickly as our music and the singers' shows were beginning to crystallize into a finely tuned mixed bag of melody, funk, and showmanship. They were becoming comfortable with us, and we with them. So comfortable, in fact, that one of the musicians in our group took a liking to one of the "Shirelles" singers. Had she not previously been involved in a long-term relationship, it might have blossomed into a lasting romance.

As we packed up equipment and loaded our two cars for the trip home, closely watched by our four guards, I silently wondered how differently the night might have been without the still-present deputies. They watched intently as we packed the last of the microphones, stands, guitars, drums, and amplifiers. When we finished loading the PA system, I thanked the deputies and told them that we were fine if they wanted to go home, but apparently they had other orders. Still, we thanked them again and got into our cars and started to drive out of the dusty parking lot toward the driveway leading out to the main road home.

As we began to pull away, I looked into my rearview mirror to see Les step out of the shadows, his aviator sunglasses catching a glint of light from the single security light fixed to a telephone pole in the middle of the parking lot. His arms were crossed and he appeared to be not happy at all. I could have kept driving, but I stopped, and as he walked toward my car, I put it in park and stepped out to speak to him. I was sure that he wasn't out at 3 A.M. to tell me to drive carefully. I was right.

Les first whispered to me in a low tone that the back road home, that he knew I'd probably take, was mostly clear of smoke, and then he told me and anyone else within earshot, "You and your friends are not welcome back in this county again unless it is to play at the high school—period!" I managed a sheepish, "Yes, Sir," as I slipped back into my car. "Please tell Mrs. Pigue that I hope I didn't mess up your evening too badly," I said and then drove off toward the highway as we pulled away for what would certainly be our last time playing at the Funland. We all knew that there would probably never be another gig in Crescent City, certainly not there.

Tired mentally and physically from the stress of playing that night under Les Pigue's watchful eye, I decided to chance the shortcut back to my bed in Ormond. Les had indeed radioed ahead and confirmed that the smoke and fires had pretty much settled down, and my shortcut was open and clear, with the exception of a short section of the road between several cattle ranches where the fires were mostly out but still smoldering. There the smoke lay heavy on the road and filled the pastures and woods with its choking thickness. That late at night there should not have been any traffic, so we decided to take our chances and make a run for it. Ralph had decided to take the longer, smoother, paved road home, but as a reckless adventurer, I decided to take the deeply rutted shortcut back the way we came.

Tim and Ross didn't care about the smoke, and their equipment was packed in the back of my Plymouth Valiant, so they didn't have much choice. It was 3 A.M., and with no traffic on this backcountry dirt road, I soon had my car up to forty-five miles per hour as we skipped across the washboard road.

Suddenly, through the smoke a car appeared ahead with its bright headlights glowing, coming toward us. The blinding glow of the headlights made it nearly impossible for us to see through the gray thickness ahead. I tried flashing my bright headlights several times, but the oncoming car seemed intent to blind me as we approached each other in the smoky darkness. Finally, the car with the bright headlights passed by, and when he did, I realized why he was intently focused on keeping his brights on. There in front of my car, not twenty feet ahead, was a massive cow that had somehow escaped her fencing during the fires. The enormous bovine was easily as tall as my car.

Tim and Ross were asleep by this time, Tim riding shotgun and Ross in the seat behind me, sharing his space with an amplifier and some of my drum kit. Tim snoozed in the bucket seat in the front next to me with his head resting against the side window.

When I slammed on the breaks, the car began spinning. The first thing that a horrified Tim O'Brien saw when he opened his eyes was the face of the bewildered cow in the window next to his head. Tim later told me that he and the cow had made eye contact in that instant, and he was sure that both were forever traumatized by the event. As I tried to keep the spinning car in the middle of the road and out of the ditches on either side, Ross woke up from a dead sleep. In his typical laid-back, deadpan fashion, he tapped me softly on the right shoulder as he watched trees and fence posts spinning by the front window and told me what a great job of driving I was doing.

How we stayed on the road is beyond me. Dumb luck often trumps lack of defensive-driving experience, but when we finally came to rest, the car was pointing in the right direction and we sat squarely in the middle of the road, as if nothing at all had happened. Even the disc jockey on WLAC Nashville seemed unshaken. We checked for traffic, front and back, and all stepped out of the car, shaking a bit at the close call we had just spun through. Wide awake now, we needed to collect ourselves, shake off the confusion, and check on the gear in the trunk to make sure it was all in one piece. When I opened the trunk, everything seemed in good order, but to my surprise, Tim grabbed a microphone stand that was near the back of the trunk and disappeared into the darkness down the road in the direction of the errant bovine. When Tim got back to the car, we didn't ask any questions as he wiped something off the base of the microphone stand in the dew-covered grass along the roadside. After a few really quiet miles of contemplation, Tim looked over at me and asked if I was a fan of sirloin steak. He added that it would be a shame to waste so much and wondered aloud if I wanted to turn around and fill my freezer? I was tempted, but I was now on a mission to get us all home, and drove on into the darkness before Farmer Brown noticed his cow had gone missing. We all assumed Tim was joking.

We played quite a few dates with Jimmy Burns's singers, including Crescent City, Haines City, Naples, and others that either slip my mind or I have purposely repressed. After five or six especially unforgettable dates with Burns's singers, the school year at Bethune-Cookman College came to an end, and so did our relationship with Burns and his stable of talented singers. Undeniably, our time with Jimmy Burns was an eye-opening experience, one that moved our band ahead musically as well as philosophically.

Race relations were a kind of unspoken plague during my teenage years in the South. In those years, racial inequality coursed all around us like a swarm of angry bees. Our brand of reverse intimidation taught me and my friends so much about life, music, and the iconic laughter embodied within us all. As White teens in the South, we broke through a good number of racial barriers, and we empowered Black musicians to work in previously "Whites Only" venues. Music in general, but particularly rhythm and blues music, is about truth, justice, and optimism. Music is the great equalizer and healer. In the last fifty-five years, at least a small portion of our Crescent City promise has been realized. I wonder if Les and Coreen lived to see it happen.

Chapter 10

The Martinique

We all grow up somewhere, but it's not where we grow up that matters, it's where we come of age. Like so many of my high school classmates and friends who came of age in Daytona Beach during the mid to late1960s, my mind is constantly drawn back to those lighthearted, carefree days of sun, sand, and music. It was a magical time when the sun seemed to shine endlessly. Those glorious days were bound together with an ethereal ribbon of music and friendship. As I retrace my footprints through the streets of my life, those days spent in Daytona Beach learning and absorbing music glow brightest.

During the summer of 1968, a soggy paper cup bulging with ice, Coke, Bourbon de Luxe, and raging hormones always rested in a puddle of condensation next to my drum set. The early years of my musical life unfolded in teen dance halls, recreation centers, frat houses, roadhouses, nightclubs, and even a few strip joints. Always gazing through a dazzling haze of stage lights and blue smoke, those summer nights seemed to never end. It was then that music became rooted in my DNA to be passed down to my children and their children, like a family heirloom. It was in the mid-1960s that I came of age, during bluebird days at the beach, and glorious nights in the cavernous, music-filled wonderland known as the Martinique.

Even now, I can perfectly recall those moments...those handful of times, late in my first years, playing in the house band at the Martinique, when the late afternoon light was at its gauzy best. Those minutes before the doors were unlocked to the waiting public for the evening, and before our band began playing each night, the very special beauty of Daytona's Main Street seems distilled instantly in a crystal clarity. As afternoon shadows stretched into twilight, the community surrounding the Martinique and Main Street became, to me, part and parcel of the city's grandeur.

As the middle 1960s mellowed toward the 1970s, the preppy smells of English Leather and Canoe slowly transitioned into patchouli and sweet incense. Those scents wrapped the heavy wetness that surrounded the Main Street community with heady fragrances that wafted to us from an unseen San Francisco.

Increasingly, hippies emerged from their "Beaver Cleaver" lives, leaning comfortably against every building, windowsill, and lamppost on Main Street, mimicking any street corner in Chelsea, LA, or Haight-Ashbury. Preppy Gant shirts with light starch, khaki pants, and Bass Weejuns of the mid-1960s slowly gave way to a gentle California vibe that spilled into the streets like sweet sassafras and molasses. Hip-hugging corduroy bell-bottoms became the fashion, with wide belts sporting leather "stash" pouches. Nehru jackets and Tom Jones shirts stippled with bright-colored flowers and bold stripes filled the eye. Some wore buckskin jackets or leather vests dripping with fringe and colored beads. Granny glasses, leather sandals or desert boots, and wildly striped pants completed the look.

The world around Main Street was populated by familiar strangers with monikers like Ringo, Karpo, Moose, Drew, Dabo, Beaver, Hair, Joy, Peaches, OJ, Mother, Phyll, Markus, Sweats, and Jaybird. Like myself, some had rooted here while others were summer visitors enticed by the vibe to stay, and some were runaways looking for a fresh start and a friendly face. Many, like Duane and Gregg Allman, inhabited apartments in the blocks of side streets that bordered the Martinique and Main Street. Music was the nail that held this gentle cosmos together. My band, the Consolidation, supplied the hammer, and the Martinique was our toolbox.

The spring of 1968 found most of my band in their late teens and senior year in high school, eager to fly away and begin the next chapter of their lives. I was quickly closing in on my eighteenth birthday, and while the entire world beyond Main Street seemed enveloped in political madness, pearls fell at my feet. Parked out in the parking lot of the Martinique was a new 1968 Barracuda Fastback that roared to life every time I turned the key. A bevy of happy girls always waited patiently at one of the tables next to the stage for my band to finish, and the prettiest one, the daughter of a Unitarian minister, rode home in my car. Most significantly, however, a recent college acceptance ensured that I would be spending the fall of 1968 in the relative safety of the South Carolina foothills at Clemson University, and not at boot camp awaiting Uncle Sam's next all-expenses-paid flight to Saigon.

Looking back now, those afternoons spent at the Martinique rehearsing and learning new music would become enduring images that would last for a lifetime—memories so unlike the average adolescent high school experience. Outside in the late afternoon glow, life teemed.

Our schoolmates did their homework, stocked shelves at Winn-Dixie, cut lawns, and practiced football, basketball, or baseball. Inside the Martinique, there was a singular world that smelled heavily of ancient cypress rafters, stale alcohol, cigarette smoke, wet mops, and damp, musty concrete. With only the brightness from a single open door bathing the stage in its limpid glow, eyes slowly adjust, but as that wonderland slowly unfolded visually, that snapshot in time emblazoned itself on my mind forever.

Often, a young blond guitar player named Duane would stop by to share licks, riffs, and techniques for bending special strings with our guitar player. Duane shared techniques that he had discovered on his own or had learned from someone who had taken the time to share with him. Duane also pontificated about his music philosophy with us and the work ethic that had made him a legend in local music circles in just a few short years. We listened intently, hopeful that his passion and fire might somehow flow across the table and into our hands. In those afternoons and evenings, Duane imparted principles that would bolster a lifetime of musical appreciation. Those afternoons and evenings that I spent with my closest friends, in the company of Duane Allman, are hours that I will take with me forever.

Most people reveal themselves very slowly, over time, while others are instantly unforgettable. Duane was, in a moment, thoroughly unforgettable. For those of us who knew him as teenagers, Duane was an iconic figure. His ability and talent glowed like an aura, although at the time he was just another character at the "musician's clubhouse" called the Martinique, or the "Q," for short.

The Martinique's humble beginnings were essentially biblical in nature. The building started its life in the early 1900s as a stable for the police horses that patrolled the beachside of Daytona Beach, before police cars. As one walks through the cavernous building today, it's not hard to imagine it as a stable, lined on each side with individual stalls. With a bit more imagination, one can see the building going from police station to speakeasy in the 1920s and 1930s. Rumors buzzed for years about Dillinger and the Barkers using secret passages from the club to the upstairs apartments for reasons known only to the ladies of the night who frequented the club in its prohibition days. Remnants of those secret passages still connect the overhead office with the main room, if you know where to look.

During the 1940s and 1950s, the Martinique was called the Martinique Palm Club. The inside of the club was decorated with large, simulated palm clusters that sat in wooden planters atop the heavy beams and supports that crisscrossed above the dance floor. During those years, the Martinique was a dance club with a full bar, beautiful stage, and sizable hardwood dance floor. Tourists would stroll down Main Street to the Martinique Palm Club from the neighboring hotels and restaurants. From its beginning, people made their way nightly to the Martinique to dance, enjoy a cocktail, meet new friends, or just bathe in the hypnotizing light from the huge, revolving, mirrored ball turning slowly in the ceiling of the ballroom. The music of that time was mostly jazz and big band flavored. Many of the famous touring bands of the day made regular stops at the Martinique.

During the 1960s and 1970s, the Martinique morphed musically with the times, and the mode of doing business changed with the wind, mostly for legal reasons. While Bill Lawler and Frank Meyer owned the building in the early to mid-1960s, the club lost its liquor license and became for a time a bottle club. A small package store was built onto the side of the building next to the office, where pints of libation were sold by Lawler himself, who had access to the club through a secret door inside his mini-liquor store. Once inside the club, after a small cover charge was paid, "set ups" could be purchased by the gathering audience for a dollar. This circumvented the necessity of a liquor license, and from that point on, the club went from bad to worse, as far as the local constabulary was concerned. The club's liquor license was renewed, revoked, and reinstated again almost weekly, and for a time in the late 1960s, there was no liquor license or bottle club at all. During most of late 1967 and early 1968, only soda was sold, and the Martinique became a glorified teen nightclub. Minimal cover charges, usually a dollar or less, were common to help offset the cost of fabulous bands that seemed to always make their way to the "Q."

The building's owners retained an endless list of astute lawyers who were well versed in the ins and outs of loophole navigation, most of whom visited the club nightly. The Martinique's legal representatives were impressively dressed denizens of the night who wore dark suits, white French-cuffed shirts, gold cufflinks, and pricey alligator-skin shoes. They drank Canadian whiskey neat, always reserved the best tables, had their pick of the waitresses, and, of course, they never paid admission.

The success and popularity of the Martinique in the 1960s and

1970s can be contributed directly to two things, the first being the quality and popularity of the music that was provided all year long from bands like the Stereos, the Allman Joys, Clarence Carter, the Nightcrawlers, B. J. Thomas, the Spencer Davis Group, December's Children, the Sir Douglas Quintet, the Consolidation, the Soul Patrol, the Newports, Whale Feathers, the Hour Glass, the 31st of February, and many others. The second and quite possibly the biggest factor in the club's popularity was its air of danger and intrigue. Most teenage boys and all teenaged girls in Daytona Beach were restricted from ever setting foot in the Martinique by concerned parents. Naturally, those who were restricted from ever setting foot in the "Q" made up 95 percent of the average crowd. Teenagers have always longed for what they can't have, and it will always be so.

There was an unwritten law at the local high schools that nobody ever mentioned within earshot of a teacher or parent how much fun they had at the Martinique over the previous weekend. There were other teen dance halls that were perfectly acceptable—the Seabreeze rec, Granada rec, the skating rink on the west side of town, and high school dances in cafeterias, but the Martinique was strictly off limits to virtually everyone, making it *the* place to be.

In short, simply forbidding access to the Martinique only added to the club's intrigue and titillation. Nobody knows for sure where the rumors of it being a dangerous place came from, but they were rampant. Surely the rumors were, in part, related to newspaper articles that chronicled the long string of legal problems that seemed to constantly involve the club's liquor license. Also, there were the rumors that bartenders rarely checked the IDs of even their youngest patrons. Before I ever had the nerve to set foot in the "Q," I had heard rumors that if you could reach the bar, you would be served. In the eight or so years that I worked at the Martinique, I only witnessed one fight, and that was a rather interesting altercation involving two very attractive ladies from Tennessee. Most people left their anger at the door, and if not, there were always muscular security guards like Jay Laing, George Karpodinis, or Moose to direct arguments outside into the night. There was simply no better place in town for the sixteen- to twenty-five-year-old crowd to meet and enjoy some of life's real pleasures. Still—"good girls" never stepped foot into that den of inequity, and if they did, nobody ever told.

During 1967 and 1968, my last year in high school, the band that I played in worked more than two hundred nights, the bulk of which were as house band at the Martinique. However, my earliest memories of the "Q" date back to 1964, when I was fourteen years old.

In 1964, Bill Lawler and Frank Meyer co-owned the Martinique, but Meyer soon grew weary of constant legal battles and didn't last long as a partner. Lawler, however, seemed to thrive on the constant challenge. Bill Lawler was a square-jawed, callously featured ex-policeman and boxer from Boston who appeared to rarely surrender to thoughts of anxiety. His fifty-something face bore the rutty map of Clancy's Ireland. Under his left eye was a jagged scar, and the bulk of his pug nose pointed east when he faced north. His skewed nose was no doubt caused by a smashing blow received in a random barroom fisticuff years before. His gray hair was military short and squarely parted to the left. Always fond of his "inebriant," Lawler nipped at single malt from a pint bottle throughout the day, weaving and bobbing as he went about his daily work. By evening, he somehow found the ability to handle business. Lawler's leathery appearance was balanced by his fatherly desire to allow as many paying patrons into the club as possible on any given night. Consequently, checking IDs was not a priority. If you were a musician or a fledgling musician, as we were, and had two dollars in your pocket, you were allowed in just so long as alcohol didn't make you conspicuous.

In 1964, at the tender age of fourteen, I was just beginning to play music with a group of my confederates, and our rhythm guitar player's much older brother, David Johnston, snuck a couple of us from our fledgling band into the Martinique to hear one of the best bands that I had ever heard. David was in college at the University of Florida at the time and in a fraternity. His advanced musical taste led us to hear many great bands in the area. David also hauled us around when we were too young to drive to gigs and helped get us booked on fraternity row at Stetson University in Deland, Florida State University in Tallahassee, and the University of Florida in Gainesville as our music developed. This night at the Martinique, David instructed us to be cool and to pay particular attention to the lead guitar player, who was, in his opinion, the best in Florida. David was dead on.

The band we saw that night was Tommy Knight and the Stereos, who were led by guitarist Jim Matherly from Tennessee. Matherly was greatly influenced by Les Paul, Bob Wills, and the old Western swing bands, though he could play just about anything, as he told me in an interview some years later. The rest of the band consisted of Johnny Ford on keyboards, Bill Sauls on bass, and Jimmy Stallsworth on drums. The

Stereos also boasted a Black lead singer, Tommy Knight, who was short in stature but filled the stage to overflowing with showmanship. In those days, you didn't often see bands with a mixture of Black and White musicians. The Stereos were top-shelf musicians, and Tommy Knight was a master showman and vocalist.

Matherly brought his band down from Knoxville to play at the Safari Beach Motel pool deck during Easter vacation of 1963 for two weeks. Local attorney and high school football coach Bud Asher, who would later become Daytona's mayor, owned the Safari, which became famous far and wide as the place to go to hear live music during Easter break while gazing at the Atlantic and meeting girls. With sand in their shoes, Matherly and the Stereos returned for the summer, landing the house-band job at the Martinique, getting paid the paltry sum of ninety dollars a week per person.

During one of my subsequent trips to the Martinique, David pointed out Duane Allman to me as an up-and-coming guitarist to keep an eye on. I had seen Duane playing with the Escorts before and I thought him impressive, but this was the first time he was acknowledged as a standout by someone who really knew music. I remember Duane leaning against the cigarette machine on the wall between the men's and ladies' bathrooms near the stage looking cool with his longish, collar-length, red-blond hair. He was trying not to be obvious while watching the Stereos, but mostly he was watching Jim Matherly. According to Matherly, Duane would stop by and listen to the Stereos often, and they would talk during his breaks. Duane was just becoming the hot kid on the block at that point, and Matherly was full of tricks that Duane wanted in his bag. Duane was beginning to experiment and expand his talent, and his sense of competitive spirit caused him to hone in on the talent that flowed so effortlessly from Matherly's fingers. Duane would watch Matherly play and go home, copying jazzy riffs and sliding R & B fills and country-flavored accents that would eventually become the basis for his singular slide guitar style years later. Duane learned a lot from Matherly, and he learned it quickly. Duane also took guitar lessons from Matherly's friend and sometime guitar teacher Ted Connors. Connors was a huge influence on both of the young musicians, as well as a generation of guitar players who were fortunate enough to study under him.

As time went on, Matherly eventually met Duane's younger brother, Gregg, who was working with Duane in the Escorts, and in October of 1965, something unusual happened. Matherly and Duane switched bands, and Matherly filled in for Duane with the Escorts all that winter while Duane played lead guitar with the Stereos in South Florida.

Gregg, Van Harrison, and Maynard Portwood were still in high school and only able to play out of town on weekends during most of the school year. Gregg and the rest of the Escorts were not quite ready to leave school behind for life on the road. Duane, however, had jobs for the band in South Florida, so Matherly joined the Escorts for the winter and used his contacts with Lawler to book the band at the Martinique on weekends, while Duane played with the Stereos nightly in Fort Pierce, Florida.

Matherly also used his connections to get the Escorts into Lee Hazen's recording studio that winter. Hazen was a gregarious twenty-something Ormond Beach music lover who seemed to have a great recipe for getting the most sound out of a band, and he was very generous with his time. He had done his stretch in the navy, and the only thing that mattered to Lee Hazen was making the best recordings possible. Hazen grew up three houses away from me in our Ormond Beach neighborhood, and then, after the navy, he moved a few blocks further away into a mother-in-law cottage behind a large estate home owned by the Troese family on John Anderson Drive. I went to school with Mike Troese. I had known Lee from the time that our family moved to Ormond in 1962. His father, Lee Sr., had a small business making seasonings in his garage called Colonel Lee's Louisiana Spice. By the end of his career, Lee Hazen Jr. had recorded thousands of songs by hundreds of artists over his career and had three gold records on the wall of his Pond Studio in Hendersonville, Tennessee, before he died.

The Escorts had recorded demos at Hazen's studio in 1964, with Duane on guitar, but Matherly, a close friend of Hazen's, suggested that the band go back to the studio and record some more music, this time with Matherly on guitar. Matherly had been an on-call studio guitarist for Hazen and had also recorded demos for him with Chuck Conlin, who later joined the Nightcrawlers as writer and lead singer.

Chuck Conlin's early demos were recorded at Bob Quimby's studio by Hazen. Quimby was another Ormond Beach recording engineer who had taken Lee Hazen under his wing before his stint in the navy. After his time in the service, Hazen worked for Quimby's Songwriter's Guild as an engineer, musician, and songwriter. Quimby, who was probably in his mid-forties at that time, had a small studio set up in the living room in his Ormond-by-the-Sea home and recorded quite a few bands there.

The Consolidation recorded a 45-rpm at Quimby's studio in late 1966, backing up a local WROD disc jockey, Ron Frasier, on two songs that he had written and wished to record. The 45-rpm contained the Frasier-penned "Summer with You" and "Another Girl," released on Catalina Records in 1967. The record is credited to Ron Frasier and the Consolidations (with Consolidation misspelled as plural). I recall setting up our equipment in Quimby's living room, and there was a reel-to-reel tape recorder on the mantle, along one wall, in the middle of the room, recording only four tracks. We learned the songs and recorded them live in one or two takes, and Frasier recorded the vocals at a later date. To our surprise, those two surf-related summer songs actually got airplay in Florida, and I remember thinking to myself, "Damn! As easy as that...we're on our way!" Well, my excitement was a bit premature.

Quimby's equipment was pretty primitive, even for those days, so when a group needed something a little more polished, they would turn to Lee Hazen for recording. Hazen was quite a bit younger and more in tune with popular music at that time. Most of the bands from the Daytona Beach area—the Nightcrawlers, and the Escorts with Duane, and the Escorts with Jim Matherly on guitar, as well as the Newports and various other groups—recorded at Lee Hazen's studio, and so did my band, the Consolidation.

Hazen preferred to record the instruments at the Martinique during the afternoons when nobody but the band was there, using his homemade mobile recording studio. This is how the recordings of the Escorts, with Matherly playing lead guitar, were recorded one afternoon during a practice session. Hazen would back a small travel trailer close to the rear door of the Martinique and run microphone cables into the building and up to the stage, recording the instruments there. Later, he would have the band record their vocals in a burial-casket shipping crate that he used as an isolation booth at his cottage studio in Ormond Beach. Hazen generally recorded two-track stereo at 15ips, which was how the Escort tapes were recorded. Most of the bands in Daytona that could afford one hundred dollars for demo tapes made their first recordings just that way.

It is a bit hard to tell who is who on the Escort recordings, but Matherly is playing guitar on the tapes that were recorded in 1965 at the Martinique and completed at Hazen's cottage, and Duane played on the recordings that Hazen engineered in 1964 entirely in his studio in Ormond. Everyone assumes that it was all Duane playing on those tapes, but that's not true. In Hazen's notes about the 1965 Escorts recordings, he wrote a note in the margin of the music chart for "Big Boss Man," saying, "Matherly's guitar playing is excellent—Duane eat your heart out!"

Hazen also said of the Martinique, in some notes about his time at King Records Studio in Cincinnati, Ohio, "There really aren't any big secrets to making a good record. Start with good musicians, good material, and a great artist. Let them set up so *they* are comfortable, and can see and hear each other easily. *Then* set up the microphones. Contrary to popular belief, you don't need a lot of physical separation to get a good sound. The tightest recordings I've ever made were in a nightclub where the musicians set up their standard way for live performing. The vocalist was standing in front of the drums; the bass amp was on the floor behind the vocalist; guitar on the left, and organ on the right. A room with high ceilings and plenty of cubic room will sound better than a small one. One such room is in Daytona Beach, Fla. The 'Martinique' is the best-sounding room I've ever recorded in...no studio has matched the sound of that magic room!"

Lee always felt strongly about the acoustics in the Martinique, and most who have played there agree with him. Music always sounds richer, thicker, and fuller in that room to this day.

As a sidebar, after Duane joined back up with the Escorts, they soon changed their name to the Allman Joys. The Nightcrawlers had a hit record, "Little Black Egg," that came out of Hazen's studio about this time. As a result of that success, the Nightcrawlers released an entire album of Hazen recordings. After the Nightcrawlers' good fortune, Duane and Gregg Allman scrambled to record their own 45 to get out to local radio stations. After all, the Allmans were much better musicians, though Gregg had not started writing seriously at this point. This all transpired during the rollout of the *Batman* television program. Several record companies intended to capitalize on the growing "superhero" phenomenon, so the Allman Joys were invited to New York City by Smash Records and quickly recorded a song titled "Batman and Robin" under the pseudonym the Spotlights, which Gregg found hard to acknowledge in later years. The song was recorded as part of an embarrassing project that included a long string of superhero-themed songs recorded by various musical groups. Very few copies of this 45 exist today, primarily because so few people ever recognized the Spotlights as Duane and Gregg's band until recently. One can only surmise that the record company became concerned about copyright issues with the name the Allman Joys and the Hershey's "Almond Joy" candy bar, so the name was hastily changed to protect the recording project. The "B" side of "Batman and Robin" was the even more forgettable "Dayflower." The Spotlight's 45 recording was cowritten, engineered, and produced by Leon Russell, Snuff Garrett, and Smash producer Lou Courtney. A subsequent, even less memorable single, "Dick Tracey," with B side "Little Orphan Annie," was released later in 1966. Both Gregg and Duane Allman would cross paths with Leon Russell later through mutual association with Delaney & Bonnie & Friends. Gregg and Russell reunited once again in 2011, joining Elton John in concert at Madison Square Garden. My guess is that they never talked about the "superhero" project after the records came out, and that partnership was promptly disavowed and forgotten by all parties involved.

So many talented musicians evolved in the Daytona Beach music scene in the mid-1960s: Duane and Gregg Allman, the Nightcrawlers, Pete Carr, Lenny LeBlanc, and Jim Matherly, to name just a few. It is natural to assume that earlier players like Matherly set the bar high for everyone that followed. Even the worst fly-by-night garage band, not to mention serious players, could not go out and present themselves as a band unit until they struggled to bring their chops up to the likes of Jim Matherly or the Allmans.

After that winter of 1964, however, when Matherly returned to the Stereos and Duane returned to the Escorts, Matherly discovered that his band had somehow become fixated on glue sniffing, and he assumed, as I did, after the incident with my car, that Duane was at the heart of the problem. This made them impossible for him to work with, and Matherly wondered just how much Duane had influenced his long-time bandmates in areas other than music. It didn't take but a few months with Duane for them to adopt a "dessert before dinner" attitude toward substance abuse. Jim Matherly found this impossible to accept, so he returned to Tennessee disappointed and without a band, while the Escorts, who soon became the Allman Joys, began playing at the Martinique, getting tight and honing their craft until Gregg graduated high school. Gregg graduated that next spring, and the Allman Joys began touring the Chitlin' Circuit of the Southeast.

My band, the Consolidation, consisted of three Seabreeze High students, Ralph Bundy on guitar; Kip Marshall and later Mike Wilson and Ross Yost on bass; myself on drums; plus one Mainland High student, Tim O'Brien, on keyboards; and our lead singer, tambourine player, and chick magnet, Carl Persis, who was enrolled at Daytona Beach Junior College—hence the name the Consolidation.

Securing long-term employment at the Martinique was not all that easy, even though we had all socialized there regularly. We filled in at the Martinique for bands here and there, but there were so many good bands in town that a group really needed to be different and stand out to land the house-band job. Up until March of 1967, we competed with other garage bands in the area, occasionally working teen clubs, the Ocean Pier, or the Safari. However, we just couldn't seem to get that long-term contract at the "Q" that was so highly prized. We had all put in our time practicing and thought it was time to start getting some better-paying gigs. Finally, in April of 1967, the Consolidation won the Greater Daytona Beach Combo Clash at the Ocean Pier, beating seven of the city's finest young bands. Things began to change dramatically for us from that time on, and I believe that was our ticket to getting more regular gigs.

After the Combo Clash, better bookings began to trickle in from the area, so we recorded four demo songs to send to prospective club owners: "Groovin'," "Get Out of My Life, Woman," "Knock on Wood," and "Gimme Some Lovin." Lee Hazen made these recordings as he normally did, recording the instruments at the Martinique and later recording the vocals in his home "cottage" studio in Ormond Beach. We also recorded the Rascals' version of "Slow Down" at BJ Sounds in Orlando that summer for an LP of Central Florida bands that was also to be sent to club owners. That recording recently surfaced on YouTube as "Slow Down" by the Consolidation, recorded at BeeJay Studios. In the summer of 1967, we did a short tour of southern Georgia with Roy Orbison's backup band, the Candymen. The group went on to combine with the Classics Four to become the Atlanta Rhythm Section.

After winning the Combo Clash, the next order of business was to audition for two nights at the Martinique over a weekend that spring. We filled the dance floor with happy feet and smiling faces both nights, and Bill Cook, who had just acquired the "Q," and his manager, bartender, accountant, and significant other, Ringo, hired us immediately.

In those days, Cook was a man about forty-five-ish, lanky, with a mop of mostly unkept ear-length, dark brownish-black hair that parted on the left and always appeared as if it had just departed a windstorm. His slightly upturned jaw gave the impression that he had a high opinion of himself in general. Before buying the Martinique, he had been a building contractor, and he always looked more comfortable with a pencil behind his ear. His dark eyes possessed a cunning business-like glimmer, though his cheeks were full and grinning, and he almost always appeared to be harboring an irrepressible chuckle. His standard dress was a tail-out, long sleeved, lightly starched Gant shirt, neatly pressed Levi dungarees, and penny loafers without socks. His gate was a quick and deliberate strut. His furniture was of a brash nature, garishly upholstered, and Cook's floors were carpeted only in lime-green/gold shag. His two closest friends were a ragtag pair of car-racing fanatics, Vernon Thurman and Tommy Roberts, or "TR," the brother of the famous race car driver Fireball Roberts.

Cook had two modes of transportation. When the sun and salt air beckoned him to the beach, he traversed the four blocks from his apartment at the Martinique to the Atlantic sand beaches in his white convertible Jeep CJ5. For evenings, trips to his attorney's office, or for an occasional boy's trip to Orlando's Club Juana, transportation was his gold Cadillac Eldorado.

Working for Bill Cook and Ringo over the years was one hell of an education in so many ways. Cook possessed surprising business principles as well as remarkable business kismet. He shared his philosophies with anyone interested in listening, usually after several drinks at the end of the night or on payday. Cook would often insist that we wait an hour or so after closing to get our little envelope of cash while he pontificated on the pros and cons of life in the small-business world. Two of those philosophies have stayed with me to this day: First, if a business acquaintance appeared to be joking, or an employee displayed wit or sarcasm, you should be suspicious because there was often an element of truth lurking behind that brand of humor. Second, Cook's basic business philosophy was remarkably simple: "Just take in more than you spend, and at the end of the year you will have made a living."

Cook's business philosophy of constantly struggling to show some kind of profit each and every week got in his way once or twice, and he eventually got the reputation of being frugal at the expense of his employees. Bands and their guests were traditionally allowed unlimited soft drinks because that old rickety building was completely without insulation, making it barely air conditionable, and thus only cool in the winter. Our dates were always allowed free admission.

One day, out of the blue, girlfriends and dates were removed from the freebie list without warning, and this didn't sit well with me or my bandmates. We all had our respective dates and girlfriends at the band table next to the stage every night, and it seemed to us that taking their Coke privilege away and making us pay their admission were reason enough for going on strike. During the spring of 1968, our high school teachers were all out on the biggest teachers' strike in Florida history, so we decided to join ranks and strike ourselves. When we came in to start playing on the night that we decided to strike, 9 P.M. came and went, and the music never started.

We sat nonchalantly at a table next to the stage, waiting for the office door to open, and it did not take but a minute or two after 9 P.M. for that to happen. The door cracked open, and though none of us wanted to stare, it was obvious that there was a head and a pair of eyes peering inquisitively out of the crack in the door. Looking back, I am sure that it didn't come as a total surprise to Cook that we were upset with his new policy, but I don't think he ever imagined that we would not be on the stage playing. Cook came unraveled in a hurry. The stage was empty, the dance floor was empty, and so was the cash register. No music and no dancing meant no money to Bill Cook, and that turned his eyes to fire.

Cook insisted on an answer as to why we weren't playing. "We're on strike," answered Tim O'Brien, our keyboard player, "and we aren't going to turn on the first amp until everyone gets free Cokes and our dates get in free." Cook came unhinged and had no idea what to do. He was totally exasperated, and his face quickly took on the appearance of an overripe tomato.

First, he fired us and told us to pack up our equipment and get out. "Fine," we replied. After all, six nights a week at the Martinique playing from 9 to 2 A.M., and then on the seventh day hosting a jam session at the Blind Pig was starting to wear us down, and we were each ready for a short vacation. When we started to unplug our amps and I unscrewed a few cymbals, Cook cooled off a bit, and then he tried to negotiate with us, which didn't work at all. We just continued breaking down our equipment, though a bit slower now. When he realized that his number-one dance band was serious and about to leave his club silent on a Saturday night, he opened the spigots and invited everyone to have a soda. While we hastily got things turned back on, he ushered our dates in the back door, where they were waiting for some sort of explanation.

I don't have a clue why he didn't carry through with his original threat...fire us on the spot and tell us to go to hell. I suppose he was an astute enough businessman to realize that a few cents' worth of Coke syrup and a few comp girlfriends were not worth losing his top money-making band. I also imagine that Ringo, who was like a band's drummer and always the peacemaker, played some part in the peaceful conclusion to the tangle. Cook may have been many things, but first and foremost he was a businessman. I always imagined that he would die with the first dollar that he ever made, and many years later, after his funeral, I found out from one of his attorneys that this was very nearly the case.

All good things eventually come to an end. In the early '70s, after all those years, the Martinique changed names and became the Wreck Bar. Changing names undoubtedly was the result of preemptive legal maneuvering between Cook and the liquor-license powers that be, but Bill and Ringo continued to run the business. In 1975, one of the first parties that I took my wife Patti to was a birthday party above the Martinique for Gregg Allman. Gregg was a mess that time, his on-again, off-again relationship with Cher blowing up on a daily basis. The Martinique, or Wreck Bar, wasn't everyone's cup of tea, and I could tell that Patti was quickly growing uncomfortable around some of the revelers who waited for Gregg to arrive upstairs in Cook and Ringo's apartment. At one point, my uncomfortable new bride looked around at a room full of well-oiled, long-haired, pot-smoking hippies and asked, "So these are your friends?" When Gregg finally made it to the party, we left pretty quickly after saying, "Hello, and happy birthday," but not before watching him being helped down the stairs so he could give playing a shot that evening. I think Patti was hoping that Cher would make an appearance, but that inflamed relationship had ground to a halt some weeks before.

I don't think I returned to the Martinique for years after that night, but in my mind, there was no place quite like it. Being in the "Q" back in the early days just felt comfortable, like a well-worn pair of jeans. Where else could a teenager drive to work on the sands of the "World's Most Famous Beach," as the sun melted into the western horizon during summers evenings, stopping at will to talk to coeds visiting from all over the entire Southeast? As I have said before, it's not so much where you grow up that matters, it's where you come of age that stays in your memory forever. I was fortunate to come of age in those perfect years, working with my closest friends, awaiting nightfall on Main Street...on the stage at the Martinique.

Chapter 11

Briefly Touring Georgia with Roy Orbison's Candymen

The summer of 1967 was incredibly ordinary and extraordinary at the same time, and the wonder of it all took cover in plain sight. Feelings of enthusiasm and excitement arrive early to beach towns. With schools shuttered for the summer, rising temperatures and escalating passions merely serve to dictate the arrival of tourist season. During the summer of 1967, sun, sand, beach parties, and music centered our lives, but eventually music became all-encompassing. The more we listened to the radio back then, the harder it was to stop. We searched for human truth encapsulated in every lyric, in every song, and the honesty we found spoke to each of us on a deeply personal basis. Unlike family and friends, songs were always there, readily available to soothe us when we had more questions than answers. The songwriters surrounding us were the storytellers...the poets, the journalists, and the critics of our generation. Writers were the keepers of the portal to our memories. They were the dreamers of dreams and those who made time stand still, causing mountains to genuflect at our feet. Our writers assigned the moments and captured the laughter and tears of our lives. They were the heirloom makers, the keepers of our secrets, and the tellers of our truth.

My high school band spun our own web of dreams and helped to make time stand still for our friends. We filled dance floors with smiling faces, gyrating bodies, and happy feet everywhere we played. Thanks to bands like ours, there isn't a baby boomer alive today who believes they are over forty-five. Most who carefully listened to the music speak still listen as if they were teenagers. What shaped this ideology is the complex essence of the music, which truly is the undeniable soundtrack of our lives. Music inspired us, made us who we are, and rode shotgun through our trials and tribulations. As a band, the Consolidation discovered and then harnessed the power of rock and roll. We laid witness to the laughter and tears of our generation, though our original intention was merely to play quality music, meet a few coeds from Kentucky, and to keep our lives between the ruts.

The magical, musical summer of 1967 brought unexpected surprises for an exploding musical world. The British Invasion of the early '60s effectively pushed many American musical groups to the back of the tour bus, but the "Summer of Love" signaled an explosion and amalgamation of unimaginable musical talent from the United States, as well as from abroad. Groups that would define not only our generation but many generations to come were established during the musical hotbed of 1967. Santana, the Electric Flag, Blue Cheer, the James Gang, Chicago, Pacific Gas & Electric, Spirit, Creedence Clearwater Revival, Fleetwood Mac, the J. Geils Band, Sly and the Family Stone, Jethro Tull, Procol Harum, REO Speedwagon, Spooky Tooth, and Three Dog Night were but a few of the countless groups that came together, influencing a generation of listeners as well as generations of future musicians. There were also incalculable less-than-successful stories like the Flower Pot Men, Tinkerbell's Fairydust, the Insect Trust, Ultimate Spinach, Whale Feathers, and the immediately forgettable Ant Trip Ceremony.

During that magical summer of '67, the music explosion that was rippling nationwide came home to Daytona Beach. As part of the Martinique family, local musicians learned from Ringo, the manager there, that her favorite local band was about to make a decision that would forever change the face of American music. The Allman Joys had joined forces with an Alabama band, the Minutes, to form a powerfully innovative and soulful band called the Hour Glass. They gathered at the house of drummer Johnny Sandlin's parents in Decatur, Alabama, where they rehearsed in his garage for a week. Fortunately, Sandlin, who would later become a producer and engineer with Capricorn Records, recorded most of their rehearsals. The original Hour Glass lineup included Gregg Allman on keyboards and vocals, Duane Allman on lead guitar and backing vocals, Sandlin on drums, Paul Hornsby on additional keyboards and harmony guitar, and Mabron McKenny on bass. Bob Keller and Pete Carr joined the Hour Glass later, also playing bass.

It is significant to mention that while The Allman Brothers Band is credited as creating Southern rock, the Hour Glass was the springhead for that musical genre. Every member of the final incarnation of the Hour Glass became, in his own way, a significant disciple of that genre, and they were all ultimately successful as a result of their association. No one can argue that Duane and Gregg Allman didn't germinate that seed, but Sandlin and Hornsby took Southern music into Capricorn studios, where they engineered, nurtured, and produced the finest of the Southern rock genre. Local Daytona Beach musician Pete Carr, who joined the

Hour Glass for their last album as a bass player, became a highly sought-after session guitar player and worked not only for the Capricorn Rhythm Section but later for many years with the Muscle Shoals Rhythm Section. Carr spread the gospel of Southern rock, helping to create such classic hits as "Main Street" by Bob Seger.

Not long after their formation, the members of the Hour Glass moved to California and began recording what was to become the first of two ill-conceived and poorly promoted albums. News of the formation of the Hour Glass spread like wildfire through the musicians in the Daytona area. This was an exciting time to be a young musician in that region. Local players were getting recognition and recording contracts, and playing legendary venues on the West Coast. Everyone hoped the Allman's magnetism might pull others with them, and they did indeed manage to propel several other local musicians into the musical spotlight. The aforementioned Pete Carr and his later duo partner Lenny LeBlanc are two local musicians whose musical careers can be directly traced to Duane and Gregg Allman and the Allman Joys. Root Boy Slim and the Sex Change Band was another group of mostly local musicians who followed the Allman Joys into the limelight. The Sex Change Band included Foster MacKenzie (Root Boy Slim) on vocals, Walt Andrews on guitar, Bob Greenlee on bass, Ernie Lancaster on guitar, Tommy Ruger on drums, and Winston Kelly on keyboards. They worked around the DC area and were discovered by Donald Fagen (of Steely Dan) and Gary Katz (Steely Dan's producer). Fagen and Katz were able to secure Root Boy Slim and the Sex Change Band a record deal with Warner Brothers, and the group recorded six albums, all totaled. All but MacKenzie (Root Boy) were local Florida players whose intention was to honor the blues/rock footsteps of Duane and Gregg Allman.

During the time that the Hour Glass was moving to California and beginning their recording sessions with Liberty Records, my band was booked to open for the legendary vocalist Roy Orbison and his backup band, the Candymen, as one of the supplemental awards associated with our winning the regional "Combo Clash" at the Ocean Pier that past April. Roy Orbison and the Candymen had already garnered worldwide recognition, and they had just recently returned from a European tour co-billed with the Beatles. These were heady times for my band. The word quickly circulated that we had been hired to open Roy Orbison's shows during the Georgia leg of his solo Southern tour. Unfortunately, when the smoke had cleared, we discovered that we were not actually opening for "Roy Orbison *and* The Candymen" at all, but only for Roy's cracker-jack backup band, the Candymen. At some point during that summer, Roy Orbison and the Candymen became disconnected. Likely, with Roy's exploding stardom, his management had made a decision to record and tour with members of the Wrecking Crew from LA, so the Candymen were no longer considered necessary.

To work with the great Roy Orbison would have been a pinnacle achievement for an unknown group of mostly seventeen-year-old musicians from Florida. Still, even without Roy, the Candymen were an extraordinary group of outstanding musicians and singers. I hurried to purchase their first solo album, *Georgia Pines,* which had just hit the record department at the local Belk Lindsey. Fortunately for us, their title song "Georgia Pines" was charting well in the United States and Europe, so we could still hang our hat on that. The Candymen tour might not have included Roy Orbison, but the Candymen were still music royalty as far as we were concerned. And, as a result of just having worked closely with the Beatles, the Candymen were able to play most of the Sergeant Pepper album while we worked with them, months before the album was released in the United States. That alone was worth the price of admission. Their new recording on ABC Records displayed a highly polished vocal and instrumental delivery. Along with their own material, the Candymen delivered forceful adaptations of an eclectic song list during their show, including songs such as "Eleanor Rigby," "Sgt. Pepper's Lonely Hearts Club Band," "A Day in the Life," "Gimme Some Lovin'," "Long Tall Sally," "The 1941 New York Mine Disaster," and a remarkable interpretation of Tom Jones's "Thunderball." Rodney Justo, their lead singer, was simply mesmerizing as a vocal entertainer and impressionist.

The Candymen began life in Dothan, Alabama, as the Webs, fronting Bobby Goldsboro. When Goldsboro left the band for a solo career, they took on Rodney Justo, from the Tampa area, as lead singer. While playing a co-bill with the Webs, Roy Orbison took an interest in the band and immediately hired them as his backup band. The Webs soon became the Candymen, named after Orbison's hit song, "Candy Man." After the Candymen broke up, their manager Buddy Buie suggested that some of them move to Georgia and work with a studio group made up of veteran Florida and Georgia musicians. There, the Candymen joined forces with the Classics IV, Dennis Yost's former backup band from Jacksonville, which eventually became the Atlanta Rhythm Section.

By the time we were to meet the Candymen tour in Tifton and

Moultrie, Georgia, we had become enthused again, if for no other reason than it was our first-ever booking outside of the state of Florida. On a more personal note, I would finally be able to add some out-of-state motel room keys to my burgeoning motel-key collection. I'm not exactly sure where I got the idea, or how it began, but from the first time that I played with the band, I kept every motel room key I was given at check-in as a keepsake. Likely, I just accidentally drove off with the first key and then quickly decided that a key collection would make a wonderful way to chronicle our escapades. By the time we disbanded and I left for college, I had at least fifty varied, mostly plastic room keys in various colors strung on a fifteen-inch length of bailing wire. The wire was bent around on itself, forming a large oval onto which the keys were threaded one by one. My key collection also included keys from Bahamas cruises and assorted, related band vacations, including a post-graduation fishing trip to the Keys with Ralph, our guitar player. When I was in college, I kept the key collection proudly displayed on a clothes hook on the wall in my dorm room as a constant reminder of the fun and travels I had enjoyed with the band. It was also a great conversation starter if and when other musicians stopped by my room to listen to some music and talk about "glory days."

Once, when I returned from college for the summer, I laid my treasured key collection carefully in its place of honor in my top dresser drawer next to other cherished knickknacks until my return to South Carolina for the fall semester. A few days later, I noticed that the collection wasn't in my dresser drawer where I always kept it. My mother, honest, steadfast Southern matriarch that she was, had found my collection and took to heart the words embossed in white on the back of each key:

> Property of "Whatever" Motel
> Drop in any mailbox. We Guarantee Postage.

That ominous message was stamped on each and every key. Naturally, assuming that they were someone else's property, and therefore not mine, my sainted mother admitted to taking each of the keys off the wire and dropping them unceremoniously into the giant blue-and-red mailbox in front of the Ormond Beach Post Office marked "Outgoing." With her moral compass gleefully pointing in the right direction, she sent the keys back from whence they came, considering her ethical duty done.

What my mother didn't consider was that she might as well have thrown them all into the garbage. I am sure that the garbage is where they ended up when they were finally liberated from the bottom of that mailbox during its yearly cleaning. Heartbreaking doesn't begin to explain the feeling of losing the only remaining tangible evidence of four years of practically nonstop excitement and camaraderie.

The family of our bass player, Kip Marshall, owned a plain white VW microbus, which seemed like the perfect vehicle for a band and its equipment headed out on the road. Kip okayed the use of his family's microbus with his parents, and plans were hatched to pack up, heading out for Tifton, Georgia, early on Thursday morning. Kip and I decided to ride to the gig in the microbus along with our guitarist, Ralph Bundy. The three of us took turns driving, riding shotgun, and riding perched atop the huge, uncomfortable pile of musical equipment that left only a tiny space for our suitcases. However, the lack of comfort only augmented our sense of adventure of the unknown.

Our "sense of adventure" quickly became dashed, as it didn't take the three of us very many miles to learn that engine-limiting governors were commonplace on VW buses from 1950 until 1967. Those diabolical devices were located between the carburetor and the intake manifold. They operated by a spring-loaded mechanism that worked a bit like a choke. When there was enough air/fuel mixture to overcome the spring tension, it cut off the gas flow to the engine, at which point the spring pulled the mechanism back again and the engine slowly reengaged. A mechanic could adjust the spring tension via an adjuster at the top of the governor: tightening to allow higher speeds or loosening to have it disengage earlier. Governors were put together with special screws with holes in the sides of the heads through which a wire was run and clamped with a lead tamper-evident seal. This made it nearly impossible for anyone to adjust the governor to allow greater speed without the owner's consent.

Back in the 1960s, it was commonplace for parents of children who owned VWs to have the dealership adjust the governor on the engine, thus limiting the vehicle's maximum speed. As was the case with Kip's VW bus, with the governor adjusted just so, it was impossible to drive faster than fifty-five miles per hour. It's hard to imagine that those sluggish, lumbering VW buses could muster too much more than fifty-five miles per hour, governor or no governor.

I had heard vague stories about VW governors. Growing up at the Birthplace of Speed, two blocks from the famous Ormond Garage, every guy and most girls learned something about automobile engines. But until Kip, Ralph, and I pulled up on Interstate-75 near Ocala, the stories about governors were just noise. Interstate-95 was still in bits and pieces during the summer of 1967, with very little of it completed in Florida. Consequently, we wove our way west on country roads past Ocala in search of Interstate-75, which divided the state from north to south and passed literally feet from Tifton, our destination. Driving at fifty or fifty-five miles an hour was fine on Florida's back roads back then, but when we pulled up onto the interstate for the first time, even rust-bucket, ass-dragging station wagons full of tourists left us in their dust. Taking turns driving, we also each learned that whenever the driver inched slowly up to the maximum governed speed, as soon as the needle pointed to that magic number, the governor immediately engaged, and the van would then slow excruciatingly to forty or forty-five miles per hour. Also, as we slowly transitioned into the much hillier area of north central Florida, it became harder and harder to maintain a constant speed, which meant the governor engaged on almost every uphill slope. There was no stopping that maniacal Rube Goldberg device from doing its appointed job, and when it did engage, the game would begin all over again. Add to that the exasperation of driving with all the windows rolled down and vent windows all pointed inward to keep the oppressive heat from turning the black Naugahyde covers on the speaker cases into an oily mess. As fairly astute fellows, it didn't take long before we felt we had been trapped in a truly unforgettable desert expedition where the clocks ticked in reverse. A lovely drive that would take a normal vehicle a little more than four hours was shaping up to take us seven and a half hours. I distinctly remember looking at my watch on several occasions, wondering if it had stopped.

Meanwhile, our lead singer, Carl Persis; keyboardist Tim O'Brien; and manager, Lee Phillips, had elected to drive to Tifton in the relative luxury of Carl's canary yellow Chevrolet Corvair convertible, with cool white leather interior. Never mind that the Corvair had been the focal point of the Ralph Nader book published in 1965, *Unsafe at Any Speed.* Carl's car embodied cool, as did he. Thankfully, Carl owned two Corvairs and never ran into the safety problems that caused that model's eventual demise. Lack of seatbelts and exploding rear-end-located gas tanks, as well as a general reluctance by the Chevrolet Company to spend money improving product safety, eventually edged Corvairs to the side of the road.

Carl, Tim, and Lee were not privy to the great sense of adventure that began for us even before Kip's VW bus made it to our city limits. Their decision to stretch out and ride up to Tifton in air-conditioned luxury was astute, to say the least. As a result of this trip, and because we lost Kip and his microbus to his family's transfer to South Florida with General Electric later in the summer, the Consolidation began looking into renting, buying, or borrowing a small trailer for our equipment. We found ourselves needing something to get our equipment to increasingly farther out-of-town engagements. When playing local gigs, we could each drive our own cars with our own equipment in the back seat or trunk, but out of town this didn't make any sense. We did borrow a small, enclosed trailer from a high school friend, Jack Tate, alias "Tater," for one of the final Jimmy Burns shows in Naples, Florida. Tater's trailer actually worked out very nicely for that trip and several others...after we sprang for two new tires to replace the nearly tread-less ones it sported when I picked it up the first time at Tater's. But beggars can't be choosers, and it turned out to be a good deal all the way around.

As good fortune would have it, Ralph's father, who was in lock-step with most of the other parents and adamantly against his son playing in the band, knocked us all out by investing in a huge Dodge passenger van that he offered to us and that we used to drive to many, many jobs around the state. Ralph's parents owned and managed a tidy apartment complex in Daytona Beach, just two blocks from the beach where they lived with Ralph and his brother, Bruce. Mr. Bundy envisioned the van as the complex's workhorse, taking snow birds to and from the airport and beach, but it worked just fine for us. The Dodge van was large: it had three rows of seating and windows all around its spacious interior. Unlike the VW, the Dodge had factory air, lots of room in the back for equipment, and, best of all, the Dodge van never knew a governor. The trip to Tifton and Moultrie would be the last time we ever used Kip's microbus for anything other than taking rubbish to the dump for his father. We did, however, manage to have a little fun at Kip's expense with his VW during our second night in Tifton.

Upon pulling into town for the first night's gig at the Tifton Recreation Center on July 6th, we checked into the accommodations that our hosts provided for us at the Hubert Motor Court. The Hubert Motor Court was located in beautiful downtown Tifton, Georgia, at 311 West 12th Street. The trip was long, hot, and grueling, and it was almost dinnertime by the time we found our motel. My heart sank a bit as we pulled into the parking lot in the lengthening shadows. We parked and walked up to the motel's office, noticing that the Hubert Motor Court must have been built in the center of Tifton when there were no other large buildings, and the city had grown-up around it. My attention was immediately drawn to three posters nailed on the telephone pole next to the entrance to the parking area. One poster advertised the previous week's show at the Moultrie Bowl: Bobby Goldsboro, the Classic's IV, and Billy Joe Royal. The next poster advertised a show booked for the next weekend at the "Bowl," which included the Gentry's, Percy Sledge, and the Atlanta Tams. A third professionally printed poster advertised the Candymen and Daytona Beach's own Consolidation at the Tifton rec tonight and at the Moultrie Bowl tomorrow night. In all our youthful exuberance and excitement, it had not really dawned on me until that moment that, ready or not, we were taking a step up to the next level of music. It was all youthful adventure and tomfoolery up to that point, but along with our first poster came a bit of hard work, as well as hard reality.

Looks can be deceiving, but not in this case. Judging solely by appearance, Mr. Hubert might likely have been the last of several owners of the property who refused to invest more than cleaning supplies, clean towels, and bar soap in the aging motor lodge. Also, judging by the sagging beds and water-stained ceiling, the Hubert Motor Court may also have been hanging on financially for a number of years. The Hubert changed hands again in 1970. But in 1967, motor courts were a dying breed of rubber-stamped, mom-and-pop motels that offered economical lodging along secondary roads in small towns across America. Built mostly before the interstate highway explosion of the fifties and '60s, their tired architecture and musty appointments were on their way out by the mid-'60s. Family-owned motor courts were soon to be replaced by large chain motels and hotels. Some still exist, using the motor court moniker, in close proximity to interstate and primary highway intersections and at interstate exits, but they're found mostly near medium-sized cities. Motor courts typically featured centrally located swimming pools, brick buildings, and cramped rooms boasting "Air-Conditioned Luxury." In the South, most motor courts were landscaped with colorful azaleas, shady pines, ancient oaks dripping with Spanish moss, and neatly trimmed, fragrant boxwood hedges.

The Hubert Motor Court was near downtown Tifton and offered very little of the Southern aesthetic nuance of a traditional motor court, exhibiting only a crumbling brick facade. The buildings were old and worn, the roof leaked, and most of the doors, locks, and hinges showed the wear and tear consistent with them being attacked by a jealous husband. Once inside our room, the peeling wallpaper was nearly as badly stained as the bedding and terrazzo floors. There was a vague damp wetness to the nose, and all four beds in the two adjoining rooms sagged unmercifully in the center, making it impossible for all but the very closest of friends to share a double bed.

We tenuously checked in, and when the rest of the band arrived (somehow we had arrived earlier...), we drove down en mass to the Tifton Recreation Center to set up our equipment. The stage was large enough for two bands, which was fortunate because the Candymen had already spread the newest and best Fender amps across the stage, and their singer had a wonderful PA system complete with Vox Super Beatle speaker cabinets, Shure microphones, a Bogen amplifier, and an Echoplex vocal enhancer. About the only thing that my band didn't eventually replicate from the Candymen was the Vox Super Beatle PA speaker cabinets. Playing on bills with bands like the Candymen was just one of many educational steps the Consolidation made along the way. We learned that weekend from one of the best bands in the South just how important vocals and vocal reproduction was. Ralph, our guitar player, also learned not to let the good-natured ribbing about his Sears Silvertone Amplifier get under his skin, however barbed.

Like most bands just getting started in the mid-'60s, our equipment was a ragtag amalgamation of whatever was readily available, affordable, and, more importantly, able to be financed with a parent's co-sign. Both our guitar player's and bass player's amplifier amplifiers were horrible, toneless, and massively heavy Sears Silvertone models. Ralph started with a black, solid-body, Montgomery Ward guitar with a white pick guard and eventually moved up to an entry-level tobacco sunburst Gibson ES-125 hollow-body guitar. Ralph's Gibson 125, a single cutaway model, sported horribly cheap pickups (the part of the guitar that converts string vibrations into electricity) but it seemed like manna from heaven at the time. Our bass player, Kip, played his lipstick pickup Danelectro '59DC bass through a cumbersome Silvertone bass rig for a nauseatingly distorted sound at any level louder than practice mode. Our singer, Carl Persis, came to us with a fairly well-crafted pair of locally made speaker columns that unfortunately required constant visits to the nearest Radio Shack to stockpile eight-inch speakers for their continual replacement. We replaced blown speakers so often in his columns that even though each tower was originally designed with ten screws holding the backs in place, the number of screws was soon reduced to four, one in each corner, to expedite on-the-fly removal and speaker replacement. The VBH speaker columns were manufactured by Van B. Harrison, the bass player for the Escorts, and Sylvan Wells, the guitarist for the Nightcrawlers. Carl's original PA amplifier was an ancient, homemade tube amp that was pilfered, kicking and screaming, from my father's home stereo system. Our microphones were mixed pre-soundboard through a small, four-input volume-control box, built by an audiophile friend and plugged into the single phone input jack on that homemade amp. An on-off volume control knob, as well as bass and treble tone knobs, were the only simple adjustments. We could only guess as to the amplifier's power output. The sound quality was remarkably rich, due in part to the two enormous power transformers mounted on its aluminum chassis next to the three power tubes.

Our keyboard player was a bit looser than the rest of us in the procurement of his equipment. We never asked where he got it, or how he was able to afford it, but Tim sported a Vox Viscount Amplifier and middle-of-the-road Farfisa keyboard, both of which needed constant volume adjustment in order to keep him from outpacing the entire band. My original drum set consisted of pots and pans from my mother's kitchen, which served me fine for early practices and beach parties. At some point, I stepped up and bought a cheap, entrance-level snare drum, drum seat, and one or two cymbals to keep time as the big money, ten- and fifteen-dollar Ormond Recreation Center gigs began flooding in. We all stuck together and persevered as we each struggled to better our equipment, and by the fall of 1967, we began to actually look and sound like a real rock and roll band...or so we thought. It was during our eye-opening trip to Tifton that all of us decided it was time to step up in earnest and get the best instruments and amplifiers we could afford. We were starting to make money and playing increasingly important gigs, so it was natural to withhold a bit from our college funds to make the band sound as good as we could.

By the time we played our first gig in Georgia with the Candymen, we had begged, borrowed, and one of us had literally stolen enough gear to represent ourselves onstage. We weren't the Candymen, certainly, but we weren't supposed to be. We were the opener and played alternating sets, and we all took Duane Allman's words to heart: we played what we knew as well as we could and we were indeed fine. There were many older teenagers and some in their early twenties at the Tifton rec who were there to hear the Candymen. But there were younger kids our age who were there for our raw energy and pure accessibility. The Consolidation had no star trappings as did the Candymen. We had not just returned from Europe on tour with the Beatles and Roy Orbison, so we were far from jaded and aloof. We were there for the sheer fun and excitement of playing for a new and different crowd. The whole purpose of our sets was to get the audience involved. We moved people through their feet and ears and pulled them closer together. Our audience seemed to melt into one gyrating form when we were onstage. We were fueled by the intensity of the audience, and we were empowered and stimulated by their energy.

For a number of reasons, it was in Tifton that I realized that this was what I wanted to do with my life for as long as I could manage, in one form or another. I wanted to move people's hearts through the music I was playing. I had experienced that feeling to one degree or another through music in church, at beach party sing alongs, and even at drunken fraternity parties, but I think it took the combination of seeing the Candymen, the Allman Joys, and the Stereos to make me recognize how it can all come together. Closely listening to those top-shelf bands emphasized that music is the voice, soul, and portal that goes straight to the heart. If you allow music to speak through the rhythms and frenzy that it creates, music in itself becomes an incredibly powerful instrument for social change.

When the Candymen came on and wowed the audience with their slick stage presence and their vocal and instrumental excellence, their audience just stood awestruck and stared, as we did. But when we went on to play our sets, the kids filled the dance floor because we were there to stimulate the audience; and so it was, everywhere we played. We were a great dance band. The Consolidation incorporated plenty of Temptations-style choreography and hip-shaking movement in our stage show. We played what the kids wanted to hear, particularly if they were interested in dancing. We played forty or fifty of the most popular songs of the day, many of which were R & B and soul gleaned from WLAC in Nashville; our style was heavily influenced by our time with the Soulsations.

That first night in Tifton seemed to vaporize into the Georgia night like magic. We opened with an hour-long warm-up set of some of our favorite music, then the Candymen played an extended set, and then we played the closing two hours. Only playing three hours total allowed us to put sets together of only our very best music. At every opportunity during the night, both bands advertised our next gig at the Moultrie Bowl a day later. By the end of the evening, many of those who had packed the smallish Tifton rec were excited and buzzing about joining us in Moultrie.

When the lights came on at midnight, a disappointed dance floor full of teenagers emptied, and our first night's audience made their way home satisfied. We managed to talk to a few new fans and then packed up our equipment and headed back to Hubert's. Unfortunately, the rooms had not changed at all since we had left that afternoon. And even though it was 1 A.M., and we were tired from the trip up from Florida and from playing three hard-driving sets of music...nothing made those swayback beds look inviting. First, we tried watching the one television station on the archaic black-and-white television set in the room. Then we played cards to pass the time. But regardless of what we did, it was impossible to get anyone to succumb to what was certainly near exhaustion at that point. Truth be known, there were so many pranksters in the band that whoever surrendered and closed his eyes quite possibly might wake up with ears full of toothpaste or a face covered in shaving cream. It would not have been the first time.

So, sometime near sunrise, those of us who weren't practically catatonic—Ralph, Tim, Carl, and I—piled into one of the cars and planned a sortie toward Moultrie in order to find better lodging for the rest of our stay in the area. There wasn't much happening in that part of South Georgia at first light. There were only a few farmers in pickups heading out to start their day, and motels on the Tifton/Moultrie highway, as we soon discovered, were few and far between. Just as the sun was high enough to begin to filter through the rows of pine trees along Highway 319 near Moultrie, the Danny Ross Motor Court came into view. It was probably about 6 A.M., and ol' Danny Ross didn't much care for four teenagers waking him from a sound sleep asking to see a room. He slammed the door in Carl and Tim's faces, but not before telling them to come back at a decent hour. Tired, angry, and exasperated, Tim leaned out of the back seat of Carl's Corvair and grabbed a nice-sized boxwood plant as we pulled slowly away from the office. Like many of Tim's antics, I'm not sure exactly how he did it, but he managed to hang on long enough to wrestle the boxwood up by its spindly roots. To this day, the herbaceous perfume of boxwood takes me instantly back to that quiet morning outside of Moultrie, Georgia. That smell also reminds me of the unpleasant feeling in the pit of my stomach when I realized we might possibly end up spending a night in the Moultrie jail. As a parting shot, Tim heaved the plant high over the fence and hedge surrounding the centrally located swimming pool, where it landed in the deep end, very closely missing the antique diving board. At that point, we decided to drive back toward Tifton in great haste and to try and find something closer to the interstate with a cleaner swimming pool.

As we pulled back into Tifton, someone noticed a billboard advertising the "new" Davis Brothers Cafeteria and Motor Lodge. Comfortable "new" rooms and cafeteria-style dining on the same property garnered our attention. After previewing a room, we booked two on the second floor for the next night, with the agreement that we could have a late check-out tomorrow and an early check-in today...like right away.

Carl turned his car back toward the Hubert. We quietly smeared shaving cream and toothpaste on the faces of Kip and Lee to wake them and checked out of the Hubert while they were busy cleaning the mess out of their ears. We got to Davis Brothers just in time to meet the traveling breakfast crowd, so we decided to join in. Ralph asked our very Southern waitress if she could tell us where the "Bowl" was located, to which she quipped, "Over there, on the shelf next to the saucers." Maybe she was somehow related to Danny Ross? After having breakfast, we all crashed and slept comfortably most of the day and into the early evening. Color TV, cold AC, and the on-site restaurant made Davis Brothers our home away from home. The rooms at the Hubert had been paid by the promoter as part of the Tifton/Moultrie deal, but it didn't matter to us. Maybe he could get a night's rent back from the Hubert tomorrow when we settled up and discussed further dates in Georgia: our original deal included the possibility of more dates in the following week. Anyway, we all relished our sleep and comfort too much to go back to that bedbug, fleabag motel. Sorry, Mr. Hubert.

From our outside balcony rooms, we watched as people checked in and out of the Davis Brothers Motor Lodge on their way to Florida for summer vacations. Station wagons bursting with excited kids and irritable parents headed south to join the festival of sunburned flesh waiting just across the state line.

We only managed to get into a little trouble at the Davis Brothers Motor Lodge. No shrubbery was harmed, intentionally or unintentionally. On that second day, while we were all getting our rest, Tim attached some sort of alarm siren to the engine of Kip's van as a prank, and, as expected, when the car was started later that afternoon, it screamed like a banshee. The prank unfortunately also destroyed the coil to which it was attached. A quick trip in Carl's car to the auto-parts store, and we were back in business, but the pranks just kept on coming, as they always did. That night, after all of the other excitement, Tim tapped me, Ralph, and Lee for a late-night prank. We slipped out of our rooms quietly and managed to push Kip's bus, fully loaded, around behind the motel. That wasn't quite enough for Tim, as he spied a pile of fill dirt that had been dumped just beyond the parking lot perimeter. We then pushed the bus over to the pile of red clay and, with an unexpected burst of energy, up on to the top of the dirt hill. In the dimly lit parking lot, it was hard to tell just how high the dirt mound was, but it looked like it would be sufficient for a teenage prank. The original intention was to merely move the vehicle so Kip might think someone had stolen his father's prize VW bus. From where the bus came to rest on top of the pile of dirt, the front and back tires were barely touching the ground, which we thought added a nice touch.

When Kip woke up and discovered his bus missing, he first went into full fluster and then into panic mode. Kip's bewilderment was hysterical, but he soon caught on to the prank as we each succumbed to contagious laughter. Finally, Tim told him where to find it, and we all followed Kip around behind the hotel, snickering, to see his ride proudly up on display for all to see. When we walked behind Davis Brothers, there was already a small crowd forming around the strange sight of a VW bus perched atop a huge mound of red clay. As time went on, the crowd swelled slightly as families began loading their cars for the day's drive, which made matters worse for Kip. As always, Tim seemed to relish in Kip's discomfort. Unfortunately, when Kip managed to get up into his bus to start the engine, it settled even deeper into the red-clay dirt pile. It soon came to rest solidly on its undercarriage. Full of equipment and an exasperated driver, the bus, with its spinning back wheels, began to take on the appearance of a box turtle resting on top of a Dixie Cup. After much pushing, shoving, and rocking, we finally had to have the vehicle towed down from its stately perch, thanks to my recently acquired AAA Motor Club card. Thank you, Dad. My father's AAA card came in handy over the years, and the next time I remember using it in a music-related incident was at the Martinique during the following Christmas when Duane and Gregg's car battery died one night after an Hour Glass show and none of us had jumper cables.

The Moultrie Bowl, where we were to play that evening with the Candymen, was our greatest surprise of the trip. The Bowl was a huge, cavernous, working bowling alley. There were at least two dozen lanes full of bowlers, with stages facing each other in the public area just behind the alleys. Large drive-thru, garage-style doors next to the facing stages allowed us to park next to the stage to load and unload our equipment. The Candymen were already set up on their stage across the room when we arrived. From where our stage was situated, we could barely see the other stage. Our puny little VW bus and Corvair must have looked as comical as our Silvertone amps to the Candymen, who sported a medium-sized moving truck, a passenger van, and a host of groupies' cars following their parade.

Again, we were to kick off the night at 8 P.M., but this night we would alternate sets, with the Candymen ending the evening. We munched burgers and drank Cokes while waiting to change in the bathroom before our first show, and we even bowled a set to kill time. I don't know why, but I only remember having stage fright twice in my musical career. The first time was at our first gig ever, which was before 2,500 people at Peabody Auditorium for a cancer benefit. The second was the night we opened for the Allman Joys and B. J. Thomas at the Martinique. Truthfully, if anyone in our band had reason to be worried, this should have been the night, but if anyone was shaken by stage fright, nobody showed it.

We were a band of supportive friends who bolstered each other and supported even the least of our flock. In the years to come, I played in many other bands, but the feeling of closeness and camaraderie that I experienced with the Consolidation was never replicated. I've played in several bands that were probably better musically and were certainly better poised to become prominent musically, but the personality factor, the friendship and solidarity, was never there like it was in the Consolidation. I remember thinking a hundred times through the years that our name ended up saying so much more about us than that we simply arrived together from three different schools.

That night, for the first time in my memory, Carl actually scratched out a working playlist from which we would work. He was planning a rousing night and didn't want to forget anything important in the heat of the moment. His list wasn't designed to be followed to the letter, but simply reflected a menu from which to pick the juiciest steaks and chops.

This set list/outline would follow us from that night on, until we played our next-to-last gig in August of the next year...which turned out to be well over two hundred shows later.

After a quick tune-up, everyone turned to me smiling, signaling that they were ready to go, and I counted down the first song with four clicks of my drumsticks. At once, we kicked into what we did the best—slick, danceable, moving rhythm and blues and soul music. Wilson Pickett's "Midnight Mover" was first on the list, and Carl quickly danced and screamed the audience into a frenzy. Ralph tucked those sweet soul licks into each line, complementing the drums, keyboard, and bass. Tim and I belted out call-and-response harmony vocals to bolster Carl's best Wilson Pickett howl. "Midnight Mover" was one of several soul songs in which we inserted our own choreography during a long, extended, rhythmical pounding of the bridge. This was a musical interlude where the band all did a Temptations-style dance step, with heads all bobbing wildly to-and-fro and the guys dancing back and forth across the stage. Glued to my drum throne, it was hard for me to do much more than add the African Twist-style head moves and shoulder rolls, but the funk in my kick drum and hi-hat cymbal did the dancing for me. Just because I was a drummer didn't mean I was not a real musician. I read music and I could whistle almost every note that Duane Allman ever played, note for note.

"Gimmie Some Lovin'" by the Spencer Davis Group was next on Carl's list. "Gimmie Some Lovin'" was a song that seemed written for a band like ours. Never mind that we had seen Spencer Davis perform that song at the Martinique with Steve Winwood singing his soulful best just a few months earlier...the song had an effect on our audience. Kip kicked the song off with that famous 12345-6 funk on the bass and I joined him on snare and floor tom-tom on the 6, to which Carl added cowbell, and after four measures I added hi-hat and a little added funk for another eight measures. At the end of those eight pile-driving measures, Tim filled the room with those amazing signature organ swells for another eight measures, and then everyone in the band came in and poured everything they had into the song. Right then, as the crowd swelled around the stage on our end of the room, we knew the audience was ours. As polished as the Candymen were, they no longer possessed our raw intensity. Most likely they had it at one time, but as they became more of a polished nightclub act, the sweat and energy that drove our music had disappeared entirely from their performances.

Ralph's vocals on "Gimmie Some Lovin'" were unearthly that night, as always. Carl supported him with backing vocals, dancing, flying tambourine, and cowbell. Then we all blended harmony and falsetto backup vocals, throwing in primordial screams when and where they felt natural. It was as if a tornado had blown into the Bowl and took over the stage and the windstorm was spreading into the shoes on the dance floor. We were having the time of our lives, and the kids on the churning, swirling dance floor felt every note. After ripping through the second verse, and when only Kip and I were locked together, beating out the rhythm and waiting for the solo to happen, Ralph, with his Gibson cranked to the max and taking full advantage of his Gibson Fuzz Tone, led the way as he decided to take a hard left, taking the song somewhere entirely different. I watched for the first time as Ralph cranked the volume control on the massive Silvertone to seven, where he paused for a moment and then did the unimaginable. When he finally stopped nudging the volume control knob up, the arrow pointed directly at ten. With great intrigue, I watched as he spun the volume control on his 125 into the stratosphere. While we all looked on in disbelief, Ralph stepped on his distortion booster and fashioned the most astonishing psychedelic version of the simple solo that I had heard him play three hundred times before. Solo number three hundred and one was decidedly different, however.

Ralph took the band down an entirely different road that night. First, he carefully loosened and then discreetly removed each and every rivet holding the aluminum roof to the building with his buttery guitar notes. Next, he returned for a second round of stabbing staccato-driven notes and blew what was left of the roof off the Moultrie Bowl. With all of us jack-hammering away at the final bridge while clinging franticly to the groove, Ralph brought everything back down into line with an amazing dynamic acumen. Leading the parade back into the groove, he pulled the music back together while jiving bandmates continued barking rhythms until he signaled an abrupt end to the mayhem by slowly raising and then slamming his guitar neck almost to the floor.

Bam! The song was finished, and our suit coats flew off to somewhere behind the stage like so many lady's handkerchiefs. We were the same band, but Ralph had managed to squeeze an entirely different sound out of each one of us. We all knew that we'd never look back. From that moment on, every one of our sets became more reckless, risky, and audacious, which empowered each musician to take whatever daredevil, tactless risk was necessary to take the show in new directions. Most new concepts, no matter how impulsive, were embraced immediately by the band and given consideration as to possible future inclusion. It was almost as if Ralph had given each of us permission to be someone other than ourselves when we walked up onstage as the Consolidation. At home and in school, we were all Clark Kent, making sure to be home for dinner by six. But when we began playing, we each retreated into our own individual interpretation of Superman...without a curfew. The Man of Steel has no curfew.

Before the crowd could react that night, Carl called out "I'm a Man," another Spencer Davis composition released earlier in 1967. "I'm a Man" flowed effortlessly because we had already laid down the groove with "Gimmie Some Lovin'." The band slipped easily back into the pocket, progressing into "I'm a Man" with a familiar full-on instrumental intro. Kip's bass and my drums locked together, with Ralph and Tim crashing down, accenting our groove. Once again, Ralph was spitting newly found fire from out of his guitar.

Not to be outdone by Ralph's vocals, Carl pulled his microphone free from its stand, picked up his tambourine, danced a bit to feel the groove, cocked his head to the left, and then reached into the rafters for those rarified Steve Winwood tenor vocals. Tim and I fell into step singing harmony background vocals and punctuating with woo-woos and whoops. Despite so much movement on the stage and on the dance floor, there was an amazing subtlety going on between the organ and guitar, the bass and drums, and the vocals floating above our heads, which made us feel that we were a whirling dervish of stimulation. Out of nowhere, toward the trailing end of the song, there came another guitar solo that Ralph insisted belonged in that song at exactly that moment. How he knew it would work, I'll never know, but Ralph's guitar began squeezing out blues-driven, rock-inspired notes like a hellhound was on his heels. This solo pushed the song from its usual three minutes to well past five. When he finally released us from his grip, the band fell silent to deafening applause.

Interestingly, Carl never bothered to learn more than one verse of "I'm a Man" and sang that one verse over and over each and every night. He just put tonal inflections and emphasis in different places each time he sang the verse, which made it sound slightly different each time he belted it out. The only reason I discovered this is that I have several live recordings of the band, and as indiscernible as his vocals were most of the time, he clearly sang only one verse over and over on all the recordings

I've heard.

But with Carl, it was never about the lyrics. He could sing the Gettysburg Address and draw a crowd to the dance floor. With Carl, it was always about the emotion and how the band was kicking in response to what he was singing. In two measures, he could make you feel as if you were screaming down the highway in a Porsche with your head out the open window, hair blowing in the wind. Nobody, as far as I know, ever accused Carl of having a great voice, but his was exactly the voice that the Consolidation needed. He fit with our band and our level of energy perfectly, and you couldn't find a better front man or a better friend than Carl Persis. Carl had a winning charisma, and he was appealing to both men and women: guys wanted to be just like him, and women wanted to spend time with him. A great singer is much more than simply perception, and Carl's performances were not only external but also profoundly internal. When he was onstage, something normally hidden deep within his soul was slowly torn loose and a tiny piece was given to each member of his audience. When Carl did what he did without a net, walking a tightrope between mistakes and genius, people got drunk on the humanity and enamored with his honesty. The only place this really happens is during a live performance, and the best place to do it is down and dirty when everyone is watching. Carl did it right, and it was always more than enough for us.

"Ain't Too Proud to Beg" was called next, and I kicked it off with a quick paradiddle role, but instead of singing, Carl broke into one of his signature James Brown-ish DJ commercial interludes, which typically lasted anywhere from ten to thirty seconds. Tonight, Carl had much to say, so his promotional interlude went on for nearly three minutes, as the band circled the airport waiting for him to bring us into the song.

"Awwwwe, Yah! Good God, Baby! We're going to do a song now by the Temptations, Yah, Baby! A song called, 'Ain't Too Proud to Beg,' Baby! Awwwwe, Yah! Good God, Baby! We're going to do it right now, Yah! We are the Consolidation from Daytona Beach. Good God! The Candymen are coming on at about nine o'clock. Yah, or 9:30, Yah! If you haven't seen the Candymen, you ain't seen nothing! Yah! That's right! The Candymen! The best is yet to come, Baby! It's all happenin' right here at the Moultrie Bowl! That's right! The Moultrie Bowl! It's gotta be the best damn place in Georgia! Yah, Baby! And you're right here! Yah! And it's all going on until about midnight tonight, Awwwwe, Yah! Right here at the Moultrie Bowl! Awe! Good God! Uhuh! All right, do it now!" And with that, Carl's typical commercial interlude was over, so the rest of us thought it was time to kick the song off in earnest. We looked for his signal to dive headlong into "Ain't Too Proud to Beg," but he was just getting wound up tight.

Carl had one more thing to say, and, as an afterthought, he hatched a plan to add some Daytona-style excitement to the tail end of the show. Out of nowhere, he became DJ Carl again, announcing, "Hey, Baby! There's one more thing, Baby! Yah! There's going to be a party at the Davis Brothers Motor Lodge after the show tonight! In Tifton! Yah, Baby! In Tifton! The Davis Brothers Motor Lodge! Yah, Baby! In room 213 and 214, in Tifton! Yah, Baby! Out by the interstate, Yah, Baby! The pool's going to be open all night long, Good God! Yah! Y'all come by if you can, now, Good God! Uha!"

Carl gave us the cue to start the first verse, "All right, band, do it now!" And this time we didn't give him a chance to do anything but start the damn song! But, oh, boy! What the hell had he done? What could we do? He was on a roll, propelled by the emotion of the music and the moment, and when Carl was on any kind of roll, emotional or otherwise, there was no stopping him. As we were to learn soon enough, a pool party at a local motel was apparently a big deal to the kids from the piney woods of South Georgia. After all, what else is there to do on a Saturday night, growing up in Podunk, Georgia, when the best you've got is stealing watermelons and tipping cows? With all the promo rigmarole out of his system, Carl finally signaled the start to "Ain't Too Proud to Beg," which went something like this...

We shifted gears to a driving, more relentless groove and filled the space between the stage and the audience with some sweet rhythm and blues, and it was graciously accepted. The musical intro for "Beg" was so generous that it was nearly impossible to break away from the groove perpetuated by the flow it created and just start singing. "Ain't Too Proud to Beg" had one of those intros that could last all night if the feeling was right, and tonight it just felt right. The drums pumped thunder, and the whole band was accenting, following Ralph's Steve Cropper-style slide-up riffs and Kip's driving bass. After ten measures of intro without commercial interlude, we were all marching to Montgomery, and then Carl began singing, "I know you wanna' leave me! But I refuse to let you go!" The band hit its groove, the music flowed, and we were firing on all cylinders. We were all locked in, pulling tighter together musically, singing background harmonies and hitting fills, and then we took a hard right, throwing gravel and spinning wheels, and then we were into Tim's piano solo. O'Brien put his fingers to the keys and started to play a progression so soulfully rich I shudder just to think about it. After Tim's solo and another bridge, we bust loose cruising down a dusty, red-dirt road, lost somewhere in the Georgia pine woods. In our mind's eye, soft musical sunshine filtered down through the pines around us as we raced the wind, spurred on by the musical expeditions that Otis and Wilson Pickett had led us on years before. As long as the intro seemed to last, the song ended much the same way, but with a slight twist. The chorus repeated for another fifteen measures, with the whole band driving to the finish line ahead, but then the song ended abruptly, leaving the dance floor full and the audience demanding more.

The rest of that set flew by similarly, twisting and turning like a dove on the opening day of bird season. As we were tying up the last few bars of the final song of our first set, I noticed that two of the Candymen were standing next to our stage, Cokes in hand, with arms crossed intently, watching us play. They were chatting very seriously between themselves, and I imagined that they were thirsting for a smidgen of our newly found energy and intensity. When we finished playing, one of them reached out and shook my hand as I made my way down the four stairs on the right side of the stage. I remember being excited and a little surprised that they were interested enough in our set to walk all the way across the room to watch. I smiled and asked, "So, what did you think? Are we holding up our end of the room?"

To which he deadpanned, "No, not really, we just wanted to watch and see if that piece-of-shit Silvertone amp that he's been overdriving, was going to explode during that set. Probably next set...It's always entertaining when that happens and well worth a short walk." His words fell like a wheelbarrow load of steaming manure dumped at my feet. I had hoped that Ralph had not heard him, but I could tell by the look on his face that he had, and then the same Candymen member added, "Maybe next set?"

Like mindless high school hazing, his parting words stung, as they dispassionately turned and disappeared through the audience toward their stage. I couldn't help but wonder what Roy Orbison had seen in them. For a backing band, they were the perfect combination of classic elegance and subdued stage personalities, but they were not at all where we planned to be in a year or two.

During our break, we were perfectly content to sit at a table near the stage on our end of the venue and sip Cokes, listening to their exactness from a distance. I don't think they even got one foot tapping at our table. The rest of the night I don't remember seeing the Candymen at all, except from our stage as they were finishing their set. They looked as small to us as we must have seemed to them. As soon as they played their last note and began to introduce us, we instantly began our second and last set, cutting their announcement off. We played our last set the way we always did, with power and excitement enough to inspire the entire audience. Our intention was to leave the crowd at the Bowl with a lasting impression, and we did. The audience quickly melted away from their side of the room and congregated at our end, where they danced and sang with our inexact but energetic band of fast friends.

Satisfied in our own minds that we had smoked the headliners that night, we packed up Kip's bus, found the promoter, got paid, and headed back toward our hotel for the night before the Candymen finished playing their final note. When we got back to the motor lodge, all was quiet and it seemed that Carl's invitation must have fallen on deaf ears. Exhausted from all that we had packed into two short days, we laid down on our beds, closed our eyes, and were soon snoring like a room full of truck drivers on furlough. At some point a few hours later, out of a dead sleep, I remember hearing our room phone ringing, and, simultaneously, the first of several soft knocks occurred on our door. I started to answer the phone as Ralph looked out the peephole, and before I could say, "Hello," I heard Ralph say, "Holy Shit, come look at this!" I dropped the phone on the nightstand and looked out a crack in the curtains to see the balcony filled with teenagers, hotel management, and even a few off-duty waitresses. The parking lot was ablaze with a parade of car lights and honking horns. "Oh, shit" was about all I could muster as I reached for the phone and summarily hung it up. Kip and Lee were now waking up, and Carl, in his paisley boxers, followed by Tim, in leopard-skin pj's, were making their way through the darkness into our room. Apparently, the Candymen's last set was over and Carl's midnight pool party was about to begin, an hour or so later than planned. The office called back again, and this time I managed to be awake enough to listen to the night manager howling through the phone. Then, another, harder, more substantial knock came on our door. When we opened it, the furious night auditor, whose only job until then had been to quietly prepare guests' bills for the next morning's checkout, burst into our room demanding to know who had invited the whole of Tift County to his motel.

By this time, the crowd was starting to thin on the balcony outside of our room thanks to the management's coaxing and the others that the night auditor had managed to press into service. Still, the spectacle of an endless parade of cars around the parking lot looking for parking spaces and the swimming pool was mind-blowing. At one point, one of our guys, much to the crowd's approval dressed only in white boxers, managed to bolt out onto the balcony overlooking the parking lot and car parade and gave the crowd a wave or two before the night auditor pushed him back into our room. The flood of young people roared its approval, but the frustrated night auditor could only shake his head in disbelief. Thankfully, the gate to the pool deck was locked and guarded, but that didn't stop the most invested and inebriated of the local citizens from jumping the chain-link fence and throwing themselves into the pool.

When the Tifton police force finally arrived, order was quickly restored and all barefooted trespassers were sent on their way. Apparently, however, the cars were still lawfully allowed to drive through the parking lot, room key or not. The parking lot drive-through went on for another half hour or so until the kids were all satisfied that there was no party to be had, at least not at the Davis Brothers pool. What a memorable night on so many different levels. One can only imagine what would have happened had that mob showed up at the Hubert Motor Court instead.

All was calm when we woke up the next morning, though we all slept in a little later than usual. Most of the Florida-bound tourists were already on the road to palm trees and paradise when we surveyed the parking lot for cars. We took turns showering and then made our way down to breakfast/lunch. If the day shift had gotten word of the previous night's fiasco, it didn't seem apparent. I felt sure that word would spread before the day was over, but we would hopefully be long gone to our next gig by then. What had happened the night before at the Davis Brothers Motor Lodge had likely never happened in Tifton, Georgia, before. A motel pool party was strictly a Daytona Beach thing, it seemed. Breakfast was quiet, and we certainly weren't about to bring it up with our waitress over eggs, bacon, and grits or cheeseburgers and fries.

The next order of business was to track down the Candymen's management to see where the next show was to be played. There had been vague talk initially of extra dates if we had worked out with the Candymen. Carl and Tim drove over to their hotel to get directions to the next gig while the rest of the band tidied up our room, packed a few things, and checked out. We were down in the office settling the bill when Carl and Tim walked in, and immediately we could tell that something was wrong. They returned unusually quiet, and their disposition made it appear as if they had been gut-punched and robbed.

"Hey, guys, what's going on?" I asked.

"They're gone," was all that Carl could say.

"What?" I responded. "Where the hell did they go?"

"I don't know," Tim said, scratching his head in bewilderment.

"They just all left this morning early and nobody seems to know where they were going," Carl continued.

"Was there a misunderstanding?" Ralph asked. "I thought we had another couple of nights to play with them? Did anyone say anything last night? I thought there were more dates on the tour, but maybe we were wrong, or maybe the rest of the tour was cancelled, or maybe..."

Then there was a long silence that ended with, "Well, shit!"

"Any way you look at it, this stinks!" Carl responded, as he shook his head in disbelief.

"You guys don't think that the pool party thing last night had anything to do with this..." Lee's thought trailed off as we all stood staring out of the large plate glass window at I-75, mesmerized for a moment, watching the cars and trucks running north and south, wondering silently which direction the tour had gone.

"Well, damn!" Carl started. "After paying for our rooms and food, we're barely going to have enough gas money to get home. So much for the bigtime rock and roll tour! Shit!"

As bad as we all felt, there was a bright spot in the darkness for me...I still had a badly worn, brown, plastic Hubert Motor Court key and a bright, new, green Davis Brothers Cafeteria and Motor Lodge key to add to my collection.

As we continued to stare out the windows in the corner of the lobby, I believe it was Tim who sank down in a comfortable chair and began to chuckle first. Next was Carl and then Lee. Ralph and Kip joined them on the couch. By the time I joined them, we were all belly-laughing so hard that we were very nearly rolling on the floor. There was never a situation so bleak that it couldn't be raised a few notches by laughter. No matter how serious the situation seemed to be, the solution was usually only a chuckle or teenage prank away, and we never got angry with each other. Never.

Somehow, we made it home with our tails between our legs, taking turns riding with Kip in the loveable bus from hell. This was simply another in a long list of learning experiences that made us all the more prepared for whatever came after the Consolidation. Whether our individual paths led to college, music, business, medical school, a mayorship, or whatever scheme Tim hatched for the next few years, after we parted ways, we each felt better prepared, thanks to our time together as a team, to outshine our teenage counterparts, who had held down humdrum jobs as babysitters or grocery baggers at the local Winn-Dixie.

Stories about that weekend in Tifton and Moultrie, Georgia, have been told and retold by all six of us in six very different ways, but the basic facts invariably remain constant. Each of our individual perspectives, however, have changed considerably as the weeks turned into months, the months turned into years, and the years into decades. Each of us has invented an author to tell the story that we are telling. It is always about the stories.

Chapter 12

Minor Crimes and Misdemeanors

Idle hands are often called the devil's playground, and that's true enough. Given time and tedium, any teenager will invariably delve into trouble. So it was for us in the waning days of Christmas vacation in 1967. Spring 1968 was on the horizon, and my band, the newly renamed Soul Patrol, was growing bored waiting for the new year to ring in and for our final semester of high school to ring out.

New Year's Eve fell on a Sunday in 1967, and Lyndon B. Johnson was president. Young Americans for the most part were listening to "Hello, Goodbye" by the Beatles, although as the decade of the '60s marched toward its end, more noteworthy and some not-so-memorable music flew from all directions. Gladys Knight & "her" Pips gave us "I Heard It through the Grapevine," Smokey Robinson penned "I Second That Emotion," Aretha Franklin unleashed her "Chain of Fools," and the Monkees and John Fred's Playboy Band dumped "Daydream Believer" and "Judy in Disguise (With Glasses)" on the airwaves, polluting the mix. *The Graduate* had just hit movie theaters across the US, while racial riots burned through parts of Northern cities such as Detroit and Chicago and antiwar demonstrators rallied against the Vietnam War outside of the Pentagon in Washington, DC.

During late December of 1967, Duane and Gregg Allman's Hour Glass band played three nights with Buffalo Springfield at the Fillmore Auditorium in San Francisco. During that time, Duane became friends with, and subsequently jammed with, Stephen Stills, and they both visited each other's recording sessions. Obviously drawn to groups of unusual Southern style, Neil Young wrote the liner notes for the Hour Glass's second Liberty album, *Power of Love*, and the album notes were "Witnessed and approved" by Steve (Stephen) Stills.

Back in Daytona Beach, as house band at the Martinique, it fell on our shoulders to ring in the new year with a midnight show that garnered at least a marginal amount of local excitement on New Year's Eve of 1967. During the fall semester of 1967 and the spring semester of 1968, my band was being booked quite frequently for fraternity parties at the University of Florida, Florida State, Stetson University, and also for local Daytona Beach Junior College Greek festivities. The primary calling card for us at these fraternity parties was the fact that we became proficient at covering music by a legendary North Carolina rhythm and blues band called Doug Clark and the Hot Nuts. Doug Clark's near-mythological band was a rhythm and blues/rock novelty act that has played party and club dates for more than sixty years.

In their earliest incarnation, the Hot Nuts started out in Chapel Hill, North Carolina, as the Tops. This group of Lincoln High School seniors quickly became popular on the college circuit during the late 1950s for their risqué song lyrics, jokes, and limericks as well as for allegedly performing in various states of undress as long as ample bail money was guaranteed. The Tops initially played for Phi Delta Theta fraternity at the University of North Carolina, Chapel Hill, and then continued on to play for nearly every other fraternity at UNC after that night as Doug Clark and the Hot Nuts.

Doug Clark and the Hot Nuts soon spread their singular brand of lowbrow, vulgar, but addictive music across the Southern United States. Their flair for telling dirty jokes and harassing audience members from the stage proved hugely successful and extremely rewarding. Although the Hot Nuts have been booked for "censored" shows as well, the crowd invariably overrides the booking agent, demanding from them the raunchy style that became their stock and trade.

The Hot Nuts' signature song is a rollicking, suggestive tune entitled, naturally enough, "Hot Nuts." Other songs that they were known by, and that my band proudly covered at fraternity parties, included: "My Ding-a-Ling" (later a hit record by Chuck Berry), "Big Jugs" (based on "Big Bad John," written by Jimmy Dean and Roy Acuff, both Country Music Hall of Fame members), "He's Got the Whole World by the Balls," "Baby, Let Me Bang Your Box," "The Bearded Clam (Is a Delicacy That Won't be Found in the Deep Blue Sea)," and one of the Soul Patrol's personal favorites, "Two Old Maids."

"Two Old Maids" allowed the entire band to participate in the self-circling vocal melee in which to tell a tongue-in-cheek joke or two. This was the only Hot Nuts composition that was not a dance song, and we would usually play it after we had taken a break to get the party crowd back into the mood. The chorus was sung a cappella, in unison: "Two old maids laying in bed...One turned around to the other and said...Have you heard the one about?" Then each band member would take turns reciting a slightly off-color joke, at which point the a cappella intro was repeated again and again until the jokes were exhausted. One of my favorites was, "Did you hear the one about the Sunday school teacher who chased her boyfriend around the church until she finally caught him by the organ?" You get the idea.

It is generally accepted that the Hot Nuts were the inspiration for the fictional Otis Day and the Knights group in the movie *Animal House*. Regardless, the Hot Nuts played a huge role in the later popularity of rhythm and blues with White college audiences. All of the Hot Nuts albums were released on the "Gross" label, a subsidiary of Jubilee Records that was created solely for the band. The list of contemporary artists that Doug Clark and the Hot Nuts influenced is long and varied but undoubtedly includes evolutionary cult bands such as the Velvet Underground, George Clinton's Parliament-Funkadelic, the Ramones, the Red Hot Chili Peppers, Jane's Addiction, and on and on.

The Soul Patrol covered and played many songs from the Hot Nuts' songbook, and because of that, we were booked at fraternity parties all over Florida and South Georgia. However, while we had no problem getting gross with an inebriated, intimate college audience, we stopped short at playing in fur-lined jockstraps, as the Hot Nuts were purported to have done on many occasions, though it was asked of us many times and considered once or twice.

At a band rehearsal in late December of 1967, we were discussing and practicing some Hot Nuts music, and, invariably, fur-lined jockstraps came up in conversation, as they always did when anyone talked about the Hot Nuts. We were thinking a lot about our upcoming performance on December 31st and what, specifically, we could do to make our last New Year's Eve show as a band memorable. We all knew that high school graduation would signal the coming end for the band, and this year needed to be as kick-ass as it could be. After all was said and done, the Soul Patrol was a close-knit group of friends who were tight and constantly in search of marginal trouble or just a good laugh. We knew jockstraps were not possible at midnight, but something a bit less risqué, but still somewhat off-color for the late '60s, might be in order. After all, our intention was to shock the audience somewhat and not to turn the midnight show into a comedy routine. Jockstraps were very definitely out of the question...fur-lined or otherwise.

After much discussion, deliberation, and comic relief, it was determined that we would take our normal 11:40 break wearing our matching T-shirts and jeans, as if it were any other night. After a quick change in Bill Cook's office, we would reappear onstage shortly before midnight wearing nothing but our Beatle Boots and paisley boxer shorts, covered by matching black London Fog-style trench coats. The plan was that after playing one song wearing our trench coats to garner everyone's attention, we would join in with the traditional countdown to 1968. At about the twenty-second mark, we would all remove our coats and reveal our boxers, to the audience's delight. Under the threat of severe adolescent retribution, we all swore not to say a word about our plan to anyone.

With New Year's Eve still a week away, we needed to jump two minor hurdles before our plan could be put into effect. First, we would need to find a store somewhere in the Daytona Beach area to buy five pairs of matching paisley boxer shorts. Carl, our fashion plate, and who knew every haberdashery in town, was unleashed on that task. Secondly, and probably most importantly of all, was the fact that we needed to ascertain that appearing in underwear onstage was not breaking any local ordinances. The last thing any of us wanted was to have to make a call to our parents at midnight on New Year's Eve to bail us out of jail for an obscenity or some other sexually-related charge.

As upcoming college freshmen, most of us were constantly reminded to keep our "Permanent Record" unblemished, whatever those were. "Permanent Records" may have been slightly overblown in conceptual reality, but the threat orbited planetary in our psyches and followed each of us like bloodhounds following a two-legged pork chop.

Just who was it who kept everyone's Permanent Records, anyway?

Where were Permanent Records kept and stored?

Was there a nationwide Permanent Record sharing system?

When, and to whom, might our Permanent Records be revealed?

These were some of the ever-present, burning questions on the mind of every high school senior in the late '60s, and an even bigger mystery to most. Of course, there was no national database in the current sense of the word in the '60s, because a database is shared between many multiple computers across a vast network. This technology had not developed at that point. While clearly on the horizon, in 1967, the term database was not in common use. The term itself was only narrowly used during the '60s by a small group of pocket-protected, computer science engineering geeks. Modern worldwide database sharing was only an aspiration until a decade later.

The reality was that in 1967, the average run-of-the-mill high school office records room served to house our "Permanent Records" in files called cumulative records folders, or CUME folders. CUME folders followed a student from kindergarten through high school graduation. The average student who didn't require much surveillance also didn't require much CUME folder space. After high school graduation, CUME folders were eventually sent to the county's central offices to be stored in huge warehouses...never to be seen again. That was the only thing "permanent" about those records. It is unclear as to how long CUME folders were stored at county facilities, but water damage from hurricanes and fires reduced many such files to a charred or moldy mess here in Central Florida.

With the advent of microfiche, photostatic copies, and computers during the ensuing decades, the specter of intangible permanent records raised its ugly threatening head again in high schools all across America. However, the passage in 1974 of the Family Educational Rights and Privacy Act, or the Buckley Amendment, took much of the punch out of the "Permanent Records" threat, giving those eighteen years and older the final word as to who might have access to their records of any kind, permanent or otherwise. The law limits access to educational information and records by public entities such as potential employers and publicly funded educational institutions, and, yes, even parents.

However, as some marginally radical high school students evolved into more overtly radical college students of the 1960s and early 1970s, the FBI began compiling detailed records, or dossiers, on some students at their regional offices. Those FBI records may have been closer to the "Permanent Records" concept of Big Brother that many envisioned and feared. The FBI offices in Columbia, South Carolina, as I discovered years after the fact, housed dossiers on several Clemson students, including me. I have never seen the actual files, but a friend who was considering a run at South Carolina politics accessed those files using the Freedom of Information Act that was passed in 1967. He relayed to several of us who had been involved in Vietnam War protests at Clemson that, much to our surprise, we were all there, tucked away in our own neat little files. Someone was indeed watching, and there was no doubt after hearing his story that, for some of us, there really were "Permanent Records"!

As close as my band was able to ascertain, in that late December of 1967, in Daytona Beach, Florida, wearing paisley boxer shorts onstage was most likely only a Class 4 misdemeanor, or, at the absolute worst, a Class 3. Maurice Wagner, the Martinique's attorney and owner Bill Cook's drinking buddy, was generous enough to explain the differences in misdemeanors when we asked him a few nights after Christmas while he was sipping scotch on the rocks at the bar. The more Maurice had to drink, the more he offered us in the form of free legal advice between sets and the more interested he became about "what the hell we had in mind?" But we remained vague as to the details of our caper. We only elaborated to the extent that we were concerned about police or overzealous beverage agents being in the club on New Year's Eve. The more he imbibed, the more the pro bono work flowed...like the fifteen-year-old scotch he was sipping.

Wagner informed us that Class 4 misdemeanors, the least serious of all misdemeanors, carry fines in some cases but generally required no jail time. A Class 4 could cost each of us up to $250, but generally they were dismissed with a slap on the wrist and a warning for first-timers. "However," attorney Wagner warned, "the federal government takes any offense involving alcohol, drugs, firearms, or sexual misconduct very seriously, and even a Class 4 misdemeanor may disqualify any of you guys from considering government work in the future. Why do you think this is my second office?"

Wagner continued on to try to shake our resolve further: "Reporting a misdemeanor does not automatically disqualify you from a security-clearance position with the government, but hiding or misrepresenting information on your application not only disqualifies you but it counts as a felony. If you guys get caught in something, I'll do my best to get you off, or depending on what it is that we're talking about, to get your records expunged. But remember, you'll still need to report all information truthfully and accurately on employment applications, and do not try to hide whatever happens from the government. Even if you think it may disqualify you, the government will eventually catch you lying on their background check every time, without fail!"

There it is again, popping up out of nowhere, the ominous, often-unspoken but omnipresent "Permanent Record" threat! "Exactly where and when is this possible Class 4 misdemeanor that you are cooking up supposed to take place?" demanded Wagner, his curiosity finally getting the best of him. Tim had cleverly established early in the conversation that we insisted protection from our employer by attorney-client privilege even though we were not technically his paying clients and Bill Cook, our employer, was his client of record.

"Well, does this scheme somehow include or make culpable my client, Mr. Cook?" Maurice questioned.

"Oh, not a chance!" Tim exclaimed, without giving Wagner's question a second thought. "We would never do anything to put Cook crosswise with the law!"

Tim's response stunned the hell out of all of us because the very reason Maurice Wagner had a permanent reserved table at the Martinique for him and his friends, plus an open, never-ending bar tab, was precisely because Bill Cook was endlessly in trouble with the law. Cook rarely opened his mail without learning that he was in some sort of legal trouble. The local Volusia County beverage agents kept Cook and Wagner continually occupied trying to cling to his state liquor license. Most of Cook's problems over the years stemmed from his inability to keep and maintain a lawful liquor license. The Beverage Department's never-ending surveillance of the Martinique and its regular denizens was a self-inflicted predicament, in my opinion. Cook was frugal to a fault and hired mostly part-time students or seasonal transients as bartenders, bouncers, and ID checkers at the door. These low-wage, pass-through, careless employees were perfect targets for undercover beverage agents sporting either fake or stolen IDs.

If I learned anything from my many years working just about every job at the Martinique for Bill Cook and Ringo, it was that if you draw negative attention from the Beverage Department, that alone will eventually spell the end of a twenty-year-old business. Keeping an attorney permanently on premises was Cook's answer to near-weekly run-ins with the constabulary. Maurice Wagner was the perfect man for the job. He was a well-respected attorney about town, he knew all the judges, and he also had several youngsters whom he could keep tabs on while spending evenings "at work" at the Martinique. Attorney Wagner also added a bit of class to the "Q" with his dark suits, gold cufflinks, manicured fingernails, diamond-studded pinky rings, and alligator shoes.

Wagner's advice didn't really do too much to calm our nerves while we busied ourselves finding the whereabouts of enough matching paisley boxer shorts for the whole band. There were still more questions than answers as time progressed toward New Year's weekend. An ominous trepidation fell over the band as we sent Carl to the National Shirt Shop on Beach Street in Daytona for one pair of small boxers and four mediums on his way to rehearsal the Wednesday before the big weekend. When Carl made it to practice at my house that afternoon with a bag full of boxers, Tim was on the phone calling the Daytona Beach Police Station to try to find out just how much trouble we could get into wearing them on a stage on New Year's Eve. The trick, he thought, was to not use names or to tip off the police about our game plan in any way.

When Carl walked into practice, we were all in my mother's kitchen, clustered around Tim, who was sitting on my mother's folding step stool/chair at the telephone desk next to the refrigerator. We were all intently listening to one half of the conversation between O'Brien and the Daytona Beach Police dispatcher.

Tim began the conversation cordially. "Hello, sir, I need some information, if you would be so kind? Can you tell me if it's against the law to wear paisley boxer shorts on a stage in Daytona..." (click!) "Shit!" Tim hollered. "He didn't even let me finish my question!"

Ralph decided he wanted a shot at getting the information, so he dialed back and this time asked for, and was transferred to, the watch commander. "Hello, yes, sir, I wonder if you can answer a question for me. I'm doing a project for school, and some of us heard about some students who were thinking about appearing onstage in paisley boxer shorts. Is this in anyway..." (CLICK) We could hear the watch commander slam down the phone on his end while Ralph returned to his conversation with no one. "Son of a bitch!" now raising his voice. "What's wrong with you guys down there?" Ralph questioned, staring into the telephone receiver, continuing to talk to the dial tone. "Do you think that we have nothing better to do than to prank call you, you assholes? This is serious shit, we need some answers!" Of course, by this time Ralph was talking to nobody at all.

Ralph was really irritated, and about the time he slammed the phone down on the carriage, nearly breaking our vintage avocado-green rotary-dial wall phone, my mother opened the door from the garage with a cumbersome armload of groceries, stepping into the kitchen where we all stood. Ralph did a quick 180 and addressed my surprised mother cheerfully.

"Hello, Mrs. Thames," he greeted my mother with his finest, most cordial voice, as he reached out to help my mother put the grocery bags down on the kitchen table. "Can we help you unload the rest of your car?"

With that close call, we discontinued our investigation for a time and helped her empty the car, hoping there might be something in the bags of groceries to feed a hungry band of teenagers. My mother fed everyone at our practices, as was usually her custom when we were rehearsing at the house. Then she would excuse herself to walk across the street to visit one of her neighborhood friends, where her world would be much more quiet.

After giving lip service to practicing a song or two to keep the adults at bay, the calls to the Daytona Beach Police Station continued. Tim wanted another shot, and he even went so far as to try and disguise his voice, but by now the story of these guys calling about paisley underwear must have made the rounds. Tim's second call went flat before he could get past, "Sir, I have a serious question." (CLICK) To this day, I can still picture Tim shouting "Shit! Shit! Shit!" while beating the receiver of our poor telephone against a stack of papers on the telephone table in perfect syncopation with his cursing.

We were about to give up on the police when I remembered the band's "occasional" date sitting quietly on my living room couch watching our folly with a smile and waiting for the music to start again. We simply didn't have time to wait until the afternoon shift change at the police station. We needed a better plan to get the information we needed and we needed it soon. Before long, my father would be home from work at General Electric to watch the six o'clock news and we all needed to be gone by the time he got home and settled into his favorite chair. As we filtered back into the Florida room to practice a bit more, I thought out loud, "I wonder if it would make a difference if a girl called next time," looking again over at the nervous young lady in the adjoining living room with a questioning eye.

Marcia was one of our Seabreeze classmates who was everybody's friend and the center of everybody's affection. Her nickname was, and still is, Peaches. There was not a person in our band, including our manager, who had not taken a run at Peaches at one time or another. To most of our male classmates at Seabreeze High School, she remained untouchable. Peaches was warm, comfortable, strikingly attractive, and wore a sweater as it was intended. If you looked for the definition of flirty, you need look no further than our Peaches. She missed a huge opportunity to become a world-class model since she had "the look" that advertisers are always chasing but never quite manage to attain. To those of us lucky enough to know her, she was just the girl next door who managed to have it all. She was also the only one outside of the band who knew our plan, but we knew our secret was safe with her.

"Not a bad idea at all," Ralph said, eyeing Peaches as we all turned our attention in her direction. "What d'ya think?"

"Oh, why not? What do I have to lose?" Peaches purred back to nobody in particular as she started nonchalantly toward the kitchen. Her attitude came as no real surprise. She was never intimidated by anyone or anything, and no matter the response from the police, she would certainly treat my family's telephone with more respect than Ralph or Tim had. Peaches settled into the seat in front of the phone, picked up the receiver, and dialed the number that we had scribbled on the scratch pad on the telephone desk. Then Peaches began to work her magic.

"Hello, sir. I'm a classmate at Seabreeze High School with the police chief's son, and I need some information for an article I am working on for *The Sandcrab*, the school newspaper. Is there someone there who can answer a few quick questions for me?"

We all waited anxiously for the reply on the other end, and when Peaches smiled and gave us a wink, we knew that we had the right girl for the job.

She continued, "Thank you so much, officer! Now here's the question. Actually, some of my friends have been calling to get the same information, and I don't think someone down there is taking them seriously. What I really need to know is this: the Drama Club at Seabreeze is planning to put on a play in the spring, and one of the scenes requires a few of the male actors in that scene to wear only boxer shorts while on the stage, for a short period of time. The question is...would this be illegal in any way?" The dispatcher she was speaking with at the police station apparently needed to consult his supervisor and asked Peaches to hold on.

"Sure, I'll wait," Peaches said to the dispatcher, as she put the lucky phone to her chest, shielding the mouthpiece from her voice.

"He's going to check with his supervisor and get right back to me," she whispered under her breath. "I think this might work," she said, continuing to whisper in a low tone, "but listen, do any of you know if the police chief in Daytona has a son, and if he does, is the kid in Seabreeze by any chance?"

With that, we all lost it and retreated into the living room with our hands covering our mouths to muffle the belly laughs, shrieks, and howling before we could return to continue to communicate with our female espionage agent. Soon, Peaches signaled with some frantic hand gestures that her contact at the police station was back on the phone communicating with her. She nodded her head in an understanding, agreeing manner, and then Peaches finally asked, "Are you sure, officer?" (pause) "Well, thank you, that's exactly the information that I have been trying to get these lug heads to find out for me all afternoon. Thank you so very much, officer, you have been extremely helpful. I'll be sure to let the chief know. Good-bye now!"

With that, she benevolently hung the receiver ever-so-gently on its carriage without a word and looked at us clustered around her with puzzled eyes and finally shook her head and offered up, "I guess you just need to use the right tone of voice when you're dealing with those guys at the police department. He told me not to worry, that as long as everyone kept their boxers on, there should be no problem at all...at least with the police."

She went on to explain, "He also offered that some teachers and parents at 'the play' might be a little offended, but I don't think you guys will have to worry too much about that happening on the stage at the Martinique. It sounds like you guys are good to go. That was actually fun, but now it's time for me to go and help my mother with dinner. Oh, and by the way, that's going to cost you guys admission and free Cokes all night for me and OJ on New Year's Eve. We wouldn't miss this show for the world," she winked again. "See ya there!"

As Peaches walked out of my front door toward her car that afternoon, she took with her our fears and anxiety concerning our suppositional brush with the law. Between Maurice Wagner and Peaches giving us their blessings, we all felt good about our chances of avoiding incarceration. With that, we polished up a few songs that we needed to practice and broke down our equipment in preparation for Friday night's show. Luckily, we called it a day just as my dad walked through the door and sat down to watch the news. After everyone left, I busied myself by polishing my cymbals and waiting for my mother to return from across the street to get dinner ready.

With New Year's Eve landing on a Sunday in 1967, the ensuing three-day weekend flushed out all of the serious drinkers in town, legally of age or not. We felt fortunate to have been hired to play Friday, Saturday, and Sunday. It was nice to have three consecutive dates at one venue so we could keep our equipment set up and ready to go all weekend long. As was the case every year, plans were put into place and orders given, though, as per usual, most of the orders were only loosely implemented. The bartenders, barmaids, and bouncers were given special instructions to be on their best guard. Cook, Ringo, and Wagner were convinced that beverage agents and undercover police would surely infiltrate the club on this, the biggest party night of the year. By this point, all that any of them could do was their jobs as assigned and hope for the best. There was rarely much wiggle room in the overall plan to keep the liquor license intact across a typically wild, aboriginal New Year's Eve, but we were all determined to give it the old college try.

As always was the case, two brand-new (to the Martinique) "salvaged" commodes were purchased, prepped, and neatly stored outside of the back musician's entrance to the club, adjacent to Cook's inside office door. Every New Year's Eve at or shortly after midnight, someone, usually Bobby Laney or Norman Spraul, would light two M-80s or cherry bombs simultaneously and flush them down the commodes in the men's bathroom. When the explosive devices went off, the ensuing explosion would rupture the plumbing or, if Cook was lucky, it would only shatter the base of the porcelain commode, facilitating much easier and quicker repair. Regardless, water would be everywhere, and it was of paramount importance to shut off the water valves to each toilet in order to circumvent a destructive flood of the wooden dance floor just outside of the bathroom door. No matter how many bouncers Cook assigned to the bathroom, there was always some sort of distraction at some point in the night, and it never took Laney and/or Spraul more than a scant moment to take advantage of a well-placed diversion. Still, a plan was in effect to keep a close eye on those two, so they were to be watched like hawks throughout the night.

Friday and Saturday were basically carbon copies of our set list for the New Year's Eve show, sans the paisley boxers at midnight, so we were well rehearsed by the time the big night arrived. We were into the music that weekend, as always, and thrilled to be playing at all, and we were looking forward to rocking the roof off the Martinique Sunday night. As I remember, it was an unusually warm December, so I brought an extra T-shirt with me for each set on Sunday, which was not usually necessary during the winter.

I played with such abandon in those days that I often became saturated with sweat by the end of nearly every set. The observant owner of the Beachcomber, a competitive nightclub a few miles from the Martinique on A1A, was a great Greek business owner named Gus Geniose. We sometimes played the Beachcomber, and that is where Gus saddled me with the dreadful nickname "Sweats." Gus's nickname was why I began the habit of changing shirts every set. As one might imagine, "Sweats" is not the kind of nickname that a teenage rock and roll drummer might want to carry around for very long.

Sunday night, the dress was white jeans with light blue J. C. Penney T-shirts, embroidered on the pocket with our initials in monogram. As was my habit, I wore one T-shirt to work and carried four more with me to play in, and I carried a fifth in case I needed an extra one after work to wear out to breakfast at Rogers Restaurant on Seabreeze Boulevard or to the Bali Junior on Mason Avenue. No more "Sweats" for me! If we were hitting the Krystal on the way home, a change was not usually required. I wore my boxer shorts under my jeans, but I never much cared for boxers; consequently, I was uncomfortable on my drum seat all night long as they began soaking up surplus sweat.

Up until our 11:40 P.M. break, there was nothing unusual about the evening other than the record-breaking crowd size and the fact that Ringo was intently guarding a huge bag of balloons that she had secured onto the ceiling to release at midnight. There was a line attached, one end to the bag and the other end looping over the rafter just above the front of the stage, that Carl was to pull at midnight to release the sea of balloons. The balloons were in plain view and were no big surprise, but nevertheless Ringo was kept busy with several foiled attempts to pull at the line securing the bag. Of course, while all of this was going on, it was comical to watch from the stage as Moose and Jay Laing snaked through the crowd following Laney and Spraul around the club like overfed undercover gumshoes on vacation. Everything was as it should be, including Peaches and her girlfriend sitting at the band table like a pair of grounded angels, stage left, between the steps to the stage and the bathrooms on the opposing wall, where they patiently sipped their free sodas.

When we left the stage for our break, we left Ringo guarding the balloons and Moose and Jay gumshoe-ing Laney and Spraul. The only others who knew what we were about to do were Peaches and her friend, OJ, and they could barely contain themselves as we passed them on our way to change. We knocked on Cook's office door and asked if we could change quickly and also asked if he would guard the door to make sure nobody barged in on us. When we finished changing and walked out of the office, all anyone in the busy club could see were five fellows wearing winter trench coats. Ralph and I headed to the men's room to see "a man about a horse," and we each got into a line for one of the two urinals near the front of the bathroom. That almost spelled disaster, because unbeknownst to the two of us, two guys fell in line behind us for the urinals and they immediately noticed our boots with apparently nothing covering our legs above. Not really sure that needing to pee was worth getting our asses kicked, we both retreated from the public bathroom to Cook's office and begged to use his personal bathroom. That was when he noticed our odd dress and began to uncover our plan, and he almost forbid it from happening.

We explained that we had checked everything out with the police and our attorney, but still, Cook's last words were, "Just be damn sure that nobody loses their shorts on my stage!"

Narrowly avoiding disaster, we joined the rest of the band and the girls at the table next to the stage and awaited our showtime, trying not to look conspicuous. At the appointed time, we all took a deep breath and marched up the three stairs to the stage in unison and readied our instruments. People here and there began to notice our odd attire about halfway through our opening number and began to crowd close to the front of the stage, pointing at our legs. The girls seemed mostly interested in what Carl might be hiding under his trench coat. Cook's office door opened a scant crack at first, allowing a narrow beam of light out, and then he opened the door and stepped completely out and stood cross-armed in the corner to watch the show unfold. Ringo eventually took her eyes off her precious balloons for a second, feeling that Carl was finally fully in charge of the string, so she stepped back a bit and when she did, her eyes bulged out at the sight of us standing there onstage in what appeared to be nothing at all but trench coats and boots. Between songs, the guys stepped back from their microphones and I stood next to my drum set, and at that point all hell broke loose.

As we removed our trench coats to oohs, aahs, and screams from mostly the girls in the front row of the audience, everyone's eyes and attention were glued to the stage as Carl began his countdown to midnight. Unfortunately, Moose and Jay were also watching us, dumbstruck by what they were witnessing, which allowed their personal charges to slip away and prepare to blow both toilets off their bases in the men's bathroom. At precisely 12:00 midnight, as if choreographed and rehearsed, the balloons fell to the floor, and the audience began popping them. When Laney and Spraul exploded the two M-80s, both resonated like gunshots throughout the club. By the time the explosions happened, Laney and Spraul had already slipped out of the bathroom area while Jay and Moose frantically threw themselves into shutting off the water valves to the two toilets. As Carl danced closer to the front of the stage, we started playing the "Two Old Maids" medley by Doug Clark and the Hot Nuts. Just then, a girl in front of the stage lunged forward, likely propelled by too much Ripple wine, and pulled Carl's boxers two inches down from his midriff. Only a quick waistband grab at the very last second circumvented what would have been certain disaster for our band and a world of embarrassment for our singer. Cook was dead serious about any of us dangling our wares in front of his nightclub. Maurice Wagner, sitting at a table on the opposite side of the stage, convulsed with laughter, nearly turning his chair over backwards. Wagner stopped laughing long enough to stand up and tip an imaginary hat in our direction. Then he joined the rest of the audience and gave us and the New Year a standing ovation.

We finished that set in our paisley boxer shorts that I'm pretty sure never saw much use after that night. Afterwards, we changed back into our uniforms just as soon as Cook could march us back to his office. We played our final set dressed as we usually were.

We returned to the club early Monday afternoon, on New Year's Day 1968, to break down and load out our gear. Amazingly, the club was mostly back in order by 2 P.M. Bill and Moose had replaced the commodes and bolted the condom machine back on the bathroom wall, while Ringo and Jay had cleaned all the tables, picked up the mess, and mopped the floors. Aside from a few colorful errant balloon shards here and there, everything was back as it should be, and Bill Cook was happy with the evening's take.

We considered, for a short while, taking our paisley boxer shorts on the road with us to fraternity parties at the University of Florida and FSU, but quickly we decided that doing so would only open a can of wiggling worms we didn't really want to expose. We had narrowly avoided a possible indecent exposure charge, and who could know if we would be so lucky going forward. Some of my bandmates, dressed merely in boxer shorts, were apparently just too intriguing for some over-served ladies to handle.

Looking back to this wonderful, carefree time, my band was simply striving to emulate the intensity and eagerness of the zany Beatles movies of the day. I am eternally grateful that Duane and Gregg Allman, as well as the other members of the Hour Glass, were busy in San Francisco and didn't wander into the Martinique that night to witness my friends and me standing onstage in our underwear. Duane and Gregg were the kind of professionals who never needed to showboat onstage or on the street. Recalling that night fifty-four years ago, other than my parents, the members of Hour Glass were the only people in the world whom I would have been genuinely humiliated to have had there that night. Of course, things always look just slightly off-kilter and a bit foggy through the rearview mirror of time. Besides, I doubt Duane would have had a pair of paisley boxers to jam in, and I wouldn't have wanted him to feel left out.

Chapter 13

Stickball Game with the Hour Glass

One early afternoon in late March of 1968, when the Hour Glass was in town playing with the Soul Patrol at the Martinique, both bands met to figure out whose equipment to use and its placement for the night. Johnny Sandlin and I would both occupy the large back riser, but because I am a lefty and Johnny didn't particularly like the thought of switching his drum kit around 180 degrees between sets, we always set up both drum kits side by side. In deference to his musical experience, much less his considerable size, I always allowed him the greater share of the riser, to the extent that sometimes I set up part of my ride cymbal on the inside edge of the go-go cage to my left. The go-go girls were not particularly fond of sharing their space with my ride cymbal, but I would have to say that I welcomed the coziness. As we normally did, Johnny set up his set of gray pearl Rogers on the right side of the drum riser, and I squeezed my set of blue sparkle Ludwigs on the left side. The space was tight, but Johnny and I always made it work.

Gregg and Paul Hornsby were very comfortable with their organ and piano setup, so that stayed. Our keyboard player, Tim, was ecstatic with the diversity of their set up, and nothing that he had would add anything of value to the mix. Gregg mostly played an L-111 Hammond console organ, owned by Paul, with the cabinet cut off and rigged on folding legs, which Gregg played through a Leslie cabinet that was miked and run through one of their 5 Vox Super Beatles. Paul primarily played a Wurlitzer portable electric piano that was amplified by one of the Vox Super Beatles. Paul also switched with Gregg from time to time on organ, and, in addition, Paul occasionally played one of his favorite Fender Telecasters, harmonizing with Duane on early Allman Brothers-style, dual-guitar arrangements like "Dimples."

Duane's guitar amp of choice at that time was a Fender Twin Reverb, as was our guitar player's, so they found room on the stage for both, sometimes stacking them one on top of the other. Until it was lost, Duane loved to play his hybrid, cream-colored 1950s Fender Esquire that had been fitted with a 1950s Stratocaster neck. A Vox distortion booster strapped to the front of his guitar completed the rig. After he lost the Esquire/Strat hybrid, he moved to a sunburst Stratocaster, but Duane really coveted our guitar player's blond-neck, robin-egg-blue Fender Stratocaster.

Duane lusted after Ralph's Strat to the point that he made a habit of coming in to play it nearly every time he was in town. Simply listening to Duane lovingly crafting "throwaway" licks on Ralph's Strat expunged whatever poker face Duane thought he was able to contrive. He relentlessly worked toward horse-trading Ralph for his ragtag but incredible-sounding Strat...but nothing worked. Ralph was tempted, occasionally, but if he wavered, we all reminded him that if Duane wanted his guitar so badly, it must have been even more special than we all imagined, and rightly so. Still, Duane never gave up trying to bargain for that guitar, nor did he stop coming by to play what became known to our band as the "Duane Strat." There will be more to this story in a later chapter...

Our bass player at that time, Ross Yost, had a new, state-of-the-art Coral bass amplifier that Pete Carr was anxious to test drive, so, as always, we used most of their gear, augmented with a little of ours. After the stage was set up, Duane, Pete, and Johnny Sandlin struggled to hang their PA columns, which consisted of the two remaining Vox Super Beatles speaker cabinets, from the rafters that crossed the club above the front edge of the stage, while Gregg busied himself chatting with a cute blond waiting at the bar. The Hour Glass agreed to use our Bogen PA amp and mixer and Carl's Echoplex voice enhancer. After enacting a stage plan, each band ran through a couple of songs to check sound levels. The Hour Glass took the stage first, checking the sound and volume levels, and then the Soul Patrol played a bit to check ours. When we finished the sound check and were packing away our guitar cases, drum covers, and amp covers, something curious happened.

From out of the dark bowels of the Martinique, Duane sauntered up to the front of the stage area, where he offered us a broomstick, sans the broom straw, and a wad of athletic tape covering something about the size of a tennis ball. Duane very innocently sashayed over to the side of the stage where we were packing up our crap and planted the broomstick into the floor, holding it with his right hand while he nonchalantly flipped the ball into the air and caught it with his left hand to garner our attention. We all stopped for a minute and eyeballed Duane, wondering what was up. Finally, Ralph asked him, "What's the deal with the ball and bat?" That is when Duane challenged us to something he described as "a friendly stickball game." When we showed a little curiosity, Duane sprung the trap and suggested that the losers buy a late lunch of burgers, fries, and Cokes at Bertie's Luncheonette around the corner on Main Street "to make the game a little more interesting." During 1967 and 1968, we learned a great deal about music, equipment, and music philosophy by just associating casually with Duane, but now he was about to school us in affairs totally unassociated with music. He was about to introduce us to a handful of minor-league life lessons.

"Why not take the bait," we thought. After all, neither brother had appeared to be the least bit athletic when they were in high school. As for our band, Carl, Ralph, Ross, and I had each lettered in several sports before music took over our lives. "Why the hell not? We should be able to cream those guys!" Or so we thought.

The Soul Patrol quickly huddled up to make sure we had enough money between us in the unlikely event of an unexpected upset. Next, we decided on positions, and then we planned our batting lineup. Tim joked that if we lost the game, the cost of lunch for both bands would probably cost us about what we were going to be paid for that evening. Then our vocalist, Carl, realist that he is, reminded us that we were being paid no money for that particular night. We were working off three hundred dollars that Bill Cook had loaned us a few weeks earlier to buy a strobe light for our lighting system. Suddenly, the game began to take on a whole new importance.

The parameters of the baseball diamond were established and consisted, basically, of the square, wooden dance floor directly in front of the stage. Duane and Gregg argued for some unusual "Midwestern stickball rules" that sounded more like cricket than baseball to us, so for the sake of expediency, we settled on rules familiar to us all. It was decided the room would be set up just like a miniature baseball field and we would play by down-home American baseball rules: nine innings, balls, strikes...the whole nine yards.

As the Soul Patrol took the field, we pulled the tables and metal chairs around the edge of the "diamond" away from the rest of the field, which made a hell of a racket, echoing through the empty club. Ringo heard us rearranging her nightclub and couldn't resist poking her head out of the office door to see what we were up to. As she emerged from the office/apartment, she shook an intimidating finger in our collective direction, warning us that when we were finished "playing," everything had to be restored to its previous pristine placement. "No problem, Rings," Duane replied. "We're just going to play a little game of stickball for lunch around the corner." Doubtlessly, Ringo had an idea about what was to happen because she hollered into their apartment to Bill Cook so he, too, could come out and watch. As we finished getting the tables and chairs out of our "field of play," Bill and Ringo as well as a few friends settled in to watch the game from the back of the U-shaped bar.

Gambling and bar owners go together like scotch and soda, so to Bill and Ringo, this was like having front-row seats to an Ali-Frazier fight. I don't know what we were thinking by taking Duane's bet, and Cook's keen interest in the game only added to my growing anxiousness. I had already lost the cost of a six-pack of Budweiser tall boys and a twenty-dollar bill to one of Cook's partners-in-crime, Vernon Thurman, on a bet that he couldn't drink a six-pack of beer at a red light before it turned green. Vernon Thurman, Bill Cook, and Tommy Roberts, or TR, the brother of the late race car driver Fireball Roberts, ran together like a pack of stray dogs, and trouble was always right on their heels.

Vernon was a huge man and an epic drinker, but, come on, who can drink a six-pack of tall beers at a stoplight, right? I don't remember who purchased the beer because I was too young at the time. It didn't matter who bought them, I ended up paying for them anyway. We placed the beers on the console between the front bucket seats in his late '60s Ford Fairlane, and then Vernon and I each placed a twenty-dollar bill next to the beer. Next, we drove out of the Martinique's parking lot a half block, to the stoplight at the corner of Wild Olive and Main Street, facing Main. We scanned the empty streets for police cars, and then Vernon patiently waited for the light to turn red. The green light turned to amber, and as the amber light turned red, he burst into action and began going to work. Like lightning, he meticulously ripped the pop-tops from each beer can and tossed them into the open ashtray. This took only a few brief seconds, and now he was ready to really go to work. What he did next was inhuman, and all I could do was gawk in disbelief.

Vernon, who was a big boy to begin with, and undoubtedly had ample room in his beer gut for a six-pack, lifted each beer one by one up to his open, gaping mouth and violently squeezed every drop of beer from the can, as he simultaneously drained the contents of each can directly into his stomach without so much as swallowing. I'd never seen anything like it. He somehow literally opened his throat and poured the beer into his thirsty stomach. What Vernon did that afternoon didn't look humanly possible. All I could do was watch in horror as, seconds later, he finished the last beer. He ripped off a gut-wrenching burp from somewhere deep inside his satisfied belly as he snatched up both twenties with a smile. He casually slipped his Fairlane into reverse, cool as a cucumber, and eased back the half block to where his car rested across from the opening to the Martinique's parking lot. There, his friends, and many of mine, cheered him wildly. Just as I stepped out of the car, I glanced back to the intersection as the offending light finally changed from red to green. It wasn't even close, and I honestly believe Vernon could have easily drained six more beers before that light turned green...maybe more. Thankfully, that was a bet I never took. I wasn't up for double or nothing that afternoon, no matter how much TR taunted me. As we settled on positions and got our stickball game underway, I began to get the haunting feeling that Duane may have talked us into another short ride to the corner in Vernon Thurman's Ford Fairlaine.

Both bands gathered around Gregg to witness him flip an old silver coin that he always kept in his pocket to decide which band would be up first. The Hour Glass won the coin toss, so the Soul Patrol took the field. Our vocalist, Carl, who lettered in every sport except women's basketball, pitched and covered home plate. Tim, who was not necessarily athletic in the strictest sense of the word but who always managed to outdistance jealous boyfriends, played first base. Ralph, who lettered in cross-country, track, and basketball, covered second base and shortstop. Third base was covered by me; I had played football and track and had been a master at slipping out of class to bowl a quick game at Bellair Lanes next to Seabreeze High. Ross Yost, who lettered in track and cross-country for three years at Seabreeze, covered the outfield between the bar, which cut off half of left field, and the right field line, which extended into the club on a line running parallel to the front of the stage. It was established that any ball hit over or behind the bar area itself or into the massive overhead beams and was lost would be considered a foul ball and out of play. Beyond that, the whole club was an open field.

To my thinking, our team was young, fit, well-conditioned, and ready for competition, but looking back over the years, I have to admit that my mind was occasionally adept at deceiving me. We had met with the Hour Glass at the Martinique to figure out the stage set up after school on a Friday in the early afternoon, so our guys were all still dressed in our preppy, short-haired, high school attire. The Hour Glass was a rough-cut, ragtag, blue-jeans-and-T-shirt kind of band during daylight hours who only dressed up for the stage after dark in their *Power of Love*-era, Nehru-style, crushed velvet jackets, Confederate uniforms, and various flowered shirts. In early 1968, the Hour Glass was several years removed from high school dress codes and our hair-length rules, so it was easy enough for us to stereotype them in their "civilian dress" as lethargic and less competitive than my band. First lesson: looks can be deceiving.

Duane stepped up to bat first, settling his lanky frame comfortably into the loosely defined batter's box. With a cold, resolute, evil eye, and nearly biting off his soul patch in anticipation of the first pitch, Duane stared Carl down, who was winding up from the center of the dance floor. Carl was somewhat surprised and shaken by Duane's determined posture and guise. When Carl lobbed his first pitch in, we all grimaced as the tape-wrapped "ball" dropped to the floor a few feet in front of Duane and rolled under a table next to the stage. We all sank into ourselves as the game started in negative territory, but for someone who had never pitched a ball wrapped in athletic tape before, Carl got the benefit of the doubt from our team. Carl's second pitch was somewhat better but still crossed the plate at around Duane's ankles and way outside.

Surprisingly, this was Duane's sweet spot, because he reached out and swung in a blinding flash. The ball disappeared into the deep recesses of the highest rafters and then reappeared magically at the far reaches of the Martinique, near the front door. Mistakenly positioned too close to the infield, Ross never had a chance to stop Duane's hit. Everyone kept one eye on Duane and one on the outfield as the spindly blond guitar player rounded second, heading full tilt for third base. In the meantime, with blinding reflexes, Ringo left her comfortable seat at the back bar as Duane rounded second, hurrying back to the front door to retrieve the ball. Ringo then managed a throw to Ralph, who then dared Duane to try for home. Duane remained unfazed and unflustered next to me on third, where he lit a cigarette as his team whooped and cheered.

Next up was Daytona hotshot guitar-player-turned-bassist Pete Carr, who hit a line drive on Carl's first decent pitch that was thankfully stopped by the bar between second and third. Ralph again made the play, but now we had a player on first and third, and Carl was facing Gregg at the plate. Twitching and shaking more than usual, Carl threw two balls right away to the mellower Allman. Then he settled down a bit and managed to throw a strike, after which Gregg decided to play the averages and watched the next two pitches drop to the floor...balls three and four.

With the bases now loaded, the biggest hulk of a man in the Hour Glass band, drummer Johnny Sandlin, stood up from where he and Paul

Hornsby had been quietly waiting. Johnny's demeanor was quite deceiving. He was a gentle, quiet man, though his face appeared to be unhinged by some unknown or unseen demon, almost as if he constantly had a stone in his boot that he couldn't eradicate. Unlike the rest of the band, who were generally upbeat and jovial, Johnny had an aura of seriousness about him that smacked of the aloofness that generally follows rock and roll stars who tend to be bored with the "normalness" of everyday life. When he stood up or moved, Johnny appeared slow, but in reality, his movements were more deliberate and unconcerned than apathetic. However, when he took his place in the band behind his drum set, his hands and feet instantly became symphonic lightning in a bottle. Apart from his appendages, only his head bobbed almost unnoticed as he propelled his band into the pocket of whichever song he was driving forward. I knew the swiftness and power that he was capable of, so I motioned to Ross to back up toward the front door of the club as Johnny made his way to the plate. Once in the batter's box, Johnny pointed the full length of the broomstick "Babe Ruth"-style toward the front door at the very farthest point in the club. If this wasn't unnerving enough for our pitcher, when Johnny's outstretched arm lowered the broomstick bat from where he had been pointing, the business end of the "bat" reached nearly to Carl's nose, from where he was pitching from the center of the dance floor. This afternoon, Johnny Sandlin wasn't the rock and roll star who would go on to share stages and rub elbows with the Doors, Janis Joplin, the Nitty Gritty Dirt Band, and Buffalo Springfield; he was playing stickball for burgers at Bertie's, and his glower only added additional posture to his somber game face and massive frame.

As Johnny settled in at home plate, Ralph and I looked back as Ross backed up all the way to the front door of the club, where he wedged his foot against the door, "running block" style. Ross also enlisted Ringo's help as an additional outfielder, stationed slightly to the right by the front of the band's storage room. Over at first base, Tim and Gregg were both elbowing and crowding each other like an overweight duo playing a single B-3 Hammond, with Tim jokingly trying to shove Gregg off the base, eager to make some kind of play. Pete talked guitar strings and such with Ralph at second while waiting for Johnny to advance him around the bases. Duane didn't have much to say to me at third, never looking down as he just dropped his spent cigarette to the floor and extinguished it with a twist of his boot. While Johnny waited for his first pitch, Duane's poker face evaporated, revealing a pursed grin that he was barely able to conceal for the first time. His smirk and the glint in his eyes spoke volumes. He knew what was about to happen, and Duane doubtlessly tasted the first bite of his cheeseburger..."Drag it through the garden, but hold the ketchup."

Before Johnny was offered the first pitch, every member of the Soul Patrol resigned themselves to paying the bill for lunch, and we hadn't so much as tasted a french fry.

When the action resumed, Johnny watched, totally lacking in emotion, as Carl pitched three nervous balls in a row. Then Carl lobbed a fourth pitch way down and outside. Instead of watching the pitch and walking Duane in for the easy score, Sandlin reached out toward first base and literally knocked the tape off the ball with the very last inch of his broomstick. Ringo shrieked as the line-drive ball flew by her head. The ball careened off the band room wall and bounced back into the middle of the huge room between Ringo and Ralph at second base, disappearing into the maze of tables and chairs. Dazed and confused, the Soul Patrol froze for a moment and watched in dismay as the Hour Glass moved freely around the bases. Ross somehow shook off his trance, which had the rest of us frozen in time, and he recovered enough to bolt from the far reaches of the club, rooting the ball out of the cast-off mass of tables as Johnny approached third base following the first three runs toward home plate. Ross would have had an easy play at the plate for the first out if Carl had not been frozen by the tornado of events swirling around him. With nobody covering home base, all that the rest of us could do was watch as Paul Hornsby congratulated each of his teammates as they crossed the plate. I think I saw Johnny smile for the first time ever that day as he followed Gregg across home plate, doubtlessly thinking, "Make mine a double cheeseburger."

With Paul Hornsby hitting an infield homer and the rest getting hits, things got out of control quickly. The landslide of hits and runs only ended when the score reached double digits without our team so much as touching third base. Hungry, irritated, and feeling a bit suckered, we called the game and begrudgingly put the room back together for Ringo. We all picked up our belongings and exited out of the back door into the afternoon sunlight on our way to Bertie's for the payoff. Our manager, Lee Phillips, was away guarding our country in the navy during this time, but I wondered if things might have been a little different if Lee had been able to play. Lee was the only member of our group who was a regular on area championship softball teams. He might have been able to make a difference...but we'll never know. On the way out into the parking lot, Duane walked past me with the well-used broomstick and tattered ball and placed them lovingly into the back of their station wagon in a special resting spot, after which he rolled up the back window and carefully locked all the doors.

The grill cook at Bertie's—Mary—took great pride in making her hamburger plates just so. Mary's burgers were second only in taste to the epic burgers created by Gus at Gus's Char Broiler, a few blocks away on Broadway in Daytona Beach. However, Mary created her hamburger plates with love, care, and an artist's eye, whereas Gus slapped your burger on a paper plate and took your money through the same service window where you ordered. Gus definitely had a slight edge on flavor because of his char broiler, and then there was Howard's Ice Cream right next door, where one could order a milkshake or soda while waiting for the burger that Gus was cooking on the open flames right before your eyes. Sadly, the creature comforts offered by Gus's ended abruptly at his service window. There were only two or three horribly uncomfortable and most times greasy, round, concrete picnic tables inlaid with shards of multicolored tile with matching curved benches out front. No comfortable tables or chairs at Gus's. His customers could only eat while inhaling exhaust-filled air as tourists hurried to beach-side motels traveling past the restaurant only a few feet from his tables on Broadway Boulevard. During the heat of the Florida summer, Gus's was not the place to take your hangover for lunch. Both burger joints were popular with local musicians, along with the Krystal at the ocean-end of Main Street, but this day, Bertie's became the Hour Glass's gastronomic payday.

There was always a certain quiet, civilized elegance to the spotless, air-conditioned lunch counter and table service at Bertie's, something almost entirely deficient at many "luncheonettes" these days. Mary's hand-formed burger patties were cooked crisp on the outside, with a perfectly juicy center. She carefully melted American cheese on each patty to a velvety smoothness. Her french fries were impeccably fried to a rich, golden crispness and then dusted lightly with salt. Each large oval serving plate was garnished with lettuce leaves, a dill pickle spear, a slice of white onion, and one slice of ripe tomato. Beyond that, the only accoutrement added was a thin slathering of mayonnaise, if desired. All other condiments were easily available family style, within arm's reach on the long lunch counter where we were all seated.

My band learned another of many life lessons at the hands of Duane and company that afternoon. This time we learned an important lesson about stereotyping. We had assumed that because, as far as we knew, the members of the Hour Glass had never been athletic in school that they would be pushovers in a game of stickball, which was baseball reduced to its lowest common denominator. What we failed to realize was that while we were practicing each afternoon in the football, track, or cross-country arenas, they were practicing their own extracurricular activity, and, in doing so, strengthening their own resolve not only in the sphere of music, but also in the arena of life. That afternoon at Bertie's, the Hour Glass relished their cheeseburgers with a proclivity that can only accompany the jubilation that follows an athletic shutout, and which can be appreciated only by those who put everything on the line in their personal and professional lives on a daily basis. The Hour Glass proved their resolve to us that day and every day going forward, demonstrating a tenacity that followed all but Duane into the next fifty or so years of their incredible individual musical careers.

That day marked, for us, the titillating period of freedom when my pals and I spent our entire summer chasing stages in and around Daytona Beach far from the concerned gaze of parents. It was long ago in that remarkable time when we were set free to navigate the fogbank of emotions by ourselves and to think of ourselves as teenagers unbridled. We bore the expectations of what was to come, shared memories of four years of past antics, and anxiously hungered for the future, more than anything. Our greatest gift was that of perspective. We each recorded the excitement and happiness that we read on the faces of friends and fans as we proceeded through the last few months of our band's relatively short career. I wanted to be nowhere else, and we knew that those snapshots in time would have to sustain us into the future.

Tapping the dopamine memory that a great night of playing releases, it's easy to imagine the five of us well-oiled and in the mood for elation and revelry. If life is a camera brimming over with quick snapshots, then bars and late-night restaurants were the keepers of our social memory banks. In returning with Ringo to the Martinique through my mind's eye, I can indulge in the sights, smells, and sounds of that time, regaining access to what was left behind. The snapshot from that afternoon of us all lined up enjoying cheeseburgers and fries while sitting at the lunch counter at Bertie's could easily have been the inspiration for Jimmy Buffett's "Cheeseburger in Paradise": "I like mine with lettuce and tomato, Heinz 57, and French-fried potatoes." In the glorious spring and summer of 1968, our days and nights in Daytona Beach spotlighted each one of us in a brightness of total indifference. That afternoon, however, we were the Soul Patrol. And we were sharing counter space and ketchup with the future of Southern music, something that we would continue to do more often as 1968 transitioned from spring to summer and then into that early fall.

Kip Marshall, Ralph Bundy, and Cecil Johnston.
Courtesy Frank Marshall

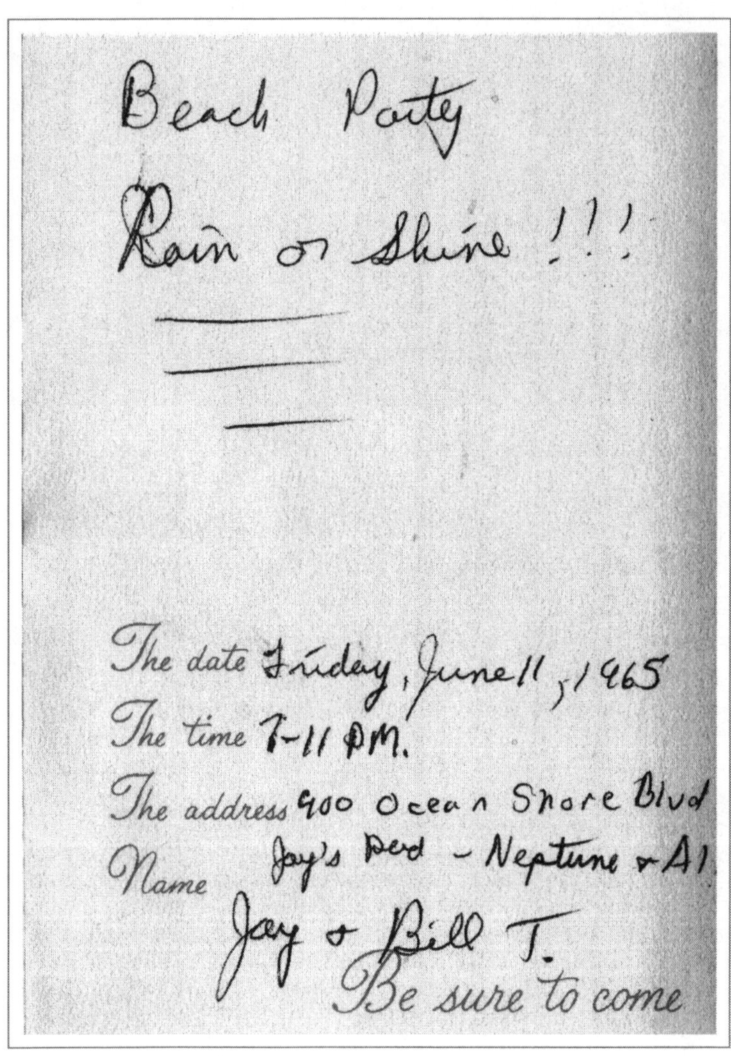
Beach Party

Rain or Shine!!!

The date Friday, June 11, 1965

The time 7-11 PM.

The address 900 Ocean Shore Blvd

Name Jay's Pad - Neptune & A1.

Jay & Bill T.

Be sure to come

Invitation to our band's beach party at Jay Laing's home.

Courtesy Marcia Cassel Ford

Early Knaves show on a flatbed truck at Ponce Inlet, Florida, for General Electric Picnic.

Courtesy Frank Marshall

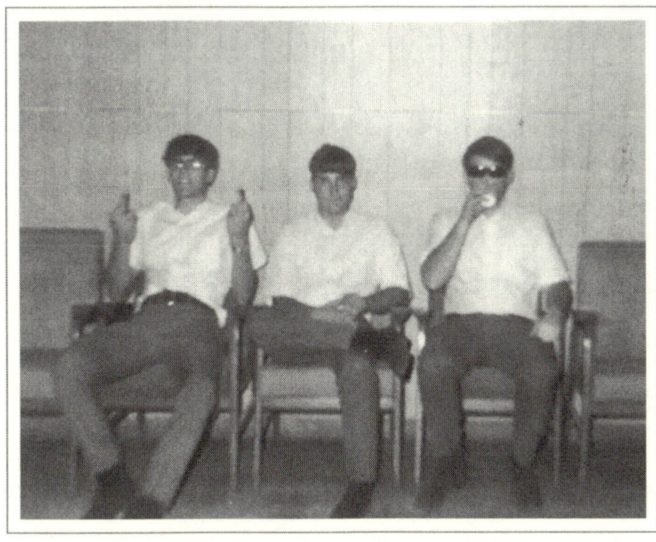

Ralph Bundy, Bill Thames, and Kip Marshall at Frank Rickards Music Center, early 1965.

Courtesy Lee Phillips

Early Consolidation practice in my parent's living room in Ormond Beach, Florida.

Courtesy Marcia Cassel Ford

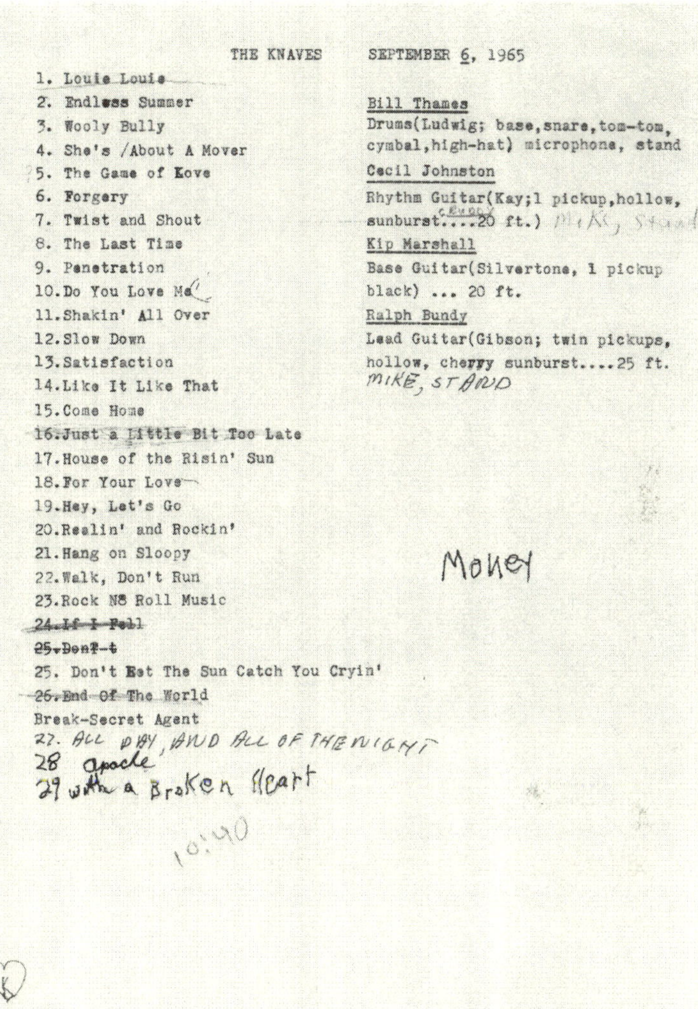

THE KNAVES SEPTEMBER 6, 1965

1. Louie Louie
2. Endless Summer
3. Wooly Bully
4. She's /About A Mover
5. The Game of Love
6. Forgery
7. Twist and Shout
8. The Last Time
9. Penetration
10. Do You Love Me
11. Shakin' All Over
12. Slow Down
13. Satisfaction
14. Like It Like That
15. Come Home
16. ~~Just a Little Bit Too Late~~
17. House of the Risin' Sun
18. For Your Love
19. Hey, Let's Go
20. Reelin' and Rockin'
21. Hang on Sloopy
22. Walk, Don't Run
23. Rock N8 Roll Music
24. ~~If I Fell~~
25. ~~Don't~~
25. Don't Let The Sun Catch You Cryin'
26. ~~End Of The World~~

Break-Secret Agent

27. ALL DAY, AND ALL OF THE NIGHT
28. Apache
29. with a Broken Heart

10:40

Bill Thames

Drums(Ludwig; base,snare,tom-tom, cymbal,high-hat) microphone, stand

Cecil Johnston

Rhythm Guitar(Kay;1 pickup,hollow, sunburst....20 ft.) Mike, Stand

Kip Marshall

Base Guitar(Silvertone, 1 pickup black) ... 20 ft.

Ralph Bundy

Lead Guitar(Gibson; twin pickups, hollow, cherry sunburst....25 ft. MIKE, STAND

Money

Early Knaves set list from September 6, 1965.

Courtesy Ralph Bundy

Kip Marshall, Bill Thames, and Carl Persis. Practice at the Thames home in Ormond Beach, Florida, early 1967.
Courtesy Marcia Cassel Ford

The Consolidation playing for members of the London Symphony Orchestra, spring 1967.
Clipping of article from The Daytona Beach-News Journal

Ralph Bundy, Bill Thames, and Jay Laing at the Pier, April 1967.
Courtesy Lee Phillips

Ralph Bundy practices in Carl Persis's garage amidst the crab traps, 1967.
Courtesy Lee Phillips

Bill Thames and Ralph Bundy at the Safari Beach Motel in Daytona Beach, Florida, spring 1967.

Courtesy Lee Phillips

Carl Persis, Tim O'Brien, Kip Marshall and (on floor) Bill Thames and Ralph Bundy at the Pier after winning the Greater Daytona Beach area Combo Clash.

Courtesy Frank Marshall

Ralph Bundy and Bill Thames at Frank Rickards Music Center with new The Consolidation drum head, fall 1967.

Courtesy Lee Phillips

Kip Marshall and Ralph Bundy at the Wedge, fall 1967.
Courtesy Marcia Cassel Ford

Ralph Bundy, Ross Yost, Carl Persis, Tim O'Brien, and Bill Thames at a wedding. This was later used as a publicity photo.

Courtesy Lee Phillips

Ralph Bundy, Bill Smith, Carl Persis, Tim O'Brien, and Bill Thames on a fishing trip out of Ponce Inlet, April 1968.

Courtesy John G. Von

Lee Hazen's "Cottage" recording studio, circa 1967.

Courtesy Lee Hazen

Lee Hazen's mobile recording studio, circa 1967.

Courtesy Lee Hazen

Ringo at The Martinique, circa 1968.

Courtesy Bill Thames

Seabreeze High School Sadie Hawkins Dance at the Americana Hotel, Daytona Beach, Florida. 1968.

Courtesy Marcia Cassel Ford

Seabreeze High School Sadie Hawkins Dance at the Americana Hotel, Daytona Beach, Florida. 1968.
Courtesy Marcia Cassel Ford

The back of my "Martinique" shirt from the summer of 1968.

Courtesy Bill Thames

Duane Allman with The Allman Brothers Band,
Peabody Auditorium, Daytona Beach, Florida,
September 16, 1970.

Courtesy Russell Atwell

Chapter 14

The Duane Allman Strat

By the time Duane Allman reached high school, he was an accomplished guitarist. He began playing the way most boys in small towns like Daytona Beach would have started. Like so many others, he began playing on an inexpensive acoustic guitar from Sears or Montgomery Ward, with a handful of thick, black, plastic picks, a scattering of extra strings, and an abundance of unscheduled time. The difference was that from the time Duane wrapped his hands around his first acoustic guitar, he proved to be as agile and imaginative a learner as any musician to ever stroke wood and strings. As Duane's ability progressed, so did his natural search for more desirable, higher-quality guitars with which to channel his aspirations. Following an extensive progression of early guitars, including three Gibsons, he finally succumbed to a Fender fetish. In a style and approach that would shadow him for much of his life, Duane landed squarely on a guitar whose looks were as unconventional as its sound. But in reality, the budding musician was all about sound. Duane's all-time favorite instrument from his formative Allman Joys/Hour Glass era, when I knew him best, was an unconventional hybrid consisting of a Fender Telecaster Esquire body (single pickup Telecaster) retrofitted with a Stratocaster neck. His hot-rod, cousin-marrying, crossbreed was accentuated by a Vox V830 distortion booster strap-on and became Duane's weapon of choice for several years. According to my memories of what I had been told, and, at one time, those of Paul Hornsby, Duane lost that guitar when it was stolen by some bottom-feeder while the Hour Glass toured the Midwest in early 1968 in support of their *Power of Love* album. In addition to my memories, Ann Sandlin agreed and told me that Johnny had lost some equipment of his own during the same episode, which supported that story.

Interestingly, though, another story surfaced years later about the whereabouts of the hot-rod Tele from Duane's brother, Gregg. According to the younger Allman, Duane traded his Tele/Strat for a Gibson J-45 acoustic that he then gave to Gregg as a birthday present. "Recognizing legitimate signs of a successful songwriter in me, Duane knew I needed a boost," claimed Gregg. Regardless of where it is today, that Telecaster with the blond Stratocaster neck still stands as one of Duane's most cherished guitars, though certainly not his most famous.

About the same time that Duane's Tele/Strat hybrid disappeared from his history, the guitar player in my band, Ralph Bundy, acquired a blond-neck Stratocaster that had been resurrected from an early restoration project out of "junk" pawnshop parts into an amazingly stage-worthy "vintage" instrument. The way I recall the story, Ralph's guitar had been purchased a few years earlier in a myriad of pieces at one of the Second Avenue pawnshops in downtown Daytona Beach by our original rhythm guitar player, Cecil Johnston, and his older brother, David. Amazingly, all of the parts for the guitar were together in a tangled mess, including the pickups, wiring, control knobs, tuners, pick guard, and other hardware. Surprisingly, nothing was missing from its cardboard box. Still, the once-proud guitar was a huge rat's nest of possibility. A war-torn tweed case that lacked the locking device was included in the deal, complete with an old leather belt looped through the handle that the previous owner had used to hold the guitar case closed.

The prevailing thought was that the guitar had been disassembled as a restoration project and abandoned for lack of time, money, and expertise...or likely all three. The whole ball of wax had been crammed into a cardboard box that was discovered cowering in a back corner of the old OK Pawnshop. The box containing the guitar parts had been folded shut with only the disconnected neck poking out of one side of the box between the flaps of cardboard, instantly giving the instrument's pedigree away to the two savvy teenagers, Cecil and David. The asking price in 1965 for a puzzle box crammed with seemingly random guitar parts was $150.

Upon opening the box and peering in, the once-stately guitar appeared to be total trash, and it wore no logos or other identifying marks. The Johnston brothers instantly recognized the sensual Fender shape and the trademark headstock as that of a Stratocaster. Doing their best to show little more than casual interest in the "trash guitar parts" in the box, David offered the clerk a check for $125 and a deal was struck. David paid the cashier while Cecil hurriedly whisked their newfound treasure out to the family station wagon, and they quickly made their getaway.

The ensuing restoration project was not going to be as easy as Cecil and David initially imagined. The Strat's once-sensuous gold body had incurred numerous dings, scratches, and gouges, showing years of road abuse, all of which required extensive patching and many, many hours of elbow grease and careful hand sanding. As it turned out, refinishing the body was the easiest part of what became a mountainous restoration project. When the chinks were patched with wood filler and smoothed, the Johnston boys had it painted by a connection at the local Fact-O-Bake paint-and-body shop for $49.95. Their friend had custom mixed the color out of leftover, arbitrary blue auto-body paints, so it didn't really match any other Stratocaster, or even any car on the road, for that matter. The color palette in 1965 apparently leaned heavily toward the light- to sky-blue color scheme. Regardless, to everyone's delight, the body turned out a sumptuous robin's-egg blue. Unfortunately, the body was the only component of the entire guitar that neared perfection, visually, from that point forward. As several weeks passed, with numerous attempts at sanding and re-lacquering the once-beautifully finished maple neck and failing to render the desired result, the restoration project began to falter. The Johnston boys grew weary of staring at the pile of pitted and corroded metal components that they could not afford to replace with new or even have re-plated locally. The decision was made to assemble their puzzle to determine what they really had and to see if the reassembled relic would actually even play.

So, with only the body looking like a fresh, new start, and little more, the junkyard Stratocaster's second restoration project was officially put on the back burner as the Johnston boys' enthusiasm waned along with their meager finances. Happily, though, while the guitar was a bit rough on the eyes, the bits-and-pieces, corroded, and tarnished instrument had a sound that was incredible...actually, better than incredible: it was unworldly and beyond all expectations (granted, our expectations were pretty low at fifteen and sixteen). Looking back, it was, to say the least, very exciting to us and to some others in town.

Only Cecil's brother David had a cursory knowledge of electrical wiring, though he was certainly no guitar tech. So, the incredible sound that we were hearing was either always hidden away in that guitar or it had been intensified unintentionally by the Johnstons' or the previous owner's attempts at restoration. In addition, the removal of a considerable amount of wood from the body in the patching and smoothing process could have possibly had some influence on what turned out to be the guitar's rich, full tone. The "Junkyard Strat," as we called it, had a wonderfully punchy/gutsy tone with that unmistakable, slightly distorted, full Stratocaster bite...a sound that was perfectly suited for raw rock and roll. That rock and roll edge was exactly what our lead guitar player, Ralph Bundy, was after and why the Junkyard Strat stayed in our band family for so many years.

Cecil Johnston had played rhythm guitar in an early iteration of our band, and, as a beginner, any old cheap guitar sufficed for those honors. But the Junkyard Strat, regardless of looks, gave Cecil a leg up in the equipment drive that our band was going through at the time and put him ahead of Ralph, who was making the best of a bad situation. After visiting a few music-store clerks in town with his father, Ralph's dad insisted that he purchase a Gibson ES-125 that they saw at Streep's Music Store in Daytona Beach. At fifteen, a guy's father wields a lot of influence, especially if financial assistance is necessary. So, Ralph was locked into the 125 by circumstances beyond his control and meager finances.

Ralph was playing the Gibson 125 when the Junkyard Strat burst into our circle of friends. Ralph's guitar had the Gibson name, but other than its pedigree, it possessed little more. The hollow body had a soft, jazzy sound that was not well suited to the edgier rock and roll, soul, and blues road that our band was traveling. Still, the Gibson was a step or two above most entrance-level guitars available at that time, and Ralph made it work. Cecil used the Strat as his gig axe for about two years in our band until he was replaced by a keyboardist for a number of reasons: a keyboard offered a variety of sounds, and also Cecil's parents rarely allowed him to play anything other than weekend nights. However, early 1968, Cecil grew tired of playing the solid-body Stratocaster because his Sears Silvertone amp had died, rendering the solid body virtually useless, so he offered Ralph a straight-up trade: his Junkyard Fender for Ralph's Gibson hollow-body electric. Ralph was hesitant at first to make the trade, but after playing the Stratocaster at a few gigs, he acquiesced and the rest of us rejoiced.

The band loved the new sound that the Junkyard Strat brought to our music, and its full, rich sound did not go unnoticed by the other musicians in town. One such musician, in particular, became drawn like a magnet to Ralph's new guitar. From the first moment Ralph laid his guitar into Duane Allman's hands at one of our gigs, the master lusted after that instrument. Like a dog in heat, Duane could smell the funk of the Junkyard Strat and hear the nasty long before he entered a club where our band was playing.

There was always an underlying current that filled the air every time Duane touched that guitar. And every conversation began with, "Young man, I want this guitar. So, what's it going to take to put her into my hands?"

No matter how Duane tried to bargain with him, Ralph's answer was always the same, "No, man, I'm sorry, it's just not for sale."

In typical Duane fashion, he took Ralph's unrelenting unwillingness to further discuss parting with his Junkyard Strat as a "maybe," and he always left their encounters upbeat and untroubled by Ralph's rebuttals. Consequently, a tradition of gentlemanly opening exchanges began between Ralph and Duane when next they met: the slapping of hands and the reciprocity and veritable quid pro quo of guitar knowledge, especially where strings were concerned. Duane was extremely helpful and forthcoming when younger players had questions about his technique or tone, and Ralph always had questions. But the serious conversation invariably returned to Duane acquiring Ralph's Junkyard Strat. "Young man, that's a mighty fine instrument you have there," was Duane's segue in just about every conversation with Ralph, and no matter how many music lessons Duane shared with Ralph, the answer never reversed course.

The sound produced by that guitar, even in the hands of a relative neophyte like our band leader, Ralph, much less in the hands of a master like Duane Allman, rang deep, gutsy, and pure, but I believe that Duane's attraction to the guitar ran much deeper than just the Stratocaster's tone. I really believe that the guitar's Stratocaster neck, worn smooth and slightly sweat-stained on Ralph's prize, reminded Duane of the neck on his old hot-rod Telecaster, the one that he wore nightly during those really rough formative years playing roadhouse gigs from Miami to St. Louis. Duane was literally married to that guitar for years, and they spent long nights together before he married his first wife, Patricia.

None of the other Stratocasters that Duane ever used, even during all of his session work at Muscle Shoals, had that smooth, comfortable, clean-sounding, blond neck. I really believe that the time-worn neck, combined with the guitar's exceptional sound, drew Duane back to Ralph's Strat night after night.

Our band, the Soul Patrol, as we became known at that time, opened for or jammed with the Hour Glass a dozen or so times during the early spring through the summer of 1968. After our high school graduation that spring, the Soul Patrol worked the entire summer as the house band at the Martinique, which meant 9 P.M. to 1:45 A.M. six or seven nights a week until the following August, when we disbanded for college. During that time, Duane developed a deeper and deeper craving to own the Stratocaster each time he and Ralph met. Many times, Duane and Gregg, but most often just Duane, came to town without the Hour

Glass band, which was in music-contract limbo during that time. The Hour Glass's two albums for Liberty Records had been disappointing money losers for their record company, so Duane often visited his mother alone while Gregg stayed in California trying to work his way out of debt as a studio musician. Back in Daytona, Duane would often come into the Martinique and ask to sit in—sometimes just to get his hands on Ralph's guitar. Gregg, who was occasionally in town, would periodically join Duane on the stage, but generally speaking, Gregg liked to take his seat next to the waitress station at the bar and nurse scotch-and-milk highballs as long as their tab was open. Duane begged, borrowed, and even suggested random trades for Ralph's guitar at times. Being courted by Duane Allman was a precarious situation for Ralph, but his answer was, invariably, "Sorry, man, no deal." We had all put too much time and elbow grease into Ralph's Stratocaster to let her go...even to Duane.

Duane Allman was the most extraordinary guitarist I have ever heard, or will likely ever hear, play. Never mind the fact that he could play just about anything, with anyone; Duane was first and foremost an incredible listener. His solos could be searing and frightful or unpretentiously mellow and melodically straightforward, but whenever someone else was playing, or a singer was doing their thing, Duane would search for all the right places to tuck a note in here or there to make the music more complete...more right. Duane's technique did not make the music more crowded or thick, like so many other musicians. He strived to add another layer that had never been imagined before. In our time playing with Duane and the Hour Glass, we learned so many lessons, but our biggest takeaway was how to "complete" a song without crowding it. Without listening closely, it was so easy to miss what Duane was doing much of the time, because when he was playing soft rhythm fills, he blended perfectly into the mood and timbre of the music. Becoming part of the forest and not the tallest tree is a nuance that is still lost on so many players. For our group of seventeen- and eighteen-year-olds, Duane's lessons were mile markers that were laid gently at our feet.

One late night in early summer, when Duane shuffled into the Martinique with a bit of an illegal smile, and our band was marginally overserved, he asked to sit in. Ralph always enjoyed taking a seat late in the evening to watch his hero hold court, so the Junkyard Strat was handed over to Duane between songs. In short order, Duane caught our attention by coaxing previously unheard notes from the instrument. Quickly, he became totally consumed in dragging us along on one of his searing "magic carpet ride" solos. After better than fifty-five years, I don't remember exactly what song we were playing, probably "Hey Joe" or just a Freddy King-style funky blues jam, but Duane was leading us around his schoolyard and we were following his lead. One thing I loved about playing with Duane was that he gave everyone a shot. I wasn't the most technical drummer in town, but I could lay down that fatback, funky groove, and Duane often asked me to kick off a jam with some funk. I liked being able to pick the tempo for once, and I am sure Duane sensed that.

Marginally compromised by whatever substance had Duane's attention other than the Strat, he had a momentary lapse and disremembered that he had tucked a lit cigarette under the strings near the first tuning key just before we started playing whatever composition it was that we were flying through. By the time Duane turned the music back over to our keyboard player for a solo and rejoined the rest of us mortals onstage, his long-forgotten cigarette had burned completely out, right where he had left it. To his horror, Duane had burned a nasty charcoal-black scar, following the cigarette's shape and contour, across the contrasting light-blond maple headstock on Ralph's guitar. Duane was instantly pained by the damage that he had done to the guitar that he and Ralph cherished. He apologized over and over while the rest of us tried to maintain decorum. Duane sincerely felt horrible and stumbled for words, promising to have the guitar neck and headstock repaired or refinished...whatever it would take to make it right for Ralph.

In reality, what Duane had done was embrocate Ralph's guitar, raising its status to that of a religious relic, at least in our eyes. Even at seventeen or eighteen years old, like every other musician in town, we all knew Duane Allman was destined to become one of the great masters of the guitar, and Ralph considered the burn mark as Duane's unique personal autograph. The entire band took turns joining Ralph in reassuring Duane that the last thing any of us would want would be for the burn mark to be removed or touched up in any way, shape, or form. From that night on, Ralph's beat-up, old Junkyard Stratocaster took on a new identity as the "Duane Allman Strat." Duane played the guitar several more times that summer, though we saw him less and less often as July turned into August. Still, he was always embarrassed about sanctifying the Stratocaster. Regardless, even after the "mishap," the undercurrent of Duane's thirst for that guitar remained undiminished.

Around the middle of July, the Soul Patrol began kicking around ideas for an advertising campaign announcing that soon we would be playing our last week together as a band. We all knew that after high school graduation those of us who were going away to college, which included Ralph and me, would leave impossible holes to fill in the Soul Patrol. With a little more than three weeks left to play as a band, we began to prepare to put on our last few shows, say good-bye to our girlfriends, and to say adieu to hard-and-fast friends who had grown together as an unbreakable unit for nearly five years. Word quickly spread, as word has a habit of doing in small towns, and pretty soon people around the Daytona Beach club circuit were talking about us leaving town. The reality of our band going our separate ways began to weigh heavily on some of us, but we did our best to soldier on; after all, the show must go on, and we all held the future in the palm of our hands.

We had so much on our collective minds that we didn't notice the group of slightly older guys who entered the Martinique through the musicians' door as we were tuning up for our show that night. As they approached the stage, we recognized the leader of the group as Duane Allman, followed by Gregg, who was toting a slender Gibson guitar case. Pete Carr and Johnny Sandlin brought up the rear, but Paul Hornsby was otherwise occupied that night and missed all the fun. It seemed odd for Duane and Gregg to show up at the Martinique before eleven or twelve o'clock, but as always, it was good to see them, and I think we were all hoping the entire Hour Glass, sans one, would ask to sit in for a set or two. That summer we were playing six nights a week at the Martinique and hosting a Sunday-afternoon jam session at the Blind Pig across town, so we were all pretty worn down as the end of the summer neared.

Duane walked over to Ralph's side of the stage and stopped while Gregg followed, laying a guitar case in plain view on the table next to the stairs to the stage. Duane didn't say a word, he just motioned Ralph over and signaled his brother to open the guitar case. As Gregg slowly teased the guitar case open, Duane's smile melted into a poker face, and his last-ditch offer poured out of that guitar case slowly, like fine Tennessee bourbon. "Look here, young man! I'm going to cut to the chase," Duane started. "No more pussyfooting around, this is it! Listen now...I'm offering you a straight-up trade! Your Strat for this beauty."

By now, the whole band was crowding Ralph in the corner of the stage where we could all see the case and hear every word. As the lid of the case slowly opened and the stage lights shown in, we stared in amazement at an incredibly beautiful guitar that shined and glistened in the spotlights. Things got real in a hurry, and the whole surreal vibe made the rest of us uneasy to be involved in the ensuing transaction. With mouths agape and our eyes bulging, it was simply impossible for our faces to contain our adolescent discomfort. Duane spoke again, suspecting that he had put a little chink in Ralph's armor. "Here, try this on, see how you like it. Plug her in and give her a shot!"

Duane picked up the glistening black Les Paul by its neck and carefully lifted it out of the case and handed it up to Ralph on the stage, who had quickly leaned his Strat against his twin-reverb and connected his strap to the Gibson as we watched in amazement. Then Ralph did the unimaginable, he actually acquiesced and plugged Duane's last and final offer into his amp. The Les Paul was jet black with an ebony fretboard, gold hardware, triple pickups, and extensive mother-of-pearl inlays on the neck and headstock. From where I stood, the guitar looked absolutely brand new. Undeniably, Duane had been in town and heard our ads on the radio and decided to make one last-ditch run at Ralph to secure the "Duane Strat" for himself, and this was Duane's endeavor to lay it all on the table.

If Duane had walked into the Martinique just a few minutes earlier, before Ralph had strapped on his Stratocaster for the night, the deal would have probably been done in that first instant, because it was obviously love at first sight for Ralph. His eyes gleamed as he turned the guitar up between practice runs to look at the neck and body, inspecting it closely for the tiniest blemish. However, the glitch for Ralph was that he had played the Strat for most of that year, and he was intently tuned in to the weight, balance, and ergonomic nature of the Strat and how the body comfortably conformed to his torso. As nice as the Les Paul looked and sounded through Ralph's Twin Reverb, I could tell that he just couldn't seem to get comfortable wearing the Les Paul. Ralph would play for a bit and then tug at the strap, trying to find a balancing point that was simply not there. We had four long hours ahead of us that night onstage, and I just don't think he could envision himself playing all that time with the Gibson hanging around his neck like a fencepost. There were other considerations as well that we started to note when we slowly began to regain our composure and huddled around Ralph to talk. Ralph carefully handed the Les Paul back down to Duane on the floor and asked for a minute to discuss the trade with the rest of us. "Sure," Duane replied, as he polished the guitar and nestled it back into its case, moving it just so, ensuring it would be in Ralph's full view from where he stood on the stage.

We clustered around Ralph in the corner of the stage considering the trade for a few long minutes without a word. Ralph took a long last look at the Les Paul, glistening in the stage lights, and finally I tried to make a joke. "She looks like she'd hurt you if you snuggled up to her all night. Your Strat looks like someone you could take to a cheap motel for a long weekend." Nobody seemed to laugh, and as we stayed huddled together, amazingly, the Gibson's bulk and comfort was not as significant an issue as I perceived in the ensuing conversation. It became all about the money, or lack thereof, and for that part of the discussion, we took our voices over to the far side of the stage, behind Tim's keyboard, where we could talk in relative privacy.

"Are you shitting me," Carl started, trying to keep his voice down so as to not increase the already-rising aggravation factor. "If he wants to trade you a new Les Paul for your Strat, your guitar must be worth a whole hell of a lot more than we think!"

Tim added, "You'd be crazy, it's got to be worth a fortune!"

Even Scott Stanley, our newest member and a hot bass player from Jacksonville, who had only signed on for our last summer together, chimed in, arguing, "I don't know a thing about Les Pauls, but that Strat has got to be worth at least the same for a straight-up trade! I don't think I'd do it."

Our vocalist, Carl, didn't really care to add much more one way or another about the two guitars, but he had noticed Ringo walk down the bar toward the stage to see why we weren't playing, and Bill Cook cracked the office door and gave Carl a "What's up?" shrug of his hands. Carl took the hint, picked up his tambourine to appear busy, and used it to motion toward the Strat, signifying that his vote was for keeping it. "Let's get going," Carl admonished us, motioning with his tambourine over toward an agitated Bill Cook and slightly confused Ringo.

It really didn't take any more convincing, so when Ralph walked down the steps toward Duane without his Strat in hand, we were all relieved and knew what he had decided. Ralph hemmed and hawed for a moment, trying to come up with every excuse in the book not to trade Duane for his guitar, but in the end it was a matter of perceived value. If Duane had brought in a newer, cleaner Strat to the trade, Ralph might have caved in, but there was just too much difference between what we thought the vintage Strat was worth and what Duane was willing to trade for it. We all just wanted Ralph to walk away and not leave any perceived money on the table.

Duane knew...He looked down for a moment at the wooden dance floor that he was standing on, and then his eyes moved slowly to the concrete floor where Ralph was standing, and then he looked back up with that same grin that he bore when the Hour Glass beat us in stickball and he hustled us out of lunch at Bertie's. As Duane's eyes met Ralph's, he did his best to put Ralph at ease. "You're smarter than I took you for. I'd have never given up that guitar either, but, you know, I had to try. We're heading to St. Louis next week to do some Hour Glass gigs, and then I have some studio work lined up in Muscle Shoals, and I thought that axe might raise my value. I understand, though. I thought this would probably be my last chance to get my hands on that guitar. Don't worry, young man, I'll find something else that'll work." With that, Duane cocked his head to the left and managed an "Oh, well" wink and then turned around to look directly at a much more disappointed Gregg.

Gregg didn't take Ralph's nix as well as his brother. What little smile he had managed quickly deflated, and he turned away, closing the guitar case and heading toward the back door of the Martinique with Duane, Johnny, and Pete trailing behind. Despite Duane's efforts to let him off easy, Ralph was shaking when he returned to the stage. His mouth was so dry that Ringo graciously brought him a Bacardi and Coke to settle him down so he could sing when we started playing. Ralph had faced down his guitar hero and told him no! We all felt better after most of the guys in the Hour Glass left the club. Sadly, that was the last time that Ralph and some of the other band members would ever speak to Duane Allman.

I have cherished pictures of Ralph playing the "Duane Allman Strat." As if it were last night, my mind and ears can still hear the Hour Glass playing "Now Is the Time," "Power of Love," and "I Still Want Your Love," among others, with Duane using Ralph's guitar. When Duane played that Strat, he tantalized and teased us all with an incredible array of throwaway licks before each song, adjusting the volume and tone lovingly. All we could do was to sit back and shake our heads. I think that he just liked to listen to the way it sounded, and he wondered what other sounds were sequestered in that magical guitar. Duane always tried to visit the Strat when he was in town. In the master's hands, it took on an almost spiritual tone. Duane's burn marks were never removed, and whenever he was onstage, all ashtrays strangely disappeared from the stage. Ralph even went so far as to lacquer over the scar, forever enshrining Duane's burn marks into the head stock of that guitar.

Duane had died in a motorcycle accident, and the Allman Brothers Band quickly gained further worldwide notoriety without him, about the time when Ralph traded the Duane Allman Strat to his brother for a semi-hollow-body Gibson ES-150, coming full circle from the beginning of Ralph's ownership of the Stratocaster. Ralph's brother, Bruce, a touring musician and bass player, needed a second guitar for his guitarist while on the road, and Ralph was in college, playing mostly in his dorm room, and he didn't have much use for the solid body anymore. The 150 was basically a thicker version of the popular ES-335 with all the same bells and whistles, but it could be played without amplification. So, again, a straight-up trade was made: Gibson for the Fender, and why not? After all, he basically traded it to his brother, so Ralph always knew that he could get his beloved guitar back any time. It was promised that the Duane Strat would always stay "in the family." Sadly, the instrument went the way of many great-sounding guitars that wind up being used on the road. Backs were turned for a split second, and it vanished after a festival somewhere in northern New Jersey.

I remember the night that Ralph told me about the loss. He was back on break from Duke Medical School, and I was finished with college, working in Daytona managing a liquor store and lounge for Big Daddy's along with our old vocalist, Carl. Ralph introduced me to his new wife, and I was dating an old high school acquaintance whom I had recently run into, so the four of us got together after I got off work for a few drinks. Ralph and I hadn't seen each other in a few years, and I had not met his wife yet, so there was much to discuss. Along with so much more, that night at his parent's apartment he told me the story of the theft of the Duane Allman Strat, but with so much being discussed that evening, the gravity of the loss didn't really sink in at the time.

On the drive to take my date home that night, I don't think I said two words. My mind was populated by two concurrent scenes alternating in my mind like electric current. The first was a recollection from March 29th of 1968. Duane Allman was standing on the stage at the Martinique playing Ralph's Junkyard Strat just a month or so before he burned/autographed the headstock, and I was engrossed by the spirals of guitar wire that crowned each tuner. Earlier that day, at sound check, Duane asked if he could use Ralph's guitar and in return, he insisted on supplying new strings. As he finished changing each string, in signature Duane Allman style, instead of chipping the remainder of the wire off, he twisted the individual strings into tight coils. That was a unique touch of Duane's, and I always found myself hypnotized by watching them bounce ever so delicately as he played, as I was that night. That was just one night of many when I tape-recorded the Hour Glass when my band opened for them. And it was just two days after my eighteenth birthday. Duane was so involved with the music that night, especially the blues, that I knew that was exactly where he was headed in life and that nothing would stand in his way. I think we all felt those same chills when Duane played. Most of the audience was simply there, captivated by the music of the moment, and that was fine too. But for myself, that night held a myriad of fine memories.

While pondering that night in March, a parallel hypothesis began to take my mind away from Duane and the recordings I made of him then. My mind began to develop the image of something that happened a few years after that night, though I wasn't there to witness. It was the night the Duane Allman Strat disappeared from Bruce's possession. My mind needed to compose its own explanation of the way the night transpired when the Duane Strat was lost. I imagined a small music festival in northern Jersey, maybe Morristown, and a crowded stage full of equipment from several bands sprawled everywhere. I could picture the usual scene: amps, microphones, cords, PA speakers, various guitars, keyboards, cases, and the belt-fastened case holding the Duane Allman Strat. I imagined the guitar safely in its case, leaning up against the back of a Marshall stack. When the show was over and the stage cleared and packed into trucks, nobody noticed that the tattered, tweed guitar case with the brown belt holding its contents intact was not in the right truck. The bands all went their separate ways that night, and by the time Bruce and the others realized the guitar was missing, they were in central New York state. I'm sure Bruce was horrified when he learned that the cherished guitar was missing, but there was little to do but wait to see if anyone from the other bands contacted them, if they even knew how. I also imagined the offending band's roadie opening the errant guitar case somewhere in Pennsylvania and staring in amazement at his newly found prize. He probably thought to himself, "It's not very pretty, but what the heck, it is a Strat, and an old one at that." He probably showed the foundling to his guitar player and made a deal for a few dollars, and a case of beer...as the new owner looked at the burn mark on the headstock, trying to fathom it.

Chapter 15

Delta 88 and the Power Off

After Gregg graduated high school in 1965 and the brothers began traveling the Chitlin' Circuit in earnest, the white-sand beaches of Daytona would draw the boys back home regularly to visit their mother, Geraldine, or to just stay in touch with friends. Both boys knew that the road was where they needed to be if they were going to follow the sound in their heads to the top, but the magical beach town where they got their start gently tugged at their shirttails. Once they got sand in their shoes, it was nearly impossible to shake it all out.

As time slipped by, however, it became harder and harder for Duane and Gregg to find the time to get back home. The road caused the gap between their goals and their home in Florida to severely broaden. As they built a fan base and became better known, the trips home to play in front of a welcoming hometown crowd became increasingly important. The releases of the first and second Hour Glass albums made getting home to claim bragging rights in Daytona Beach all the more important to the two brothers. In the fall of 1967 and the winter of '68, their record company, Liberty Records, had the Hour Glass spending most of their time on the West Coast in California or taking dates in the Upper Midwest. Occasionally, though, they booked nights in the Southeast, closer to home and the beach town they loved.

Sometimes Duane and Gregg would blow into town alone with time to spare. Other times, they brought the rest of the band to the beach—Johnny Sandlin, Paul Hornsby, and Pete Carr. When the Hour Glass came home to Daytona Beach to play, there was always a show booked at the Martinique nightclub on Main Street. The Martinique was their second home in Daytona. One such show coincided with the release of the *Power of Love* album. The show took place, as discussed before, on Friday, March 29th. That show also served to celebrate the Daytona Beach album-release party for *Power of Love*.

Posters reproducing the album cover hung like hundreds of race-week banner flags from the ancient pecky cypress rafters in the Martinique. Handbills were posted on telephone poles all around the Main Street area by street kids who were promised free admission, and the two

Daytona Beach rock radio stations, WROD and WMFJ, ran promos about the Hour Glass show almost constantly during the week before. It was a triumphant homecoming for Gregg and Duane, and the town's musical community intended to support their hometown boys.

Daytona Beach had a few musical sons who had brushes with stardom and marginal recording successes, like the Stereos (Jim Matherly, guitar), Whalefeathers (Lenny LeBlanc, guitar and vocals), and the Nightcrawlers (Chuck Conlin, vocals, and Sylvan Wells, guitar, and Tommy Ruger, drums), but no other local musicians had done what the Hour Glass had managed to do: Duane and Gregg's band had recorded and released two albums for a major record label. That was a big deal for Daytona Beach, and a serious bragging point for the rest of the city's musicians. By the spring of 1968, the original Nightcrawlers had long scattered to colleges and joined other bands all over the South. "Little Black Egg" had charted higher than any single that the Allmans would release until they were part of The Allman Brothers Band. Still, the Hour Glass recordings were just a vague hint of things to come. By 1968, Duane and Gregg had outdistanced all the other "local" bands hands down in the turf war.

Two weeks after the March 29th *Power of Love* album-release party at the Martinique, and just a week after the April 4th slaying of Martin Luther King Jr., the Hour Glass performed another show in Daytona Beach on April 12th. Bill Cook promoted the show, but it didn't take place at his club, the Martinique; instead, it was performed several blocks away at the Neptune Room. The Neptune Room, or the Neptune A-Go-Go, as it was called in 1968, was an intimate nightspot situated on the north end of the massive Daytona Plaza Hotel, directly on the beach. The reason the second date was played at the Neptune A-Go-Go was because the Martinique had lost its liquor license, which had, by 1968, become almost a monthly occurrence. When the Hour Glass played that second date, they were even tighter, sharper, and much more bluesy, because it was closer to the April 22nd Fame Studio recording date in Muscle Shoals, Alabama, where the Hour Glass had been woodshedding, hell-bent on making those recordings the best representation of the band's ability and direction. Their intention was to record in Muscle Shoals and return to Liberty Records with something more representative of their live shows.

Throughout this time, Duane and his brother would often whip into town, just the two of them, to see their mom or to take care of other business. Regardless, Duane would invariably stop in at the Martinique during the evening to offer his talent to the house band for a set or two. The sight of Duane walking into the club would strike fear into all but the guitar player in the band onstage. The guitar player knew that all he would have to do was hand off his guitar to Duane and pray that his strings and amplifier would make it through the night. The rest of the lucky band could only hang on and pray. So it was, a regular schedule at the Martinique was a double-edged sword of sorts. It was not easy in the beginning for me to get comfortable playing with Duane, though we had known each other for years.

On nights that he stopped by to play when our band was onstage, Duane would breeze through the front door and chitchat with Ringo and Bill Cook, but eventually he'd begin to snake his way over to the stage through the crowd, greeting old friends along the way. When he made it through the audience, Duane would just stand down in front of the Soul Patrol, at our guitar player's side of the stage, watching him play, until our guitar player would cave in and offer up his reconditioned Strat.

For me, watching Duane make his way to the stage was like being forced into a line that was loading for a newly improved and redesigned breakneck, supercharged roller coaster. The watching and waiting frightened the hell out of me, but when I had that ticket in hand, and Duane was ready to play, I knew I was in for the ride of my life. My stomach would churn, and no matter how hot it was onstage, the sweat running down my back would turn icy cold at the sight of Duane heading our way. I recall hoping that the six-string roller coaster operator on his way through the crowd would stop short of the stage and lose interest in playing, but that almost never happened. The other members of my band all felt similarly because we never knew what Duane was going to pull out of his musical hat. What he offered once he was onstage and ready was almost never anything that we had ever played before. Duane was a master of curveballs and sliders. He spent his life digging through stacks of dusty record albums, searching for remotely popular compositions that he could refresh with an interesting twist.

Duane introduced me to Jimi Hendrix on one of those fanciful nights...and the only thing I could do was hang on by the seat of my pants, trying to enjoy the ride. You can just imagine what it was like to hear those classic Hendrix tunes for the first time, not from a stereo system but coming out of Duane's guitar, only I was seated next to him, expected to play them...off the cuff. He had a way of drawing out the best in other musicians that he played with. There was a monstrous soul in that man's heart, and it always gave him pleasure to watch the rest of us learn what he had to teach. There is no doubt that his influence on my band was so profound that by the end of that summer we actually had contacted and were considering an audition for the Johnny Carson Show. If someone had just bottled up Duane's essence and spread it evenly over the world, it would be a far better place to live in today.

Sometime during the late winter of '68, before the *Power of Love* album was recorded and subsequently released in late March, Duane and Gregg paid one such impromptu visit to the Martinique. They tripped in late one night at very nearly closing time. The mostly local crowd was on the small side, as was normal for that time of year and that time of night, and, of course, the Allmans' appearance had not been advertised—they just showed up, as they often did. Gregg seemed road-weary that night and took his normal seat near the end of the bar by the waitress station, nursing a scotch and milk, trying to shake off hours on the road. Duane, on the other hand, was his normal charge-ahead, explosive bottle rocket self, looking for something or someone to light his fuse.

He gradually worked his way up to the left side of the stage, where the friends of my band and our girlfriends sat. He chatted a little while, keeping one eye on Ralph and his robin's-egg blue Strat. Once Duane had caught Ralph's attention, he gestured "Hello," and with a single finger motion then pointed to himself as if to ask, "Is it my turn yet?" Duane cocked his head and raised his brows, dropping his head slightly, in a questioning sense. Ralph had little recourse but to relinquish his guitar, but as for the rest of us—we were about to be schooled in how to play fox and hounds. And just like that, the chase was on.

As Duane shaded his eyes from the stage lights and looked out into the sparse audience, our singer, Carl, excused himself quickly down the opposite set of stairs on the north side of the stage, smirking and waving his tambourine to the rest of us as he left. Then Duane turned around and explained to the audience, as he saw it, in his best deep-bass, Southern-baritone, fatherly voice, "All right, boys, let's whip this crowd into shape!" Duane tested the volume of the Strat and Fender Twin Reverb with a few chanks and throwaway licks and then began snapping his fingers to a hellish tempo. He bellowed instructions while he did this: "Shuffle in G, okay?" When he was sure everyone was in line with him, he continued snapping and began counting the song off, "Uh-one, Uh-two, Uh-you-know-what-to-do!" With those last ten words, we all left the station, drawn into Duane's own musical tornado for the duration of the night. One by one, we all climbed on board with eyes wide with excitement and slightly tinged with terror.

Hendrix, Butterfield, Cream, the Blues Magoos, Otis Redding—one after another, Duane would pull out this and that from each album he had tucked away somewhere in the back of his mind. A little stage direction here and a subtle hand motion there and a..."You boys know such and such, in whatever key, don't you?" The reality was that no matter how scared we were, we also felt like we were pretty hot shit and must have sounded pretty damn good with Duane out in front leading the charge. I'm sure Duane raised the rest of us a step or two above our normal level of playing. It is nearly impossible to quantify how beneficial those nights were for a group of seventeen- and eighteen-year-old musicians with stars in their eyes.

Duane would get us cooking and then, when he was sure that we were comfortably in the groove, he would step up to the front of the stage and curl the toes of his shoes over its front edge. What came next was pure unadulterated Duane Allman throwing his entire being over to the music, as if he were alone in the universe. When Duane decided it was time to step out front, he forced his whole body and soul out through his fingers. He contorted from shoes to shades and every visible muscle tingled with excitement. His face, though, underwent the most severe transformation of all. When he reached for those notes that didn't live on anyone else's fretboard, Duane's neck would stretch and bend forward and his head would tilt still further forward and twist about 45 degrees, angling down toward the neck of his guitar. Next, his forehead would furrow deeply, his eyes would nearly close, and his mouth would open slightly, with his tongue writhing inside his mouth. As the notes began to flow, his lips parted and he mouthed the sounds of those notes as they began flowing from his amplifier. Then his eyes opened slightly, allowing light to shine into his world. All of these gyrations gave the impression that Duane was in some exotic, nameless pain that appeared remotely sexual in nature. On close scrutiny, though, his facial contortions coincided precisely with the notes that he was stretching out to produce. It appeared as if the notes he played were being wrenched from somewhere deep within his psyche and quickly distilled into the area between his chin and hairline, magically transforming into a kind of rhythmic facial ballet. I distinctly recall wishing that I had a recording of that night, which very well might have been the catalyst for the subsequent recordings I made of the Hour Glass and my band.

Closing time at the Martinique was 2 A.M. sharp. Carl normally gave last call at 1:30 A.M. and ended our last set at 1:45 so the waitresses and bartenders could usher the drunks out the door by two. On this particular night, Duane was on his own timetable, and he blew right past what should have been last call with "Get Out of My Life, Woman" by the Paul Butterfield Blues Band. Then, without stopping or missing a lick, he held a hellish sustained note for what seemed like two minutes, bending the note ever so slightly, marking the upcoming tempo, and then flowing into a slow, bluesy version of "Hey Joe" at around 1:55 A.M. We had no recourse but to fall into place. The music was beginning to become something very different from what we were used to performing, and it was refreshing to stretch out and play something other than dance music. With the excited crowd gathered around the front of the stage and securely in Duane's hands, the music was just beginning to cook, and he had no intention of stopping short of genius. So, on we played...two o'clock, two-fifteen, two-twenty-five...we just followed Duane's lead and tried not to look at our Timex's.

It didn't really matter to Duane, or to my band, and certainly not to the audience, when Cook turned on the houselights and then shrieked from the side of the stage, "You need to shut it down, goddamn it, Duane! The cops are at the front door!" Duane didn't hear Cook; he only heard the music in his head that he was chasing, and so he just kept on playing and pulled us along with him on his journey. I was only seventeen and more than a little nervous at the sight of Daytona's best constabulary filing in the front door with flashlights flashing in the shadows, but still Duane played, oblivious of the impending peril, and he even took the current number up a notch or two.

My younger brother, who was only fourteen at the time, had snuck into the Martinique that night and he remembers well when the police turned the power off to the building in a foiled effort to get Duane to stop playing, and so do I.

All at once, everything went black and we all stopped playing—all of us except for Duane, that is. In the dark silence of the cavernous Martinique, lit by only the two red "Exit" signs, a few flashlight beams, and a very few battery-powered floodlights, the people who had pressed up against the front of the stage holding cigarette lighters were treated to some of the finest guitar playing of that time. Looking back, it was truly amazing how loudly Duane played that Strat—without any amplification. He just wouldn't stop, and for eight or ten measures, I clicked my drumsticks together helping him keep time while a few in the audience did the same by clapping quietly as Duane wound up his solo at the end of "Hey Joe." I think it was Ralph who finally pried the guitar from Duane's hands, allowing him to slowly return to the stage in the Martinique that night from wherever it was that he had gone.

We watched from the stage as policemen with flashlights ushered the last of the customers out of the Martinique at nearly 3 A.M. One of Daytona's finest (and I mean that with the deepest, most sincere respect, RIP), Sam Etheredge, issued Cook what was probably his umpteenth "final warning." Soon, the power to the club was restored from the main breaker box outside, and the houselights illuminated the inside of the smoky club. It wasn't a pretty sight in the least...

It looked as if a tornado had torn through the club and had moved everything out from in front of the stage so that the audience could either sit or dance directly in front of the band. Tables and chairs were turned every which way, and paper cups and cigarette butts had been strewn everywhere. It took a united effort by everyone to return things to normal.

While the rest of us straightened up the mess, Duane and Gregg slipped out through a side door next to Cook's office, only to find their gray Delta 88 languishing with a dead battery. The battery was so dead and the night was so cold that even my jumper cables were useless. I volunteered to call AAA and use my parents' membership to get a tow truck to come out to see if they could get the car started. The operator at AAA asked that we go back outside in the winter cold, open the hood, and wait by the car until the truck arrived...which would be sometime in the next hour.

It was a cold January, especially for Daytona Beach, so pretty soon Gregg, blowing warmth on his hands, slipped back inside where there was a warm barstool, friendly barmaids, and plenty of scotch and milk. So, I waited by the car, shivering, with Duane. It wasn't long before Duane sadly disappeared into the club along with everyone else, only to emerge a few minutes later with two stiff bourbons and an illegal smile. We leaned back on that cold boat of a car and sipped bourbon, discussing music, and Duane chased away the cold with insights and personal experiences. By our second drink, Duane began explaining chapter and verse what it took to "make it" in music or in the pursuit of any other worthy livelihood.

It didn't take me long to realize that to be a musician of the caliber of Duane Allman, it took more than the willingness to stand out in the cold and wait for a tow truck to arrive, but that was part of it: dues were dues. To really persevere, it would take at least the same thousands of hours of practice and playing that Duane had put in over the years. As the experts say, it takes ten thousand hours of hard work to successfully hone your craft, regardless of what it is. Between Duane and the Bourbon de Luxe, the lecture was becoming pretty persuasive, so I found myself willing to give it a shot. I had been listening to Duane play for scarcely more than four years, and it was mind-boggling how far he had progressed in such a short period of time. From listening to the Escorts playing surf music to what I had been a part of that very night—Duane's musical journey had been truly remarkable, and, of course, the best was yet to come. Consequently, the conversation that night eventually turned to how he had become so damn good so fast.

That night, Duane gave me a glimpse of what his life had been like in California, where he had spent months in near isolation honing his craft and determining which way his personal compass was pointing. "If you want to make it, really make it, and not just be another lounge act, here's what ya gotta do each and every day—I shit you not, this is serious shit, man!" With that, Duane started a lecture on that frosty night that warmed my soul, and I hung on his every word.

"You've got to wake up, brush your teeth, and practice, then have yourself some coffee, and practice some more—have lunch, and practice some more, and have dinner, and practice some more. Ya get my meaning?" Duane continued his sermon: "Maybe after dinner, you want to go out for awhile and listen to some cats play something different, but when you get home, you practice what you heard that night that impressed you while it's still fresh, and you go to bed thinking about it, and wake up and do it all over again the next day. You have to treat it like a job, but it's not a job, it's so damn much more than just a job. Work at it for at least eight hours a day or it's just another f***ing hobby, and you might as well be building model airplanes with your thumb up your ass. But the cool thing is...while you are doing all of this, you just naturally start going down the right roads. If you are going to make music your life, you'll make certain important decisions, you see...along the line. And if you make those decisions in a logical manner, the top is the only place you can wind up."

I always remembered what it was that Duane said, but frankly, at seventeen I didn't fully comprehend his meaning at the time. Only maturity would eventually allow me to better focus on the conversation that we had and the depth of its meaning. Eventually, like some of Duane's other life lessons that were laid at my feet as a teenager, I took my time implementing his suggestions.

I clearly remember looking at Duane and thinking that I'd do anything to be just half the musician that he was...Anything, that is, except to practice every waking hour or to leave my cushy home and my solid future. I knew that realistically I was probably not going to make music my life, but what he had told me that night tucked nicely next to some other "fatherly" advice he had given me just a few short years earlier. Still, I would wind up, like so many musicians from my era, sailing through life with one foot onstage and the other in the business world, making a comfortable living but taking no chances.

When Duane brought me a third drink, the conversation lightened up considerably. A few minutes later, the AAA truck came ambling up Wild Olive, and I hailed them into the parking lot. They had a super heavy-duty battery jumper/starter, but the driver advised me that the owner had better buy a new battery the next day. Doubtlessly, they either bought a new battery or appropriated one the next morning, because they certainly didn't get that car started again without a new one.

That wasn't the last time Duane and Gregg stopped by to play, and we opened for the Hour Glass three or four more times in the next eight months, but it was the last time I had a chance to sit down and have a meaningful conversation with Duane until November of the following year at the Thanksgiving weekend Turkey Trip concert in Atlanta, which was my first-ever Allman Brothers show.

Those nights in 1968 were heady times playing with Duane and Gregg and the Hour Glass at the Martinique. I suppose that Duane's deep sensibility is why I eventually became so excited to get a chance to play with him. It didn't matter to Duane if I played slightly out of time here and there, just as long as I tried to do my best. Traditionally, whenever there is a train wreck onstage, everyone automatically looks back at the drummer. Even if it's entirely someone else's fault, it doesn't matter: they all look at the drummer. Duane wasn't like that. There was never an aggravated look on his face, at least in my direction. He was just content to be playing, so he made the best of whomever he played with...and he made whomever he played with better.

Duane Allman was a Venus flytrap, closing tightly over all of the emotions, memories, and hopes of that era. He captured devotees wherever he went as he moved from club to club and town to town. Duane drew fans in with his words, but his bait of choice for musicians was his love of music. What Duane created was undeniably fulfilling his legacy. Even all these years later, he is consistently voted into the top three of rock guitarists. His music gets inside of you, and your body naturally begins to move, even if you are just sitting in a chair. It can't be helped. You are either on the bus or you are off the bus. You either get Duane Allman or you don't, and if you do...it's because he touched you with his live music or his recordings somewhere deep inside your soul.

There was a time, and it seems like it was not all that long ago, when we had the potential to be truly *changed* by just one song. When the right song emerged, those changes came fast and furious. I miss that era. Radios exposed us to what was worthy in music. We knew a history-changing song when we heard it. And we had great respect for the musicians who wrote and performed this music—the Beatles; the Rolling Stones; Janis Joplin; Crosby, Stills, Nash & Young; Joni Mitchell; The Allman Brothers; and many others. But now there are no DJs and fewer radio stations pointing to the facts and providing space for social commentary; music today appears to be in complete turmoil. I love hearing great new music, but it's challenging to find substance. I wonder if I'm the only one who feels that way. Back in the 1960s, we listened intently to music that inspired us in so many different ways. I've never forgotten that music or how it made me feel and how it changed the world.

When I pull up popular music of the '60s and the '70s on my phone, I feel that warmth spread through my soul, reminding me of the power of music to expand my senses and what that means to me. As I listen, the whole of 1968 spools through my brain. Where I was...where I was going...what I was doing...who I was with...during those chilling winters and sizzling summer nights at the Martinique, under a formidable shadow shaped like Duane Allman.

Chapter 16

Closing Time 1968

On so many occasions during the waning days of my band playing at the Martinique in the glorious summer of 1968, Duane and Gregg Allman often found their way back there from whatever musical adventure they were pursuing. They were always anxious to share their new horizons with those of us who would listen. During this time, the Hour Glass was trying to extricate themselves from their recording contract with Liberty Records and Bill McEuen. At the same time, the band was trying to make what money they could while playing around St. Louis. This was also the beginning of the exciting time that Duane would play his first sessions at Muscle Shoals. Gregg's horrible solo recordings with Liberty Records in LA without the Hour Glass were released, and nobody seemed to care. When the Hour Glass disbanded for good, Duane briefly moved back to Daytona, moving in with his mother while searching local bars for the sound that he could hear but could not quite touch. Duane was the relentless English pointer on a pheasant hunt, the weathervane on the barn roof of the music industry. He searched out and found great music as if born with a divining rod in his hands, and he always gathered great friends. During this time, Gregg remained in California, for the most part, and continued to write, alone and downhearted. But he, too, drew in a tight group of the right friends.

As they regularly did when they were back in town, the two journeymen musicians would stop by to sit in with our band, which simply added more to my personal angst of leaving behind the musical unit that the Soul Patrol had assembled. The brothers Allman were often home from the road with their slowly fading Hour Glass band in July and August, bringing with them Johnny Sandlin, Paul Hornsby, and Pete Carr. As was the case as summer grew long in 1968, the brothers would be home in Daytona between visits with friends or trying new music in Alabama, Georgia, California, Missouri, and Florida. This was an awkward, confusing time for Duane and Gregg, but for my band it was an awe-inspiring time to be drawn into fresh new music at the speed of life. For those of us fortunate enough to have had time playing with Duane Allman, and in so doing being drawn up close and personal with his music, the enjoyment came from riding along in the slipstream of his energy.

However, the real bonus was later listening to his stories unfold in the raucous brainstorming sessions that invariably followed a night's work, cloistered in Bill Cook's office, relaxing.

When back in Daytona for just a few days, Duane and Gregg often crashed with their mother, Geraldine, or "Aunt Gerry," as the musicians and management around the Martinique affectionately called Mrs. Allman. Occasionally, Aunt Gerry would follow her boys around to listen to them play. She especially enjoyed the red carpet that Ringo laid out for her at the Martinique. Ringo and Aunt Gerry had a special relationship in those days, and Ringo always did her best to make her feel welcome and comfortable in her club. These visits home allowed Duane and Gregg time to hit all of their old haunts looking for new musical reach. The Martinique, where we were playing that summer as house band, was usually one of the stops on their nightly excursions around town looking for someone interesting to jam with. These grand nights working with the Allmans and the other members of the Hour Glass afforded us a unique opportunity to play and enjoy the newest music, under the tutoring of Duane and Gregg Allman. The importance of Duane's perceived attention to our band was monumental. Most nights, Duane would join our band by himself, singing and jamming for hours to favorites of his like "Hey Joe," "Fire," or "Born in Chicago" while Gregg practiced his pickup lines. Pete Carr had old friends and family in town to occupy his time, and Paul Hornsby met a cute little blond surfer girl named Linda who captured much of his time. Johnny Sandlin derived great enjoyment watching his buddy Duane improving his chops by the minute, and he seemed to prefer listening to Duane with the ears of a producer than to play. Sandlin once shared with me that "sometimes it was really painful to listen to Duane when he was just starting to play slide guitar...kind of like listening to a kid trying to play violin." Sandlin continued, "I guess I just didn't get it when he was just starting out." So, during many of those summer nights, we had Duane all to ourselves with the exception of when he was developing his slide chops in private.

Those nights sharing the stage with Duane Allman in the waning months of the summer of 1968 were magical, life-altering events. Duane was undeniably stretching toward the sound that he had dreamt about, deep in the recesses of his mind, from his early days of playing in Daytona Beach at the Pier, the Martinique, the Surf Bar, George's Place, and so many other dives that influenced the music that he was aspiring to create. Being party to that creative process was an extraordinary experience, but it was just another fragment of life in that bubble.

Watching Duane unscrew notes from his fretboard those nights was like watching a musical architect giving birth to an unprecedented lyrical master plan. Every phrase and lick was pushed to the surface by his fingers, captured by his strings and guitar pickups, forced through his cord to his amp, and then bulldozed out through his speaker cabinet like one huge, shuddering convulsion. Each and every note was, to Duane, of paramount importance. Each and every note worthy of the pain and anguish that he put himself through in order to manipulate and extricate that reclusive note from the refuge of his psyche. The agony and passion on his face was evident as he conjured notes to the surface that were, until those very moments, undreamed of and unheard before. To observe Duane play was nearly as provocative as hearing the notes themselves, and the ever-growing confederation of musicians who showed up to watch all knew from the beginning that they were listening to cutting-edge originality. Duane was every bit the innovative young master as was Beethoven or da Vinci at his age.

During those mind-blowing nights in the late summer of 1968 when Duane and Gregg would make their way from the front door of the Martinique to our stage, they were only seven months shy of putting together what would soon become the finest, most original band in the world. The two brothers had outpaced their most recent band, the Hour Glass, and while the Hour Glass was undeniably the springhead of the sound that became known as Southern rock, that configuration did not produce quite the sonic brushstrokes that Duane searched for. Still, Pete Carr, Johnny Sandlin, and Paul Hornsby were part of the amazing structure from which Duane and Gregg's music would develop and emerge. Moreover, each member of the Hour Glass continued on to become integral elements of the Southern sound that spawned Capricorn Records and forever changed the direction of the Muscle Shoals sound.

Hornsby and Sandlin became elemental cornerstones of Capricorn Records in Macon, Georgia, and Carr became an influential studio guitarist in Muscle Shoals, Alabama, bringing to bear a dominant melodic sound that would forever influence the future of the "Muscle Shoals sound." We were fortunate to have all five of these incredible musicians visiting the Martinique often during 1968. Listening to them play, getting to know each man, and working with them will always stand out as the musical highlight of my developmental years.

During those ordinary nights that summer, when Duane and the

Hour Glass were elsewhere, as close to 1:30 A.M. as possible, Carl would announce to the audience, "Alright, people...head to the bar...it's last call for alcohol. And don't forget," he would continue, "Tip your bartenders and waitresses!" If there were announcements about upcoming events or special bands, this was the last opportunity to sneak in an advertisement, but Carl was pretty good at rapping about such things between songs and at the end of each set. Besides, by the end of the night, most of Carl's words of wisdom or affirmation fell on inebriated ears. Looking back, it might have been more practical for Carl to offer fewer words of wisdom and a few more words of prayer.

Fifteen minutes later, when the notes of our final song had been fully absorbed by the pecky cypress wallboards surrounding the stage, Carl would make the first of two final announcements: "Remember, you don't have to go home, folks, but you can't stay here," or his surrogate evening closer, "Remember, if you can't be with the one you love...love the one you're with! Thank you and good night!" At that point, there would be fifteen minutes to clear the stragglers out of the club, but our night's contribution was essentially exhausted and we were officially off duty. Those who were amplified shut off their amplifiers, leaving the PA running in case reminders needed to be announced about closing time, and I would access my tattered drumsticks and drumheads in case I needed to make a run to Frank Rickards Music Center the following day for a replacement supply of Slingerland 19-LNT drumsticks and Remo drumheads. Then we would walk down off the stage talking about the night's show, good and bad. We'd say bye to a few stragglers, grab a drink at the bar, and try to wind down and relax a bit, collecting our dates if we had any.

After another fifteen minutes, at the witching hour of 2 A.M., and after the last drunk had been peeled off the floor and turned out into the shadows of Wild Olive and Main Street, Ringo would lock the Martinique's front doors. The houselights would come on, instantly illuminating the ghosts of a thousand dancers and as many broken promises as those spirits fought to disappear into the shadows of darkness surrounding the rafters and gloom high above the dance floor. At this time, within reason, the club was ours to do with as we wished while we watched the bartenders, barmaids, and other employees begin to file the previous five hours of chaos into either the walk-in cooler or the garbage. Cook, Ringo, and Wendy would retreat into the office where the evening's take would be counted and divided between different piles. Some would go to the bank the next day to pay bills, and some would go to the band or other employees if it was payday. The bulk of the cash, however, would make its way to the trunk of Cook's El Dorado Cadillac, where it would be transported the following morning to Cook's attorney's office safe...where the cash would patiently await a rainy day.

As was our habit back then, we would each change into our fifth dry shirt of the night, scoop up our girlfriends, and head to Rogers Restaurant for a quick, late-night bite to eat. Playing high-powered rock and soul music for five hours to a raucous audience of boogaloo-ers and head shakers stimulates unexplainable hunger pangs in teenage musicians, and the excitement of playing terrific music with wonderful friends only reinforces the need to continue the excitement flowing. Rogers was one of three all-night restaurants in Daytona Beach at that time, and the one where most musicians preferred to dine and commune after work. There, we'd meet with other bands from other nightclubs in town to laugh at and harass each other until our stomachs ached from cackling and we were finally full enough to throw in the towel and make our way home.

Quite often, weed-stoned or severely over-served customers from local nightclubs would stumble into what we considered our private late-night clubhouse. They would quickly become targets of innocent forms of flippant adolescent gang-style harassment. Near catatonic drunks, hovering precariously over jellified, half-consumed, hot roast beef sandwiches would be snapped back into the moment by being pelted from every direction with spit wads, shot peashooter-style through soda straws, followed instantly by earsplitting laughter. The protection of one's own food was of paramount importance. Sad was the unfortunate person who got up and left his food unattended to use the restroom before finishing his last bite.

One night in particular, our first bass player, Kip Marshall, excused himself from the table soon after we ordered. While he was absent, a thick and frosty chocolate milkshake was delivered to his place at the table while he used the bathroom. The shake had been served up in a tall, old-fashioned soda fountain glass, and the whipped cream and cherry garnish gave Kip's milkshake the appearance of being perfect in every way. When he returned, ketchup from one of those handy squeeze bottles that dotted the tables had been stealthily squeezed into the center of the thick shake, leaving nary a visible trace. The milkshake was so thick that the ketchup was hidden from view in the center of that icy chocolate column. When he returned from the washroom and took the first long pull on his straw and got a mouthful of ketchup instead of chocolate milkshake, the laughter and backslapping spilled out onto the sidewalk in front of the restaurant that night. Kip can thank Tim O'Brien for the idea, but me for implementing his plan. The thought of that night still makes me laugh out loud. In those days it was best to remove all the condiments from your table before stepping away for any reason whatsoever.

On another night, while I was engrossed in conversation with someone to my right, Tim smoothly and nimbly filled my shirt pocket to near overflowing with sugar without my noticing or feeling a thing. When I finally realized Tim's ruse, it was nearing time to leave, so I quietly paid my bill and walked out the front door to dump the sugar out of my pocket without making a mess inside the restaurant. In front of Rogers's plate glass window, which was next to the front door and checkout register, was a bus stop bench that functioned as such during the daytime but at night was often a resting place for drunks as they moved from one bar to another looking for drink specials. This night it was occupied by a slouching heap of near-comatose, whiskey-swilling humanity who could scarcely communicate. Not wanting to give Tim an ounce of satisfaction, I used the inebriated man's placid form to conceal myself from the customers inside the restaurant, turning my T-shirt pocket inside out and emptying my pocket full of sugar very innocently onto the pavement in front of the man. To my absolute amazement, my "human shield" bolted up from a near horizontal position, instantly rejuvenated as if given a whiff of smelling salts, and was vertical and ready to fight. He was trying to stand erect but the alcohol affected his equilibrium and he began to sway ever so slightly. Then, much to my surprise, he threw up his dukes, "Marquess of Queensberry" style, and challenged me to a fistfight right there on the sidewalk. By the time the rest of my band had joined me on the sidewalk, I had calmed my wobbling sparring partner down a bit. Apparently, he awoke and had become very agitated by my dumping a white substance out of my pocket in close proximity to what he perceived as his "space." As only a drunkard can do, he pointed to me with a very shaky, very dirty, crooked finger, declaring in slurred speech again and again to all who would listen, "That guy! That guy right there! He poured something at me! That guy! That guy right there in the blue T-shirt. He poured something right at me!" While everyone else was laughing hysterically, the man noticed that we all had blue T-shirts on, which just confused the issue. I delivered a quick apology on my behalf, fisticuffs were narrowly averted, and once again peace was restored to Seabreeze Boulevard. Scenes such as these repeated themselves over and over in those early-morning, alcohol-fueled breakfasts across the summer of '68 and well into the future.

Old or young, seasoned or not, no group of local musicians in Rogers Restaurant was exempt from our harassment and hounding, with the exception of those sitting at any table occupied by Duane or Gregg Allman. While the two Allmans and their bandmates generally preferred fourteen-cent hamburgers and fries from the Krystal for a late-night snack, occasionally they graced us with their presence at Rogers, where a burger, though much larger, would set you back $1.95. Still, everyone was fully aware that they were off limits from our childish high school bullshit. Duane and Gregg's stage presence emanated the very essence of cool, and their unflappable coolness surrounded them wherever they went. That aura enveloped them in a no-nonsense, no-bullshit, near-frosty temperament. Consequently, if they arrived, usually late, at Rogers, a more subdued atmosphere fell over the restaurant. Like so many other lessons that we gleaned from the brothers, those who were observant were schooled in a sense of maturity and cool, from which we all grew immeasurably.

To the uneducated eye, the roadhouse stages of our lives were a contorted web of cables, smoke, and stale alcohol. But those stages, as well as late-night restaurants, serve many functions to budding musicians: preschool, shelter, and sources of sustenance. Those places are the building blocks of all that is important to music. Sometimes, late at night, you are at the buffet...and sometimes you are the buffet. Duane and Gregg Allman taught us the difference. They also taught us that the American stage is the world's largest, most dynamic smorgasbord. Literally, the S&S Cafeteria of entertainment, just so long as you make your choices wisely.

Chapter 17

Goodnight, Louise...I'll See You in My Dreams

August 10, 1968. The end of the Soul Patrol's exhausting, spring-through-summer, six-nights-a-week sprint to the finish line at the Martinique was exacerbated by our hosting a weekly Sunday-afternoon jam session at an old Daytona roadhouse, the Blind Pig, which nestled comfortably on the wrong side of the tracks. During that arduous last year of our existence as a musical troupe, we all somehow managed to finish school, most with honors, even though we played more than two hundred nights out of the previous 365. Included were thirty-seven straight beer-fueled nights as resident house band at the Safari Beach Motel pool deck during the stand-alone epic spring break of 1968.

The Safari was the epicenter of Daytona Beach's spring break action in those days, though the Martinique was its first cousin. We filled the Safari's pool deck to overflowing each night with college kids from schools all over the South. It may have been an exhausting row to hoe, but the laughter, camaraderie, and memories left us each with a knapsack full of retrospection that would last the average teenager three lifetimes. From our perspective, the future was so bright we practically needed to wear sunglasses in bed. By the end of that summer, I was eighteen and still in full possession of that crazy edge of a teenager...full of swagger and cheap bourbon.

As significant an outcome as disbanding was to my bandmates, there was no unforeseen, conscious, decision-making process that evolved one day to dissolve the band after four years of moving together as a tight unit. We had all continued down our own individual roads with the clear understanding that after we graduated high school, those who were so inclined would transition smoothly to postsecondary education. There was never any thought or any consideration that the end of the band would unfold any other way than for us to simply walk into the future individually. Even when Carl's mother insisted on contacting the Johnny Carson organization to arrange an audition in our waning weeks. We were steadfast in our sprint to the end. School was of paramount importance to most of us, and while the fire and excitement of playing every night was undeniable, it was just that...and we were all able to look beyond the adolescent stimulation and burning enthusiasm. Regardless of our collective viewpoints regarding continuing education, we intended to go out with a bang. The decision to relinquish our hold on the Martinique's stage for our chosen paths forward was no justification for simply walking away from years of camaraderie without lighting the fuse on a final box of fireworks on our way out the door.

Sometime in mid-July that summer, each member of the band was paired up with another and ordered down to the WMFJ radio studio to record tapes advertising a huge going-away party for the Soul Patrol to run for two weeks before our last night. The radio script was kept simple and short, and went like this:

"Hi, I'm Ralph, and I'm Bill, from the Soul Patrol, and we want to invite all of our friends to come down to the Martinique for one last huge going-away party for the Soul Patrol!"

Then the Boss Jock from WMFJ took over the microphone and finished the clip, announcing:

"The Soul Patrol has rocked the Martinique like no other band, and this is the last week to dance and listen to the Soul Patrol! So come on out and say good-bye to one of Daytona's most popular bands ever!...The Soooouuullllll Paaatrrroooollllll!!!!" (With lots of reverb and echo thrown in at the tail end for extra effect.)

A single copy of those tapes still remains after fifty-five years, gifted to me as a going-away present by the DJ. Copies were included for anyone interested in this piece of old Daytona history as a gift, along with the Hour Glass and Soul Patrol recordings that I made in March of 1968. Also included with our final weeks' advertising recordings is the single version improvised by the DJ for our keyboardist because Tim was a no-show for those recording sessions at WMFJ.

At a point in my life when I was content to watch time flow by at the pace of Grand Canyon erosion, all of a sudden, out of nowhere, the end was at hand. There was nothing any of my bandmates or I could do to slow the locomotive that had latched to our destinies, and we were pulling into the last whistle stop on our high school musical journey. We were all on a collision course with dramatic futures, and those futures sparkled with a bright optimism as we clearly looked beyond our final summer together, blinding us to the pain leaving might cause.

Our going-away parties at the Martinique continued all night, every night for two weeks. We closed our tenure at the "Q" with each night's momentum building like a late-season hurricane, picking up strength and energy from the ever-increasing throng. In addition, our final week roughly coincided with the official end of summer break for most college and high school students. That week quickly evolved into a last chance to "burn it down" one more time, and as the week progressed, the parties picked up momentum as word spread about the ensuing musical carousel. Friends and classmates who had danced and romanced to our music for the previous four years showed up in droves to wish us well, thanking us for all the years of memories and fun.

The building crowds danced the Funky Broadway and the Boogaloo all throughout our final week. There was no escaping the furor and emotion. One night, near the end of our last week, I broke into an impromptu, funky, fatback, pseudo-drum solo during Wilson Pickett's "Funky Broadway." Carl switched off the PA and moved all the microphones up on the riser behind me on the back of the stage for safekeeping. He did his best to keep things under control while the rest of the band fled the stage just in the nick of time. Next, Carl alone joined me, breaking into his best James Brown-inspired hip-shaking, head-swinging, trance-like dance moves, and then he invited the audience to join the two of us onstage. The entire stage quickly filled to overflowing with crazy dancers insisting that the funk and roll that we launched last well over forty-five minutes. I did my best to accommodate Carl and his dance-crazy crowd with an extra helping of fatback kick drum, ear-splitting, rim-shot ghost rolls, and funkier than thou, sassy, high-hat backbeat. Carl drove the masses onward by hammering the two and four counts on my best crash cymbal with his rapidly disintegrating tambourine that finished the night shredded into nothing more than toothpick-sized wooden shards and scattered, flutter-floating jingle-jangles. The adrenaline emitting from the stage quickly spread, caffeinating the club and spreading the dance itch past the front door, eventually overflowing out into the street. Night after fun-filled night that last week at the Martinique, more and more people filled the club as word spread of the fun and excitement. Everyone wanted to be part of the musical orgy, and those crowds only served to feed our adrenalin and emotion as we played. Our swan song became a final weeklong marathon of music, emotion, and adolescent postpubescent excitement, never to be fully replicated in my lifetime and burned deeply into my mind forever.

Much to our collective wonderment, that last week became so much more than the standard hype that our radio advertisements promised. What transpired that week, primarily of our own making, was my first and likely most profound advertising lesson in a lifetime that would soon become crowded by weekly advertising and business promotions. The radio promotions that burned up the airwaves likely stirred up about 20 percent of the business those last two weeks, but word of mouth and quality of product drew the rest of the crowd...Period! End of conversation. Years later I attended an advertising seminar, and the first lesson we were taught was that when a person opens a new business, advertising—newspaper, radio, and television—is of paramount importance because that's where 80 percent of your new business will come from. After you are established, it switches 180 degrees, and advertising only accounts for 20 percent of new customers while word of mouth draws in the other 80 percent. I learned that lesson at the Martinique at the age of eighteen, as my band advertised our shirttails off and discovered the people that we drew were former friends and customers.

When we finished our final performance on that last Saturday night at the Martinique, the huge audience of friends and fans gave us several standing ovations, begging for, and receiving, two encores. Local Main Street constable and all-around friend of teenagers Sam Etheredge winked us happily past the 2 A.M. curfew this, and only one other, time. We opened our encores by dipping into the deep water for a perennial crowd-pleaser—an extended version of one of the band's longtime barn-burning favorites, "Gimmie' Some Lovin'," by the Spencer Davis Group, with Ralph on vocals, lead guitar, and deep-throated screams. After which we closed the night with Otis Redding's "Try a Little Tenderness," giving it all we had and extending the ending by several bars and raising the volume level to "That's all we got!"

After our final encore fell on downhearted ears, begrudgingly, one by one, the audience was directed out of the front door, reluctantly leaving us behind on the bandstand with little more than dim stage lights and sweat-filled pockets overflowing with memories. Our dates still occupied the table to the left of the stage for the last time, dutifully guarding our drinks from the waitresses who were busy clearing the tables. Bill Cook and Ringo immediately approached the stage when the club emptied, planting seeds of a "reunion week" or two in December when most of us would be back in town for Christmas break and we would all be in desperate need of spending money. The reunion suggestion pleasantly surprised us all, and we agreed to give it the old college try. Bill then penciled us in onto their calendar so as to tentatively hold the week before and the one after Christmas for us to play if we could all manage to be back in town and free of other obligations. Tim, Carl, and Scott would likely be playing in other bands then, but they agreed to try to keep those dates open. Only Scott was a maybe, so a plan was laid.

Even with the plans of a band reunion and rekindling of our disappearing musical friendships, something all-important seemed to have been sucked out of the air around us that night. We would be soon leaving the Martinique, our home away from home and musical clubhouse, and it was just beginning to leave a mental mark on us all. Each of us had made our way to that night from very different neighborhoods, and on different paths, but the primary things that brought each of us to the Martinique that night were tenacity and our love for the music, as well as each other.

It was abnormally quiet as we broke down our equipment and packed it out into our individual cars so we could play the following afternoon's jam at the Blind Pig. I'm sure I wasn't the only one quietly reflecting back to the merriment and excitement that we had all experienced and what our group had developed into during the past four years. We developed from a mostly out-of-tune, ragtag group of beach-party, amateur guitar strummers, and by the force of sheer determination, we practiced and became a tight band of seasoned professional musicians that kids all over the United States would never forget listening and dancing to. Those kids may well have forgotten our band's name through time, but they will never forget the palette and brushes that we afforded them to paint whatever masterpieces represented each of their teenage years. While on our road, we had nurtured friendships that extended well beyond our six. We had become accepted and admired by other local musicians and had been mentored by the likes of Duane Allman, Johnny Sandlin, Paul Hornsby, Jim Matherly, Pete Carr, and Gregg Allman. What we had achieved was an amazing accomplishment for a group of young teenagers, and this felt tantamount to winning a regional or state athletic championship. We even sported a towering trophy to help document a portion of our achievement. It would take most of us years to replicate that sense of accomplishment and success that we had attained by the tender age of eighteen. These thoughts and more coursed through my mind as I schlepped my drum cases out into the night one last time that summer. Like the stack of spiral notebooks packed full of journaled notes, set lists, dates, and nightly compensation that Ralph so dutifully chronicled, his historical workbook held clear, concise recollections of camaraderie divided neatly into mental file folders.

That "burn it down" summer at the Martinique, playing every week while spending Sunday afternoons hosting a jam session at the Blind Pig, gave us an education in mental strength and endurance that we barely thought possible. The Blind Pig was located on the southwest corner of US-1 and Madison Avenue. The Pig's legendary owner, Cadillac Jack, was near the top of our list of prominently notorious club owners whom we had worked for. The Sunday jams at the Pig were always fun, and Jack paid us thirty-five dollars each plus a meatball sub after our first set and two pitchers of frozen daiquiris to split. Our in-kind compensation package almost made all the moving of equipment for one afternoon's thirty-five-dollar gig worthwhile.

On our last Sunday jam at the Pig, August 11th, the day after our final night at the Martinique, we invited our many friends from the Martinique to spend a lazy afternoon listening to us play some of our favorites from the previous four years. Afterward, Cadillac Jack gave each of us, along with our thirty-five-dollar paychecks, a Budweiser beer pitcher and six matching Budweiser pilsner glasses for our college dorm rooms, which was quite a score. This time, when we packed up our instruments, amps, lights, and sound system, it would be the end of the Soul Patrol, at least for the most part. We all made a point of getting together during the following week before those of us who were leaving town packed up and abandoned ship. There were lots of laughs and also a few solemn moments of reflection. There would be no more sweltering practices in Carl's garage surrounded by a dozen or so crab traps, or in my living room, keeping one eye open for my father, the General. And there would be no more listening to new records from Ernie's Record Mart on Ralph's console stereo to glean new material for the band to learn. Of course, we would, as time allowed, get together here and there to play or jam together when back in town, but it wasn't until that December that we flew again as a flock. When we did get back together again to play as a band, it was surprisingly different and it exposed a refreshing individual eagerness to surprise each other with new and exciting changes in personal music tastes. After all, we had all been set free in August and no longer confined by the music that we all knew as bread and butter, and we were bursting to try our new tastes out on our former bandmates.

While attending the local college, Carl, Tim, and Scott continued playing in Daytona that fall, having formed a new band with some local cracker-jack musicians and working at the Martinique in our stead. Ralph, determined to become the doctor that he became, would woodshed mostly in his dorm room between studying and jamming at fraternity parties, maintaining his chops. I smuggled my drums into my dorm room after an early trip home that fall and formed a band primarily made up of sophomore antiwar sympathizers at Clemson University called the Old Florida Rum Company. My new group was created from musicians like myself who had left successful high school bands, including one former guitar player who had worked, for a time, with the early Amboy Dukes.

Christmas break of 1968 was a welcomed respite after an exceptionally demanding first semester away at Clemson. Interestingly enough, as footloose and fancy-free as my high school years had been, I found adjusting to college life, with all its trappings, challenging, to say the least. I was afforded as much, if not more, freedom as I had in high school, and I had nobody to answer to when I dragged my butt home but my roommate...and Ed didn't really give a damn. We both had a period of trial and error to work out the bugs of living with endless time to channel into positive arenas. Time management and simple conflicts between class scheduling and extracurricular entertainment became my primary nemesis. By Christmas, I needed a break from the bluebook funk of my first semester away from my best friends, and the Soul Patrol's upcoming reunion was exactly the medicine I craved.

The Soul Patrol had always been big on making and keeping promises. Long before we all got home that December, we decided to keep our promise to bless the Martinique's staff and our old fans with a reunion show. The Soul Patrol reunited for a final time, settling on one Saturday night during December. We had originally talked about a week of shows, but Carl and Tim's new band was working at the Martinique full time, and their band didn't want or need a week off during the holidays. Everyone in our last incarnation made the show except for our last bass player, Scott Stanley. Our original bass player, Kip Marshall, had been playing in a South Florida band since he moved to Ft. Lauderdale with his parents. The band he had been playing with was similar in style and composition to the Soul Patrol, so for the fun of it, Kip made his way back to Daytona for the reunion show, and the band was complete once again.

As much fun and camaraderie as we had shared over the years, I don't remember ever playing to a more welcoming crowd and having as much fun as we did on that reunion night in December—four months after we thought we had said our last good-byes. It didn't take but a few jokes, and a few Cokes, to fall back into our old routine, and it felt so right. There was a unique bond that revealed itself and was shared by all, and always will be. There is a rarified magic involved when old friends reconnect after a time apart. In high school, we saw each other every day, but as time passed, it became much rarer than that. However, the connection was palpable, and camaraderie is one of the tonics that makes life worth living.

The band arrived at the Martinique in the early afternoon, and we ran through a few of our songs that had changes that might trip Kip up, and we smoothed out as many wrinkles in our harmonies as possible. Other than Carl, the rest of our backing vocals had rusted somewhat in the past four months. We also brought a new song or two to the band as our individual music tastes developed. Ralph was delving heavily into Credence Clearwater Revival by then, so we worked up "Born on the Bayou" for his Florida Institute of Technology fraternity friends in the audience. We added a few Doors compositions that everyone was familiar with and quickly learned "My Pledge of Love" by the Joe Jeffery Group for Carl, to satisfy his funky jake leg.

The night itself was fun and loose, and if there were missteps along the way, nobody seemed to notice or care. I don't remember any major train wrecks, though there were a lot of laughs. The primitive video that our manager, Lee Phillips, and his brother-in-law Russ Atwell produced that night confirmed the lack of derailments. At one point during the night, Carl called for "Light My Fire" to be played next, to which Kip responded in horror, "I don't remember the chords!" To which Carl replied with a chuckle, "It doesn't matter, I don't remember the words, either!" That's the way the night went: just like always, we supported each other, and the least of us was raised up in the process. Even Kip, who had not played with our band since the spring of 1967, stepped up and handled his bass chores like a champ. Kip and Ralph made a point of playing next to each other so Kip could get his cues and any missing chords from Ralph. Playing that night, it was as if no time had passed between our winning the Battle of the Bands in April of '67 and Christmas of '68. Even those few new songs that we managed to work up on the spot for that one show were performed with an untroubled elegance and a funky suaveness. Being together onstage again was like being on the tilt-a-whirl on the Boardwalk with an old girlfriend...all we could do was smile, hang on by the seat of our pants, and take whatever the night threw our way.

Carl was entirely unchanged as he stepped into the spotlight, as if we had all simply taken a week off for finals. He danced and shook and growled each song, belting out the soulfulness that we had all grown to know in the previous four years. Carl rooted us all to the stage. He bound us in place, keeping the five of us from washing out to sea. Without Carl Persis, we would have been a mat of driftwood floating aimlessly on the Atlantic tides. There were times when we didn't always appreciate what it was that Carl brought to the stage, but make no mistake, a great band depends on someone like Carl to root them and keep everyone moving in a positive direction. He was equipped with a special kind of cultural X-ray vision that kept him constantly alert to the details and signifiers of the audience. Carl judged the perfect placement of our song list as the night and the crowd's emotion shifted. He propelled the band through each set as if following the audience's mood with halogen fog lights.

Tim was Tim, and more often than not, he pushed the volume pedal clearly to the metal, requiring the rest of the band to turn up in order to meet him even halfway. Asking Tim to "Turn it down" was fruitless, so we eventually submitted to his lead-footedness. His keyboard prowess, however, moved with a rare urgency in contemporary piano and organ. It was hard not to notice that Tim was the most improved by our absence. Where so many musicians get gummed up is in the traffic just shy of the last turn. Tim's chops were smeared with the sticky residue of Black musical history and contemporary White blues. His playing and vocals drew in fans, snagging them like flies to flypaper. Tim always knew which notes to play and which notes to leave un-played.

My soulful fatback drumming had not suffered from lack of practice, and from early November until Christmas break, I had been practicing with my college band, learning new music and writing with various musicians at Clemson. Our fledgling South Carolina band was moving into a different direction from the Soul Patrol, but a four-count backbeat is the same no matter from which genre the music is plucked. I had been moving slowly into a much different musical neighborhood while away at school: Buffalo Springfield, Poco, Eagles, Jackson Browne, James Taylor, the Hour Glass, and a new band that had caught my ear, Gypsy. With all of this new music swirling around in my head, I still nestled into the pocket with my old band as if our last gig had been yesterday. I even surprised myself by the speed and ease with which the songs came back and found their way to my drum heads and cymbals. We had played such a grueling schedule for the past year, with more than two hundred gigs, that those songs will likely go with me to my grave.

As far as Ralph was concerned—our pillar of strength and invincibility had changed very little in the past four months. His guitar playing was rock-solid, and he was the same vestige of strength that he had always been. However, because of his time working with records almost exclusively, his touch took on a sensitive, emotional feel as his fingers moved effortlessly across the strings of the Duane Strat, evoking the sounds of hearts bleeding softly in a gentle rain. Ralph was always in charge musically, and the video recording that I have of this night clearly demonstrates his ability to lead the band down new or old musical alleyways with the nod of his head or the raising of his pick hand. We were complete again, and the music that night was better than any of us imagined possible. Still, as rewarding as it was to get together with the Soul Patrol again, I felt a vague eagerness to return to South Carolina and explore new directions with the Rum Company.

During the second semester of my sophomore year, the Rum Company played some huge outdoor concerts during Vietnam War protests at our college. At one point in late spring, several of the members of my band discussed playing at a large antiwar rally in Piedmont Park in Atlanta. The rally was cancelled by the Atlanta City Commission, and the rally's organizers were scrambling to find another place to hold the weekend-long event on short notice, so we invited all interested individuals to the Clemson campus for music and other antiwar activities. We thought it was a brotherly thing to do, but our fundamental misstep was not running the idea past the university's administration for permission beforehand. So, when the gathering got out of hand, we did our best to keep our heads low and maintain decorum as best we could. When more than four thousand hippies from all over the South descended on the Clemson University campus in one weekend, unannounced, the president of the university demanded the names of the responsible parties and the finger-pointing began. Naturally, there were dire consequences for our actions. Even though the president of Clemson, Dr. R. C. (Bob) Edwards, had been my father's roommate many years before, my bandmates and I were in a world of trouble. Even the close family connection to Edwards could do little to diminish my glaring transgression, which led, in part, to an inauspicious compulsory withdrawal for a semester from the university as well as a severe tongue-lashing and forewarning concerning my future at Clemson University from the president. Needless to say, my concert-promoting days at the university were finished, but for the time being my drum set remained in Clemson.

The rest of that fall semester found me waiting for the beginning of my spring semester suspension, searching for some classes to take at my local junior college back home, and laying low in my dorm room to avoid attracting the administration's further ire. A second and third administrator, Dean Walter Cox and Assistant to the Dean Nick Lomax, were alerted to my situation, and the two kept a close eye on my whereabouts from their offices in Tillman Hall, which was literally yards outside of my dorm window on A-8 in Johnstone Hall. We literally waved to each other daily until it was time for me to slink away to Florida with my tail between my legs. Before my exile back to the Sunshine State began, my roommate Ed and I began searching for off-campus housing. The heat was beginning to become too much to bear on campus.

Then, during my semester off back in Daytona, in December of 1969 and early 1970, the unexpected happened: disco raised its ugly head in America, at which time Carl and I found ourselves working together once again: Carl spinning records while a sixteen-year-old Black drummer, Lorenzo Laws, and I kept the beat alive. We were back at the Martinique once more. Bill Cook had the wild idea that if he paid a drummer or two to play along to the records that Carl was spinning, people outside of the building would think that they were hearing a "live" band and flock into his club. Damn if it didn't work, at least for as long as disco lived on the airwaves in Florida.

Back on that familiar stage again, I remember Ringo's admonition to Carl to let the music settle like ripples on a pond between songs before diving headlong into the next track. I remember the brightly colored lights under the dance floor gliding smoothly across that platform in perfect-colored unison. Those lights faded into a fog of cigarette smoke floating like ghosts above the raised Plexiglas dance surface. I often think of Drew, behind the bar mixing drinks, with his nostrils raised to the crowd, staring intently into the gray fog, wondering what that new scent could be and knowing that it was the scent of so many things that matter.

That spring became an alternating gumbo of work and entertainment. At one point, I was able to stretch a night off into a road trip across the state to hear The Allman Brothers Band with a Dodge van full of absolutely bat-shit crazy friends. Gregg was under the weather that night but Duane and Berry sang in his stead. Reese Wynans, the Allman Brothers' original keyboardist, sat in on Hammond organ and piano. The concert rocked and satisfied my soul, even without Gregg's powerful vocals. That night spilled over into the breaking sunrise as we limped back home, full of wide-eyed wonderment and Ripple wine.

Back at the Martinique, the music that unfolded was a delicious cocktail of whatever Carl decided he liked at the moment, just so long as it had funk and soul enough to fill the dance floor. Lorenzo and I were only hog-tied by our ability to keep up the funk, so we were allowed a grand mix of musical tastes, mostly from the Stax catalog. Playing drums along to records in a public setting at the speed of life was also an incredible experience for both drummers as far as cadence and tempo was concerned. There was no room to drag or pick up the beat...the pocket was right there in our ears, and Lorenzo and I knew to keep up with whatever record Carl threw on the turntable. My disco partner and I split drum duties, alternating songs unless one or the other got a song that the other percussionist particularly enjoyed playing, but our styles were remarkably similar. We were both fatback, funk-inspired, rhythm-producing machines who could at any point inspire feet to dance across that beautifully lighted dance floor.

Occasionally, I would slip a favorite non-funk inspired album into the mix and hope that Carl would not notice. My country rock side occasionally showed through and some Poco vinyl would magically appear in the mix, but a quick tongue-lashing by Bill or Ringo would straighten Carl's course so that we would stay in rocky water. From my side of the stage, Drew, Carl, Ringo, Lorenzo, Wendy, Bill Cook, Moose, and George Karpodinis all bobbed through the night in perfect harmony, keeping the tempo awake with their step and floating like fog-shrouded apparitions that slipped momentarily in and out of my line of sight.

As summer school back at Clemson became close at hand, in late June I began feeling odd pangs of homesickness for my alma mater, and I was feeling the need to play catch-up with missed opportunities. Calls were made and promises offered, so I left for my second home once more with my drum set packed carefully in the trunk of my car. Everything is a learning experience, and what I discovered during my semester's exile away from Clemson was twofold. College inspired and nurtured a humanity and social militancy deep within me that required to be set free, and I discovered that I play music for the same reason that I breathe: because music is both spontaneous and essential to life. Those two lessons were extracurricular in nature and originated far outside of the covers of any of the textbooks on my shelves. They were lessons born of a charitable, tolerant upbringing and years of euphoric musical camaraderie, culminated by a singular birthright forged in that grand old Daytona Beach roadhouse, the Martinique.

Chapter 18

Cops and Other Angels

Memory so often burns brighter than reality, and leaving well enough alone only gives authority to fantasy. When there is nothing left but a shoebox full of letters and a handful of Instamatic photographs of the bluest eyes ever captured on film, the mind is free to wander. This is an often-told story around the lobby of the Heartbreak Hotel. An amazing spirit-force can blow through once in a lifetime...twice, if you are charmed, turning the universe upside down. Then, only months later, that force can vanish like the fragile leaves of fall. As time passes, there will be the realization of how simply being with her allowed for a better person to emerge. Afterward, there will be weeks and months when the burn of that loss will flair at the slightest familiar fragrance or sensation. Heart-wrenching devastation can spell doom to a college freshman far from home unless he has the good fortune to run into the two people who are willing to put a stranger's best interest before theirs.

Jim Croce's widow, Ingrid, said once about "Operator (That's Not the Way It Feels)," one of her favorite songs by her late singer/songwriting husband, "Everybody has to have their heart broken at least once or twice before they can have a real relationship." Croce's chart-topping song "Operator" was inspired by his time in the Army National Guard, where he did his basic training in 1966. Croce was stationed in South Carolina, far away from his home in the North. Lonely and homesick, he recalled endless lines of soldiers waiting to use the few pay phones on his base, many of them calling home to their wives or girlfriends to confirm whether or not their "Dear John" letters were indeed authentic. And, as if calling your girlfriend to see if she had abandoned you wasn't heart-wrenching enough, back in the days of pay telephones, the heartbroken and despondent were required to navigate those troubled waters through the ears of an often-curious operator as their intermediary. Released in the fall of 1972, Croce's "Operator" spoke to me on a very personal level.

Like a freight train barreling down the track un-engineered, the waning days of August 1968 came, and I left home for college with all my hopes and dreams tucked neatly into my footlocker. For a time, Jasmine stoked my fire by writing me tender letters every day from her bedroom back home. From day one on the Clemson University campus, my unwavering daily practice was to rise with the first pale, ashen light of dawn, excited to tumble headlong into another exhilarating day of self-exploration and discovery. Hitting the floor and moving about my room surreptitiously so as to not unsettle my snoring roommate, Ed Alden, I would hustle through the military's three all-important S's that I had gleaned from years of instruction by my military family and my West Point Youth Camp counselors. After the important issues were completed, it was time to dress to impress for the day: Gant shirt, Farah khaki slacks, Gold Cup socks, and Bass penny loafers allowed me to blend inconspicuously with the human mélange of 1968 freshman classmates at Clemson. I often grabbed a hearty breakfast with other early-risers from my hall whom I would meet while sneaking quietly out of my room (so I wouldn't wake Ed) on the way to Harcombe Commons, the military-style, regimented dining hall that I always passed on my way to classes. Winding our way through D and E halls, our parade would pick up steam and growing numbers of hungry students weighted down with books and spiral notebooks. Finally, we would reach the dining hall, where we were greeted by steaming trays of scrambled eggs, grits, toast, bacon, sausage, and coffee. Juice, milk, cereal, biscuits and jelly, or a quick doughnut were also available, depending on time and hunger. Even something as mundane as breakfast took on a singular spark as I watched in amazement as my South Carolina brothers mixed everything on their plates (scrambled eggs, grits, toast, bacon, biscuits, and sausage and gravy) into a steaming heap, and then devoured the hodgepodge like hungry dogs. The freshman five was alive and available to all in Harcombe Commons.

Morning classes began at 7 A.M. sharp. They lasted forty-five minutes and usually ran back-to-back until 11:45 A.M. My earliest classes were invariably located at the farthest point on the campus from my dorm room, and those days always drizzled. The sun never shone before ten on my mornings, and winter was always right around the corner, or so it seemed. It actually did not rain much in the upstate of South Carolina, but those long walks gave my mind time to drift back to the girl I left back home, and mental clouds often shadowed my walk. Lunch was generally my first break of the day, after which afternoon classes and science labs sporadically filled my time from 1 to 4 P.M. When afternoon classes or labs were over, it was time to meet like-minded friends for *Star Trek* viewing at the student lounge over the loggia, which housed the only televisions (black-and-white) for half a mile. After an hour of watching Kirk and Spock challenge us to "go boldly where no man has gone before," it was time for supper back at Harcombe Commons, once again, which was just two flights of stairs down from the TV lounge. The only other dinner options on campus were trekking all the way back across campus to the dining hall amidst the East Campus women's dorms, or to buy a burger, grilled ham and cheese, or fried bologna sandwich at the campus canteen, located adjacent to Harcombe. The canteen didn't offer the variety of healthy dinner options that Harcombe Commons offered, but it did offer a decidedly more diverse and bohemian level of conversation.

"Downtown Clemson" offered Dan's Sandwich Shop for food and the Study Hall, which also offered beer as an additional benefit for those over eighteen years of age who were willing to make the two-block walk into the downtown area. After supper, the options included heading back to D-3 for some time to shoot the shit with friends or to walk one building south of the dorms to the campus YMCA for a dime movie or pool game until it was time to head back to D-3 to put in some time studying. Later, as lights began to dim all over the dorms, it was "rack time." Time for reflection, contemplation, and mentally engineering plans for the future.

During my freshman year at Clemson, the only major concerns on campus were lack of air conditioning, lack of student parking, and the limited, unpleasant food choices in the dining hall. Possibly, it was the lack of television news or rarity of national newspapers, but the issues of the day outside of our microcosm were of little consequence to most of Clemson's students. Aside from seceding from the Union, South Carolina had never been a trendsetter in American history. But as 1968 began to shift gears into 1969, the Robert Kennedy assassination as well as that of Martin Luther King Jr. and the Chicago Democratic Convention riots began to paint the future with a much harsher brush. Even the sheltered Clemson students began to take notice.

Things began to change slowly in South Carolina in 1969 at first, but change was in the air and more and more of my friends sensed the transformation and moved slowly in its direction. Longer sideburns, mustaches, longer hair, and even beards began appearing around campus, especially at the bridge table at the Johnstone Hall Canteen. Campus radicals such as Gary Ligi held court in the canteen and planned the first student demonstrations at Clemson University in protest of the Vietnam

War. Those initial demonstrations were not well accepted by the rank-and-file South Carolinians, and most of my friends at that time were on the fence about the war and student involvement. Most were preoccupied with having dates for football weekends, and all marched into the history of those tumultuous times without much groundwork or preparation.

Nobody offered maps to help us navigate through the exhausting mazes of the '60s. When my high school class's footsteps had echoed across the wooden stage of Peabody Auditorium a scant four months earlier, we joined quite literally thousands of other high school seniors who stepped innocently into an unpredictable future. We graduated to become one of only two American generations that waged war on each other. However, this war would be the only war to ever be fought by Americans on both foreign and domestic soil. Certainly, we were all free to choose sides, but bystanders were scorned for their neutrality, and there was a stiff price to be paid for indifference; that price was often alienation and estrangement. There were few survivors of this war as it was fought on American soil, only casualties and virtual prisoners of war. The veterans returning home from Southeast Asia were often physically and mentally scarred forevermore.

While many moments during the late '60s were captivating and some magnificently beautiful at the same time, there was a cloud of smoldering darkness that hung just above the horizon. Those of us in Clemson, South Carolina, were swept into the future by this wave, and we were carried under by circumstances that we scarcely understood. The Vietnam era was one of the most mindless periods in our country's history. Strangely enough, many of those whose lives unfurled through that period felt acutely alive, and, as a result, many began pursuing a wildfire existence, caring little for their futures. Those who withdrew from the debate were often ignored in silence, floundering invisibly as much of the country's youth fed upon themselves.

Freshman and sophomore men at Clemson University were never scheduled classes after 2 P.M. in the afternoon on Thursdays to allow for Army and Air Force ROTC drills—a requirement at Clemson stemming from the college's long history as an all-male military institution. Cadets, as we were dubbed by the ROTC department, were bemoaningly required to register for and complete menial two-credit Military Science 101 and 102 courses. In those classes we were taught how to fieldstrip, clean and load our weapons, outflank the enemy, and march as a group in near-perfect unison. As part of the Military Science classes, cadets were required to spend Thursday afternoon every week marching with a six-pound, standard military-issue, fully functional, semiautomatic M-1 Garand rifle, complete with a clip that was fully capable of holding eight rounds of 30-06 ammunition. We marched into the future in one of two uniforms...short-sleeved summer uniforms or "full dress" winter uniforms that included long-sleeved shirts and green dress blazers. Both uniforms were issued at the beginning of the school year and came complete with military-issue, spit-polished dress shoes that felt as if they were constructed of rigid plastic that begged tender feet to blister and bleed.

For many of us, a quickly developing bonus of being in college during the Vietnam era was avoiding military service or, upon graduation, passing seamlessly into the service as a first lieutenant in the army. In those years, the draft meant an all-expense-paid, two-year stint in Southeast Asia. Until the draft lottery was enacted on December 1, 1969, the much-coveted "student deferment" was the major benefit of college enrollment and more than enough reason to keep one's grades up for most male students at Clemson. Still, dressing up on Thursday afternoons to play "army" during that tumultuous time was also a chance to dip a toe in the Mekong River without actually stepping foot on Vietnamese soil.

I began to grow my hair out a bit after my initial freshman "rat cut" and was often asked by the gung-ho, upper-class ROTC officers, "Don't you support the war, Rat?" To which I would reply, "No, sir, I don't support the war but I do support the men fighting the war! Don't put that patriotic bullshit on me. I was born into the army and have spent my entire eighteen years in an army family. How many years have you lived on army bases?" If that wasn't enough, I would flash my still valid army-issue dependents ID card.

During Thursday afternoon drill, while the minions were standing at attention on the parade field for what seemed like endless hours, the upper-class platoon leaders constantly warned, "Don't lock your knees, you'll faint if you do." But if, like me, a cadet was lucky enough to stand in a squad line near someone who was prone to fainting, a helpful cadet could gladly lend a hand to one who fainted, helping them to a comfortable spot under a tree where they could be fanned by their own hat until they were able to walk back to the dorm. The whispered words of encouragement were always, "Stay down."

Another ploy to avoid the endless hours of monotony during

Thursday drill was to remove all but two nails from the heel of one of your drill shoes. The offending heel could then be easily kicked off, on cue, whereas a poor cadet had no choice but to limp back to the dorm, heel in hand, to somehow repair the offending shoe. Cheap tricks? Absolutely! But in the era of the Vietnam War before the lottery draft, anything to circumvent the established chain of command, albeit college ROTC, was clearly within the accepted field of play.

Wedged somewhere between the exciting and the mundane, I *always* found time each and every day to write two letters home to the girl I left behind in Florida. Unless rained out, the first letter was written before lunch beneath the shade of an ancient oak tree on a bench in the open-air amphitheater in the center of campus. If there was rain, I could always find an empty classroom or laboratory from which to write. Before lunch I would mail my first letter from the post office underneath Harcombe Commons. Later in the day, I would often stop at the same morning bench on the way back to my room from afternoon classes to compose my second letter. After written, I would paste a five-cent stamp on the preaddressed envelope that I usually had stashed somewhere in my books, and I would slip my afternoon letter into the red, white, and blue post office box outside the door of the P.O. under Harcombe Commons.

Before time and tide had placed so many hours between us, I could probably count all the letters that I had written in my entire life on both hands and still have fingers enough left over to play an E-chord. In my exciting new world, there was so much happening every waking moment that I couldn't wait to journalize it all, and those journals took the form of letters home to Jasmine. Words seemed to write themselves and appeared to fly out of the wet end of my much-prized, jumbo-cartridge, black-ink-filled Parker T-ball Jotter. Two quick pages of whatever paper was handy (usually torn out of the back of a spiral notebook), filling both front and back written before lunch and two or three more pages written before dinnertime, was about average. I was so well pleased about my newfound ability to burn through letter paper that at first I didn't notice that, as the trees began covering the campus in a blanket of fragile brown leaves, there wasn't always a return letter in my post office box. I went off to college that fall, discovering an eagerness for longhand, and at least for a while, she wrote me sweet letters back, charged with desire and emotion.

Sometime in late October, her letters cooled and became less about passion and more about how long her days had become with me so far away. She also mentioned a nice boy that she had met in her fourth-period class. By early November, my impassioned letters home suddenly became entirely unanswered and she left me with nothing but a shoebox full of letters written in disappearing ink. What I had failed to realize was that while my days were filled surfing the cresting waves of excitation, I had left Jasmine sitting alone on the beach to grind out her senior high school year in emotional exile. So, by the time I noticed that my mailbox was empty more often than not, her letters discontinued altogether.

Desperation fell like the chill of a cool mountain rainstorm, and the hardest thing for me to comprehend was that she had virtually vanished from my life as suddenly as she had entered. I simply couldn't imagine that she had abandoned all of our plans for the future. Our relationship was the most important possession that I had brought with me to South Carolina, but what I had failed to see was that she needed to be something more than a framed 5 x 7 photograph sitting prominently like a trophy on my shelf. After the letters stopped, Jasmine also became unavailable to talk when I called her house on the customary day and time. With all communication now cut off, I felt as if I was going through my days and nights blindfolded.

A sense of total abandonment overwhelmed me, and I actually considered walking out to the highway to thumb my way home. Then, out of the blue, a letter from her house on Idlewood Drive lit up my mailbox. My fervent hope was that she had simply been busy with midterm exams of her own or in the middle of an overriding senior project that was taking all of her time. When I tore the letter open, it was as if I had been blindsided by a pop quiz on a chapter I had not read. What I held in disbelief was my very own personal, much-disparaged, and highly maligned "Dear John" letter. Like a wall of stones held together with sand for mortar, everything that I knew began to crumble again. In the thirty-seven seconds it took me to read her letter, my life changed on the spot.

Sitting alone in that post office with my thoughts in my hands, it was unimaginable that my life could turn upside down in a matter of weeks and that my one and only life plan had vanished into the first chilling evening of fall. Suddenly, I was alone in a world so cold and empty that birds refused to sing, and the excitement that brightened my every day was instantly reduced to drab shades of gray.

Tears are few among males in my family. They are as rare as gold bars in the dark vaults where our grief is stored. The bright palette of fall had at once become the season of the witch. I watched for a moment as students bustled by outside of the post office, making their way to dinner or back to their rooms. Some entered the P.O. to check their 5 x 5-inch square metal mailboxes, and I fought the urge to warn them off. The contrast was suffocating. Shutting my eyes for a moment, I tried to clear my head of the noise and disturbance, but the air was filled with human static. Neither world, the one on the outside nor the one that I opened my eyes to, was tolerable to me. My world and the one outside chaffed my psyche like flint on steel. The choices were simple: sit and smolder like a slow-burning fuse, imprisoned by a newfound ball and chain, or put the mindless river of humanity behind me somewhere in the night. I left the chaos of humanity, my only home, behind as the post office door closed slowly behind me.

For endless hours I wandered aimlessly about the buildings and classrooms of the place that I had loved. All I wanted was to escape from the nightmare, return home to Florida, and make things right. Walking holes in my shoes, I still couldn't make sense out of what had come to pass. From a distance I watched a world where a handful of students were awake at 3 A.M. studying while I was awake slowly dying. Still clutching my "Dear John" letter, I saw parts of the campus on my pointless journey that I never knew existed, and I made excuses to be anywhere but in my room until I was too exhausted not to sleep.

Word spread quickly the next day on D-3 that I was one of the walking wounded. I was not the first freshman to be steamrolled and shell-shocked that semester, but for me it came at a particularly bad time, just at midterm exams. Luckily for me, I had a plethora of experienced upperclassmen around me, and I soon became overwhelmed with expert advice for the lovelorn as well as copies of previous midterm tests and mimeographed copies of current tests provided by my dumpster-diving fraternity friends.

It was Thursday of a football weekend, which meant no Friday exams or Saturday classes, so after much serious kibitzing, counseling, and encouragement, the general consensus was that I needed to hitch a ride to Rabbit Martin's liquor store in Pendleton to buy a bottle of hooch, which I needed to drink to try and forget the past nine months ever happened. There were likely better strategies offered and most assuredly worse, but at least it was a game plan, and at that point in my life I was happy that at least some course of action was in place.

Riding out to Rabbit Martin's had become a rite of passage for underage students at Clemson, and a visit on a Thursday before the Friday rush normally assured a fairly decent selection of alcohol. Rabbit Martin's wasn't a liquor store in the traditional sense, but it worked if you were under the legal drinking age, which was twenty-one for hard liquor in South Carolina. A student could buy beer or wine at eighteen in the state, but my complete and total annihilation required a more high-octane-charged solution.

Rabbit was a short, quick Black man who lived in a nondescript wooden shack set just off the Pendleton highway. Rabbit's house was set back into the trees, leaving just enough room for one or two cars to pull off into the red-dirt front yard. The front room of his "home" housed an amazing supply of intoxicants in a variety of categories, sizes, and price ranges, and Rabbit was not concerned much, if at all, by the age of his customers. The ability to see over the makeshift counter which blocked his front door from entrance was apparently the only age restriction at Rabbit's liquor store, and all Clemson students were welcome, especially freshmen. Rabbit Martin's livelihood depended heavily on the university, and most freshmen and sophomores banked entirely on Rabbit's inventory for weekend recreation. Rabbit relied on this unique codependence to keep his liquor sales alive, making this symbiotic relationship a match made in heaven...which is where you might wind up if you drank too much of his legendary 190-proof Everclear Grain Alcohol. Everclear was the key ingredient in P. J., or "Purple Jesus," a favorite celebratory concoction that students generally reserved for major festivities or sometimes simply mindless debauchery. This day, I needed only something that would set my chickens free and then rock me to sleep and not knock me out completely for the weekend.

A deal was struck, and Rabbit's shaking hands slipped me a fifth of Bacardi Silver Label. Rum and I had long been acquainted, and Bacardi Silver Label was the favorite drink of my high school rock and soul band, the Soul Patrol. Bacardi often accompanied the band on road trips, stashed in an air vent situated next to my left leg in the 1968 Plymouth Barracuda that I drove everywhere before leaving it behind when I left for college. While traveling, our favorite mixer was either a Coke or lime Icee from Magic Market or a similar-flavored Slurpee from 7-Eleven, whichever was available. "Fill my cup about 3/4 of the way, please," was the common request.

Today, however, I stopped on the way back to the dorm for a small bag of ice and a two-liter bottle of Fresca citrus-flavored soda as a mixer.

Back in my room after drill, and after enjoying a fortifying dinner of meatloaf, mashed potatoes, and gravy at Harcombe Commons, I mixed a batch of the intoxicating ingredients in my trophy Budweiser pitcher. My mixture was a bit on the strong side, and the concoction was offered to my roommate and the four guys who lived on either side of our room. By the time I had mixed and dispatched four pitchers full of rum and Fresca, the Bacardi bottle was nearly empty and the rum had taken a firm grasp of my friends. The party had become much more spirited and bright than I had anticipated. As the only one incapable of out-drinking the melancholy, on one of my trips to the bathroom down the hall, I slipped away from the revelry and merriment with a full tumbler of my concoction in hand, plus an extra shot of rum for good measure. I drifted again, alone among the spiderweb of sidewalks, lost in my thoughts. I had hoped that the further into the rum I delved, the more that my mind would allow me to erase. Unfortunately, that's just not the way it works. The mind is a cruel taskmaster, and the deeper you wade into the darkness, the harder the mind focuses on the rocks and roots beneath the water ahead.

The further I wandered into the night, the more arduous my melancholy became, like wheels within wheels. My mind never would allow forgetting, but a healing of sorts did begin with the first of two extraordinary miracles that followed each other in relatively quick succession.

As I continued wandering through the night in a semi-drunken stupor, two Allman Brothers compositions began to crowd my mind: "Little Martha" and "In Memory of Elizabeth Reed." As a result, I somehow found myself in the Fort Hill Cemetery above Death Valley football stadium, where I looked to Duane Allman and Dickey Betts for some quiet and solitude. Simply following their lead into the darkness, there was no other reason that I stumbled into the cemetery except to find sanctuary from the fraternal heartbeat of overflowing dormitories. In the cool darkness of that peaceful place, no one would see my tearful sulking. Until tonight, with Duane and Dickey's prompting, the thought of sitting alone in a cemetery had never once crossed my mind, but I could not bring myself to enjoy the good-natured company of my friends back in the dorm. I imagined that the Allmans likely communed in Rose Hill Cemetery to get away from the ruckus at home. Communing with Clemson's past among the headstones seemed somehow dark but fitting. Dante himself could not have described a more vivid hell.

Sitting on the headstone of a long-dead biology professor, staring out into the shadows and darkness while sipping the last dregs of my drink, I had not noticed the Clemson police officer who slipped up behind me smoking a cigarette.

"Excuse me," the officer said, framed in a haze of blue smoke. "Are you aware that this cemetery closes at sundown?" Mildly startled but reaching for a Winston myself, I just shook my head no.

As I fumbled with my lighter, the officer flipped open his silver Zippo and pushed the yellow flame under the business end of my cigarette, illuminating my face. "So, what's going on with you tonight?" he continued.

"Well, yesterday I got a Dear John letter from my girlfriend," I started, with my voice cracking and pained. "I was under the impression that we were going to be married at some point, so I'm kind of trying to sort things out," I continued, as I gazed again out into the darkness searching for something to focus on. I took a deep drag off of my cigarette and continued, "I just needed to get away from everyone and everything and this was the only place I could find without a constant parade of people coming and going at every minute." Looking around and then gesturing down at the headstone I was resting on, I went on. "It's quiet here, and Ole Professor Long here and I have been locked into a pretty heated one-way conversation about my future as a biology major here at Clemson. Did you know that the biology building is named for him?" I questioned.

"Yes, son, I did," the officer replied, his own voice trailing off as if in deep thought himself. Then he startled me and unnerved me deeply with what he said next.

"I spent two years studying in that building as a botany major myself until one day I got a similar letter from the girl I thought that I was going to marry back in Charleston." He continued, "Let me tell you, from the moment I quit school I've regretted that decision every day of my life. I know all of these buildings on campus and most of the names on these headstones, and I've seen my share of guys just like you. I know one thing is true...throwing in the towel isn't the answer. That I can promise you! And you are sadly mistaken if you think for a minute that there's enough whiskey or moonshine in Pickens County to wash your problems away. Getting back on track will just take time, and keeping your nose in your books will help, believe you me."

As a light misting rain began to fall through the massive white oak trees that stood guard over the graves in Fort Hill Cemetery, we both dropped our cigarette butts on the path next to Professor Long's grave, signaling a time to make some sort of move. The officer slowly extinguished the fading glow of both cigarettes beneath his shoe and then put an assuring hand on my shoulder as I rose from my granite resting place. "What do you say?" he started. "It's almost nine-thirty and it's starting to spit rain. If we hustle, we can make it up to the canteen before it closes at ten. I'll bet that I can get Ben to make us a couple of his famous chili cheeseburgers, with fries and a Coke, before he shuts down the grill. You're going to need to soak up whatever it is that you've been drinking tonight, and I'll have him put it on my tab."

Alone, surrounded by the weathered headstones and moss-covered monuments in the eerie darkness of Fort Hill Cemetery, I could have easily slid deeper into my funk. Luckily, this kind member of the Clemson constabulary, who could have just as easily arrested me for public drunkenness and trespassing, snatched me from the cavernous arms of despair and filled my mind and belly with hope. I really didn't know how to answer, but his offer sounded much better than explaining away my arrest in a cemetery to an unforgiving father and the president of the college, who also happened to be one of my father's closest friends. So, I nodded and we left the cemetery, walking up the long hill beside Johnstone Hall and D-3 to the canteen, which was located in the middle of the maze of Johnstone residence halls, dubbed the "tin cans." Once at the canteen, we each feasted on a huge platter covered with thin-cut french fries and burgers smothered with mustard, onions, American cheese, and Ben's homemade chili. We washed it all down with a large soda fountain Coke served in the company's iconic red-and-white, wax-encased paper cups.

I don't remember ever seeing that policeman on campus before or since that time, but he was one of two angels whose appearance helped me begin to put my life back in order that fall, though it took a while to drive that break up completely out of my mind.

When I got back to my room that night, someone must have noticed me being walked up the sidewalk from the cemetery by the police, and everyone had assumed that I had been arrested or at least given a severe tongue-lashing at the campus police station. I just told anyone who asked that I had lucked out and gotten away, which is basically what happened. All in all, it was a good night...no crime, no foul, and I was another step closer to getting my life back on the straight and narrow. For me, this was no ordinary break up.

For the next three weeks after receiving my Dear John letter, I would take the same nearly worn-out paper roll of quarters down to the wooden phone booth tucked into the corner of D-3 every few evenings, and especially Fridays, to attempt calling Jasmine. Taking the first four quarters out of the ten-dollar roll, my habit was to leave three in a stack next to the open roll of quarters on the small counter inside the booth and put one in the wall-mounted Western Electric/Bell System three-coin rotary-dial pay telephone mounted on the wall inside the booth, next to the accordion-style folding door. At the top of the prepay-style telephone, there were three plainly marked coin slots to choose from: one for quarters, one for dimes, and one for nickels. Any combination of the three would work as long as the sum totaled the cost of the call as determined by distance and the Bell South operator who placed the call. After sitting down and depositing my first quarter in the slot, I would pull the folding glass-and-metal door on the front of the booth closed, which turned on the inside light signaling that the phone was now in use. I would then wait for my first quarter to make its long way through the coin-chute mechanism. Somewhere deep inside of the antique black-enamel telephone, my quarter could be heard nicking and scraping metal guides as it made its way noisily through the internal workings of the phone. The quarter would ultimately strike a bell and a bright *ca-ching* would ring out. Then, almost simultaneously, a final click would signal that my coin had been accepted and was now in the possession of Southern Bell Telephone and Telegraph Company. The alternative was for bent coins or appropriately sized metal washers called "slugs" to be spit out like a slice of sour orange and disgorged unceremoniously into the coin-return slot. There was always the unsettling fear of even the most pristine and newly minted coin being rejected for some unknown reason.

When the quarter had successfully made its way to wherever purgatory held the coins captive inside the telephone until a call was completed, I was free to summon the operator and choose from the three basic pay phone choices:

1. I could make a collect call where the receiver of the call would be billed for the charges (usually reserved for calls home to Mom and Dad, or my sister in New York).

2. Arrange a very rare and cutting-edge credit card call (which was not for me, as I was only trusted with a benign Gulf Oil Company gas

card).

3. Or the caller could just pay for time in three-minute blocks, costing four quarters per block, in so renting time, equipment, telephone lines, and operator services from "Ma Bell."

My choice when calling home to Jasmine was to always prepay in three-minute increments, ultimately using the entire ten-dollar roll of quarters that I allotted myself each week as well as any other high-denomination coins that I could glean from my change jar.

With my first quarter accepted and the dial tone now ringing in my ear, it was time to begin my call by hailing the operator. I would finger the "O" operator hole on the rotary-phone dial and twist the daisy wheel from its bottom right position all the way around past all of the other numbers to the left, stopping at the ergonomically curved chrome finger stop. As I withdrew my finger, the device would spin back to the left, returning to its original position on the bottom right of the face of the phone.

When a call was completed and the receiver handset cradled, all of the coins that now belonged to Southern Bell dropped en masse into the chrome-faced coin vault for safekeeping until a telephone-company employee with the appropriate key could come by and empty its contents. Occasionally, a destitute student would find his way into the coin vault, rendering the phone "Out of Order" until appropriate repairs to the security of the phone were completed.

After a few rings, there would normally be a chipper, "Hello, this is the operator, how can I help you?" To which I always replied, "I'd like to place a person-to-person call to Jasmine," and then I'd give the operator her number and wait for her to dial the number from her station.

If I listened on my end closely, I could sometimes hear a ringing faintly in the distance through the miles of transformers, relays, and wires between the phone a few steps from my dorm room and Jasmine's kitchen phone in Florida. Then the familiar voice that made my heart skip would answer, "Hello?"

Before the "Dear John" letter, I imagined Jasmine sitting next to the phone waiting for my call. In better days, her excited voice always sounded as if she had been running as fast as she could to answer the phone, afraid that the telephone would stop ringing before she could lift the receiver. The operator would ask for her by name and she would answer, "This is She!" and then the operator would tell me to "deposit three more quarters for the first three minutes," and the sound of quarters representing priceless time would move one at a time through the mechanism, eventually ringing that exciting bell deep inside the telephone. When the first three minutes passed, the operator would break into our conversation and advise me, "Please deposit another dollar for three more minutes." This continued over and over until my roll of quarters was nothing but an empty crumpled paper tube. Often, I would have a few extra coins in my pocket and could sometimes stretch the call out to fifteen minutes of bliss because it was always heart-wrenching to have to say good-bye.

After her letters stopped, my days became mountains to climb, and the disappointment of attempting to call Idlewood Drive occurred with less regularity. As hard as it is for a young man to face personal rejection, the specter of being rejected through an intermediary absolutely rubs salt in an otherwise agonizing wound.

"I'm sorry, sir, but there's no answer at that number today," the operator's voice would often bemoan. Or she would say, "The party with which you wish to speak is not available, I'm very sorry." In either case, the operator would relinquish her hold on my initial quarter and my lonely coin would make its way through the mechanism, circumventing the coin vault, and appearing back to me with a brutal clunk as it entered the coin-return slot. I would slip that offending coin and the three others that I had stacked at the ready on the ledge back into my unused roll of quarters. Slinking back to my room with a full roll of quarters in my hand was discouraging and demoralizing.

One evening, after I had hung up from a particularly gut-wrenching attempt to reach her, I sat in the phone booth for an extra minute or two because I was fumbling and having trouble forcing the unused quarters back into their paper roll. The end of the coin wrapper had become flimsy and thread-worn from overuse. Paper coin rolls were normally intended for one or two uses before being thrown away. One end of my coin roll had become somewhat tattered from forcing coins in and out. When I finally got my coins situated, I started to walk slowly away from the phone booth, but before I could take five steps, I was startled by the phone that I had just hung up beginning to ring. During my freshman year, if the phone rang on our hall and anyone was walking past, it was their duty to answer it and summon the recipient to the phone booth. So, when I heard the telephone ringing, it was my duty to answer it. Stunned, I immediately recognized the voice on the other end as that of the operator who had just helped me try to place that call and apparently several other failed attempts in the previous days.

Apparently, the operator had noticed a predictable pattern in my calls and could detect an unquestionable note of desperation in my voice. Probably breaking every rule in the Southern Bell Telephone operator's handbook, she took a chance that I was as desperate as my voice had led her to believe. She took herself off-line, going on break, and immediately called my pay phone number back from her break room in the Greenville telephone offices thirty miles away. Startling me, at first she asked me if I wanted to talk that night or just get coffee sometime when I happened to be in Greenville.

Like my mysterious policeman in the cemetery, that Southern Bell angel pulled me back from the brink of desperation on that cold, troglodytic night, opening her heart and giving me her private number. I did call her on that special number a few times and met her in Greenville one Saturday afternoon, hitchhiking to town and then walking to Darrell Floyd's Sandwich Shop for lunch and conversation. Her name was Trish and she was knock-dead gorgeous...the most beautiful forty-something-year-old angel to ever help mend a love-shattered heart. I never learned her last name and I never learned where she lived, but she told me she would always answer her phone if I called if she was at home. She added that if I left a message on her code-a-phone, she would return my call right after work, and by God, she meant it. I had to hitchhike to Greenville until I finally sneaked my car to South Carolina after Thanksgiving. Until then, Trish would always drive me out to the edge of town on HW123 near Whitehorse Road, where I was sure to get an easy thumb-ride back to Clemson. That fall, she allowed a glimmer of sunlight to break through the storm clouds that had enveloped my world, and she probably got me through midterm exams when everything in my world had turned hopeless.

Sometime between Thanksgiving and Christmas vacation, while I was struggling to study for my first-semester final exams, there came a knock on my dorm-room door one evening, announcing that I had a person-to-person call down at the pay phone. Pleasantly surprised, I assumed it was Trish from Greenville checking in. When I picked up the receiver my heart sank. It was Jasmine. Almost as if I had lost the ability to reason, what I imagined might be a "pleasant and very platonic" conversation wrapped itself around my tongue like endless winds of masking tape. So many things were spinning in my brain, but the disconnect between my mind and my tongue grew ever wider. Finally, the more we ignored the past eight months, the harder it was for meaningful conversation to ensue. Like a self-centered idiot, I found it futile to sound anything other than dejected and melancholy, which likely fed her resolve. Long before I could actually see the spark disappearing from her eyes, I could sense the indifference in her voice when we spoke on the phone that night.

There was nothing to do. The spark that a few short weeks earlier could spontaneously combust into passionate wildfire was lost as resolutely as a dime chilling in a winter snowbank. There was no point in deliberating or groveling to try and ignite one last spark of lightning in our shared bottle. That last spark had been consumed, and nothing was left now but cold, gray ashes, and I could sense a chill closing in around the phone booth. She agreed to meet during Christmas break to discuss our future together. When I did visit her, we tried to establish a normal platonic relationship, but we both seemed fidgety and distracted, a constant reminder of something missing.

One's life never follows a straight line from beginning to end. The geometry of human existence is far too imperfectly scribed by time and tide to allow a straight line into its intricate system of laws. For two years I drifted aimlessly in the shadow of my loss, and I flogged my own back with thorny branches of my own invention. Riding a narrow mountain ridge, I jumped from one crest to another, avoiding the valley at all cost. Truly, my path had become a skill to be nurtured. Executing time carefully allowed gentle continuous progression—as I turned the volume of life slowly up to ten, then eleven, and then twelve. And that was alright. The alternative became unthinkable. Miss a curve in the road and the decline might not be fatal, but it could entail serious stumbles and falls. In the dawning of my realization, there was simply no time to be traveling east on a westbound highway any longer...or to spend one more night sitting on a broken carousel waiting for the horses to begin to move again.

Ours was very nearly the different kind of relationship that I imagined burning with a clear furious energy for years to come, but that fall I had rolled the dice and instead of seven, they came up snake eyes. Simply holding her in my arms brought the best and most exciting moments of my life back to me in a flood. Vagueness and confusion filled my life for more days than I imagined before that shadowy bellyache healed completely.

Then, when I least expected it, the passion that I imagined vanishing forever from my life reappeared like a flash. Through the service window to the Yardarm Restaurant in the Treasure Island Hotel, a blinding light appeared while I was mixing a whiskey sour on the rocks. It took nearly six years, but in that fleeting instant, the fog vanished and a Yankee lady with the smile of a goddess and angel eyes illuminated my path to the future.

Chapter 19

The Turkey Trip in Atlanta

Two brothers...two musicians...one future...one dream. For two ordinary brothers, this geometry could easily have driven a competitive wedge between the two. But these were not ordinary brothers and the term "sibling rivalry" was nowhere to be found in their phraseology. From the onset of their musical career, Duane and Gregg Allman would go out into their world each day and strive to surpass what they had accomplished the day before. Chasing a life obscured by smoke and mirrors, the brothers cautiously worked their way through a veritable Rubik's Cube of musical genres, learning early that the ticket to the top was combining their exemplary talents with their inherent originality. The brothers were stylistically unparalleled by their peers, but for years conditions and venues rarely improved—but somehow their music always did.

The music industry will draw all the lines it wants, but there is only one clear path to the top, and the brothers instinctively knew the manner in which to advance their passion. As far back as I can remember, Duane and Gregg were never conventional musicians. They were always the Swiss Army knife of local musicians, but their breaks came slowly and their struggle never stopped. For the two brothers, there was invariably another town and another stage down the road. Their goals were like the horizon that they admired but could never quite reach. Duane and Gregg could only aim whatever band they played with toward their true north and admire the prize as they drew closer. They were determined from the start that their stage presence would embrace no heroics or cool-guy postures. The road to the top would be slow, thoughtful, and oftentimes painful. Still, Duane and Gregg knew that the road to the pinnacle of the music industry would take them through a series of chess games...not rugby.

Their musical perspective took more than a decade and thousands of rugged, lonely miles to reach. Then, one afternoon, with equipment crammed into the dining room of a rented hippie house on the south side of Jacksonville, everything they had worked for unfolded before them. The brothers knew instantly that they had found the sound that they had been chasing toward that unreachable horizon, and the sun rose brightly on a new day. Who better to show us a new genre of true Southern music than two musicians who, after all, had lived for a melody line that only the two carried in their hearts. That fateful afternoon, jamming with what would be their destiny in Jacksonville, everything jelled, and the brothers knew immediately that all of their hard work, searching, and hours on the road had finally been rewarded.

Without hesitation, they packed their Econoline Van and headed north. Capricorn, Macon, and a new music-based religion were waiting, and the second piece of their life-sized puzzle slipped into place. As spring turned to summer, there was still much work ahead, but their goal was becoming as clear as Duane's vision. The summer of 1969 turned to fall as the band created a history for themselves across the Southeast and beyond. They worked the dives of New Orleans, up through the Delta, and wound their way through the northern reaches of Georgia and extended their reach farther, into the chasms of New York City and the barrooms of Long Island and Boston. They never forgot their loyal, local audiences, stopping in Daytona, Jacksonville, Orlando, Tampa, Miami, and every town in between that would have them. The band grew tighter and closer by the day, testing the limitless bounds of their newfound musical spirituality.

November of 1969 brought the release of their first album with their new band and with it the earth, moon, and stars aligned and their trajectory appeared limitless. Even the winter chill and relatively lackluster record sales didn't impede their tireless advance forward. While other touring bands closed up shop and warmed their feet up by the fire until the spring festival season, the Brothers kept up their relentless schedule, playing anywhere and everywhere that hungry ears beckoned. The band's buzz spread across the South like wildfire. This was the destiny that Duane had visualized from the beginning. He and Gregg advanced to meet their musical future, instead of waiting for it to come and pluck them off an empty stage back in Daytona Beach.

Languishing in a kind of bizarre parallel universe located just two short hours up Interstate 85 from Atlanta, Georgia, there was a budding hippie striving to chart his own path forward. Agonizing in solitary confusion in the small university town of Clemson, South Carolina, I leveraged academia for its own destiny and possibilities. In 1969, the distance between Clemson and Atlanta was more realistically measured in years than by the ticking of a wristwatch. Chances are fair to middling that today the differences remain likewise similar. In retrospect, it would be hard to imagine two cities more dissimilar in 1969, however, there were a smattering of striking resemblances.

Atlanta miraculously raised itself up from the ashes of its Civil War nightmare to reimagine itself as the rising Southern star of the Peach State. In her own devastating nightmare, Clemson's entire physical manifestation was jeopardized by hundreds of feet of hydroelectric floodwaters in the 1950s. Plans had been drawn and work was underway to create a Duke Power Company reservoir where the town of Clemson and the university stand today. The reservoir threatened to submerge both beneath hundreds of feet of Savannah River floodwater. Clemson University and the neighboring community were spared annihilation by an engineering marvel in the form of an intricate, innovative dike system surrounding the campus and town, thus protecting them from the newly established Lake Hartwell Reservoir.

By the time I was a first-semester sophomore at Clemson in the fall of 1969, Atlanta had become an astonishingly diverse microcosm of counterculture lifestyles, particularly for a Southern city established so resolutely in the traditions of the Old South. Clemson's shoes dragged slowly through the Carolina red clay. Begrudgingly, the state and its citizens were slowly following suit, though with a less conspicuous contingent of hippies, flower children, and free-spirited students. Generally speaking, though, most of the free spirits at Clemson University hailed from well outside of the rural South.

A healthy bohemian, free-thinking lifestyle slowly spread across college campuses all throughout the United States, fueled, in part, by the antiwar sentiment during the Vietnam conflict. Traditional Southern, khaki- and oxford-wearing, Weejun-shod Clemson students began hungering to slip into bell-bottoms, flowered shirts, and huarache sandals to test those waters.

Clemson nourished two prominent communities of hippies during the late 1960s. However, small communities of like-minded students eventually began to advance into this traditional Southern college community even in university-owned student housing. Clemson's conclave that most closely resembled a traditional hippie commune was the gentle people inhabiting the Clayton House. That historic house occupied a heavily wooded property located at 107 Dogwood Drive in the centermost lot of the dogwood- and azalea-studded former faculty housing district. The Clayton House did not simply materialize out of the crisp mountain air as Clemson's famous "Hippie House." It began its long transformation as a modest three-room structure in the early 1900s. By the late '60s, when the heads and hippies moved in, the Clayton House had grown through additions into a massive ivy-covered brick structure encompassing twelve student apartments as well as bathrooms, kitchens, and other common spaces. Professor Clayton, an architecture professor in the early 1900s, bought and then added to the original three-bedroom structure. The now-rambling house eventually became the first "rooming house" of its kind, to accommodate architecture students, when students were first permitted to live off-campus. By 1969, the Clayton House had transformed itself into the genteel focal point of Clemson's counterculture lifestyle. Uncommonly tranquil, these apartments became the most sought-after housing units for hip Clemson students, with openings only coming at graduation, if then.

Visitors to the Clayton House were met by a tapestry of stippled sunlight filtering through a huge canopy of pastoral oaks. The vague murmur of stringed instruments and the delicate scent of marijuana wafting from the apartment windows above painted a beckoning canvas. Comfortable overstuffed chairs and cushions of every color spilled out from the common areas onto the mossy-brick walkways and ancient gardens that surrounded the old house. It was "The Place" near campus to meditate, explore life, and scrutinize the universe.

The other major conclave of transplanted hippies spread like summer molasses through a strip of ancient farmhouses that backed up to the Southern Crescent railroad track just beyond the Highway 123 overpass, beyond Clemson's city proper. Elm Street's small one- and two-bedroom, craftsman-style cottages with wraparound porches lined both sides of that bucolic lane and were ideal for free-spirited students with space and impunity on their minds. Those small cottages gradually became populated by shaggy-haired college kids weary of dormitory constrictions who longed for a place to groove with some elbow room. Elm Street was, on a nice day, in easy walking distance from the campus, and the Southern Crescent served as an ever-present alarm clock for slackers who relished their sleep. The residents kept sleepy porch dogs, Cheshire cats, as well as the odd chicken or domestic duck. Soon, this quiet lane became populated on both sides of the street by agreeably minded, bell-bottom-clad longhairs, peasant-dress-wearing hippie chicks, and less conventional South Carolina students edging toward a laid-back lifestyle—allowing their hair to curl beyond their ears. Vegetable and herb gardens of every description began dominating the landscape around homes that sported windows billowing with brightly colored tie-dyed window curtains. Carole King, Dylan, Donovan, CSNY, Traffic, the 5th Dimension, and the Youngbloods all shared turntables with a relatively new group from Georgia, The Allman Brothers Band. A balm of sweet patchouli oil, ganja, and pungent purple incense danced like smoke ring angles on the lightest breeze.

Atlanta's interurban "Strip" community stood in refined contrast to the Clayton House and Clemson's countrified Elm Street neighborhood. Clemson's counterculture communities attempted a similar, elegant sophistication, but Atlanta's Strip was the counterculture equivalent of a twenty-four-hour state fair the size of New York City. The wide-eyed action was pedal to the metal, nonstop, and all-inclusive for those who passed through its turnstile.

In those days, Atlanta's Strip took shape on Peachtree Street near the Krystal and the Middle Earth Head Shop. By 10th Street, the Strip was percolating intensely. In these middle blocks there was the obligatory drugstore that offered hungry denizens of the night twenty-four-hour, ninety-nine-cent breakfasts. The Strip continued to pulsate until about 12th Street. Beyond 12th, the Strip began exhausting itself, slowly dissipating to around 24th Street...the freaky people's shortcut to Piedmont Park.

The Strip was more than a hippie gathering place and head shop-infused group of city blocks. It was the place for the hip crowd to be seen and to carry on the overt or covert business of its community. Of course, there were a plethora of hippies along the Strip, but the sidewalks were also populated by all forms of hipsters, hawkers, outlaws, pimps, dealers, Jesus freaks, rednecks, bikers, Hare Krishnas, and even followers of the Guru Maharishi. Young teen hippie street urchins, eager to scale the financial ladder, sold the *Great Speckled Bird* weekly tabloid on street corners. Hawkers, peaceniks, and thieves were all unified under a singular banner of peaceful cooperation.

For me, no trip to Atlanta in the '68, '69, '70 era was complete without a stop to explore the wonders of the Strip. Free weekends away from the rigors of studying and a car to get me anywhere within driving distance of ten dollars' worth of gas often morphed into trips to Atlanta for a night or two. Those trips became increasingly frequent during the summer and fall of 1969. Though I had an aunt and welcoming cousins in Atlanta, I often traveled incognito into the bowels of that hippie community, making the Strip my home away from school. I sometimes crashed in a spare room at the editing house for the *Great Speckled Bird* magazine on 14th Street, a block from Piedmont Park. "The Bird" was a counterculture publication that was the only local source for news beyond the conventional media. People around Atlanta, in North Georgia, and the surrounding states depended heavily on the Bird .

The best way to navigate the Strip and not miss anything, or anyone, was to find a suitable place to stash your car and then to burn shoe leather. There was much to see, as the Strip was a bustling commercial ganglion connecting everyone of interest to the counterculture community. In its heyday, there were shops on both sides of Peachtree Street where locals and visitors could buy and sell items unique to the community's needs. Shops carried daily necessities such as rolling papers, pipes, sandals, clothes, candles, incense, black light posters, *Zap* comic books, and other counterculture literature. Much of the inventory sold on the Strip was handmade or recycled by local craftsmen and artists, targeting well-off suburban followers and counterculture wannabes. There were also drugs, both harmful and benign, if you knew which rock to kick. The Strip was where the straight and hip worlds merged effortlessly together in commerce, becoming the Greenwich Village of the South. Like the Pied Piper, the Strip also drew young ears to the center of Atlanta's burgeoning music scene, pulling musically minded people deeply into that vibe.

Undeniably, live music brought shape and form to Atlanta's nightlife, and much of that music was born deep in Atlanta along the Strip. Musicians from all over the Southeast were instinctively drawn into Atlanta's swirling undertow of prophecy unfulfilled. The Allman Brothers and Goose Creek Symphony were regulars playing free concerts in Piedmont Park on clear Sunday afternoons. Eric Quincy Tate (EQT) and a young Lynyrd Skynyrd band, as well as other local bands such as Hydra, the Hampton Grease Band, Kudzu, and Darrell Rhodes, played nightly at clubs like the Bowery. The remnants of both Roy Orbison's Candymen and Dennis Yost's Classics IV were about to find their way together to form a new Atlanta super-group, the Atlanta Rhythm Section. There was always something musical happening twenty-four/seven. If visitors couldn't find what they wanted in the clubs, there were always impromptu jam sessions popping up in whatever city park or empty building had electric power and at least one unlocked door or gate. The complexity and creativity of these fledgling Atlanta musicians continues to amaze and inspire generations of musicians. Some never made their way out, making Atlanta their permanent home. Others returned to their native turf with a hip pocket full of knowledge, while others scattered their musical prosperity to the wind, embracing communities all over the United States.

Early in my first year in college, I discovered that if a person lusted for top-shelf live entertainment, Clemson, South Carolina, was definitely not the place to spend your Saturday night. Two hours away, Atlanta's music scene was exploding, and Atlanta was just close enough to Clemson for a quick musical road trip. My generation knew full well how fortunate we were to come of age in such a flourishing musical microcosm. We watched on mostly black-and-white television screens as the Beatles arrived, pushing surf rock to the side while thoughtfully allowing folk rock and protest music their space. During that time, we experienced a swelling of soul and jazz and the unavoidable emergence of psychedelic and acid rock. In the days when we owned transistor radios instead of smart phones, we became instantly excited by whatever emerged from one small six-inch speaker in the dashboards of our car. Back then, if a person wanted to know which direction the wind was blowing, they would listen to their radio. Music began to explode in directions that became almost incomprehensible.

The Allman Brothers' eponymous album was released on November 4th of 1969. Try as I would, I could not get the disc jockeys at Clemson's university-owned radio station, WSBF (lovingly nicknamed "whizzbiff"), to play any of the music from Duane and Gregg's first Allman Brothers album. To know that the Allmans' promo album was resting, unplayed, on a shelf in WSBF's studio and that someone had arbitrarily determined that it wasn't worthy of sharing was just one more reason that I eventually decided that I had been barking up the wrong educational tree.

My nightly conversations with WSBF's program director usually went something like this:

(PD) "Hello?"

(Me) "Yes. Can you play something from The Allman Brothers' new album? All my buddies and I would sure like to hear some of that music, and *Rolling Stone* magazine is saying it's pretty interesting."

(PD) "You're kidding, right? We don't play that kind of crap. We're a popular music station. How about I play something by Creedence Clearwater, Strawberry Alarm Clock, or the Tams instead?"

This was the usual response from whichever unenlightened program director or disc jockey answered the phones in the studio three floors above my dorm room. Frustration abounded.

Then one day I got the word that the Allmans' debut album was available in Clemson's campus bookstore. I flew down eight flights of stairs with a week's worth of beer money clenched tightly in my hand to buy my very own, personal copy. I probably didn't need to run...mine may have been the only copy they sold that week. No matter, I barely touched the stairsteps on my way down to the bookstore. Shortly, I was back in my room, trailed by a gaggle of like-minded friends, including the members of my college band. The cost of my very own permanent piece of The Allman Brothers history was...$4.79.

We quickly settled into my dorm room, where everyone waited anxiously for me to drop the needle on the shiny disc, still encased in mystery and cellophane. The album cover, like a religious relic, slowly made its way around the room, where Stephen Paley's photography left a room full of college sophomores thunderstruck. The photographer's flair for pairing the emotional tension of the music with his photographic art was exceptional here. The entire album was purposely underexposed, which lent an honest air of mysterious uncertainty to the band.

After we all had digested the cover for clues and information, the folding jacket was put to good use as some uncombed herb was cleaned and readied for the big bong. Nobody was thirstier than me to find out what Duane and Gregg had morphed into from the Hour Glass, but first things first. When the audience settled in comfortably and was amply buzzed, I took a deep breath and set my stereo's tone-arm mechanism into motion. It seemed as if the pops and crackles coming from my speakers would never become music, but when they finally did, nothing in my mental database prepared me for the initial bars of "Don't Want You No More." The music surged through my speakers, literally enveloping my dorm room and rattling each of us to the bone. *The Allman Brothers Band* tested forevermore my capacity to listen judicially to almost any other music of that time. A wondrous new genre of music drenched the walls of my room in a rich, textured coat of musical notes. Like disappearing ink, when one song concluded, we were straining our senses to hear more.

The Allman Brothers' initial release was so incredibly different from anything that I had ever heard that it was as if the band had developed a new musical vocabulary all their own. The Brothers were gnat's-ass tight, and the twin guitars rang out like conjugal visit bells to lascivious convicts. Gregg's passionate, smoky vocals challenged the two drummers and single bass player to drag his audience toward an unseen cliff. He reached out with a velvet hand stretching out as far as possible and then stepped out into space, drawing us all into "It's Not My Cross to Bear." The gravel-throated, wolf-howl scream kicking off "Cross to Bear" still rattles me every time I hear it. Quickly following the opening couplet, "Black Hearted Woman" and "Trouble No More" redefined rock and roll and blues forever in my music dictionary. Those initial four cuts blossomed into a roadmap to the very future of Southern music.

Flipping the album over and threading it anxiously back over the spindle, we discovered more of the same on side two, in one sense—but, in reality, there was *so* much more. "Every Hungry Woman" opened our ears to call-and-response, twin-guitar harmonies and more of Gregg's whiskey- and gravel-drenched vocals. It was apparent that there would be no stopping their vision and drive. Next, "Dreams" unfolded, stretching out melodically like graceful satin sheets barely touching a curvaceous silhouette. The magic carpet ride that The Allman Brothers hijacked us on with "Dreams" wove a musical tapestry that floated in the air delicately like the blue-gray smoke of fine Indian incense. Then, jarring us all awake from our mental dreamscape, "Whipping Post" took flight, destroying the delicate, smoke-ring magic of "Dreams" in a most intoxicating way. "Whipping Post" became the final dance of the night, at which time the album was hastily flipped back over and the roller coaster left the station once again.

Like spontaneous combustion, we all became instantaneous, lifelong fans of an as-yet-unseen band whose live sound was still shrouded in musical mystery. Another more profound change took place, but only in those of us who were musicians on that day. I watched self-doubt quickly enter the eyes of my musician friends as each track trumped the one before it. Right then, to one degree or another, we all began considering our wherewithal and worth as accomplished musicians. A musician's lot in life, unfortunately, is to compare himself to other musicians—penis envy of the most insidious nature. From that point on, no matter what I thought of my personal ability as a musician or how much I enjoyed watching an audience light up when I played, I knew that for me, music was never going to be more than a ship that had left the dock without me while I occupied myself by filling out college applications.

All my college friends knew about the Hour Glass and my earlier ongoing relationship with Duane and Gregg, because that vinyl was always in constant rotation on my changer. If my friends sat still for more than a moment, they would be regaled by story after war story about the glory days of my early music career back home. Some were football stars or track stars, and I had the Allmans. They knew the pride I felt knowing Duane and Gregg, so I found it hard to admit to any of them that I was initially deeply shaken by what I had heard on that first Allman Brothers album. The music blindsided me with its raw grittiness like nothing I had ever heard before from the brothers. Regulating my mind to this incredibly different music was going to take some work. No matter how many times or how hard I listened, I could find little or no Hour Glass in those notes. Like a junkie, it took me some time to become comfortable with the frightening edge of the newfound music hidden between the grooves of that album, but still I came back again and again for more. The addiction was all-encompassing and complete.

Inflamed by the Allmans' initial recording, the entire conversation quickly turned to finding a way to hear The Allman Brothers Band "live." I knew that catching a live show was just a matter of time and an itch that would require attention. What the others didn't understand, but I knew from past experience, was that whatever Duane and Gregg produced in the studio was a mere trickle of the raging flood storm that their live shows promised to deliver. I was ready, willing, and able to face that flood...or so I thought.

By November of 1969, I had spent fifteen months in the musical wasteland that was Clemson, South Carolina. I was beyond ready for a serious road trip to hear some music, just as long as it didn't include the omnipresent Carolina beach music. Any worthwhile road trip would do, but if it involved hearing The Allman Brothers Band, so much the better. I knew full well that there was not a snowball's chance in hell that they would be playing a concert in Clemson anytime soon, unless they learned some Top 40 hits of the day...doubtful. When my first opportunity to hear the band came, the show was beyond my wildest dreams.

The Old Florida Rum Company was the name of the college band that I played with in South Carolina during the fall of 1969. That entire band was anxious to hear The Allman Brothers after listening to their first album. Hearing my war stories added a personal note to the prospective adventure. By the fall of 1969, I hadn't seen my old friend and music hero, Duane, to talk to since he had nearly tantalized my guitar player, Ralph Bundy, into trading a Les Paul for Ralph's Stratocaster in the late summer of 1968. With all the mind changes brought on by college and life's swinging gates, the jams back in 1968 seemed at once like distant memories. The two brothers and I had missed each other on multiple trips back home, and now they had become bona fide, five-star celebrities. The Allman Brothers Band had played at least three dates back in my hometown of Daytona Beach during the eight months from their inception to the first album release: one at the Ocean Pier; one at my old high school, Seabreeze Senior High; and one at the old National Guard Armory.

Hearing stories about their Daytona Beach shows that I had missed that year from Ringo and my hometown music buddies just sparked my interest and eagerness all the more to wade deep into a live concert. What little I knew about The Allman Brothers to that point I had basically learned from Ringo, *Rolling Stone Magazine*, and the Daytona Beach music grapevine. Without exception, my lighthouse for unadulterated information about Duane and Gregg was always Ringo. She saw them each and every time that they were back in town and searched everyone, everywhere for any information about "her boys" when they were on the road. Every musician who worked on the Martinique stage was part of "Ringo's boys," but Duane and Gregg were a step above the rest. From day one, Ringo had lavished Duane and Gregg with affection, and they felt it. Duane and Gregg returned her affection in kind. So, whenever I was home, I looked up Ringo first for the latest dope.

In addition to keeping me in the know whenever I was back from school, no matter how briefly, Ringo was also my primary source for stop-gap employment to keep a poor college kid afloat between classes. Anytime I showed up at the back door, Ringo always found something for me at the Martinique: filling in for a drafted drummer, tending bar, working the door, working security, building a lighted dance floor, or even repairing plumbing and mopping floors. That marvelous lady invariably found some way for me to make a little money whenever I needed some cash...anytime, that is, but the Thanksgiving break of 1969.

That Thanksgiving break, I planned to stay in Clemson for the week prior to Thanksgiving, determined to redirect my academic trajectory from the quiet solitude of A-828, my dorm room. I desperately needed to immerse myself in missed study opportunities and unread assignments in preparation for the semester finals that were just three weeks away. I was not entirely happy to be stranded by myself in a bleak, deserted dormitory, studying and listening with one ear to the door for footsteps echoing down the linoleum hallway. The majority of my friends and classmates were heading home to be with families, decompressing and feasting together in warm houses. Sadly, my intention was to pay penance for slacking off, and I needed to make up for missing classes and chapters unread from that fall. Normally, I would pack my car at the slightest hint of a long weekend to join my family and old friends gathered back in Daytona Beach. Beyond reconnecting old friendships, my mother's cooking was legendary and she never failed to send me back to school with a less-than-epic "care package" of homemade cakes, holiday cookies, and other goodies whenever I returned to school. This holiday, finals loomed large against a short time frame, and I was steadfast in my struggle to cling to a renewed determination for success. As tempting as my mother's Thanksgiving dinner table would surely be, I was dedicated to putting in some much-needed hours studying. So, I resisted the urge to drive eight hours home and then a few days later drive the same eight hours back to school with nothing to show except a full belly and slipping final grades. My plan was to bury myself in books and martyr myself to uninspired dining hall fare, celebrating Thanksgiving with Campbell's Turkey Noodle Soup and bologna sandwiches.

My plan and willpower stood unwavering until the Saturday morning before Thanksgiving when Bill Laffoday slipped onto the eighth floor and threw a live hand grenade through my open door. Like a runaway midnight milk truck crashing through a living room uninvited, Laffoday burst through my door dragging John Adams behind him, chanting lyrics from "Riders on the Storm." Until that unsettling moment, I wasn't aware that Laffoday was even on campus. His family lived less than two hours away in Charlotte, so I assumed that he would be at home celebrating Thanksgiving week there.

Adams's family lived in Laredo, Texas, but unless our band was practicing or gigging, I rarely heard from John. He was normally as unassuming as bathroom wallpaper, and if he had been just carrying in a book or two to quietly read, he would have been more than welcome. While moderately irritated, I wasn't terribly surprised to see Adams show up. Still, I knew that I had to get them out of my room or I would never get back to studying. I also knew that Laffoday meant trouble. Laffoday always meant trouble.

Bill Laffoday was my band's kaleidoscopic lead guitar player and John Adams shared lead and rhythm duties unobtrusively on guitar. John, in his wire-rimmed glasses, had a soft-spoken, studious, professorial appearance and usually kept to himself unless chemically stimulated, which instantly assured him, to the point that he considered himself longtime friends with perfect strangers. John's perennial corduroy jacket, sporting dark elbow patches, added to his serious professor-like appearance, but upon closer inspection, his perpetually burnished, blood-reddened eyes revealed the true nature of his character.

Laffoday was undeniably the most flamboyant musician I have ever had the pleasure to work with. I had worked with more than one cleverly camouflaged peacock over the years, but Laffoday was the whipped cream and maraschino cherry that crowned that particular sundae. His deportment consisted of one thundering exclamation point after another. He used his swagger, good looks, and long, straight blond surfer mop to accent the physicality of his well-rehearsed demeanor. Laffoday never passed an inhospitable mirror.

So, as I was funneling notes and information together in preparation for a week's laborious studying, in through my door rudely exploded two friends cleverly disguised as a carload of circus clowns. In typical fashion, Laffoday wordlessly made a quick lap around my room, took in the sights, and then dropped a week-old *Great Speckled Bird* newspaper into the center of my semester's research. The paper was conspicuously opened to a page containing a huge advertisement for a weekend-long music festival in Atlanta called the Turkey Trip, circled twice in yellow highlighting marker. The Turkey Trip, I deduced, was happening this very weekend in Atlanta. The mini-music festival was scheduled for Friday and Saturday night at an empty Duke Tire warehouse on the corner of 11th Street and Peachtree Street, right along my beloved "Strip." Today being Saturday, the Friday night show was already music history, but there was enough time, they insisted, to put together a quick road trip to Atlanta, if there were willing takers.

"No, No, No—Hell, No!" was my first reaction. "Don't even start that shit with me," I begged, looking up quickly from the yellowing journal to assess the power of my proclamation, which was beginning to sound more like a plea than a proclamation, even to me.

"I'm here this week to study and that's what I intend to do...ALL WEEK LONG! THAT'S IT! Don't try to talk me into going anywhere. It's just not going to happen," I proudly insisted, with an unusual flair and determination.

After scanning the advertisement one more time for more information about the bands booked, I continued sheepishly, "Just for shits and giggles, what time does the music start tonight?" I asked, casually looking at my watch and scanning the paper again, inspecting for otherwise concealed information.

Then it happened: the tiniest of cracks began to form in my unshakeable armor. "I'm just curious, you know, if there is even the slightest chance that we can make it down there in time for the show and make it back tonight? That way I would have all day tomorrow to finish my preparation. Shit, I'd really like to hear The Allman Brothers!"

My words trailed off and I looked up to see how serious Laffoday and Adams were as they both hustled toward my door. The last words I heard from Laffoday as I started scanning my closet for something clean to wear were..."So, we'll take that as a yes. And if we're going to do this, we'll have to check with Rob Sands to see if he's game."

Robert Roy Sands, aka Rob the Cowardly Lion, played bass in the Old Florida Rum Company, and a more in-the-moment, party animal had never populated the hallowed halls of Clemson University. Rob's New England accent followed him to the Palmetto State, making it nearly impossible for him to pronounce the letter "A" without dragging that lowly vowel out into three excruciatingly long syllables somehow resembling "oull." My roommate's last name was Alden, and he forever became Ed Ooouuulllden to Rob. Never mind that his bushy, dirty blond hair, mustache, and conjoined mutton chop sideburns rendered him the perfect camera double for Bert Lahr's Cowardly Lion from the Wizard of Oz. His uncanny resemblance gave Rob no choice but to live his life in character. Rob had been banished from the dorms, but he and a like-minded roommate, Craig Ellifson, rented a trailer on the outskirts of Clemson on the Central Highway, with their own phone, so it was easy to get an enthusiastic, "Oh, hell, yah!" from Rob on the concert road trip to Atlanta.

Less than two hours later, a car packed with four long-haired musicians looking to burn their first doobie of the day while swilling Ripple wine and blasting music from my eight-track tape player were headed up the I-85 on ramp toward Hotlanta. Thankfully, Atlanta and the Strip were only two bottles of Ripple and a couple of eight-tracks away. What could possibly go wrong?

Two hours later on the dot, we pulled off I-85 at the downtown Atlanta exit and wound our way quickly around to Peachtree Street and then headed in the direction of 14th Street. The first order of business was to visit the little family grocery around the corner from the *Great*

Speckled Bird house for additional bottles of Pagan Pink Ripple wine. Then we headed back outside into the fall air to buy a twenty-cent copy of the Bird from the hippie kid on the corner. With that done, we drove back around to the Bird House and asked if there was room for four tonight. As was normally the case, the editor obliged with a smile and a nod. We deposited two fat joints and one of our three bottles of Ripple on his desk, and leaving the car parked out front, we headed out into the night on foot.

Saturday's version of the Turkey Trip featured a smorgasbord of hot Atlanta bands opening for The Allman Brothers Band, including special guests the Knowbody Else band, who subsequently changed their name to Black Oak Arkansas. The Hampton Grease Band was slated to warm the stage next, and finally, The Allman Brothers Band was scheduled to finish the night as the headliners.

As was often the case in those days of sketchy promoters, questionable venues, itinerant start times, and uncertain lineups, concerts were often painted in interesting shades of unpredictability. Shortly after starting our trek up the Strip in the direction of the tire warehouse, where the show was supposed to be held, my buddies and I learned that the venue that we were marching toward had been condemned hastily by the city in an attempt to thwart another "devil-music extravaganza."

The act of condemning buildings in an effort to prevent music shows had become such a commonplace occurrence in Atlanta that we weren't at all surprised by the political move, though we were disappointed. Promoters and fans learned to roll with the punches, so it didn't take long to get the hot tip about the relocated show. The location had been hastily migrated to the ballroom in the Georgian Terrace Hotel across the street from the Fox Theatre in downtown, which actually turned out to be a bonus. Unfortunately, start time was also moved up from 8:00 P.M. to 6:00 P.M., and the admission price exploded through the roof from two dollars to three, which, in fact, drove some away. The change in location posed us a minor logistics problem, but the time change had us double-timing it back to my car in order to catch any of the opening acts. Time was tight, and the show was probably three bands into the night in downtown Atlanta. So, instead of blocks away, the Georgian Terrace Hotel was miles.

As luck would have it, we made it to the Georgian Hotel and found parking in the back just in time to hear the final jarring, disharmonic notes of the Hampton Grease Band as we lined up outside of the door that led to the admission table. It would be another fifty-four years before I would see Col. Bruce Hampton again. The next Bruce Hampton show for me would be in 2014 at the Holiday Hootenanny at Little Five Points in Atlanta. His final notes at the Hootenanny rang similarly outlandish to the ones I heard at the Turkey Trip, but that was Bruce's shtick. Regardless that we missed nearly three hours of music, in our minds the admission charged was calculated from the first notes of The Allman Brothers Band. All the other music was simply bows and lace on someone else's wedding gown.

We stumbled over each other as we handed over our three dollars to an incredibly statuesque apparition at the door, dressed in a lavishly embroidered chiffon peasant dress. Her costume was accented with hand-sewn glass beads that matched the multiple strands of love beads that disappeared mysteriously into her generous cleavage. We were all jockeying to make inroads until the mountainous security guard/bouncer/boyfriend fresh from the local gym asked us to kindly keep moving, which we all gladly agreed to do, except for Laffoday. Finally, we urged him to break off his romantic interest as we pushed him through the hallway, which opened into the right-hand corner of the large rectangular ballroom.

No tables or chairs were available, and there was nothing but elbows and security guards close to the stage, so we found a little space against the back wall where we watched as the roadies and stage crew busily made changes, readying the stage for The Allman Brothers. The room was packed well beyond capacity, but we planned to eventually snake up closer to the stage after the music started. Although as the crowd swelled, it was looking more and more like where we were was where we were going to be for the show. I assured the guys that the back of the room was an ideal vantage point from which to listen and watch the band. It was a big room but not huge, so we staked out our space against the back wall and waited for the fireworks. But none of us were prepared for the significance of what we were about to see and hear.

All the members in my band, like myself, had come from better-than-average, well-established, working bands from our respective hometowns. As a group of long-haired musicians invariably do, we found each other in a sea of crew-cut, khaki-clad preppies at Clemson. The first question invariably was "What do you play?" It didn't take us long to begin talking about putting a band together and amassing equipment from back home. Eventually, we commandeered a late-night practice space from a friendly music-department head who also made available full use of several good-sized auditoriums for free shows and concerts. We had free run of the place until we offered up the university to four thousand hippies as a suitable alternative space for a hurriedly cancelled anti-Vietnam War rally that was supposed to take place one weekend in Atlanta. That overstep considerably changed the timbre in the university's attitude toward the Rum Company and its members. We learned that day the hard way that there are downsides to the old myth that "It's always easier to beg forgiveness than to ask permission."

Bill Laffoday had spent some time playing with the Amboy Dukes in one of their earlier incarnations. The fact that Laffoday understudied Ted Nugent, the Sultan of Spectacle, came as no big surprise to any of us. Adams and Sands both had at least three years of continuous stage time before hauling their equipment to Clemson to join the Rum Company. Early in our relationship, I had regaled my prospective band with stories of Duane and Gregg from back in Daytona. I had bragged to my new bandmates that the Soul Patrol had opened for and played with the two brothers from time to time, which was becoming more and more impressive as their notoriety built from the Hour Glass to The Allman Brothers Band. What I failed to mention was that there were very few musicians from Daytona that had not worked or played with Duane and Gregg at some point in time. The Brothers rarely passed up an opportunity to sit in and jam with just about anyone, anytime. By the time we had all made it to our first Allman Brothers concert, Duane and Gregg had become bona fide rock stars. Quite naturally, my buddies were goading me to "prove" that I really knew them, and their insistence in that regard was unrelenting.

Thankfully, their coercing and nagging slacked off when the stagehands put the Hampton Grease Band to bed and made sure that Duane and Gregg's equipment was powered up and ready. Red Dog made a final sweep of the stage, checking everything. As he left the stage, I watched Red Dog deposit what looked like a small empty glass bottle and a few spare picks on the corner of Gregg's Hammond. From the same side of the stage, The Allman Brothers Band quietly and resolutely walked up from our left to take their places onstage.

Duane and Gregg appeared little changed from the way they looked the year before in Daytona. There is that blinding instant when you run into old friends who have become famous and a world of questions swirl through your mind. I had one such moment when I saw Duane onstage at the Turkey Trip.

"Would Duane find time to talk to a fellow musician from back home after the show?"

"Did Duane still lust over my guitar player's Stratocaster, the storied and deeply admired Duane Allman Strat?"

While my time had been adequately engaged for the past year, it was abundantly obvious that we were gauging time spent by two entirely different modes of determination. Duane and Gregg's year had been spent cresting the summit of Mount Everest while I had been meandering in the foothills. Upon listening to their recording, it was instantly obvious that they had found the musical voice that they had been searching for. This night, my friends and I were poised and ready to hear what their year on the road had condensed into, from the stage.

Unlike the Hour Glass's spartan stage setup, The Allman Brothers' equipment crowded the stage's capacity with Fender and Marshall amplifiers and speaker cabinets stacked, balancing like cordwood, against the drum riser just behind. It was as if each musician and roadie had brought four amps, and the monitors that fronted each microphone and musician were something entirely new to me. The band appeared confident and composed as Duane fine-tuned his guitar to Gregg's Hammond and tested his volume with a few of the same throwaway licks he had teased audiences with from the Martinique's stage back home. Gregg's hair was a bit longer, making him even more statuesquely handsome sitting intently at his Hammond B-3. Behind Gregg, a polished walnut Leslie cabinet hummed like a penned-up rodeo bull itching to release impatient notes on its audience. This being my first Allman Brothers concert, I knew the other four players only by reading their names on their record jacket and from what I had heard on that one album; I had yet to meet any of them. When the band was satisfied with their setup and tuning, Duane motioned to the side of the stage where the promoter of the weekend's shows was patiently waiting. It was his last chance to make announcements, promote other shows, and introduce the night's shining stars.

The promoter took to the stage, and it was soon apparent that he had a trainload of affection and appreciation for his headlining band. He confidently walked in front of Gregg's Hammond and carefully removed Duane's microphone from its stand, sliding the switch to the on position while Duane rested his arms on his Les Paul and took a step back to intently listen to what was said. The Allmans' were the weekend's headliners, so, as is normally the case, the promoter made a few housekeeping announcements and ran through a long list of bands to be thanked, not only for tonight's show but for the entire weekend as well. After offering that long list of recognitions by heart, he stopped, pausing for an extremely thoughtful moment, gathering his thoughts as he gazed into the dark recesses above the audience. The crowd was anxious, but it was clear that the promoter had something important to say, so the audience settled back, showing obvious respect. Bracing himself against the microphone stand with one hand, his voice became that of a seasoned radio announcer, taking on a thoughtful, deliberate tone as if to prepare us in advance for what would be a concert of exceptional merit.

When his introduction began to roll, he launched into a near sermon-like oration that remains, to date, the most sincerely heartfelt introduction of The Allman Brothers I've ever heard. When the promoter found his footing, he shared with nine hundred of his most intimate friends his thoughts about a group of musicians that he was unmistakably enraptured by.

"Atlanta is the home of The Allman Brothers. They're technically from Macon, Georgia, but Atlanta is their home, but if you remember last summer and last fall, some of the kinds of things that The Allman Brothers did for us...the free mini-festivals in Piedmont Park...a couple of gigs at the Georgian Terrace and some other times...The Allman Brothers can make things happen, and they're going to make things happen here tonight. The Allman Brothers play blues, and blues is traditionally the kind of thing that makes you feel a man's sorrow, but The Allman Brothers play the kind of blues that makes you feel happy, instead. They make you realize that, through their lyrics, we all have our blues, like everybody else...but with their music, they bring us back together into one, and make us feel good and bring us all back to one, with one another. This'll make up for a lot of music that hasn't happened lately, and people wonder why we don't have more concerts but this is it...(pause)...well...Welcome The Allman Brothers Band!"

With that, thunderous pent-up applause erupted like the top of a mountain blowing off as the promoter exited the stage to his right, tapping on Gregg's Hammond and nodding to Gregg in approval on his way off the stage. It would not be until the following summer at the Second Atlanta Pop Festival in Byron, Georgia, that I would recognize the promoter from the Turkey Trip as Alex Cooley, Atlanta's beloved Mayor of Music. Cooley went on to become the South's most courageous and successful promoter. A few years later, he transformed the Georgian Terrace Hotel's ballroom into "Alex Cooley's Electric Ballroom" and went on to feature The Allman Brothers Band prominently at the Second Atlanta Pop Festival the following July. Alex Cooley knew of what he spoke.

As the audience continued to applaud Cooley's introduction, Duane stepped up to his now-vacant microphone. As he nuzzled up to the mic, he raised his pick hand for a few words, and again the applause and impatient crowd noise subsided out of an abundance of respect.

Then Duane Allman's Southern-fried, baritone voice responded to Cooley's introduction: "The man says we play the blues and I guess that's partly true. We'd like to start with a blues for ya about Mama and that lamp that she turns down low."

Duane's voice finished his introduction, descending into the basement of his deepest bass baritone voice, dropping down rich and sweetly and stretching the word "low" into a three-syllable, semisweet stretch like summer taffy. Before he took another breath, Duane turned partially to the band, snapping the fingers of his left hand in time as I had heard him do a hundred times before, counting off their opening number. Instantly, the band belted out the first five notes of the first number in response, as Duane slid something onto his left ring finger, and magically we were hearing music played in a different language, a language that none of us could speak or begin to explain. The entire band repeated the opening five notes, again and again, while Duane's slide inserted aces and kings exactly where they were meant to be. Regardless of the number of times we had heard that first album, nothing amply prepared any of us for the musical anaconda that refused to give up its crushing death-grip on us for the next four hours.

As this initial firestorm unfolded into a slide guitar and blues-shuffle euphoria, this unrestrained group of musicians, The Allman Brothers Band, brought us immediately to a music genre entirely unimagined before. While still befuddled by what we were hearing from Duane, and before we could blink or comment, the other guitar player, Dickey Betts, joined the fray, trading straight guitar licks back and forth with Duane before melding like warm whiskey and syrup into a harmony guitar solo reminiscent of the Hour Glass's live "Dimples" harmonies between Duane and Paul Hornsby. Duane and Dickey left the Hour Glass in a dust cloud of fragmented musical notes.

The four of us became psychologically nailed against the back wall where we fought to breathe as Duane slipped the glass slide back onto his ring finger and led the band through a maze of previously uncharted guitar notes. Clearly, we were the only four people in the Georgian Terrace ballroom that night who were not familiar with the opening selection, because by the time the band was five notes in, the audience had broken into a frenzied bedlam that did not entirely subside until the band played the final note of their final song...some four hours later.

When that first tune finished, I turned to the excited stranger standing next to me and posed the rhetorical question, "What the hell was that?" To which the excited stranger replied, "That was f**king 'Statesboro Blues,' that's what that was!"

For four more hours The Allman Brothers laid down arrangement after incredible arrangement of mostly original, new-to-us, or simply unrecognizable covers of blues standards. We followed as best we could in blind confusion as there were no roadmaps marking the twists and turns on this new musical super-speedway. This band was running over newly laid blacktop at breakneck speed in exciting, uncharted directions. I had no idea what to expect next, but it was clear that The Allman Brothers Band had abandoned the Hour Glass band somewhere on the road between Macon and Atlanta.

Gregg found his voice in this new sect, and in the year since I had heard him play, his keyboard chops had increased tenfold. Duane was equally advanced, and he seemed well pleased and comfortable with Betts as a coequal counterpart. Both guitarists provided energy for the other to feed from as the two players led the band up a twisting mountain road, song after song, switchback after switchback. But as innovative as Duane, Gregg, and Dickey were, the rhythm section caught my ear not long after those intricate melody lines lost me in a firestorm of bluesy, razor-edged power rock.

It was the drums and bass that jumped out front and anchored the band, penetrating my body. Butch Trucks, Jai Johanny Johanson ("Jaimoe"), and Berry Oakley were nothing less than a relentless herd of charging buffalos. Those three balanced and complemented each other in endless counterpart of thunderous poetry. The entire band was otherworldly, and though we didn't know the names of many of the songs they played, we genuflected, kneeling at the altar of the passion involved in each and every composition. When it seemed like their first set was ending, we felt stripped bare and laid open, but we had to have more of this new music. We joined a new secret society of magnanimous fans, relenting our cool and joining in the bedlam. There simply had to be more and we joined in that call.

After almost two hours of nonstop, mind-bending music, Duane announced to the audience, "We're going to wipe the sweat off, so we'll be back in a few minutes."

The guys and I headed to the bathroom to offload some Ripple, and then, shaking our heads, we ventured out into the parking lot to recharge our batteries and to somehow talk about the first set. We each had our theories about the music, but frankly it was hard to make any sense out of what we had just heard. Listening to The Allman Brothers Band play live for the very first time was as if we had all mistakenly stumbled into a quantum physics class and the professor asked us to describe our thoughts on the subject before we could explain that we were looking for Freshman Bird Watching 101. We tiptoed through a minefield of adjectives for the next twenty minutes, but truth be known, we simply could find no words to describe the indescribable. Duane and Gregg's new band left us huddled like jabbering idiots, shaking our heads in the chilly parking lot.

The only explanation that I could offer was that back in Daytona Beach, right from the beginning, we all knew that this was the destiny that Duane and Gregg had chosen. Step by step, we knew that Duane and his brother would rise up to become an elemental component of the American music scene. And tonight, we were there to bear witness that The Allman Brothers' train was pulling out of the station and those driving the train waited for no one.

With our ears still ringing from two hours of nonstop music in overdrive, we tried our best to adjust our thought processes to this new musical vernacular. We soon found ourselves developing certain adaptive behaviors while in the presence of such amazing talent. The chief of these was glancing back over our shoulders toward the ballroom, listening intently for telltale musical notes as regularly and reflexively as a motorist driving down a bustling interstate highway might check the rearview mirror. So, a few sips of Ripple and a few tokes later, we begin to hear drummers testing the backbone of the stage and guitars tuning, which signaled that it was time to hustle back inside. It was time to listen to more of what it was that we did not understand. Back against our section of wall again, with one foot firmly on the floor and the other bracing us against the wall behind us, we were recharged and ready to follow these marauders wherever their music led.

The second set was a driving mixture of solid rock and slow jazzy blues, like "Stormy Monday," one of the few selections that we all recognized. Interestingly, when Duane and Gregg had the audience drawn into following them as they carefully laid out a smooth, melancholy, soft-sand blues, things would change in a matter of milliseconds. The band would allow the audience no rest, and they would instantly ignite another instrumental fuse, twining the two guitars with Gregg's nimble keyboards while the light show matched the intensity of each and every note. Each member of the band meshed together like teeth in a gear, fitting perfectly with the others and filling the exact sonic space that their instrument was built to occupy. As gracefully as a flock of starlings in a murmuration, the band moved as if connected together, twisting and turning and changing direction at a moment's notice so as to become all that was possible...no more, no less. Amazingly, though, as each member fluidly transitioned into a solo, that transition was as smooth as water slipping calmly over moss-covered rocks. The intensity would gradually increase, building into wild rapids before a profound change could be imagined.

The two drummers brought a tsunami of talent and virtuosic percussion while playing with a subtle concept that contributed not only to meter but the sheer power to positively impact the group. The bass player changed hats, becoming four musicians in one, as quickly and smoothly as a chameleon changes color: thundering bass one minute, delicate guitar counterpart the next. Then he unleashed unrelenting backing melody, segueing into thumping percussion whenever and wherever positive accents became necessitated. Of particular interest was the way the band would feature the bass player's melodic, chord-like bass lines and then unleash the "if you'll scratch my back, I'll scratch yours" percussion section, tearing at the audience like a pack of hungry wolves. Like no other bands of the day, The Allman Brothers Band accepted the rhythm section as full-blooded members of their congregation and not simply afterthoughts. Butch, Berry, and Jaimoe percolated and stewed like a concrete mixing truck driving along behind the band, blending their portion of each song to the right consistency until the time for them to lay a fresh foundation of bottom. Whenever that happened, the rest of the band stepped happily aside and allowed them as much elbow room as they required.

The second set continued with all the power and individuality as the first and the music flowed through my soul and beckoned me to it like a carnival barker. It was apparent that the brothers were making the music history that they promised, and I had been watching their parade form from the staging area. Listening to this new musical genre unfold was like trying to play catch on a wooden roller coaster. All any of us could do was to take in as much as the music gave us while struggling with the ever-increasing lateral momentum.

We shared a commonality of musical history, Duane, Gregg, and I, which went far beyond what happened during that four-hour concert and even beyond our history back in Daytona. It was the inter-mutual awareness of turning off a paved road into a gravel parking lot. We felt a common excitation build as our bands unloaded station wagons and vans full of equipment and gathered around each stage with each member staking out his space and territory for the night. I will always share the universal excitement derived from the journey to the destination. Everything that goes on before the gig and everything that happens afterward are part and parcel of the brotherhood of the road: from the drive to the show and the load-in of the equipment to the celebration after the performance, each new stage is an adventure, and each audience generates its own unique stimulation. We shared a unique brotherhood that only working musicians understand.

The three-dollar admission to the Turkey Trip bought far more than entrance to the Georgian Terrace Ballroom that night. I had, in effect, purchased a winning trifecta ticket: initiating my college band's first exposure to The Allman Brothers live while sharing in that initial exposure myself and experiencing the ultimate thrill of watching two of my hometown journeymen skyrocketing into the future of music with brothers of their own. The exhilaration was exhaustive and complete—comparable only to the exhilaration of standing naked against a full-bore Atlantic hurricane.

When I thought that the music had taken us as far into the future as possible, another bend in the road sprang forth from the minds of these geniuses and bowled us over like four duckpins balanced on the edge of time. Appearing like an apparition from the smoke and chaotic twisted finale and the bounding timpani cadence of one arrangement, there morphed a breakneck paradiddle drum roll, building into outrageous speed, performed by timpani and snare. The twin percussionists were soon joined by Duane, Dickey, Gregg, and Berry, slowly, one by one. When the smoke and musical confusion began to clear, what materialized was the vaguely familiar fifteen opening notes belonging to Donovan Leitch's popular composition "There Is a Mountain." Before I was able to fully purge my mind of the ethereal whisper of Donovan's opening flute lines, The Allman Brothers Band banished that translucent melody into the back of my mind forever.

The four of us could only stare at each other with an overwhelming wonder in our eyes while grinning ear to ear as we slowly began to realize that the trap was springing on a wondrous musical one-liner. Still, we stumbled to process just what we were hearing as the music led us onward through twists and turns beyond our wildest imagination. Total befuddlement, exasperated by the intoxicating audience buzz, sent us into a musical region far beyond our limited sphere of knowledge. The Allman Brothers Band guided us through the turnstile to Duane's own personal magic carpet ride.

Nothing about this renewed arrangement had anything even remotely to do with Donovan Leitch's composition with the exception of the first and the last fifteen lines. The orchestration changed direction as quickly and sharply as a block of Frank Lloyd Wright architecture. While always vaguely threatening to break back in the direction of the original theme, the music reached toward Mr. Leitch several times but could never connect. The theme from "There Is a Mountain" sustained its drive for well past an hour and had something for everyone in the audience, all of whom swelled and applauded wildly with each and every twist and turn.

"Mountain Jam," as it was dubbed, was without a doubt the longest continuous musical marathon I had ever witnessed outside of a full protracted symphonic performance. However, no traditional symphony in my experience ever played breakneck compositions offering a balls-to-the-wall, torrid music gumbo percolating on the highest burner. Duane removed any doubt that we might be lulled into snoozing as if we were before the Atlanta Symphony Orchestra.

Percussion? Oh, Hell, Yes! "Mountain Jam" was brimming over with percussion neatly folded into drum solos as Jaimoe and Butch flailed nonstop at breakneck speeds. They were quite literally the foundation of this composition. The two drummers traded licks in a focused hornet's-nest tsunami of subtle power and energy, positively controlling the intensity and dynamics of the entire band.

Berry Oakley wailed on his bass as if it were an indestructible six-string guitar on steroids, with all the melody and emotion of a virtuoso guitarist. He joined the two drummers during their solos, feeding on the intense interplay between the two. When Oakley joined the fray, the three became a melodic steamroller of tempo, percussion, and unison.

Gregg no longer played his Hammond B-3 with a traditional approach. He assaulted the instrument aggressively, demanding his own territory in the spatial arena. With Gregg's normal laid-back demeanor out the window, he aggressively violated notes not normally supported between the black and white keys.

Duane and Dickey stretched out, playing mostly straight guitar harmonies and individual solos until Duane once again picked up his slide from its resting place on Gregg's Hammond. That is the precise moment that the number charged into fourth gear, cruising wildly over the hilltops, applying the brakes only to tip his hat to Betts, as Duane's partner was handed the solo baton at a full gallop. At some point, from out of the melodic pandemonium, came the distinctive cry of a wounded bird from Duane's guitar as he played notes not found on any other fretboard anywhere in the world. The experience of hearing The Allman Brothers Band play for the first time brought with it countless indefinable musical experiences!

Another momentary nod to Donovan's theme flickered for an instant near the midmost portion of the piece, but it quickly morphed into a thin slice of "Will the Circle Be Unbroken," after which the jam continued on and on, picking up more speed while spinning in Bruce Hampton-style concentric circles. When it didn't seem possible to keep up the pace any longer, Duane and Dickey gave the percussionists a short reprieve with some chicken pickin' that didn't require much in the way of backing as they morphed into a twin guitar and bass-driven nod to Bo Diddley. While Dickey and Duane laid down the basic premise, Oakley churned tastefully in the background, never allowing the guitarists to step too far out on a weak limb alone. Soon the three explorers Bo Diddley'd their way back into the central theme, as Duane, Dickey, and Butch dragged the band back into the original melody, rejoining the others in a flutter of guitar and bass counterpoint. Quivering on a pinhead of bent-note harmonies, pulsing ripple-swing bass, flaming guitar, aggressive organ, and drum crescendo, these futuristic rhythm blasters played every note known to the Luther's craft, nodding here and there to some of their favorite musical influences until they finally conceded to the original Donovan melody, "There Is a Mountain." As the guitars harmonized, the finale drew them all together, climbing a short ladder, rung by rung, to the final note. The audience, which had by now become a congregation of faithful, became maniacal—partially from exhaustion and partly from a contact high generated by the band that we had all been watching for what had been, now, more than four hours.

The crowd noise and applause swelled like a land-falling hurricane. When the applause died back somewhat, a delighted Alex Cooley appeared back onstage. As he did, Duane, Dickey, and Berry were already tuning for what they knew would surely be their encore. Cooley asked for another hand as Duane gave him the thumbs-up sign. Then Cooley put the rest of the evening into the hands of the congregation: "How 'bout it? You want some MORE?" Cooley bellowed into the microphone. And the audience erupted once again.

Duane finished his tuning chores and took the microphone back and explained with an impish grin, "This next song we're going to do is a little bit out of character." Then he counted off the beginning song of the two-number couplet that opened their initial album that had been living on my turntable back at my dorm at Clemson. Those songs even the four of us recognized as we joined into the fray. The audience was treated to "Don't Want You No More" and "It's Not My Cross to Bear." As those songs rang out through the ballroom to everyone's enthusiastic approval, we all looked at each other, and it was then that my buddies and I felt that we had passed through the Atlanta initiation of the Allman Brothers fraternity.

We knew that this time the show was over when those two songs concluded. Truthfully, nobody could have possibly asked for anything more. The hour was late and we were all physically and mentally wasted, rendering us beyond the point of limping all the way back to Clemson. By this point, there was no need to hurry anywhere. The four of us froze at our vantage point against the back wall as we watched the audience file slowly out of the ballroom. Finally, as the room mostly cleared, Laffoday turned to me with a taunting stare that broke the uneasy silence, sneering, "Hey, Thames, if you really know those guys, why don't you give us a little verification. I'd like to meet that guitar player you say you know...the one with the glass finger."

To their collective amazement, I walked directly across the empty dance floor and hopped up on the small stage behind Duane, who was busy drying his guitar and putting his equipment to bed. I startled Duane, and one of the roadies started to hassle me, but Duane waved him off.

"So, what's happening back home," Duane asked, extending his hand, not vertically to shake it, but horizontally, palm up, to slap me five.

Duane and I spent some time catching up on friends that we both hadn't seen in a while, and just to irritate Laffoday, I didn't offer to introduce Duane to my three chums, now standing at the front edge of the stage with their tongues hanging out. Actually, I did little more than explain to Duane that this was my new band in South Carolina. I told him that this was the first Allman Brothers Band show for any of us and that the Donovan tune was simply beyond amazing! Duane smiled and said, "Yah, that'll sure catch you unawares, hearing it for the first time...Really liked it, did ya?"

"Yah," I replied, "Nothing tonight sounded in the least like the Hour Glass."

An emphatic "Good, man" was Duane's only reply as he smiled, knowingly.

It was obvious that he was wired and enthusiastic about the music that night. As I learned much later, he had plans for the soundboard recording, but it wasn't until fifty years later that the tape would materialize through the eons to make its way into my hands. As providence would have it, the soundboard recording was guarded for decades by Johnny Sandlin, whom Duane gave the recording to the next day in Atlanta for safekeeping. The precious tape was stored away and forgotten for nearly fifty years until it was rediscovered by Sandlin and passed from him to Captain Skipper Littlewood. Capt. Skipper digitized the recording and mastered the incredible music, returning it to Sandlin. Then my two friends, Johnny's wife, Ann, and Skipper's widow, Renee Littlewood, put the recording into my hands as I was writing this chapter of my book, which by happenstance hinged on that particular concert and that tape.

While Duane and I were up on the stage briefly talking after the Turkey Trip, I nervously picked up one of Duane's spare picks from its resting place next to his magical glass bottle that rested on the corner of Gregg's Hammond. I fiddled with the pick while we chatted about Ringo and her status as manager of the Martinique and musical mother of all Daytona Beach musicians. The pick was marked "Fender Thin" on one side and Allman Brothers Band on the other. It was just an ordinary pick like most others, but it happened to belong to Duane Allman. At the time, I had no intention of keeping the pick, it was just something to occupy my hands.

We talked, dodging roadies, until Red Dog dollied up the B-3, snatched up the Coricidin bottle and the other picks, and began to haul the Hammond away. At that point, we said our good-byes for what would be the last time. Duane's pick found its way into my pocket and later into my wallet as a permanent keepsake from that night. I saw the Brothers with Duane a half dozen times before he was tragically killed in the motorcycle accident, but I never had another opportunity to stop and chat that I recall.

Duane and Gregg eventually both became unapproachable celebrities who rarely set foot back in Daytona Beach together. I had later heard that Duane had grown somewhat egotistical, but that was never the Duane Allman I knew. As he hurried off in the direction of the soundboard to retrieve what later turned out to be the recording of that monumental concert, I told him I'd tell Ringo and Bill hello for him and he nodded in agreement.

After listening to that concert recording, all I can surmise is that Johnny Sandlin must have determined that the recording quality and microphone placement weren't up to his exacting standards, but not so the actual music. He then likely filed the recording away in the back of his busy mind, thinking that a better-quality live recording would certainly be captured later. In my experience, the forcefulness of that night's show was never again equaled.

Outside in the near-deserted parking lot, the late November air was crisp and good as the night's adventure continued. All but a few of the earlier crowd had found their way out of the massive parking lot behind the Georgian Terrace. Of course, there were the obligatory small groups of people huddled together trying to extend their high. We piled back into my car and turned down toward the strip to see what was shaking. It was now nearing 1 A.M., and we decided to get our two bottles of wine's worth of sleep at the Bird House and then head back to school early in order to salvage some tiny semblance of what was once a determined study weekend. It appeared that the show pulled a lot of people away from the Strip, so it didn't seem worthwhile stopping or cruising more than past the mostly empty streets to the Bird House. We slipped into my regular room and split the two beds, kicking off our boots to catch some Z's.

About two hours into a great dream, Rob, my bed partner, poked me and pointed to the girl that was sitting on my side of the bed munching a box of Kentucky Fried Chicken that was resting on her lap. She had neatly aligned and gingerly balanced her condiments on my stomach.

This explained my craving for my mother's epic fried chicken and biscuits. I think my new friend may have jokingly suggested that I join her in a breast, a thigh, or a leg. We chuckled as she munched her chicken, and then the young lady asked if we were interested in exploring something that would blow our minds—the recently opened but as yet nearly deserted Underground Atlanta?

"At 4 A.M. nobody will be there," she began, "and we can have the whole place to ourselves to explore. You guys won't believe what I'm about to show you," she theorized out loud. She tried to explain the concept of a city beneath a city to no avail, but still, the concept seemed interesting and worth the time to explore as long as we were already awake. After all, this had already been a pretty incredible day...so why not make it epic?

What the hell, Rob and I were awake by then, and Underground Atlanta would put us a little bit closer to Clemson with our boots on when we were ready to pull out of town. So, we rousted the others, slipped back into our cold boots, and headed back out into the night, scrubbing the sleep from our eyes with our knuckles. The fried chicken lady and her friends had their own car, so we followed their lead into the bowels of Atlanta and on into an area I had never seen or heard about before. The entire area was crisscrossed wildly by hundreds of railroad tracks.

When we finally stopped crossing train tracks and parked, I began to sense what working in a West Virginia coal mine was like. Being a bit claustrophobic myself, I was beginning to wonder why I had agreed to explore an endless cavern of blackness. The area was not just dark, it was totally devoid of light. Our friends assured us that the area was completely lacking in operational train or subway tracks, so that was a positive. Our guides assured us that our cars were safe where they were parked and that no trains used this particular section of track any longer. I was naturally a bit skeptical that they were actually keepers of the city's train and subway schedules, but still we followed their flashlight glow through the inky darkness toward a faint light in the distance across a few more train tracks. I recall thinking that we were headed east, but I had no idea where we were or where we were headed, so if the flashlights died, so would we. We were locked beneath an eerie diesel and electric netherworld that smelled of stale diesel fuel and the burnt-chlorine smell of electric ozone gas.

As our eyes adjusted to the darkness, we emerged from the rail-

carpeted cavern into an opening that was no longer crisscrossed by the minefield of railroad tracks. In a few moments, we were walking down the center of an alleyway between dust-covered buildings toward a dimly lighted street ahead. We walked out on to what appeared to be the main street of some long-forgotten ghost town with a roof of concrete covering everything in view. We learned that night that this was where Underground Atlanta had recently opened, a Disney World of sorts for young adults from Atlanta. For now, the street was lined on both sides with architectural features forgotten a century earlier but that had somehow survived intact. The amazing architecture included decorative brickwork, granite archways, ornate marble, cast-iron pilasters, hand-carved wooden posts, and gas street lamps. There was a curious mixture of a handful of newly opened, customer-ready businesses and underway construction, but most of what we were seeing were long-closed, dust-covered storefronts with windows still sporting long-forgotten business names etched across dusty glass in barely visible gold leaf paint. At this point of its development, Underground Atlanta was a startling vista like nothing I had witnessed before or since.

There were fully functioning gas streetlights on this long main street shedding an eerie lipid light on the panorama before us. Two cherries crowned this whole outlandish sundae. On one end of the main street, near where we entered through a perpendicular alleyway, was a full-sized antique streetcar resting on a flatbed trailer. The streetcar was named New Orleans. On the other end of the street, much to my astonishment, resting gently on its side like a lounging, long-toothed Collie, lay a genuine Mercury space capsule—like the ones I had seen numerous times before at Cape Canaveral (now Cape Kennedy) when I was a young teen. Nobody has ever explained to me how one of NASA's six manned Mercury space capsules managed to land in Underground Atlanta. During that crazy-wild Atlanta night, these polar-opposite apparitions were just two more bizarre twisted pretzels presenting themselves in less than a twenty-four-hour labyrinth brimming over with still-unfinished tangles, turns, and snarls. Catapulting four hippie musicians who had been living in an entertainment wasteland like Clemson, South Carolina, deep into a metropolitan city like Atlanta for a night was surely bound to produce some odd rabbits tumbling out of whatever top hat tilted to the absurd.

The scene was so ludicrous that I would not have been surprised if John Glenn had stepped out of the shadows that night, but instead of a Mercury astronaut, our voices startled Mike, a sleeping security guard who stepped groggily from out of the shadows behind the streetcar. Mike had laid down his life guarding as many deserted buildings as he deemed necessary for one night. He was using the streetcar to protect himself from a block party for sewer rats as he snoozed after the few businesses that had been open closed for the night. The jovial Black security guard, dressed smartly in a rent-a-cop uniform, approached us and assessed our threat, as we did his, while we kept our eye out for a quick exit. To our collective surprise, the security guard, whose full title was Officer Mike Gallagher, offered to give us all a flashlight-guided tour of the city below the city, which we eagerly accepted.

Mike explained how it all began right after Sherman burned Atlanta during the Civil War. After Reconstruction, the train tracks that connected Atlanta to practically every city in the United States became problematic for downtown pedestrian and automobile traffic after the introduction of gas-powered buggies. In 1928, a "twin-bridged" viaduct was completed that raised the street level over some of the downtown by one and a half stories, and a five-block area was completely covered by a concrete shelf. This submerged the original street-level storefronts, allowing access to the original levels from old Lloyd Street at one end or from across the railroad tracks on the other end, from whence we came. This brazen design allowed streetcars as well as passenger and freight train lines to access those ground-level tracks unencumbered.

As construction went forward, merchants moved their operations to the second floor of their buildings and turned the original ground-floor storefronts into basements for storage and delivery service. During Prohibition, these "basements," being obscured from the city above, became prime sites for speakeasies. Soon, juke joints with music and illegal drinking became commonplace. The plethora of legends and stories about these illegal speakeasies led two Georgia Tech graduates to formulate a plan in the late 1960s to convert the unused underground level into an entertainment district—thus Underground Atlanta was born.

Officer Mike knew his Atlanta history and kept our interest, but time in the city was growing short, and no matter how entertaining the tour was, history would never be more than just that, and I needed to concentrate on chemistry, not Atlanta history. I glanced at Sands and he concurred, giving me that "My ass is dragging, so let's move it along" look. So, we excused ourselves and thanked our tour guide and somehow found our way back to the car, following our chicken-munching friend back to the surface. We bid Atlanta a fond farewell, putting the city lights squarely into our rearview mirror.

The plan was to stop at the first rest stop that we came to after clearing the city proper to catch a few more Z's. Sands and Adams, in the back seat, were already snoring and Laffoday was not far behind, becoming hypnotized as the brightly colored city lights flashed by his window. I planned to sleep until the rising sun became impossible to ignore and then limp back to campus to try and somehow trick myself into getting back into study mode.

Despite our good intentions, bad luck threatened to capsize our ship of fools once more on the way out of town. The first rest stop northeast of Atlanta on I-85 was closed for "modernization," and the entrance had been heavily barricaded. Refusing to take no for an exhausted answer, I drove slowly past the rest area while eyeing the nearly finished improvements. None of us required the normal services of a rest area, but I really needed a quiet spot to close my eyes for a short time. Besides, it was completely deserted, so I pulled to the side of the interstate beyond the "exit ramp" and then carefully but quickly backed into the rest area. Once on the freshly tarred parking lot, it was easy to find a dark corner in which to hide. The four of us slept like babies until we were roused by a faint tapping on my fog-covered driver's side window. As I wiped the condensation from my window, the uniform of a Georgia State Highway Patrolman began to materialize.

Back in the '60s, just the sight of a highway patrolman's uniform would strike fear in the hearts of a car full of sleeping hippies, but we were college hippies, which I think bought us a measure of exoneration. Regardless, the patrolman was polite as I rolled down the window, and I reciprocated in kind. He asked what we were doing in a barricaded rest area that was under construction. I explained that we were just four tired college students heading back to Clemson who had pulled off for a little sleep before I dozed off and ran off the highway. The officer smiled and pointed toward the exit in front of us and told us that he was heading up the road toward the Buford exit for some coffee. He emphasized that he would be back in about thirty minutes and we had better be long gone when he returned. My only reply was a military-style "Yes, Sir!"

We watched through exhausted eyes as he pointed his patrol car toward the encroaching pastel sunrise while we each picked a tree to water. As I was irrigating a stately oak near a stack of construction materials, I reflected on the mad escapades of the past nineteen hours. Smiling, I knew that we had experienced the genesis of a lifetime of Allman Brothers appreciation. There would be other concerts and other crazy friends, but at least for me, the previous nineteen hours would be unparalleled.

The quotient of jubilation is easily determined: you simply divide what you have by what you expect. What we had was a primal Allman Brothers concert, played in their adoptive hometown with the band clearly nowhere close to their apex but nonetheless experiencing a skyrocketing upward trajectory. What we expected...was a better-than-average night of music. The quotient that we arrived at was nothing less than an unforeseen musical awakening.

Music was a huge part of the life I had chosen, and I was determined to find a way for the music that I loved to accentuate my formal education. I had hoped that music would lead me out of my own self toward a significantly brighter world. In that world, unimagined experiences would exist and the unexpected might be experienced without need for copious reflection. The Allman Brothers music became, for me, a metaphor for this electrifying, unreflective, freestyle life of music. Compared with all other concerts in my lifetime, this one was unforgettable.

As I pulled away from the rest stop, slowly gaining speed to join the deserted sunrise highway ahead, nobody spoke a word. We were each absorbed in the past evening's influence on our self-worth as musicians while gradually overcoming the effects of cheap wine and devil weed.

After a few minutes, Laffoday momentarily looked away from a spectacular breaking fall sunrise ahead, checking to make sure Sands and Adams were asleep in the back. Now gazing out the passenger window to his right, looking at nothing in particular, his facial expression morphed slowly from wistful to brooding. When he finally spoke, his was the most significant commentary concerning the previous night.

Speaking to nobody specifically, he cast out a thinly veiled, passive-aggressive stipulation concerning the Old Florida Rum Company going forward. Laffoday verbalized what we had all been thinking in the most basic of terms: "We all need to make an important decision when we get back to school," he declared emphatically. "We're all going to have to practice harder and write better music or we're going to have to decide to put in more time at the library."

Postscript 1

As I was writing this book, I had numerous discussions with Ann and Johnny Sandlin about the music that Johnny was involved with over the years. At some point, the discussions naturally turned to The Allman Brothers, and I confessed that I had arrived to The Allman Brothers table late. I explained that I never had a chance to hear them play live until more than a year after the Hour Glass left Daytona in late summer of 1968. I told them that the first Allman Brothers Band show that I attended was around Thanksgiving of 1969, and that the show was in Atlanta, at a weekend concert called the Turkey Trip.

I told Johnny and Ann that this was when I finally had a chance to hear The Brothers, and the show was incredible. As I recalled, the one thing that separated that show by miles from every other Allman Brothers Band show that I have seen since was the "Mountain Jam" that night. I remember telling Johnny and Ann that, at the time, I didn't even know the name of the incredible composition that I was listening to. It would only be later that I would begin to put names with faces and titles with songs.

We kept talking, and Ann told me, fifty years later, that a tape had surfaced in a box in their garage and that the tape had been cleaned and mastered by Capt. Skipper Littlewood. I still was not clear about what she was talking about, but we were having this conversation about soundboard recordings, and Ann was telling me about a recording that Duane gave Johnny the night after a show somewhere in Atlanta. Ann was trying to date the tape and put a venue with it. What finally turned on the floodlights about her recording was Johnny's description of the band's version of "Mountain Jam" being over an hour long and how it was played at breakneck speed from beginning to end, top to bottom.

Ann eventually sent me a copy of the recording, and along with hearing Alex Cooley's introduction, I determined, without a doubt, that this was the night that my buddies and I were at the Angora Ballroom at the Georgian Terrace Hotel for the Turkey Trip. As soon as I heard the way "Mountain Jam" took off and never touched ground until the end, I knew that it was undeniably the same night—no doubt in my mind, whatsoever. Rob Sands later concurred.

I asked Ann to imagine what it was like standing in that room at the tender age of nineteen, along with my close friends, two guitar players and our bass player, listening to that groundbreaking, innovative, unworldly music for the very first time while it was being played that very night. What an incredible indoctrination to The Allman Brothers. We were hard-pressed not to climb the walls, and I'm sure we weren't the only musicians in attendance who were so incredibly impressed. That explains why my friends could not believe that I knew Duane and Gregg and goaded me into approaching Duane that night. After all, by 1969, the Brothers and I weren't exactly traveling in the same musical circles.

The mystery of the supercharged "Mountain Jam" was solved, and I had been there to hear it as it was played that night in Atlanta. It was an extraordinary weekend of music that I would never forget for a myriad of reasons.

Postscript 2

There is another story woven into the fabric of this story but not connected umbilically to that night. I kept moving that pick of Duane's through a long series of wallets for years as a reminder of what I had and what we all had lost. Fast-forward to about 1986, and I'm back home, living in Ormond Beach, when I found out my guitar player from high school, Ralph Bundy, the man who had owned the Duane Strat, had been stricken by a terminal liver condition. Ralph and I were always close, and as time went on, his condition worsened to the point that he was flown up to Walter Reed Army Hospital for treatment several times and was put on a liver-transplant list. That September, he was told by his doctors to have "Christmas" with his family that month because he might not make it to December without a new liver. I gave Ralph that pick of Duane's for a "Christmas in September" gift that year, along with a misty explanation of its lineage over cocktails one night.

Fast-forward again to 1998, and Ralph's doctors thankfully had discovered a miracle cure for his condition and he recovered completely. Ralph was one of the handful of patients in the US who had the same liver condition and were concurrently being treated for occasional gout. The doctors discovered that the gout treatment somehow cured the liver condition. Go figure, his liver cure came by way of rum and Coke, kinda, sorta.

Ralph and I were in his home studio a few years later recording "Somebody Loan Me a Dime" in 2003. I was drinking way too much Crown Royal, because I volunteered to do the vocals and they were not going well. I was having a hard time getting the phrasing right. The drinking became contagious, and, as always, the conversation turned to Duane and our shared histories. I asked, while pouring both of us another Crown on the rocks, "Hey, Ralph, you've never mentioned that pick of Duane's that I gave you...What did you ever do with it?"

He looked at me with an uncertain, perplexed look on his face, and replied..."What pick?"

Chapter 20

The Allman Brothers at Littlejohn Coliseum September 11, 1971

First, just a little South Carolina/Clemson background: The campus of Clemson University was a bucolic study in perspective and point of view during the late '60s and early '70s. Members of the counterculture's musical constituency, or "Heads," who lived in South Carolina through that era while attending Clemson still shake their heads in disbelief at the dichotomy in everyday circumstances surrounding those remarkable times. Dressing against the tide in bell-bottoms and sandals and sporting long hair always drew catcalls and even the occasional egg, launched covertly from almost any open dorm window or from behind any tree.

The source of this defamation was unquestionably Southern students, known to the out-of-state Northern student population as "Grits." The term Grits had less to do with the white goop that always took up space on a breakfast plate and more to do with the deeply "Southerfied" person who might be seated next to you at breakfast. The term Grit (a single Southerner) was frostily bestowed on those Southerners whose lack of tolerance constantly aggravated other peaceful, nonviolent students. In other words, Grits were generally considered by the diplomatic, counterculture, hippie-type population (Heads) of the university as "redneck peckerwoods" with shit for brains who loved to prey upon the peaceful/liberal population. A Grit's uniform of choice consisted of khaki pants, blue oxford Gant shirts, and either tasseled loafers or Bass Weejuns—also known as penny loafers. Still, Clemson was and is a pulchritudinously landscaped and thoughtfully designed campus located in the rolling foothills of the Blue Ridge Mountains and situated on the shores of Lake Hartwell. Clemson University had also been a military college from 1893 until 1964, and the sum total of its historical backstories explains much of the yin and redneck yang associated with that fine institution. In spite of the university dropping its military association in 1964, as a freshman in 1968, ROTC was still a two-year requirement for all males.

Perspective swirled around Littlejohn Basketball Coliseum like the questionable fragrance of the blue/gray incense smoke that permeated the dorms on the night of Saturday, September 11, 1971, as The Allman Brothers prepared to play their first concert on the campus of Clemson University. On one hand, there was the hallowed student organization that had hired The Allman Brothers Band, the Central Dance Association, or CDA, the members of which suffered horribly from buyer's remorse on the night of The Allman Brothers Band concert. Coincidently, CDA was predominantly made up of dyed-in-the-wool South Carolina, beach-music-loving Grits. On the other hand, there was the audience—mostly made up of students and young nearby residents who were, for the most part, members of a growing counterculture. They came to the Clemson campus with the awareness that they would be provided an evening of spectacular music. The Allman Brothers Band worked their musical magic that night, totally unaware of the complex steps and circumstances that led up to the fact that they were even so much as invited onstage in Clemson, South Carolina.

More importantly to this chapter, and so many stories to follow, the conversation that ensued between Duane and Dickey after the concert that evening in Littlejohn Coliseum proved incredibly insightful. Sadly, that foreshadowing offered a brazen and unique explanation as to why Duane Allman would die on a lonely two-wheel crossroad in Macon just weeks later. But, in reality, Duane's accident wasn't necessarily, as many have speculated, because of his love of speed or because of some twisted "death wish." Duane may have died simply because he ignored a mechanical malfunction that, until recently, has gone unconsidered.

In the late 1990s, while perusing my old 1971 Clemson yearbook with my longtime Clemson roommate, Ed Alden, I found a copy of the school newspaper that I had saved for more than fifty years. The newspaper had been published a week after The Allman Brothers Band Concert in Littlejohn on September 11th. Reading that article again, which at that time was twenty-seven years after the fact, stopped me in my tracks. As soon as possible, I called Ann and Johnny Sandlin, who were equally blindsided, and we all agreed to keep the information under our hats for the time being. Ann and I were in the talking and planning stages of writing individual books, and that newly found information might just be beneficial to one or both of us. It was an interesting scenario that had not been considered before then, so we just put it to bed and I closed my yearbook and put it back on a shelf.

My memories leading up to that concert and of the concert itself, along with the *Tiger* article published on September 17, 1971, by associate editor Tom Priddy, were the combined genesis for this story. The end of this chapter was inspired by actual events as witnessed by myself and reported by Tom, however, some of the final scenes and dialogue have been dramatized under the supposition that my theory was indeed correct.

Preamble to the Littlejohn Show

The khaki-clad members of Clemson University's Central Dance Association scrutinized The Allman Brothers concert fretfully from an empty press box high above and across from the stage in Littlejohn Coliseum. From their perspective, what they were witnessing on the stage and on the wooden basketball court was frightening. White paper cups soon began to overflow with brown liquor and Coke that gradually took on a stronger and stronger chemistry as the CDA members watched in horror as the evening's music unfolded. The CDA's sole function as a student organization was to hire wholesome entertainment for "dances" before and after major school and athletic events throughout the year, and it was abundantly obvious to all of its members that they had screwed the pooch this time, right out of the chute, by hiring The Allman Brothers Band.

The more music that the CDA listened to, the more they drank, and the more they drank, the deeper into depression they all slipped. Perspective and point of view became a tough and bitter bite for the CDA to gnaw on that night. One by one, unspoken questions began clouding their minds as they continued to watch the show:

What were we thinking?

Whose stupid idea was this, anyway?

Was this horrible "dance" ever going to end?

Will we be blamed for bringing an onslaught of hippies to the Clemson campus?

Can we blame it on the band or the booking agent?

Why are no couples dancing on a dance weekend?

Why are the couples just sitting on the dance floor or standing, nodding and swaying to the music?

Will we be held accountable for the haze of blue smoke that's blanketing the entire coliseum?

Are we going to run out of bourbon before the show is over?

And the most terrifying question of all, God forbid— will the student body demand more such concerts?

The CDA sensed that they were in deep shit, and they knew it all began, innocently enough, the previous fall semester.

I recall the trouble for the CDA starting nearly a year before The Allman Brothers concert in Littlejohn Coliseum, when several CDA members knocked on my friend Chipper Lowery's dorm-room door. It was early in the fall semester of 1970, and Chip's room was already overly crowded with the usual suspects who had stopped by to covertly burn a "J" before catching the current *Star Trek* episode at 5 P.M. in the student lounge. After *Star Trek*, the munchies always dictated a communal flow downstairs for dinner in Harcombe Commons dining hall. Chip and his friends were toking up while listening to the new and hauntingly different Crosby, Stills, Nash, & Young album, *Déjà vu*. As they barged into Chip's room, interrupting David Crosby's classic "Almost Cut My Hair," the uninvited CDA members immediately killed our buzz and gawked suspiciously as they pondered Chip's confusing décor and sonic accompaniment. "Hippie music to be sure...And what the hell is that smell?"

The unconventional way in which Chip's room was decorated and the suspicious-sounding music caused them to stop dead in their tracks. Chip's walls were covered with an assortment of black light posters. Tie-dyed bedsheets fashioned into makeshift curtains covered most of the single window except for the lower section, which held a typical box fan. A red parachute bloomed from the ceiling like a huge hibiscus flower, completely consuming the single room light that barely filtered through the silk. Reed matting covered the floor instead of carpet remnants, like most of the other dorm rooms in Johnstone Hall. Chip's room was as close to a hippie pad as you could possibly expect to achieve on campus, and its unconventional appearance did not go unnoticed by the uninvited CDA guests.

Looking back, Chip Lowery's red herring room wasn't even remotely discreet or inconspicuous. To top it all off, on this sticky August afternoon the large box fan pointed out the window in the opposite direction than normal, making the strange scene seem even odder. Of course, the fan's reverse placement served to exhaust any illicit smoke fumes outside instead of into the hall. It worked well...

The CDA had been distributing music questionnaires, two per room, throughout the dorms. Basically, the questionnaires asked students what kind of "dance music" they were interested in hearing on various historically established "dance weekends" scheduled for the following year. Because of the uncommon music playing on Chip's stereo and the "Keep on Trucking" T-shirts and the bell-bottom jeans worn by his friends, the CDA immediately pegged us as the kind of troublemaking, nonconforming music subversives that Mr. Khaki-Leg Penny-Loafer was beginning to loathe immensely—the kind of people who dared to buck the good old boy system. The kind of people whose numbers were growing steadily, by the day.

Apparently, that fall there had been some complaining about the quality of the music by some of the other "out of state" rebellious troublemakers. Times and tastes were changing, which was fine with us in our little corner of South Carolina. The beach music of the Grand Strand was slowly giving way to the blues of Haight-Ashbury and Macon. However, the CDA and a majority of the South Carolina students were not quite ready to trade in their Gant shirts and Bass Weejuns for dashikis and sandals. A quick perusal of the CDA's music questionnaire reassured me that this particular cat had no real intention of changing its spots. Unfortunately for the CDA, the growing number of "music subversives" included people with just simply good musical taste who were used to a little better grade of music from their FM radio stations back home. Many thought a visit from some of Macon's music scene would do the college good.

The questionnaire had little boxes for students to check next to suggested favorite groups that might be in a price range suitable for a midsize college with several thousand dollars a semester to spend on entertainment for the following year. Students were asked to check ten favorite groups and return the questionnaires to a box located next to the CDA office by Sunday afternoon, or else someone would stop by each hall on the following Monday evening to make sure that the questionnaires were each filled out and all duly accounted for.

Their choices included many groups that had played Clemson in the past. The selections were not really all that bad, just a little dated and offering little or nothing fresh or cutting edge: the Tams, the Four Tops, the Beach Boys, the Swinging Medallions, James and Bobby Purify, Booker T and the M.G.'s, Solomon Burke, Jerry Butler, the Chambers Brothers, the Chi-Lites, the Drifters, Al Green, Clarence Carter, the Isley Brothers, the Righteous Brothers, the Four Seasons, Gary Puckett and the Union Gap, and the Association.

At the bottom of the page, well beyond all the beach music/R & B/shag groups, was a lonely line marked "other" that looked to the world like an afterthought, or at the very least, a lame stab at musical equality. Apparently, there were other like-minded individuals who thought that "other" meant groups like Deep Purple, the James Gang, Poco, Cowboy, Goose Creek Symphony, and, of course, The Allman Brothers Band.

Mr. Preppy/Joe College came to my room Monday night knocking on the door after dinner looking for the questionnaire that had been shoved under my door while I was at Chip Lowery's room the week before. My stereo was on, and, as usual, there was the normal stack of LPs on the changer waiting to drop and settle tunefully under the needle. The records that spent the most time on my record changer at that time were the two Hour Glass albums, Paul Butterfield's *East-West*, the Beau Brummels' *Bradley's Barn*, and The Allman Brothers' mesmerizing self-titled debut album.

Dressed in a smartly starched oxford shirt complete with a neatly pressed locker loop, the CDA representative almost gagged when he saw that among others, "The Allman Brothers Band" had been written in on that last line of my questionnaire. He was equally surprised to see The Allman Brothers Band written on the one that had been left for my roommate, Ed Alden, who had been recently dubbed "Fast Eddie the Hook" after winning everyone's money at a recent all-night poker extravaganza.

Joe College practically wore the starch out of his collar shaking his head negatively in disgust. The corner of his mouth turned up and he sucked air between the two top teeth near the corner of his mouth, making a sound that could only be perceived as abject repugnance. Finally, the overdressed chicken-shit, rat-bastard began to speak to my roommate, who wasn't even in the room.

"You can tell Ed when he gets back that when we hire a rock band like The Allman Brothers to play for a dance weekend here at Clemson, the Tiger Marching Band will play 'Who the Hell'd Have Thought It' on the fifty-yard line in Death Valley. Where does he think he is anyway, Berkeley?"

"Did you say Berkeley?" I replied, trying hard not to let my aggravation level pass the sucker-punching point. I reached over and lifted the needle off of "Norwegian Wood" right in the middle of Duane's electric-sitar solo and hastily laid the arm down on the cradle as I started in on my unwelcome guest. "Shit, you'll never catch me or any of my friends mistaking this tiny redneck pile of cow manure for Berkeley! Berkeley? Are you shitting me? Yah, right!"

About this time, the August heat and the realization that I would not have an interesting thing to do until my next trip to Atlanta, 120 miles to the west, started to get to me, and I took it out on my unwelcome guest. "Here, take your bullshit questionnaire and get your penny loafers out of my room and close the door behind you. I have a test tomorrow. I'll be up all night studying, and you're wasting both our time...shit, Berkeley, really?!"

Apparently, the CDA representative didn't know when he was being thrown out of a room, or maybe he had just never been told to leave before.

The Littlejohn Coliseum Show a Year Later and the Icy Foreshadowing Afterwards

What a difference in perspective a year makes. The greater part of the audience in Littlejohn Coliseum was enjoying a rare treat. A local band, Lion; Wishbone Ash; and The Allman Brothers Band opened many eyes that night as to the future of music in the upper echelon. What we heard was some of the best music that had ever graced the Clemson campus. Unfortunately, some came to Littlejohn Coliseum to dance to the likes of the Tam's, so there were those who left unsatisfied. The CDA, however, was looking down at the stage from the opposite end of the same kaleidoscope and seeing something entirely different. Little did the members of the CDA know that The Allman Brothers concert marked the beginning of the end of more than eighty-two years of Clemson "dance weekends." Music was changing, and now it was time for the Central Dance Association to step aside and let some real-deal, legitimate, cutting-edge music and cultural experiences begin to bloom on campus.

Starting late because of a local opening act by the name of Lion and, later, a spellbinding set by Wishbone Ash, The Allman Brothers show blew right past midnight in a hurry. Their second set evaporated into Sunday morning like the miasma of smoke that cast its blue haze over the mammoth Littlejohn Coliseum. A fog of illicit smoke thickened despite the best efforts of a bank of exhaust fans working feverishly at the opening of the visitor's locker room tunnel across the floor from the stage against the opposite wall.

With everyone except the knee-walking, drunk CDA on their feet enjoying the hell out of the show, The Allman Brothers Band churned through the last encore of an inspired performance. Turbulent and frenzied, the last few lines of "Whipping Post" built to near pandemonium while Duane Allman's bending strings begged questions and Gregg Allman's tortured keyboard screamed answers. This musical tug of war culminated in carefully measured volcanic bedlam that finally erupted, casting notes to every corner of the arena. The music melted slowly away into a mellow, solitary Butch Trucks timpani drum roll, pulsing with orgasmic emotion that signaled the beginning of the end for this night's Allman Brothers Band concert.

Gregg swept his long blond hair back over his right shoulder and out of his dripping face while he reached deep down into his diaphragm one last time. He braced himself against his Hammond organ as if to hold it down in the windstorm that he knew was about to swirl around him on the stage, and then he delivered the closing benediction.

Towering over and a little to the right of his microphone, with his face and eyes turned left, Gregg moaned so softly at first that he could barely be heard over the soft timpani roll building in the background. Teasing the audience and the band with a tasteful whisper, Gregg lamented softly, "Good Lord, I feel like..."

Gregg's vocals begged Butch to answer again with his building bank of timpani, and he did...slowly building the thunderous roll into a deafening roar, which fell off once more as some in the crowd shouted their encouragement. Gregg stepped his vocal up ever so slightly, this time scarcely singing above a whisper, but slightly more forcefully with another half spoonful of expression..."Ooooooh, I feel like..." His vocals dropped away again at the end of the phrase, leaving Butch ample room to echo the emotion he was grinding out each time a little more forcefully.

Finally, with the conviction of a sinner on his knees repenting his most horrific sin at heaven's gate, Gregg added a final compelling benediction, drawing the words out into an almost insufferable duration. This time Gregg stood his ground and his voice thundered across the floor, up the walls, and into the press box where the CDA's rubber knees were quaking, but no one understood quite why..."Ooooooh Lawwwwd...I feeeell...like I'm Dyyyyy-yyin...!"

This time the patiently waiting band eagerly joined Gregg and Butch, one by one, note by note, building one last time, higher and higher, louder and louder, to what sounded like an unsustainable summit.

Duane led the climb, punctuating the throbbing bedlam with wounded-bird flurries that somehow lived within only the six strings of his guitar. Dickey strummed jazzy bumblebee/hornet's-nest fill chords, louder, faster, and higher as the end of the night drew near. Berry Oakley now coaxed notes from his Fender bass that weren't on the instrument's fretboard, punctuating unseen turns and steps on the steep path home with brazen Godzilla guitar chords. Gregg leaned heavy hands on both keyboards of his B-3 and pushed the volume pedal to the floor, sending his Leslie speaker cabinet screaming and the horns spinning centrifugally as if climbing out of earth's orbit. At this point, both drummers blanketed every skin within reach and sent cymbals fluttering in the crazy-frenzied flashing stage lights as if it was their last show on earth.

The conductor of this runaway train, Duane, stepped away from the band, turning his back to the audience and pedaling a chord near the end of his fretboard. His arms began to spread from his sides while he backed out further toward the front edge of the stage. The maestro of mayhem took one final sweeping look around the stage and raised his head ever so slightly in order to gather the attention of everyone in the band. When Duane was convinced that everyone had given the signature white-noise Allman Brothers ending as much as they possibly could, he then commanded one more step higher. The band gave him the one he asked for and then offered another giant step toward the stratosphere. Smiling from ear to ear and making eye contact with the entire band at once, Duane pointed his guitar neck up to the roof and dropped it smoothly, almost to the floor, and for a moment everything was quiet. The once-frenzied stage lights melted rapidly into total darkness. Only random "Exit" signs illuminated the mammoth building like red fireflies twinkling on a summer night. The entire coliseum was whisper quiet and dark, with only the soft rumbling stir of hushed voices.

For that moment time stood still, and there was relative stillness as the last notes of "Whipping Post" tapered off, echoing serenely between the walls of Littlejohn and trailing off toward the mountains into the early South Carolina morning. The audience and the CDA stood shell-shocked, not comprehending for a moment the innocence in mayhem that they had just witnessed. Then, as if instantly awakened from a hypnotist's trance, the audience erupted into thunderous applause. Above, in the CDA box, a lone pair of knowledgeable hands began to clap, but sneers from the other members quickly quieted the lone dissenter.

Duane became acutely aware of the audience for the first time this evening. He turned, grabbing a microphone with the last three fingers of his right hand, with his pick still between his thumb and first finger. Pulling the microphone to his mouth, Duane acknowledged the individuals around him with his cupped left hand and uttered his first public words of the night: "Barry Oakley, Dickey Betts, Butch Trucks, Jaimoe, Gregg Allman, and I'm Duane Allman. Thank you...! That concludes our set."

With that, Duane, Dickey, and Barry quickly unplugged their guitars from their amps and made their way to the back of the stage to stairs that seem to lead only into the blackness. The audience was still on their feet clapping, whistling, and screaming their approval, and even up in the press box, a single CDA member from Georgia hooted his endorsement.

Meanwhile, Gregg shut down his B-3, closed his songbook, and followed the guitar trio into the darkness, carrying his precious songbook in his right hand. Butch and Jaimoe each tossed a pair of nearly destroyed drumsticks to some hot chicks in the front row who appear excited by the gift, and then followed Gregg into the shadows. Butch glanced back at the girls who were now waving frantically, and Jaimoe unsympathetically shoved him ahead through the locker room door, shaking his head sardonically. Jaimoe and Butch joined the rest of the band in the men's basketball locker room, stage right, where the Central Dance Association had supplied sandwiches, drinks, chips, and the obligatory M&Ms with the red candies painstakingly removed by ladies-in-waiting with tender young fingers.

Duane looked businesslike, having changed into a dry black Triumph motorcycle T-shirt, and he methodically wiped down his Les Paul flame top. He slipped it into its case and then turned his attention to the bright red SG Special that he had come to enjoy playing slide on—polishing the front and back, he paid special attention to cleaning the remaining five unbroken strings. Duane rested on a long pine bench beside his two guitar cases, one on each side, with his back against some lockers, carefully untangling the broken guitar string from the tuning knob on the bottom of the headstock of the SG. Leaning forward, he took a sip of his drink, which sat on another bench across from him. He repositioned his cup of Coke nearer to, but at a safe distance from, a small stack of square paper packages containing an array of new guitar strings. There was also a small pile of Fender Thin Allman Brothers guitar picks beside the replacement strings and an aerosol can of Finger Ease. An old pair of Sears Craftsman side-cutting pliers completed his traveling repair kit.

Settling comfortably back into his makeshift workshop, Duane seemed oblivious to the clamor of the departing crowd and the commotion of the roadies outside of the locker room door. The Brothers took a rare moment to relax after a concert before the roadies packed up everything for the four-hour drive back to Macon, and Duane seemed to be making the most of it. Absorbed in thought, he curled the broken guitar string around his finger, unwrapping it and curling it back around his finger again, over and over, until all of a sudden he looked over in Dickey's general direction and blurted out something he had been chewing on for a few days.

"You go foolin' with motorcycles long enough," he told Dickey, "and you know, you're gonna take a screw every time—that's just the way it is. That new Harley that I just got has a stuck throttle and I can't figure out how to get it workin' right. It don't back off when I go off the throttle—a spring or somethin's stuck. I've tried workin' it to death with oil, but I'm just about to where I don't trust the damn thing anymore."

"Damn, Duane," Dickey replied in a Southern hippie drawl, "We've got, what, nine bikes between us in the band? Call someone and get the damn thing fixed or get a manual that'll break it down for you part by part, piece by piece. Hell, someone's gotta figure out how to keep all them bikes running. You're the one with his face stuck in a book all the time, you figure it out!"

Duane looked up from his finger, which was turning bright purple/red in little spirals where the high E-string had cut off the circulation to his pointer finger. He looked over at Dickey, who had just finished wiping down his Goldtop Les Paul and was easing it into its velvet-lined case.

"Naw!" Duane said, "Man! As far as stripping it down and getting all greasy goes, I'm not going to do it! No damn way, I got no interest in that."

"Suit yourself, man," Dickey droned. "But you just watch. If you don't get it fixed right, that son of a bitch is gonna throw you off like dirt on the street one of these days! You said it yourself, 'You go foolin' with motorcycles and you're gonna take a screw, every time.' Suit yourself, Duane, but when it happens, then we're all gonna have to lay-up, waitin' for you to mend, and we're just starting to make some real money. What if you break your arm or something? Ah huh. I'm gonna sound pretty damn foolish out there playing harmony licks with myself. Right? And another thing, while your broken arm is in a cast, am I supposed to all of a sudden learn how to play slide? Shit! Ya just better get the damn thing fixed—or get rid of it!"

"Screw it, man, it'll be okay. I'll figure it out," Duane retorted as he tossed the mangled guitar string free-throw style at a wastebasket as it exploded into a mangle of wire in midair. The wad of tangled silver wire landed in the wastebasket next to where Berry was cleaning his bass all the way across the room, thus signaling that it was time to change the subject.

"Hey, Berry, we almost got 'Blue Sky' right tonight—almost," Duane remarked in his bass player's direction; the statement was obviously meant to get under Dickey's skin, which it did, so Duane continued, "I don't for the life of me know why that's such a hard song to nail live? Ain't all that damn complicated—it's just different, that's all. It's got that country thing going, ya know, it's just not rock and roll or bluesy enough."

Berry, the consummate peacekeeper, just smiled and slowly looked up from polishing his own four strings toward Duane, and then he looked at Dickey, who was now frowning through his mustache, cocking one eye and appearing more than just a little pissed.

"Hey, Duane," Berry replied, "I thought that we hit that one tonight. Almost got it right? Nah, we nailed it—at least Dickey and I did. Man, 'Blue Sky's' just one of those tunes that rolls rather than rocks. Butch and Jaimoe's got it down now, too. Hey, the whole damn place loved it from what I could see. Of course, with those new stage lights I can only see ten feet in front of me." Berry's smile was so infectious that Duane, Dickey, and Berry were all smiling at each other before Berry could close the tweed case on his Fender bass.

Gregg, Jaimoe, and Butch all of a sudden appeared out of the shower room where they had been listening to the motorcycle talk while toking down the last of a Columbian fatty that a fan had handed Gregg as the concert ended. Gregg, with that illegal smile on his face and a happy-go-lucky bob in his step, said what everyone was thinking as he buried his hand in the bowl of M&Ms. "Damn college kids, man, they have the money, the hottest cars, and always wind up with the best shit and the grooviest chicks."

Butch was just about to bust a gut laughing and reiterated what Gregg was saying as he grabbed a handful of chips, crowding Jaimoe's hand from the bowl, "I think that one day I'm going to go to college to see what the hell the big deal is. Man, they don't look or talk any different than the rest of us but just look at the shit they smoke and the cars they drive! Momma's precious little thing—Shit! If momma only knew," Butch testified mockingly and then looked at Gregg and Berry with a swagger and self-confident air to his headshake. "Hey, what do you say we hang around outside by the truck and see what appears out of the darkness. I'm not in a great big hurry to get back to Macon. I could use a little strange."

Jaimoe, the only Black person in the locker room, the only Black person at the concert, and possibly the only Black person for twenty miles around the Clemson campus, looked up at Butch. Jaimoe seemed content to settle back on a bench near Duane with one ear open as he munched on half a ham sandwich with half a turkey sandwich balanced on his knee next to a cup of Coke. Jaimoe finally looked up from the buffet on his lap toward Butch, Gregg, and Berry with a highbrow, unsympathetic, fatherly look, and piped in, pointing a drumstick-calloused "you just watch" finger in their general direction. "You know if you go screwing with the girlfriend of one of those redneck peckerwoods, someone is gonna get their ass kicked—or a whole bunch of someones are gonna get their asses kicked. Snaking the girlfriend of one of those big football-playing ruffians will get your ass kicked every time. A little bit of strange just ain't worth it, ya see what I mean? Take it from someone who's been on the shit end of the stick. I'd suggest we just pack up, get in the 'bago, and head back home. No damage done this time out—all the petals stay on the rose. This part of South Carolina just ain't no friend of mine. It's not like Macon or Daytona Beach. This is Easy Rider country."

Duane piped in again, winding another string around his finger and looking very serious. "You just don't know, man—growing up back in Daytona it was the shits, man, if you were Black you weren't even allowed on the other side of the bridge where the beach is after dark. No shit, man! Don't let the sun set on your ass in Daytona Beach on the wrong side of the river—no jive—I shit you not. That's what they told the Black cats back in the day.

"A lot of that's changed now, but that's the way it was when we played the Pier with Abe and the Houserockers—and that's only been like six or seven years ago. Seems like the blink of an eye, man. We used to have to drive the Black players back across the bridge when the gig was over. No stoppin' for nothin', just back over to Second Avenue and on home. There was only a handful of Black dudes in Seabreeze High

School when we were there. The Black high school, Campbell, had all the good players, man, Abe Alexander, Floyd Miles, Lindsey Morris...all those cats. Man, those cats could all play better than anyone in any of our dime-a-dozen White bands. And me and Gregg we played surf music, man, white bread all the way. Beach Boys shit...that was like the worst...Beatles songs and all that slop. Same old shit, man."

Red Dog, being careful not to interrupt any conversations, came in and picked up the guitar cases and looked around to make sure there wasn't any more equipment laying around. Duane and Jaimoe started toward the door. "Come on, man," Duane tells Jaimoe, "Let's head out to the Winnebago, I want to rap with you 'bout something."

As Duane and Jaimoe stepped out of the dressing room and made their way to the exit sign on the wall, Duane noticed something vaguely familiar about Littlejohn Coliseum, though he'd never been there before. It could easily have been every other stadium, or coliseum, or gymnasium that they had called home for a few hours in the past two and a half years. As they walked outside, the night air was thick and heavy with the smell of Lake Hartwell in an early Sunday morning September fog. So heavy, in fact, was the air that it seemed as if they were the only two who could breathe the heavy wetness. The two walked out into the night and stood for a moment next to the waiting Winnebago and packed equipment van. The parking lot was empty and the street lights were shutting off one by one. Duane leaned back against the side of the vehicle and rested the heel of one boot behind him on the side panel as the stars became brighter as more and more lights turned off and their eyes adjusted to the darkness and the clearing sky.

Duane was quiet for a time, letting his strawberry hair fall back as he looked up into the night sky studying the sheer number of stars that were visible to them now that they were so far away from any city lights. Duane seemed to look past the stars deeply into the night sky.

"Hey, man, you know something, Jaimoe? We're just about there...we're that damn close," Duane said philosophically, while holding his two fingers as close together as he could while still letting the light of a tiny star shine between them. "Do you see all those stars up there, man? One day we'll be up there like that, and sell as many records as all those stars put together, and we'll have a following just like that—thousands, man, I can feel it every night that we play. We're getting tighter and we're playing bigger gigs every time out. One day, if we keep up like we're doing, we'll pack our shows and then we'll be able to take it a little easier. Man, we gotta keep doin' what we're doin', and writin' what we're writin', and playin' the way we're playin', and if we do, we just can't lose. The music is starting to grow and take on a life of its own. You and Butch, man, you were kickin' tight. Barry is layin' it down like a third monster guitar, and Gregg's writin' is getting better each time we go into the studio. I'm telling you, if we don't screw it up, it's gonna happen this time, I just know it, man. This is it! The thing about this band that has been missing from other bands that we've put together is that each cat has the power to pull the other cats along. Man, that's some powerful shit!"

Duane turned from the sky and looked an obviously doubting Jaimoe in the eyes. "Hey, man, I'm serious, this is what we've all worked our asses off all these years for, and it's just about payoff time. I'm loaded for bear and ready for business, and everybody better wake up to that fact!"

Jaimoe dropped his head and turned away from Duane, opening the door to the Winnebago, and started to climb in. Duane grabbed a very surprised Jaimoe by the belt to stop his escape and quite nearly jerked him out of the truck. "Hey, man, I'm not kidding! This ain't no jive shit!"

"I know, Duane," Jaimoe said meekly as he finished stepping back onto the pavement. "It's just that I'm a little worried that you have these big plans, and I'm not so sure that I see all that you see in that sky up there. Man, it's a little scary to me. Those are the same stars I've been wishing on since I was a little kid."

"Scared? Is that what it is?" Duane questioned with a cynical smirk. "Jaimoe, I've been scared before, plenty! Being scared hangs a lot of people up and keeps them from what they could be. Ain't nothin' to be scared about! It's just us now, and we're all heading together down the same road for once, that's all. Man, if you're scared, then step into my office and I'll tell you a couple of stories about being scared and what that can do to you. Hop into our 'tour bus' and let's work this out on the way back to Macon. Let me tell you a couple of stories about where I grew up and some of the scared cats I left back home. Where is the rest of the band, anyway? I sure hope that baby bro and Butch didn't follow Betty back to her dorm."

Perspective makes an interesting story extraordinary and an extraordinary story remarkable. In no other industry does perspective play a larger role than in the music business. From top to bottom, attitudes and impressions are solid gold. Very few localities harbored more worthless points of view than the upstate of South Carolina in the late '60s and early '70s. There were two very dissimilar perspectives working vigorously against each other on September 11, 1971, but only one band walked away from that stage in Littlejohn Coliseum victorious when Saturday night became Sunday morning. One question still begs answering: was that sticking throttle on Duane's bike the reason his story ended on that devastating day, when Duane laid his bike down?

Chapter 21

A Modern Revival

About the matter at hand, my curiosity ran soul deep. I had seen the photographs in *People* Magazine. I read the article, then I looked at the picture again, and I read the article again...this time more carefully. I found myself just staring at the newsprint that spelled out his life...his legend...in short neat paragraphs and well-constructed sentences.

As his protégé, he had always been a torpedo speeding through my life, just beyond yesterday. From the outset I knew that he could hold a congregation like no other but I also knew that human frailty would be his downfall. I lacked his faith...the faith that it would take to follow him through his life of anguish. His life had become an unsettling string of flaming bridges, so one morning, I left.

That morning, Reverend Keys had given me a new silver dollar to preach an extra sermon in the afternoon. I wouldn't earn that dollar. I wrote a short note and left the coin on top of the note. Climbing down from the locomotive that was his life, I left owing him nothing.

Settling down to a quiet congregation in the suburbs, I took no chances. Like a runaway train, he continued to burn up the tracks of his life, relentlessly chasing the devil from town to town. In all these years, he never left my mind. I watched from a distance as he stirred congregations in churches and tents all across the South. Deep in my thoughts, I felt compelled to stand once more beside my old friend and bathe in his dynamic strength. I felt the need once again to experience it all for myself, with my own eyes, and with my own ears...to feel the energy once again and to experience that dream.

Certainly, neither happy nor curious, my wife voiced her contempt in the car. "Why are we doing this, one more time, again? Is there no end to your optimism?" Just this once I wanted to prove her wrong. She knew full well that I harbored a deep admiration for the man inside the revival tent. For what his life had been—up one day, then down the next—over and over again, each time slipping a little further into the depths of despair. Temptation constantly pulled at his coattails. So often he would confuse heaven with a taste of sin...trying again and again to pull himself away, but he always came back for one last taste—hundreds of times.

Staring aimlessly out of the car window, she reminded me with her voice of reason, "If he can't find redemption himself, how can he possibly save others?"

"My dear wife, you know that no one earns passage to glory without a measure of suffering and pain. Why, then, should it be different for him than any other flesh-and-bone man?"

She smiled that placating smile that quickly turned to a smirk. Lately, though, the rumors had changed from bad to better. The road he was on seemed a bit straighter and a bit more positive. Still, the need to satisfy my own curiosity burned deeply, now more than ever, before it all disappeared. Why else would I find myself staring up at his huge revival tent on this cold February evening?

From the makeshift parking lot we made our way toward the entrance of the tent. Intoxicating, rhythmic music coming from just inside drew us closer. Inside, people were swaying to the beat as we stepped into the cavernous enclosure. Excitement momentarily gave way to astonishment as I surveyed the enormous congregation. Evidently, we were not the only ones who had turned out on this cold February night to see if the man behind the familiar wooden altar had himself found salvation. People crowded into every corner of the enormous canvas room. Emotions inside were soaring. Excitement and a muffled buzz spilled over everyone. The kick reminded me of past years when Reverend Keys had been young and exciting...when crowds had thrilled with exhilaration. Word spread quickly in those early days. Believers and nonbelievers alike filled churches in every city where he and his entourage had preached. His rise to the top of the mountain of transfiguration had been incredibly swift but so had been his plummet into near obscurity. For the good Reverend Keys, the light of glory was fleeting and never really securely in his grip. Tonight, however, the old-time feeling was everywhere.

Looking around the congregation, I saw people of all ages, many too young to remember Reverend Keys in his glory. Only a very few could have possibly known him as I did, when he was just another good preacher in a town full of extraordinary preachers. Those attending tonight were curious but they were unquestionably here for the word, and they wanted to hear it from the master. The congregation impatiently waited to hear from the man who had fallen as low as a man could fall. Some hoped to find his singular perspective uplifting—I did. Some hoped to help lift the crown of piercing thorns from his head and some, as always, were here to sit in judgment.

When the curtain finally parted, Reverend Keys made his way unhurriedly with the choir and musicians to the altar. He seemed somehow less tall, slower and more deliberate in his gate. His blond beard had become stone gray. His brow seemed furrowed from the relentless battles that he faced daily with unrelenting demons. Still, unquestionably, the fire in his eyes still blazed. The congregation, now all on their feet, with chairs discarded like matchsticks, edged slowly forward to heed the message. A peculiar quiet fell over the crowd as they watched him make a few adjustments to the altar. As Reverend Keys looked up, his steel-blue eyes pierced the soul of every person in the congregation. From that moment, time ceased to exist. Communal hearts shared a rhythm as old as time itself, and the canvas surrounding us all began to breathe in perfect unison.

Then, without warning, the guitarist, as if possessed by a tempestuous demon, struck a mournful, hellish chord which cued the stoic Reverend Keys and shook him from his earthly trance. His expression turned instantly to rage tinged with pain. The message came thundering from his mouth and it was a haunting mixture of fire fueled by thunder and the devil's feathered jewels.

His words, like an earthquake, shook each and every person down to their foundation and caused most to tremble and shake. Quaking, shuddering, and pulsing with the heady intoxicating rhythm of his accompaniment, the congregation moved from side to side as if to help shake the ever-present monkey off the back of Reverend Keys. Again and again, he anointed the congregation with words of hope, wisdom, pain, loss, and tragedy. Words only imaginable by someone who had lived through the fires of hell and had only now caught a fleeting glimpse of glory. He had stared Satan in the eye and survived to tell the story, and tell that story he did. We were all hanging on his words, waiting for the message. When it came crashing down around us, it was deceptive in its simplicity: you must first pass through the darkness before climbing the mountain of redemption. His words raised my soul. Years of sadness and doubt were washed away instantly, and I felt sanctified again.

His voice was clear and powerful and his words forceful. His eyes were intently focused, and he was obviously in charge, for the first time, of his own destiny. He horsewhipped everyone, he struck something within me. His was the only story, the only light in our darkness, the only road home.

I could see in her smile and in her eyes that my wife was becoming slowly converted. Years of contemptuousness and distrust gradually fell to the floor like ashes. As the choir began singing "Will the Circle Be Unbroken?" I gathered my courage, still not fully convinced of her total conversion, and asked, "What do you think? The sermon is nearly finished, would you like to slip into the back to have a few words with an old friend?" "Sure," she said, "I think that would be nice." So off we went, like two kids trying to sneak into the circus.

Getting in wasn't hard at all. We slipped, unnoticed, under the edge of the tent and simply walked to the side of the stage where invited guests were standing. There we finished watching the sermon as if we belonged there...and quite honestly we did belong. In all those years, I had never lost faith in his dream. Optimism had finally torn down years of doubt, and it was obvious that he was back. I hoped that I could tell him just that. Twenty-two years had passed without a single coherent conversation with the good Reverend, but something told me that tonight would be different.

Reverend Keys gave his final benediction and then it was over. Deacon Miles walked off of the stage first and made his way over to us, soaked with sweat. The good Deacon reached out to me with a warm hand and a smile. We had prayed for just such a night many times. "It does my heart good to see him doing so well," I told my old friend. "I know," he said, grinning and nodding, "I can see it in your smile."

We made our way over to the man of the evening. He was soaked with sweat and worn from giving so much of himself. He had filled the air with life—his life. For the moment, the battle was all out of his piercing blue eyes. He wore the haggard look of a man trying to bear the weight of everyone else's sins but who could barely abide his own. Still, we both knew that the world outside was a hungry lion, and that trouble stretched over him like the cold night sky.

I wondered if he would recognize us. Slowly, he became more at ease, then his shell cracked like a stubborn oyster. We spoke of the midnight masses that we had held together and of funny things that had happened along the road. The stolen equipment, accidentally intentional shootings, and the car that left him stranded in the middle of the night...and we spoke of his wonderful new perspective.

Soon, though, weary eyes told me that he was trying to politely wrap up our conversation. Workers around us were busy packing away his life in boxes and crates. They would reverse the process in the next town, and the next, and the next. Silently, I wondered, "Was this the road that he had chosen or did that road choose him?" I caught a glimpse of his life in one transient moment—the Baptist circuit rider, the brother to us all who had lost his own brother to the game. The midnight rider and the man on an endless highway to his own destiny. Sadly, I knew that his lot in life was to leave a small part of himself in hundreds of cities and at thousands of revivals just like the one tonight. One cold morning, when he had nothing left to give, he would pass through this life, and his words would live forever.

The three of us said our good-byes, smiled, and promised to meet again. We shook hands, but I somehow knew that it would be years before we would come together again. There was so much left to say. Unspoken words hung in the air like snow that refused to fall. As we turned to leave, he reached out and gently seized the elbow of my shirt, gaining my attention. Reverend Keys closed one eye and motioned for me to step out of the lighted hallway and over next to the curtains out of the glare. My wife walked on for a few steps, giving Reverend Keys and me the privacy that we sought. "Listen," he said in a soft, loving voice, while resting a weary hand on my shoulder, "I have thought of you often all these many years. I know that you feel as if you have forsaken me. Do not! I am pleased with the road you have traveled and we both knew it had to be. While here, we are only allowed a choice in the little things...the rest is our destiny. We both heard the Word, you and I, but we heard it differently. It's as simple as that." His words caused me to tremble...

With that, he reached into his pocket and pulled out a shiny silver disc so worn that the engraving was barely legible. On an altar covered with silver dollars, I would recognize that coin at a glance...it was mine, the one that I had returned to him thirty-five years ago. He gently placed the coin in the palm of my hand and closed my fingers around it, saying, "When your problems become mountains, and there seems to be no end to it, look at this coin and imagine all the places that it has been...all the trouble it has seen. Let it be your salvation, it has served me well!"

Without another word, he turned, and slowly pushing the curtains aside and glancing slightly upward, he walked down the narrow hallway, never slowing or turning back.

The strength went out of my legs. I turned, searching my wife's eyes for support. Emotion swelled up in me like a tornado. Clutching the worn coin in a death grip, all my doubts were suddenly vanished.

Silently, we walked arm in arm out into the bitter cold. Frost had covered the grass in a carpet of brittle white crystals. We stopped for a brief moment but neither could speak. I held my wife tightly, feeling the familiar warmth that had always given me comfort. As I gently rubbed the satin smooth coin between my fingertips, I could feel the decades melting away.

Chapter 22

A Lesson Carved in Stone: Duane and Me

Even today, at age seventy-two, on rare occasions, that shadow-filled, aching feeling in the pit of my stomach appears from nowhere like a sucker punch from the past—that nauseating feeling that comes home to roost whenever I step in front of an audience of any size to speak or perform. Everybody knows what I'm talking about; that feeling that your stomach is trying to squirm its way up into your throat on its way to abruptly emptying its collection of violently churning butterflies. Even though it's infrequent for me these days, just thinking about the way it makes a person feel, and how it can change an individual's physiology in an instant...Well, it's enough to torpedo an otherwise benchmark occasion. Stage fright can manifest itself so severely as to become a make-it-or-break-it moment in a person's life.

To a young, unseasoned musician, stage fright can be a terrifying and career-altering emotion. Merely the anticipation of playing an important show can wrestle an otherwise normal human to the ground and render them a stuttering, trembling, sweaty, dizzy, dry-mouthed heap of anxiousness. There are countless self-help volumes chockful of suggestions to help moderate the condition. Simply knowing that stage fright is normally worse in anticipation of a performance and that it often dissipates once the curtain rises is key to making it through an important performance. At this stage of life, I can normally deal with those emotions, but there was a time, as a teenager, that stage fright quite nearly cost me my job, my closest friends, and the single most thrilling night of my early musical career.

I began playing in a garage band like thousands of other kids whose only goal in life, back in the early 1960s, was to emulate the Beatles. Starting out with an inexpensive Harmony F-hole acoustic guitar, I began to learn basic cord patterns and simple songs of the day. Early gigs were played with my buddies at beach parties on Friday evenings just up the street from my house at the base of the Neptune Beach approach. We would get together with a record player, a bonfire, a few blankets, and some early groupies to play and sing until our fingers were aching and blistered. I had heard from a pair of hot-shot local guitarists, Duane Allman and Pete Carr, about a guitar teacher who had taken them under his wing, Ted Connors. I wanted badly to take lessons from Ted. The speed at which Duane and Pete had become excellent players under his guidance had not gone unnoticed by the other fledgling guitar players in town. Unfortunately, when I called about signing up for lessons, Ted said he was solidly booked, which meant I was on my own. I was doing okay on guitar but not really excelling, and it was time for our beach-party band of seven guitar players to start dividing up the duties. If we were to become a serious rock and roll band, we needed to diversify somewhat. A band with seven guitar players and no bass, drums, or keyboards simply wasn't going to work unless we were aching to become a folk-singing, minstrel group. We already had too many mediocre guitar players showing up every Friday, so I began to pay attention to drummers in all the popular groups of the time.

Before moving to the sun and surf of Florida, I had played woodwinds in my junior high school band in Arlington, Virginia. My best friend in the band sat near me in the drum section, and his father was a serious jazz drummer who played in the clubs of northern Virginia and Washington, DC. What I really wanted, when I moved to Florida, was to join the drum section in the school band, but it was full with a waiting list. I decided that playing drums in the rock band that we were trying to hatch would be the next best thing, so I quickly moved from my cheap guitar to my mother's old pots and pans and convinced my bandmates that if I could keep a beat, I had promise as a drummer.

So it began. We would get together like so many other bands of that period and practice in empty garages, or in living rooms, or on back porches of parents who were working during the afternoons. We gradually gravitated to the different instruments necessary to pull off a real gig: Ralph Bundy settled, quite naturally, on lead guitar; Kip Marshall moved on to bass guitar; Cecil Johnston played rhythm guitar; and I played pots-and-pans percussion. The other three guitar players were encouraged to continue on and to start another band of their own, which they did. Occasionally, others would try to invade our practices, but our band was beginning to solidify nicely with those four members, and, as a not insignificant benefit, we were all getting along really well as friends.

We were just getting our equipment-feet wet, but it soon became apparent that a drum set manufactured by Revere Ware just wouldn't do the trick in a real-world job scenario. I soon graduated to an inexpensive snare drum and a more or less toy high-hat cymbal. I made that do, but with real jobs looming on our horizon, I saved my money during the summer of 1965 and headed to the music-equipment Mecca of the East Coast, New York City, where I knew I could find something to keep from being bounced out of our fledgling band, newly dubbed "The Knaves." So, in August of 1965, I flew to New York. My sister lived with her husband in Gramercy Park, and the next day I set out for Manny's Music Store on West 48th Street to buy a real set of drums with real cymbals to bring back to Ormond Beach.

My mission to New York was threefold: I would roll my musical shopping spree into a sibling visit and a quest for my first real professionally tailored suit. As far as the suit was concerned, my parents insisted on charcoal and let my sister and brother-in-law know that it was to be gray in no uncertain terms. I, on the other hand, lusted for an iridescent, slightly greenish suit much like the ones I had seen Wilson Pickett and the Four Tops wearing on *Hullabaloo*—my parents won that round. Selecting the drum set, however, was entirely my choice, limited only by the sum total of my summer's lawn-mowing compensation.

Stepping into Manny's Music Store back in the 1960s was a life lesson in music history all in itself. At any time, members of the Rolling Stones or the Beatles might be in Manny's looking for the newest and best equipment for their next tour. Anyone and everyone flocked to Manny's for the latest equipment and the maximum discounts. The showroom was scarcely twenty-five-feet wide, but it was also at least four times that deep, and the entire left side of the center aisle was lined with drums of every description: Ludwig, Slingerland, and Gretsch, every color and combination imaginable. My eyes immediately focused on the Ludwig section and the other name brands quickly faded from my view. Ludwig was good enough for Ringo Starr, and I had dreamed about the Ludwig logo on my bass drum from the Beatles' first appearance on *Ed Sullivan*.

This was my first time in a real music store full of generous options, and I wanted to play it cool, but it didn't take long before puppy fever struck and I locked in on a set that I really wanted. Imagine the shock when I turned to the waiting salesman after just a few minutes of looking, and with no test drive, told him, "Wrap 'em up!" I selected a blue sparkle Ludwig trap set, lightning-fast Ludwig Speed King pedal, four Zildjian cymbals, hardware, sticks, cowbell, and gig cases. I had roughly $350 to spend, and never in my wildest dreams did I think I could walk out of Manny's with a complete set of premium drums for that amount. The price tag on the Ludwigs was an astonishing $350, marked down from $425, so I was excited beyond belief and more than ready to lay down the cash. My brother-in-law, Doug, yanked me off of cloud nine and back into reality, however, by giving me a serious lesson in New York City bargaining that day.

Doug stepped in and burst two bubbles in a New York minute that afternoon with the first outright lie I ever remember him telling. He told the salesman that all I had to spend was $240, which would have to include shipping back to Florida. My heart sank and I could feel my eyes welling up. I knew that there was no way in the world that I could get that set for $240. I had looked all over Daytona, and similar sets sold for way more than $650, not including cases or hardware. I thought this was a great deal, and Doug was about to wake me from my three-way Ringo Starr/Ludwig fantasy.

My head lowered and my hand covered my grimacing mouth. In my mind's eye, I pictured someone else walking out of Manny's with the drum set that, until a moment ago, had most assuredly been mine. When the salesman told him absolutely not, Doug quietly nodded to him, winked at me, and motioned with his head toward the door, saying, "Let's go back to the other store and make the deal there." What the hell is he talking about, I thought—what other store? Manny's was the only music store I had been to, and the only one I really knew about in New York City. Horrified and dejected that I would return to Florida without a set of drums, I pulled myself away from the set that attracted me like a flute on the lips of a snake charmer.

It was all starting to become clear as I watched Doug move ever closer toward the front door. I had begun to think that my father had secretly conspired with Doug to keep me from becoming a musician so I could become a college football star. He had surely put Doug up to this. It made perfect sense, but it happened so quickly and blindsided me so completely that I had no time to mount a reasonable defense...It was all part of a devious adult scheme. All I could do was to follow the conniving son of a bitch as he left. I sheepishly followed my brother-in-law toward the void that was surely to be my life without drums: no friends, no fun, and no female fans.

I believe Doug had his hand on the handle of the front door when the salesman hollered from the back of the store where the manager's office was for us to stop. He quickly made his way through the clutter of drums and stacks of amplifiers and guitars from the back of the store up to Doug and me. With an annoyed look in his eye, he told us, with a frown, that the manager had okayed the deal—only we would have to pay for the shipping at that price. There simply was not room for Manny's to sell the drum set and ship it to Florida for that price. Doug seemed to be thinking about this much too long, but apparently he was just toying with the salesman a little more, and when he realized that they were firm on the final price, he said, "Okay, you've got a deal. We'll pay the freight." Only then did I begin to breathe normally, and the Florida tan slowly returned to my face. As I recall, the salesman seemed to be having the same problem.

I still have the receipt from Manny's for my drums: August 19, 1965, $240.00 for everything. Shipping was to be air-freight collect. Oddly, I don't remember a thing about the suit other than it was dark-charcoal gray and "equally fashionable at a wedding or a funeral," as the salesman reassured me. When I returned to Florida, my drums followed a few days later, and after an exciting afternoon of group assembly and tuning, my band's practicing and rehearsing took on a fevered, though much louder, pitch. I was the last member to acquire his chosen instrument, so now we were good to go.

To a man, each member of our fledgling band brought something positive away from playing for a crowd of dancing, smiling faces that stirred our souls. As an upstart band, we played for birthday parties, sock hops, Bar Mitzvahs, cotillions, teen-center dances, and high school and fraternity dances in order to gain experience and to make a few dollars along the way. We played just about any place that paid a few greenbacks, and quite a few that paid nothing at all, except for all-important goodwill. We were not too choosy about how much we were paid, which meant that we worked a lot. Our band played just about anywhere and everywhere for the first two years, but what we really wanted, more than anything, was to land a prestigious job at a nightclub in Daytona Beach called the Martinique.

The stage at the Martinique was "owned" by two local bands, the Nightcrawlers and the Allman Joys. From time to time, however, the Allman Joys, who were getting better by the day, began to get booked out of town more and more regularly. Later, the Nightcrawlers all graduated high school and scattered to pursue college or other bands, which further opened musical doors for our band. Slowly, we worked our way into the Martinique and began to play whenever the Allman Joys or the

Nightcrawlers were on the road.

By early 1967, we were getting enough bookings to require a manager and booking agent, and in early February, our chosen manager, Lee Phillips, got a call from the owner of the Martinique, Bill Cook, asking us to open a Valentine's Day dance and concert. Our band, the Consolidation, would open the show at 8 P.M. The Allman Joys would, in turn, warm the stage for B. J. Thomas. And after B. J. Thomas completed his show and encore, we would return to the stage to finish out the night.

The rest of the band bubbled with excitement, but I was more than a little rattled by our good fortune, and I did the worst thing that I could possibly do: I internalized and began to absorb my emotions. The news of our booking spread through our friends like wildfire. Everyone was positive that we had finally made the big time; everyone, that is, except for me. Among other things, I was worrying that we might have taken too large a bite out of the elephant in the corner of the Martinique. After all, we had never played on the same stage with the Allman Joys, much less a national touring act like B. J. Thomas. To make matters worse in my terrified mind, Thomas had recently released his first top-ten album, and the single "I'm So Lonesome I Could Cry" was receiving constant radio play. His album was a favorite of mine.

My major stumbling blocks were twofold and menacing: the Allman Joys' drummer and B. J. Thomas's drummer. Bill Connell, who played for the Allman Joys, was a serious rock and roll drummer who could get a crowd on a dance floor simply by tuning his drums. Connell had long hair and a real rock and roll attitude. I hadn't been playing long enough to develop either. To make matters worse, B. J. Thomas's amazing drummer, Jimmy McCormick, was originally from Daytona. He had moved to California and quickly became a widely admired, in-demand studio drummer. He still had contacts in Daytona and Jacksonville, so rumors began to fly around music circles about how incredibly fast McCormick played paradiddles. No such rumors flew anywhere about my ability. Hell, I could barely play a paradiddle at that point.

By the time Valentine's week arrived, McCormick, the seasoned professional, had been raised to demigod status among the musicians at my high school, and the buzz spread to the two other schools as well. I was petrified at the thought of being shown up by two professional drummers and was getting queasier by the hour. Soon, I had worked myself into such an emotional funk that for the first time, stage fright made an appearance and threatened to stay put until the cows came home.

About midafternoon on the day of the show, I showed up alone and shaking at the Martinique to set up my drum kit. The truth is, I didn't sleep much the night before, and I had been physically sick from the moment my feet hit the floor that morning. The only lighting was two dim stage lights, and the rest of the club was pitch-dark. The only other lights were the red "Exit" signs over the outside doors and a few small dim lights over the bar.

McCormick, the alpha drummer, had naturally taken the center portion of the back riser, spreading his dazzling chrome-and-black-pearl set in every direction. Connell had set his kit up on what little space was on the left side of McCormick's set. I pensively squeezed my set on the right side of the stage, all the while trying to fight off the feeling that I was about to step off into the abyss.

When I was finished setting up and tuning my drums, I walked out onto the dance floor to survey how the stage looked. By now, my eyes had adjusted somewhat to the darkness, and the rest of the stage setup seemed a bit clearer. From the middle of the dance floor, my set of blue sparkle Ludwig drums that I treasured seemed small and insignificant. What was I thinking, anyway? I had been playing drums for scarcely two years, and six months of that had been on pots and pans. How could I possibly get up on that stage and play before two of the finest drummers in the business? What was I thinking? I shuffled off the dance floor and sank down into a convenient chair at a table next to the corner of the stage. There, I buried my face in my hands, hoping nobody would walk in, and considered my limited options. Sinking deeper into a quagmire of despair by the minute, I didn't notice the blond guitar player who was standing behind me just out of the dim light. He had been at a small table back near the bar, where he busied himself restringing his guitar for the night's show.

Trembling and quaking from the sheer weight of the psychological load, I began to shake my head from side to side, softly moaning every swear word I knew and trying hard to shake off the horrendous feeling of impending doom. I truly think that I was on the way to some sort of adolescent train wreck when a voice came out of the darkness, and the blond man who had been watching me all this time stepped out of the shadows. It was Duane.

"Hey, there, young man, what the hell's going on with you," Duane asked, half smiling as he sauntered over and slid into a chair at my table...cool as could be. Duane's molasses-smooth baritone voice took me by surprise at first, coming from that lanky twenty-year-old, but at the same time I took comfort in his reassuring Southern brogue. Duane crossed his arms and his eyes pierced me as I tried to find somewhere else to look. He quickly dissected the situation, and I'm pretty sure that he knew what was chewing on me before I had a chance to speak. He looked me squarely in the eye again and gave me a reiterating "What's up, man" snap of his head, lifting his chin in a questioning fashion, which was my cue to unburden myself.

I began unloading while he just listened quietly. "Man, I have no business even thinking about playing here tonight. The other two drummers are just way out of my league," I started. "I think I am going to go home, get sick, and then go to bed. Man, I don't think I can come back here tonight to play." My voice trailed off into the darkness, and when I finally looked up, Duane's normally gregarious, smiling face became serious, and his eyes pierced me right down into my soul. He leaned forward in his chair, put a firm, fatherly hand on my shoulder, and gently began to speak.

"Listen here, young man," Duane started, "I've heard you play and you can kick. I love the way your drums sound, man! You're just young, that's all. Don't let all the talk and shit get you down. We all started somewhere...even McCormick. Come on up here on the stage for a minute and let me show you what I'm talking about."

I obediently followed Duane up the three wooden stairs on the side of that old dusty stage that was shiny black from years of sweat and grind. We made our way through the maze of equipment and cords on the stage to the drum riser in the back. Duane tilted one of my cymbal stands to the side just enough to make room for his slim profile to step behind my set. Slowly, he sat down behind my kit and found the pedals while picking up the sticks that were resting on my bass tom.

It took Duane a moment to get his bearings because I set my drums up left-handed and catawampus. Then, with a consenting look, he slowly began to hit my bass drum over and over with his left foot. Each time he slapped the kick drum, he smiled and tilted his head to the side as if the sound made him somehow feel better or took him to another place. Then, one by one, he tested the sound of each tom-tom, the snare, and each cymbal.

As the drumsticks bounced off of each drum and cymbal, there was more head-cocking and smiling approval until the sound drifted softly away into the recesses of the Martinique. Coming from the best musician that Daytona Beach had to offer, I considered Duane's silent, prideful endorsement high praise. The longer he flailed, the better I felt and the better my drums began to sound. Finally, Duane gave the bass drum one last thunderous slap. That kick of approval resonated through the entire Martinique with only Duane and me to hear it. The punchy snap of my bass drum sounded completely different from the front side where I was standing than from the back side of the drums where I normally heard them. I began to smile for the first time that week, and my stomach started to settle a bit.

Duane laid my sticks down and we made our way off the stage, back to the table next to the dance floor. Before I had a chance to sit down, Duane started to prime me for my lesson. "Man, I love the way you have that bass drum tuned. Out on the dance floor it'll feel like a train running through your chest—I mean to tell ya, man, that kick drum just sounds so cool!" When we had been up on the stage, I felt exactly how the sound seemed to drive itself through my chest, echoing all the way to my spine. I could actually feel, for the first time, exactly what Duane had been talking about.

With a tone of voice somewhere between preacher and father figure and with eyes that commanded respect, Duane continued with the most important lesson I learned that day. This was his most serious music lesson and something I will never forget. "Look here, man," he started again, "I have something to tell you, and I hope you'll listen to what I have to say, because I'm telling ya, it's important shit, man. Here is what I know. When you're playing in front of other musicians or anyone else that you are trying to impress, never, and I mean never ever, try to play something that you don't know for sure you can absolutely play! Stick to what you know and play it with as much soul as you can. Man, it's as simple as that...I shit you not! I've heard you play before, and I know that you can cut it. Just slide into the pocket, nice and simple, and keep the groove going and you'll be fine. Just don't stick your neck out and don't try to show off to nobody and you'll do just fine. Now, I'll see you back here tonight, right?" What could I say? I really didn't have any choice but to agree...Duane was the man.

With that, he stood up and walked over to the bar to latch his tweed guitar case—a second later he vanished out the door, leaving me to contemplate the music lesson that would become a life lesson. I never forgot what Duane Allman said to me that afternoon or how utterly fantastic it felt to play that night on the same stage with the Allman Joys and B. J.

Thomas. That night in February of 1967 remains one of the greatest musical nights of my life, and all of these years, I have carried Duane's advice in my heart like a lucky coin. On occasion, I've shared his wisdom with young musicians whom I've noticed in the same circumstance.

Duane died just a few short years after he and I talked that afternoon in the Martinique. We had talked on many occasions before he died, and I always listened intently to anything he had to say. But on that February afternoon in 1967, it felt like he had saved my life. He taught me and my band a tremendous amount about music and life through the years, but that day, when I was young and green and scared, he was there for me when I needed him, and that has made all the difference.

In 2003, my wife and I drove to Macon, Georgia, for the first time since Duane was tragically killed in a motorcycle accident in 1971, for GABBAfest. There, we met some new friends, most of whom never really knew Duane when he was alive, but it was obvious that his philosophy and spirit were alive and well among those who love his music today in Middle Georgia. My wife, Patti, and I drove out to Rose Hill Cemetery early on a bright clear morning before we left Macon to pay our respects to Duane and Barry Oakley...two monster musicians who both died far too soon. As I leaned over Duane's grave to read the engraving on the stone, I felt his hand again on my shoulder and I was warmed by what I read:

> I love being alive and I will be the best man
> I possibly can. I will take love wherever
> I find it and offer it to everyone who will
> take it. Seek knowledge from those wiser
> *and teach those who wish to learn from me.*

Chapter 23

The Cradle of Southern Rock: The Tale of the Tape

Join me as I ramble back down memory lane to the cradle of Southern Rock...On one Saturday afternoon, in late October of 2003, I was looking for an excuse not to finish the list of chores that my wife had laid out for me that weekend. My favorite college football team was not being televised, and it was getting harder and harder to look busy straightening up my desk.

I know what you are going to say: "2003 simply cannot possibly have anything to do with the epicenter of Southern Rock!" And you're absolutely 100 percent correct...but humor me, if you will, while I fill in some important blanks. Hopefully, by now y'all have noticed that there is always more to the story than just the story. So, let's get back to the tale at hand. I think that you'll agree it's an important one!

Earlier that Saturday, all of my yardwork had been finished, and all of the burned-out lightbulbs had been dutifully changed. The only item left on my wife's kaper chart, the one item I had been putting off for weeks, was to clean out the last of three bedroom closets. I finally acquiesced and begrudgingly began cleaning out and straightening up the back section of that last bedroom closet. In the very deepest recesses of that room, behind stacks of irreplaceable pieces of my life's history that I hadn't touched or seen in years, a brown cardboard box caught my attention from the very darkest back corner. Weeding through stacks of sacred memorabilia that appeared to stand guard in front of the box, I finally made room and was able to put my hands on the box, which had followed me through at least seven physical moves. Regardless of its contents, at this point questions began to swirl around this mysterious pasteboard box. There must have been a good reason I dragged that box around for three-quarters of my life without so much as taking a peek inside. Was it simply worthless, adolescent junk or was it the repository of all things I wished disremembered?

The afternoon was beginning to stretch out toward dinnertime, but curiosity got the best of me, so I dragged the old box from its longtime resting place and placed it on a bed near the window where some decent light could illuminate whatever prizes awaited. As curious fingers carefully unfolded the top flaps of the box, the first thing I discovered were some great old photographs of my parents before they both grew old and gray. These pictures caused me to pause for a moment because they are both resting now, overlooking the Pentagon, in Section 11 of Arlington Cemetery. The photos had been taken on the banks of the St. Lawrence River in upstate New York, overlooking Canada, during the reception at Patti's and my wedding. I look again with renewed interest into the magical box, and there I found an envelope full of nearly forgotten photographs and negatives of my high school rock and roll band. Those photographs were of the band that was going to make us all famous...the band in those photographs was comprised of my four best friends marching from stage to stage through our teens. In my mind, that band was like none other, before or since, but in reality, it was remarkably similar to thousands of groups that chased the Beatles' prompt into the late 1960s. Still, we were different. The band in those photographs was young, fresh, eager, and wildly determined. Nobody had yet told us that the world was not ours for the taking. We were, to the man, full of piss and vinegar and determined in our musical commitment and backbone.

That same envelope also produced pictures of a few old girlfriends as well as the band's most loyal and determined of our groupies. Deeper into the treasures was a yellowed, timeworn, two-page, handwritten invoice, numbers 15695 and 15696. The invoice was dated August 19, 1965...It caused another deep pause and a sigh of realization. That handwritten invoice was from a fall visit to my sister and brother-in-law's apartment on Gramercy Park in New York City. That invoice chronicled one of the happiest days of my life. It was from Manny's Music Store in New York City, and it was written for a complete set of Ludwig drums, including four Zildjian cymbals, hardware, pedals, stands, sticks, mallets, brushes, and hard-shell cases. The cost of a complete set of teenage dreams in 1965 was $240.35, not including shipping. The cost of collect air freight to Ormond Beach, Florida, from New York was estimated by Manny's at a paltry thirty-five dollars.

With a new charge of excitement, the digging resumed, as layers of trinkets and mementoes flowed forth, producing more exciting flashbacks on what had been an otherwise humdrum Saturday afternoon. There were photographs of faces whose names had evaporated through the years—coworkers, short-time bosses, managers, and such, and there were also photographs of people whose names will remain forever in my memory. People like Ringo, Bill, Moose, Wendy, Gus, and Ben the Bartender. As I dug deeper through the layers of years, the mementos became more and more interesting and more eclectic.

Finally, I dug through to the bottom, underneath the layers, past old empty wallets, worn-out pocket knives, and other keepsakes that have now become hazy and muddled by time. At the very bottom, I came up with an old, vaguely familiar seven-inch Scotch 140 magnetic tape box. I turned the box over to look at the names of the songs scribbled on the back, and suddenly the fog lifted, and a flood of memories flashed across my mind like a freight train hell-bent for Macon, Georgia. There in my hands was a very old, very rare, very historic "live" concert recording of the Hour Glass, featuring Duane and Gregg Allman, Johnny Sandlin, Paul Hornsby, and Pete Carr. On this tape recording, Gregg, Duane, and Pete are playing for their hometown Daytona Beach audience in their favorite nightclub, the Martinique. In less than a year, the brothers would form the most famous and dangerous rock and roll band in the world, The Allman Brothers Band. The tape was recorded only a few weeks before the Hour Glass would drive to Fame Studios in Muscle Shoals, Alabama, at Johnny Sandlin's insistence. There, they recorded the bluesy demo tapes that included the foreshadowing "B. B. King Medley" that a shortsighted Liberty Records would ultimately reject as not "mainstream or commercial" enough. The tape in my hands was also recorded just a few short months before a twenty-one-year-old, way-too-cool-for-Daytona Beach Duane Allman would begin to make a name for himself as an explosive studio guitarist at Fame Studios, recording with such greats as Clarence Carter, Wilson Pickett, Aretha Franklin, Boz Scaggs, King Curtis, and Herbie Mann, to name just a few. The tape recording chronicled a totally misunderstood phase in the musical history of Duane and Gregg Allman, a time when they were recording what was generally considered white-bread, West Coast, pseudo-psychedelic pop music at the insistence of their record company while they were playing music so profoundly out of the ordinary that it would ultimately transform them into the most polished and powerful musical group in America. What I was holding was an extremely rare, 24-carat nugget of rock and roll history and, quite literally, the missing link to the band that, by the time four years had passed, would write their name in permanent marker on the annals of music history. Sadly, the iconic leader of both the Hour Glass and The Allman Brothers Band, Duane Allman, would never see his twenty-fifth birthday.

This was not the first time I had seen or held this tape. The night of its recording, after that show, I listened keenly to that tape over and over again in my bedroom while I awaited the sunrise. The very next day, I took it to a local recording engineer and audiophile to whom I paid the outrageous amount of ten dollars to copy the reel-to-reel tape onto eight-track format so it could be used in my car stereo. That eight-track tape followed me from one car to another until it broke for a final time and was discarded, while the original recording was stored in one of my bedroom drawers. That tape followed me to college, where it was played for bandmates and was eventually assumed lost or recorded over, along with another, separate tape that had been recorded on a different night at the Neptune A-Go-Go, about a month later, in April of 1968. That second tape had been recorded much the same way, in an old nightclub on the north end of the old Daytona Plaza Hotel, directly on the beach in Daytona. That second tape was assumed lost as well, but there is always the chance that it still exists somewhere in a still-unfound box of memories. Of course, the hope is that the second tape will also turn up and that music will be heard once more. Still, this was a great day and a great find...and my excitement was irrefragable.

Now, for the sixty-four-thousand-dollar question: what does one do with an extremely rare tape recording like this one, once it's been rescued from time? That's a fair question. So, what did I do with it? Naturally, a solid plan needed to be hatched and implemented.

First, I would need to find a knowledgeable recording engineer to archive the original tape and convert it to the more modern, digital format before it disintegrated into a tape box full of oxide shards, plastic, incense ash, and teardrops. A smart person would find someone old enough to have an in-depth history of working with tape and who is comfortable with that medium in a time when tape is considered passé. This knowledgeable recording engineer would need to have access to 1960s vintage tape machines in order to remove the original signal carefully from the old tape before it disintegrates. The tape's owner would need to find an expert not only in analog tape but also computers, so that once the tape was archived digitally the engineer could then go to work using twenty-first century technology to glean as much pertinent data from the original recording as humanly possible in order to wind up with a respectable finished product. This recording engineer/tape expert/computer wizard should also know enough heavy hitters in the recording industry so that if the project ran into trouble, he could get on the phone and have an answer to any questions that might arise in a matter of minutes. So, this recording engineer/tape expert/computer wizard/music-industry networker would have to be a person with recording feet planted firmly in the twenty-first century, musically, while still having a deep abiding respect for where modern music originated and how it got to where it is today. This superhuman, techno-retro, prodigious, Herculean wizard should also be humble enough to know when it was time to say: "That is as far as I can take it...let's run it over to the mastering house and see if they can do more." It would also be nice, as a sidebar, if this recording engineer/tape expert/computer wizard/ music-industry networker/music historian/contemporary musician/Herculean/ humble man could also make suggestions as to legal counsel to weed through the mountains of possible questions and pitfalls, if such were needed. And, finally, if at all possible, you would want to find someone with the patience of Job to answer the myriad of silly, senseless, repetitive, and ignorant questions that a recording neophyte like myself or anyone else might ask. It wasn't long before I found myself looking for a recording engineer/tape expert/computer wizard/music-industry networker/music historian/contemporary musician/Herculean/humble man/ attorney-savvy/patient/tolerant/persistent/genius. Sounds like I had painted myself into a pretty ridiculous and insurmountable corner, from which to fight my way out, right? Actually, the solution to all my problems was a simple phone call away.

The natural assumption is that the owner of that rare recording would call a large studio with a huge staff of highly qualified technicians, or you might think that the tape owner might put the recording in the hands of a studio that specializes in tape restoration and the archival of rare recordings—the kind of business that charges hundreds of dollars for each and every hour's work. It wasn't necessary to contact a huge corporate recording entity for the job at hand at all. There were actually two such studio owners in my orbit who fit that exact description.

One was Danny Lee Ramsey, whom I had only met a few years prior and who lived in Nashville. Danny Ramsey is father to Patti's and my goddaughter, Savannah, and ex-husband of Rebecca Ramsey, the daughter of my close friend and Rotary brother Norman Miller (now deceased).

The other recording Einstein, Johnny Sandlin, I had met a year before the tape was recorded, in 1967, and he had actually played drums for the Hour Glass and was playing drums on that very tape. Sandlin later became the chief recording engineer and producer for Capricorn Recording Studios in Macon. After getting Capricorn up and running, he subsequently opened his own studio, Duck Tape Studio, in Decatur, Alabama, with his wife and business partner, Anathalee, or simply Ann. Unfortunately, I hadn't seen or talked to Johnny but a handful of times in the thirty-three years since that recording was made in 1968. So, I ended up calling Danny Ramsey at Little Hollywood Studio in West Nashville.

Danny graciously cleared some studio time for me, so I flew the historic tape to Nashville and delivered it to Little Hollywood Studio. From the moment I arrived, I was made to feel as if this were the most important project Danny would work on that year. Other than running out for occasional supplies or disappearing upstairs for a few hours of sleep at night, Danny stayed in the control room at Little Hollywood almost constantly guzzling Coca-Cola® and living on little more than crispy fried bacon and soda for the next four days. The project was not only historic but, from my perspective, it was technically mind-boggling.

My tape was recorded in March of 1968 at the historic Martinique nightclub on the corner of Main Street and Wild Olive Avenue in Daytona Beach. It was recorded on an old stereo/mono Wallensak T-1500 tape recorder set on the stereo setting. Even though the recorder was programmed to record in stereo, I only had one microphone plugged into one of the two input channels, which means the tape was recorded only on one channel...and on only one-quarter inch of the available half inch of tape. To make matters worse, the tape was already an old, badly worn tape when I originally got my hands on it. The old Scotch recording tape came to me by way of a stack of used and taped-over tapes that my father brought home from work. All these tapes had been recorded on, over and over, multiple times. Finally, the real kicker was that the tape itself was originally intended for speech and not music. Speech tapes are, unfortunately, thinner by design than music-specific tapes, making them inherently more fragile and easily prone to scratching, tattering, or, God forbid...breaking. Another deep concern was that tapes this old can only be played a few times before the oxide layers that contain the recorded signal begin to deteriorate and literally flake away. Danny cautioned me from the beginning that even the most benign of these problems could spell total disaster for the entire project at the seemingly most insignificant bump in the road.

Regardless, when I arrived, Danny was anxious to get to work. We got comfortable in the control room that would be home for the next few days, and then Danny asked me to show him what I had brought with me from Florida. I handed him the box containing the tape, and he studied the unopened box carefully before he gingerly opened it to explore the contents. Danny found the loose end of the tape and attentively examined it, running the fragile tape through his fingers, after which he carefully examined his fingertips for shards before even lifting the reel of tape from the box. When he was satisfied that there was a reasonably good chance that the tape would not disintegrate before his eyes, Danny delicately threaded it on a reel-to-reel deck that was sitting on a pedestal in the center of the control room, like a newly arrived head of state.

We both took a deep breath as he turned the toggle switch to "play." As the old tape came to life once again, it began to crackle, hiss, and buzz. The first song that came from the studio speakers was a disappointing cover of the Doors' "Light My Fire," and the singer was definitely not Gregg Allman. Danny looked at me oddly while at the same time trying not to burst out laughing. I'm sure he was concerned and confused, but at the same time, with all of my talk and hype about the Hour Glass and The Allman Brothers, he just couldn't decide whether to laugh at the music and risk hurting my feelings...or assume I had picked up the wrong tape. So, Danny's initial concern came across as a combination of confusion and hilarity as a strange voice stabbed wildly at Jim Morrison, flailing at the most well-known of the early Doors songs.

"Oh, yah, yah, yah," I explained while chuckling a little. "That's my high school band, the Soul Patrol. We opened for the Hour Glass on a handful of nights in 1968, including this one." The night of the show, I recorded my band's two sets as well as the Hour Glass's two sets. Our concerns about the fragility of the tape caused us both to scratch our heads to try and figure out a way to somehow get past my band and into the meat of the Hour Glass music before something catastrophic happened. Otherwise, we would have to listen to one set of the Soul Patrol's music on this side of the tape and another set on the other side before we could access the Hour Glass music. My best suggestion was that unless we wanted to risk the tape breaking by fast-forwarding it, we were going to have to sit through two entire sets of this pretty mediocre music before we'd get to hear both Hour Glass sets.

However, Danny, who was always two steps ahead of me, replied, "Not necessarily...I think I can release the tape, wind it forward using a pencil, and not risk harming the tape. I can even wind it across the tape head so that we can hear when the songs are over. Or, if you want, I can record your band too, and you'll get a BOGO, but we'll still increase the chances of something happening to the tape—it's your call!"

"Why not," I said, "I'm feeling lucky!" I decided quickly, and actually, this had been my original intention back in '68—to record our band for posterity. Recording the Hour Glass was really an afterthought, a secondary bonus that I was hoping now might pay dividends. So, Danny recorded our set, and after almost an hour, we finally came to a place on the tape where it was obvious that the music took on a different tone and quality. When we got to the Hour Glass's first set and listened to the first few notes of that historical music, I could see the wheels turning in Danny's brain, and then a worried expression began to spread across his face.

"What's up, Danny?" I questioned. Was there something happening to the tape that we hadn't expected? Could the project be over before it started? Was there something about the tape that I couldn't see or hear that spelled disaster for the project before it even began? He was looking increasingly concerned by the second as he made hurried changes to the recording controls. Danny was making me more and more uncomfortable the more he fussed with the controls. He stared at the tape recorder on the table between us and began to shake his head from side to side and frown. Slowly, as Danny Ramsey's world percolated, he began to vent his concern.

"Ya know, Bill, this is too important a recording to lift off this old tape with this machine of mine. It's a great tape player, and I've cleaned the heads and tweaked it the best I can, but there are much more professional, studio-quality analog tape machines out there. I don't have one and I am not real sure that I can come up with one either. There is one guy up in Hendersonville who just might have the machine we need, but I don't know him at all, and from what I've heard, he's kind of a hermit. He'd be just about our only chance. I understand that he rents out his huge collection of vintage recording equipment." Thankfully, this sounded more like a bump in the road to me than a full-blown disaster, and what he said next brought a sigh of relief from deep down inside.

"Bill, you may know this guy who lives and works over in Hendersonville. His name is Lee Hazen, and I think he's originally from down in Florida somewhere near you." With a Cheshire cat grin I replied, "Yah, Danny, I think I've heard of him. As a matter of fact, Lee and I grew up three houses apart in Ormond Beach, and my band cut our first professional demo tapes in his Cottage Studio, the same studio where the

Escorts, the Allman Joys, the Nightcrawlers, and just about everyone else in town cut their teeth at studio recording."

The small cottage in Ormond Beach where Lee had lived and made his recordings after he returned from his stint in the navy was a small mother-in-law's cottage situated behind a good friend and high school classmate's house, Mike Troeses. Mike's historic old home was less than three blocks away from our old neighborhood and was located on John Anderson Drive, facing the beautiful Halifax River.

"Danny, do you know how to get in touch with Lee? I'll call him right now. Lee and I go back a long way, and it would be great to catch up." Danny made one or two calls and quickly got Lee's number from another recording engineer, and after a short chat on the phone, Danny and I were on our way up to Lee's Pond Studio in close-by Hendersonville, Tennessee, to visit with my old friend and to tour his studio and massive recording-machine collection. Lee's home was on Old Hickory Lake, which is a very large, winding lake and reservoir in north central Tennessee that was formed by damming the Cumberland River, which flows gently through Nashville on its southern side. Old Hickory Lake is anything but a pond, but Lee jokingly referred to the beautiful impoundment as "his pond," and the name stuck, becoming, in turn, the name of his recording studio.

Over the years, Lee had collected two of nearly every electronic tape recorder ever made, dating back, in fact, to the time before magnetic tape, when they instead used magnetic wire to record. His collection was neatly displayed, two-deep in most instances, lining the entire inside walls of his living space. Lee himself remained much as I remembered him from his early recording days in Ormond Beach, thirty-five years before. His straight blond hair was beginning to gray and thin a bit, but it was still combed straight back. His neatly trimmed "navy issue" full beard that he sported when he returned from the service was much the same as I remembered it from all those years ago.

Lee grinned ear to ear and couldn't hide his excitement as he handed me a cassette tape labeled "The Consolidation 1967" as we walked through his front door. What Lee gave me was a copy of tapes that my early band had recorded as a demo at Lee's Cottage Studio. Those cassettes were intended to be used as attention-getting, demonstration (demo) tapes to mail to prospective clubs in the Central Florida area. The copy that he gave me that day sounded as good as I had remembered it being in 1967, but what really amazed me was that he had kept our masters lovingly stored away after all these years, right next to the masters that would later become important album releases. After we discussed what he remembered about our recordings, he then surprised Danny and me both when he played his only remaining copy of the early Allman Joys tapes that he had recorded in the winter of 1965. The Allman Joys tapes had been recorded in Lee's Cottage Studio while Duane was AWOL, playing guitar in South Florida with Tommy Knight and the Stereos, while Gregg was finishing his senior year in Seabreeze High School. Lee related to me the story of selling the original master recording tapes to Joe Bell. It turned out that Bell was one of the owners of *Hittin' the Note* magazine and was the managing partner for the twenty-four years of its existence. When Lee met him, Joe Bell was acting as intermediary for Gregg Allman, who desperately wanted the recordings and did not want them released to the public under any circumstances. Gregg didn't like his voice at that time, and he didn't much care for the song selection either. Lee told me that Joe had offered him enough money for the recordings to pay off his mortgage, and he was gleefully happy about that. Joe and Gregg allowed Lee, under the agreement, to keep one copy of the Allman Joys sessions for his own personal use—not to be duplicated under any circumstances.

Personally, I did not concur with Gregg's assessment of the songs that I heard on those recordings, or his voice, and I thought those sessions were certainly important historically, if nothing else. We all surmised that Gregg was not comfortable having those recordings in the public domain because it was not Duane playing guitar, as most had always thought. Instead, the Stereos guitar player, Jim Matherly, had stayed back in Daytona, having taken Duane's place in the Allman Joys and playing on their recordings as well as their club dates at the Martinique. At that point in time, it was almost impossible to tell the two guitar players apart. Matherly was somewhat of a guitar inspiration to Duane as well as a host of other young musicians in town, including Pete Carr. I imagine that if Matherly's story had never seen the light of day, no one would have ever known their secret. But Lee certainly knew the difference, and he went so far as to give me a copy of the recording notes from those early sessions, where he had handwritten remarks in the margins. Remarks like, "Just listen to that solo [referring to Matherly on "Big Boss Man"]. Eat your heart out, Duane!" Lee was quite close to Duane and Gregg as well as most other musicians in town, and he had nothing but respect for Duane as a musician. He was also somewhat of a historian and was adamant about keeping the record straight and the facts intact. However, some good-natured heckling was always in order back in those days, as chronicled in his recording notes.

Anxious to get back to the task at hand, when Danny and I finished our tour of Lee's collection and recordings, Danny selected the perfect commercial analog recorder from Lee's huge collection. I photographed some historic 45s that Lee had on his desk. He also allowed me to photograph an exact duplicate Wallensak T-1500 recorder to the one that I used on the recordings, as well as the same offensive, less-than-adequate Electro-Voice microphone I had used. After paying Lee a hundred dollars for rental until we were finished with the project, he then made some suggestions as to how he would approach the project. Lee recommended that we make two copies of the signal and match them back together slightly out of phase and then redirect the resulting signal into two-channel stereo on the final digital copy to replicate the intensity of a true stereo recording. Lee told Danny that he had used that process several times in the past with mono recordings, though with mixed results, depending on age and tape condition, but it often rendered a better final product. Advice taken, the three of us took the stairway down and toured his basement studio where we found a gold record hanging proudly on the wall behind his recording console for work done on England Dan & John Ford Coley's original gold-record releases.

On the way out through his garage, we walked past Lee's parents' red 1964 Cadillac DeVille convertible, with its spotless white-leather interior. I had watched that car entering and exiting our neighborhood multiple times each day from the front porch of my parents' house on the corner leading out to a main Ormond Beach thoroughfare. Lee rarely used the Cadillac now, but he kept it lovingly enshrined in his garage and spotlessly clean. Lee's dad had worked for General Electric in Daytona Beach as an engineer and consultant on the Apollo Project, as had mine and many of the other men who built houses in our neighborhood. Lee Senior also maintained a cottage industry on the side for as long as I can remember, making and bottling "Col. Lee's Louisiana Seasoning." Col. Lee's seasoning is a savory blend of "Cajun-style" spices that he blended from huge drums of raw spices stored in his garage. Back in the day, everyone who lived in Ormond Beach had at least one bottle of the spice mixture in their pantry. Lee gave me a complimentary bottle to take with me and also noted the website listed on the back label as the only place in today's world to find Col. Lee's spice mixture. Released like a genie from its bottle, I unscrewed the top and breathed in a lifetime of my mother's kitchen smells buried deep within my childhood. I left Lee's house that day taking much more than the recorder that I had come for.

Back at Little Hollywood Studio, Danny went to work carefully disconnecting and removing his original tape machine and replacing it with the Ampex Professional half-inch studio model recording machine. Adjustments were made to ensure that the quarter-inch tape would wobble as little as humanly possible while it was making its way across the sensitive, hair-trigger tape heads. When Danny was satisfied, he went to work carefully threading the tape back on to the new machine. Danny was concerned that, given the age of the tape, it might not last for a second pass across the tape heads, so he took every precaution possible to ensure that one pass would be sufficient to get as much of the signal that was concealed in the tape as possible. So, armed with every type of tape cleaning and repair system known to man, Danny backed the tape carefully up and began to play and simultaneously record the music that we heard coming out of his studio speakers—first the Soul Patrol, and then the Hour Glass. Listening to my band playing when we were all seventeen and eighteen years old took me back to the time and place that I have always considered the epicenter of my musical life. It was the time when it all started, and the time when friends that I met along my musical road would follow me through my entire lifetime.

With the Soul Patrol's first set safely on tape, the first Hour Glass song to emanate from the speakers in Danny's studio that afternoon immediately took me back and focused me squarely on that weekend in late March of 1968, just three days after my eighteenth birthday. The flood of memories was so vivid and complete that it was almost as if it had all happened just the weekend before. That had been a monumental weekend in so many respects. It was also the weekend that, at a birthday party given by a girl who was a little more than a good friend, I got a deeper look into Gregg Allman's questionable, slippery side.

Phyllis Smith, a girl that I was kind of sweet on, threw me an informal birthday party on that Friday before the Hour Glass show on Saturday. The party was at Phyllis's sister's house in South Daytona. Phyllis and her older sister, Gloria, lived in a small two-bedroom house in South Daytona on the mainland side of the Halifax River. Their house was located almost directly across the river from where Duane and Gregg's mother, Geraldine, lived in Daytona Beach Shores. My band and some friends stopped by the party for a drink or two that evening and so did most of the Hour Glass at one point. Phyllis and I were sitting on the couch getting close when Duane and Gregg arrived. Gregg made a beeline for Phyllis and sat beside her on the other side of me...and that was that. A few minutes later, they disappeared into the back of the house, and it was "party over" for the birthday boy.

Phyllis and I weren't really that close at that time, though I was leaning in that direction, so there was nothing much to be mad about, but it is telling that I remember the incident in such detail, always keeping him at arm's length going forward. Really, though, what kind of fellow snakes a guy's date at his own birthday party? From that night on, I always respected Gregg musically, but I admired the man that Duane was so much more, and that helped cement our casual friendship. In reality, had Duane not banished stage fright from my life a few years earlier when my band opened for the Allman Joys and B. J. Thomas at the "Q," I might not have been playing at the Martinique three years later to record those Hour Glass sets.

If you step back and allow your life to chart its own course, it will generally flow smoothly from the brim to the dregs. And if you can detach yourself from the day-to-day reality of life and pay attention when something important happens, you will often come to the realization that everything happens for a reason. Events are always taking place in each of our lives, but when something monumental happens, people don't always notice, or understand, or even accept it. Listening to that music recorded in 1968 returned me instantly to that time and place and made keeping my mind on the project at hand nearly impossible. There were too many dots to connect between 1968 and my trip to Danny's studio in Nashville. As I connected each dot, I suddenly realized that they each marked a point on the straight line that was my life. It was a good thing Danny was somewhat detached from the night of the recording of those fragile tapes, and the history leading up to and surrounding those rare recordings, as well as the future.

March 1968—and the times were certainly a-changing. A near-volcanic pressure that had been building beneath the music scene in America was nearly ready to erupt and spew forth a whole new musical genre. Musical groups such as the Hour Glass had clawed their way to the pinnacle of their respective mountains and were searching for new musical vistas to explore, other musical roads, and other musical cohorts with whom to define those new musical directions. All of the strange twists and turns that led our two bands to that Saturday night gig at the

Martinique in Daytona were serendipitous to say the least...a strange, inexplicable series of luck, flukes, and happenstance that started around 1964 and carried on through the night of March 30, 1968. Even today, fifty-four years later, the events leading to that night and the recording of that music have guided my path in many respects to this very day. There are certain moments that will mark a life forever, if you are watching.

Back to the show: Gregg and Duane Allman, Pete Carr, Johnny Sandlin, and Paul Hornsby were already beginning to imagine, in March of 1968, that there were other musical directions to explore. Of one thing they were absolutely certain—the path that Liberty Records had forced them to take was not their path. In March 1968, the *Power of Love* album had been released by Liberty, and while somewhat closer to their vision of the future, the new record was not the road that Duane and Gregg knew would ultimately lead them to the music that they had heard in their hearts and knew was possible from the time that they picked up their first guitars. It was hard for the band to be overly excited about the *Power of Love* recordings because their hearts were not into the crisp, white-linen, West Coast pop sound that Liberty Records demanded of them. Gregg and Duane's hearts were drawn home to the South, and the South meant the blues of dirt roads to the Allmans as well as the rest of the group. Still, the new album had been released, and it was their responsibility as professionals to play the gigs to support that effort, regardless of their personal feelings.

With their band in tow, Gregg and Duane made that trip home to Daytona Beach in late March of 1968. Coming home, for the Allmans, would allow the band to rest, clear their heads, renew friendships, play a date or two, and make decisions that would ultimately affect all of their imminent futures, as well as the futures of countless others. Unknown to Duane and Gregg at the time, their brief intermission would soon cast the small Middle Georgia city of Macon into the forefront of international musical focus for the next fifty years. So much of what would become music history would revolve around this simple visit home for the boys.

Soon after coming into town, as they always did, Duane and Gregg stopped by to visit with Ringo and Bill Cook at the Martinique. After the customary haggle, handshake, and hug, the date of March 30th was selected for an album release concert at the "Q." Duane and Gregg loved to play at the Martinique. It was their second home in Daytona and held very special memories for them. The acoustics in the Martinique were superb, as attested to by Lee Hazen, who, as part of his established recording technique, almost always used the Martinique as a studio to record the instrumental portions of his projects. All of Lee's band recordings during the early to late '60s were recorded first with only the instruments captured on tape on the Martinique stage in the quiet afternoons. The lead and background vocals were recorded at a later date in Lee's Cottage Studio. Lee told me that he felt that he got better results recording the bands in their normal, comfortable stage setting rather than scattered around in a studio helter-skelter. Lee always dreamed about buying that building and turning it into a huge recording studio, however, Miami and eventually North Nashville pulled Lee Hazen in different directions, and he left Daytona behind.

My band at the time had morphed into the Soul Patrol and was tapped to open for the Hour Glass on that Saturday night in March of '68. We were basically the house band at the Martinique, having played seventy-eight nights there in the past nine months, and we were poised to play another hundred and twenty or so nights before our departure from the Daytona music scene for college in mid-August of that year. However, we were called on to open for the Hour Glass for a quirky reason entirely that spring. We had borrowed three hundred dollars from Bill Cook to buy a strobe light for our lighting system, and we were paying him off by working three nights without pay. According to my guitarist Ralph Bundy's impeccable records, the date with the Hour Glass would be our last unpaid night as Bill Cook's indentured servants. Other bands wanted to play that night, but we got the call simply because we were free of charge. For the album-release show, each band would play two one-hour-long, alternating sets, with the Soul Patrol opening and the Hour Glass finishing out the night.

On the Saturday afternoon of the show, the two bands met at the Martinique to figure out how to situate all of the equipment on the stage without having to move things around too much between sets. As was his nature, Duane surveyed the situation and quickly hatched out a stage plan. Duane decided that we would mostly use the same setup, using the best equipment from each band. Because I am left-handed and couldn't use Johnny Sandlin's drum set without taking it apart, we situated both sets on the massive riser behind the main stage. Gregg and Paul Hornsby would supply the somewhat-portable modified Hammond organ and Leslie tone cabinet, along with their portable Wurlitzer electric piano, amplified by one of several Vox Super Beatle amplifiers they owned.

Duane would use his trusty Fender Dual Showman amp, and Ralph Bundy his Fender Twin Reverb. There were two guitar amplifiers onstage, and because Paul Hornsby played some guitar during songs like "Dimples," he asked to use Ralph's Twin Reverb and the slick Fender Stratocaster that Ralph had recently finished rebuilding. Pete Carr and Ross Yost decided to use Ross's big new Coral bass amp, with its six ten-inch speakers, simply because Pete liked its sound. Hour Glass was using an impressive-looking but quite muddy PA system that consisted of two Vox Super Beatle speaker boxes and a Super Beatle Head to power the system. Our vocalist, Carl Persis, donated his Echoplex reverb unit to the massive PA system, allowing the PA to be as muddy as it could possibly be. With that, the setup was complete. The equipment placement required no equipment movement at all between sets. The premium equipment setup simplified things onstage for everyone, and it was actually Duane's decision for us all to use the state-of-the-art mix of equipment that prompted me to record the evening's music.

My group consisted of three high school seniors, Ralph Bundy (guitar), Tim O'Brien (keyboards), and myself (drums), and two Daytona Beach Junior College students, Carl Persis (vocals) and Ross Yost (bass guitar). We had decided a while ago that our group would break up at the end of the summer of 1968 when the graduating seniors left the area for college. Musically, we were nearing our pinnacle, and using the Hour Glass's equipment would make us sound about as good as we ever would. So, that afternoon, after sound check, I decided to haul my father's General Electric-owned Wallensak T-1500 tape recorder to the gig, set it up on the bar near the waitress station, and record our band—and maybe, if there was enough tape left, I would record the Hour Glass too.

That evening, I showed up with a new date named Debbie, who definitely was not Phyllis, and I showed Debbie which button to push to start the tape moving across the recording heads. From behind my drum kit, just before our first set, I gave her the signal and she started the tape rolling. When we finished our set, she stopped the tape on cue, and when I thanked her for her services, I was delighted to see that the first side of the tape was less than half used. I thought that there would be more than enough to record the first Hour Glass set. Unfortunately, as I was to learn many years later in Danny Ramsey's studio, the reason I was getting so much recording time from the tape was because, unbeknownst to me, the recorder was set to record at half speed. A slower recording speed is all well and good for recording inconsequential lectures or speech recordings, but a slow recording speed is not the most effective approach to chronicling important music and vocals...another problem.

When Duane and Gregg's band took the stage, as was their custom from the early days, they said very little. Each musician looked as professional as possible while making minor adjustments to their individual instruments. Gregg slipped behind the massive Hammond organ that seemed to dwarf Paul Hornsby, who played the smaller portable Wurlitzer piano situated to the left of the Hammond at 90 degrees. Pete Carr plugged his Fender Precision bass into the waiting Coral amp, adjusting the tone and volume. Johnny Sandlin made final minor adjustments in drum placement and he was ready to rock and roll. Meanwhile, Duane had plugged his Fender Tele/Strat hybrid into his Dual Showman amp and he began to limber up his fingers. In those days, Duane played a custom Fender guitar that consisted of a Fender Esquire body fitted with a blond Stratocaster neck. Duane's hybrid guitar sported a Vox distortion booster strapped on the bottom of the body, below the knobs, and back just in front of the tailpiece. He could coax some amazing tones and sounds out of that setup, and though he occasionally had to replace a JBL speaker or two, his Fender Showman amp produced the punch that would send his notes straight through the waiting audience's bodies.

Duane's throwaway licks that night were enough to make any self-respecting guitar player hang his head in shame, and I am sure that they were intended to give the hometown crowd a taste of what was to come. I looked over at my guitarist, Ralph, and all he could do was stare with his mouth half open and shake his head in approval. Moments later, I looked over at Ralph again as Duane continued his warm-up with those amazing throwaway licks. I believe that was the first time that I had ever heard an expletive of that nature used to describe something indescribably beautiful, breathtaking, and astonishingly different other than in a sexual context. The way Ralph lamented that simple term seemed to stretch the simplest four-letter word into four syllables.

When the Hour Glass began their set, we were all awestruck by what we were hearing. We had not heard them play since the fall of 1967, and the growth of the band in eight or so months was astonishing. They opened the first set with three songs that I had never heard before. Those mystery songs would be recorded at Fame Studios only a few weeks later as demos and were ultimately released on the album *Duane Allman: An Anthology*: "Ain't No Good to Cry," "Neighbor, Neighbor," and "Gone Much Too Long." As they performed that March night at the "Q," the harmony vocal duet on "Gone Much Too Long" found Duane and Gregg seemingly pulling soulful blues from the old Cypress rafters above the dance floor. The next song they played was an in-the-pocket version of "I Don't Need No Doctor," which has become a Daytona classic. My younger brother, Bob, played the Hour Glass version of that song for thirty years, learning it off of an eight-track copy of this recording that I used to play in my car. Gregg's vocals on "I Don't Need No Doctor" stretch out in new bluesy directions, and the band displays the tonal dynamics that were to become The Allman Brothers' cash fund.

The next song, "To Things Before," is the fifth song, and, interestingly, it was the first selection from the *Power of Love* album. Duane announced it simply as "off of our second album." Here, Duane kicks into high gear and pulls notes seemingly out of heaven, where only the angels and recording engineers have been blessed enough to hear them before this night. It is interesting to note that even though they had just released the *Power of Love* album, the Hour Glass chose to play four songs that were not from that album that they considered better to lead off their show. Next came another song from the "new album," as Duane introduced "I Can Stand Alone." Here, Gregg's vocals and Duane's soaring guitar seem to collide in midair, entangle, and then explode somewhere in the dark recesses of the Martinique's ceiling. It seemed that the Allmans had developed the ability to propel their music into an incommensurable dimension—a new latitude that was at the same time both tonally exquisite and emotionally frightening.

The next song was groundbreaking from any standpoint. Paul Hornsby stood up from his normal place behind the portable piano and picked up Ralph's waiting Stratocaster guitar. After a quick cursory tuning, Duane and Paul played the first harmony guitar licks I can ever remember hearing in a musical piece. The Hour Glass's version of "Dimples" that night, with Duane on vocals, showcased what was to become The Allman Brothers Band's most widely recognized, distinguishing characteristic—those amazing, ephemeral twin-harmony guitars.

The music coming from the stage at the Martinique that night was heartrending, exciting, and infinitely different from anything that any of us had ever heard before. While from the earliest days the Allmans had treated us to something new and different on a regular basis, tonight's music was something else entirely. By this point, everyone in the room was sitting cross-legged on the dance floor in front of the band, with incense sticks burning, wondering what could possibly be next. "Dimples" was so significant and breathtaking that Duane probably felt he had better bring the audience back to reality, so they reached way back and played a wonderful Ray Charles version of Paul McCartney's "Yesterday." Only a group of confident, seasoned professionals such as the Hour Glass could pull off playing "Yesterday," and it was magnificent for both Gregg's vocal and the band's musical approach.

Next came the title song from the new album, the Eddie Hinton - penned "Power of Love," followed by another selection from the new album, "I Still Want Your Love." Again, Gregg's soulful vocals showed the promise of what was to come in the not-too-distant future. To end the set, Duane and Gregg reached back to the Allman Joys songbook and played one of Gregg's favorite Otis Redding songs, "Try a Little Tenderness." The set went longer than I had expected, and just as "Try a Little Tenderness" was about to end, after two Redding-style false endings, the tape ran out on the first side. Consequently, the last ten or fifteen seconds of "Try a Little Tenderness" is missing. Sorry, y'all, I'm a drummer, not a recording engineer!

Duane thanked the audience, announced that they would be back in an hour for their final set, and that the Soul Patrol would be back up for another set. While Duane was making his announcements, I turned the tape over and readied the tape machine for our next set. A few minutes later from up on the stage, I signaled my "recording engineer" to start the recorder again to capture our last hour, and we began our final, energy-charged set of the evening. When our set was complete, we nearly had to track down the Hour Glass. They were so busy in Bill Cook's office talking about their upcoming set and their set-list preparation that they didn't realize we had stopped playing, or maybe they had simply tuned us out. After a few minutes, the Hour Glass huddled up in Cook's office for a pep talk by Duane and Gregg, and then it was off to the stage. Duane carried the hastily written set list with him and slapped it down on top of brother Gregg's organ with a contagious cat-that-ate-the-canary smile. Duane knew that he had the perfect set list, and as fire flew from his fingertips, the show lifted off from the stage like the Apollo 13 spacecraft.

The entire tone and character of the second set was vastly different from the first one. Hell, it was different from anything I had ever heard before, and different from anything that anyone will ever hear again. The band had most certainly gone through a period of attitude adjustment while they were offstage, and whatever mood-altering substance they had imbibed paid dividends to the waiting audience. The congregation in the Martinique was treated to music on that perfect March night that has only played a handful of times to a live audience, anywhere. Most of the fans came that night for Budweiser, but what we were all treated to was a little taste of Heineken.

I was so spellbound by what I was seeing and hearing that I almost missed recording the very beginning of their first song. I told you I wasn't a recording engineer! The instrumental warm-up jam that they played to lead off their second set was the nucleus of what would become their stock-in- trade: jam-based noodling that Duane built from a spark into a wildfire. The full band warm-up jam featured mostly Duane and Paul Hornsby limbering up their fingers for the show ahead but also included mini-solos from Gregg, Pete, and Johnny Sandlin. From that opening selection, it was obvious that we were listening to a performance that was profoundly distinctive and incredibly powerful.

After the warm-up jam, they switched gears and played an old familiar Otis Redding composition from their Allman Joys songbook, "I Can't Turn You Loose," but this rendition was steeped in far more power and attitude than ever before. Duane and Gregg had apparently finally peered past the bend in their road, and they intended to drag us all along with them over this dusty, dirt-top country road that would eventually lead into an enormous musical breakthrough scarcely a year later.

Next up, they pulled another old Allman Joys favorite from their musical hat, "Keep on Trying." The vocals on "Keep on Trying" always captivated me because this is the only duet I ever recall hearing Duane and Gregg singing together. Duane's vocals answering Gregg's, along with Duane's authoritative guitar accents, make that song a classic in the deepest sense of the word. They then slipped into something a little bluesier with "I Wanna Know (Why You Treat Me So Bad)." Then, when they had the audience mellowed and relaxed in their seats, along came a few late-night surprises.

If anyone has ever argued about who brought "Nobody Knows You When You're Down and Out" to the Layla sessions, this version, with Duane wailing on guitar and the band climbing up and down the scale to the finale, should settle the argument once and for all! This 1968 Hour Glass arrangement is identical to Clapton's iconic 1970 version on the Layla album, and the guitar licks are all Duane Allman, pure and simple. Duane brought it to Clapton, and not vice-versa. Next came a cover so exceptionally different that it is hard for anyone but the most avid Duane

Allman fan to explain. Neither Johnny Sandlin, Paul Hornsby, nor Pete Carr remembered playing this song, thirty-five years later, when I first played it for them in Sandlin's Duck Tape Studio in Decatur, Alabama, in 2006.

Pull out your old vinyl album collection and listen to the original version of Dionne Warwick's "Anyone Who Had a Heart." Listen closely to the saxophone solo, and then listen to Duane's guitar solo on the Hour Glass version contained here. It becomes immediately obvious that, as friend and Maryland art and music critic Alex Lynn would tell you, "Duane Allman was profoundly influenced by horns...and saxophone in particular." Duane's Vox Distortion booster and his Telecaster/Stratocaster hybrid emulates the original baritone saxophone solo on Warwick's recording faithfully. I've listened to this recording over the years, and this one song has always haunted me; I don't even need to play it to hear Gregg's vocals and Duane's tasteful guitar work today. "Anyone Who Had a Heart" was my first concrete indication, while I was still just a teenager, that Duane Allman was indeed a profoundly multifaceted and intensely complex multidimensional musician.

The next segment of the show was anchored by the medley that would be recorded just a few weeks later at Rick Hall's FAME Music Studio, and which would ultimately cause the Hour Glass to tell Liberty Records to "go take a hike." The "B. B. King Medley," while only played to a live audience a few times, was the direction that Duane and Gregg sought to steer their ship. The shortsighted powers that be at Liberty Records would ultimately reject the Muscle Shoals demos as "not interesting enough." Consequently, just a few short weeks later, the Hour Glass, one of the most interesting Southern groups of the late 1960s, would disband, and its members would go their own way on the same one-way street. During that music-charged night in late March 1968, Duane, Gregg, Pete, Paul, and Johnny kicked the roof off of the Martinique with such a down-home bluesy rendition of the "B. B. King Medley" that I have talked about hearing that song on that night to other musicians for fifty-four years.

The next song was one that they reached the deepest into their musical bag of tricks to find. Bobby Blue Bland's "Love Light" was a rousing staple from the Escorts days that followed Gregg all the way to *The Gregg Allman Tour* album and beyond. On this balmy spring night in March of 1968, Duane and his brother were proudly showing off their new material and their new direction, but they also knew that many of their old fans were in the club, and those fans came to hear something familiar as well. The seminal Hour Glass/Allman Joys/Escorts devotees in the audience who had followed the brothers to the Martinique that night had been on the bus since 1963, and most would follow until today. So, this night they played some of their old familiar material, not for themselves, but for the loyal fans who had done much to propel them into the future. Even those older standards, while familiar, were played with dangerous new arrangements and interesting, powerful new twists.

The final selection of the night, "Dimples," began as a faint echo from the first set, but the second time around, this piece was played differently, with a threatening new titillation and an ominous, almost perilous foreshadowing of what was ahead, just around Duane's bend in the road. It was the musical magma that would ultimately lead to the eruption of The Allman Brothers Band onto the international music scene. Again, Paul strapped on Ralph's Strat and again he stood next to Duane and played "Dimples" with its trademark harmony-guitar licks. This time, when the song ended, it was a taunt, another false ending right out of Otis Redding's soulful bag of tricks. It was here that Duane sealed the entire Martinique and its occupants into his personal time capsule and transported us all forward a year into the future for a glimpse of what he and Gregg had in mind for the future of Southern American music.

In that short year and beyond, Duane would make his mark forever on the music industry by playing on countless studio tracks in Muscle Shoals, leaving his legacy on hundreds of recordings and musical genres. Also in that short year, The Allman Brothers Band would form from the ashes of the Hour Glass, from which several other top-notch Southern bands would form. The remaining members of the Hour Glass band would go on to individually influence the very framework of Southern music well into the next century.

We were all treated that night in late March of 1968 to a visual and aural sampling of a musical/jam genre that would ultimately become The Allman Brothers Band's stock in trade. Fans who never listened to the Hour Glass live but listen to their studio recordings and to those of The Allman Brothers Band would often ask me, "How did the Hour Glass band ever became The Allman Brothers Band?" The answer to that question has never been found in the studio recordings of either band. The bridge between the two groups is undeniably found in the live versions of each band. The excitement, fire, and agonizingly tender soulfulness that would ultimately become The Allman Brothers Band is here in these live recordings for anyone to hear.

So, sit cross-legged on the floor in front of your stereo speakers on a comfortable cushion, turn the volume up, turn down the lights, and repose into tranquility with your closest, like-minded friends. Then prepare to let the past wash over you on its way to the future in comfortable surroundings. Imagine that you have been whisked away to a nightclub full of kindred spirits where black lights, strobe lights, patchouli oil, and incense pave the way for the music that follows. Take in the sights, smells, tenor, and dynamics of Main Street and the music that blanketed us on that night in 1968. Enjoy this priceless slice of rock and roll history that I have faithfully guarded for all these many years. Those clustered around you on the dance floor in front of the stage, elbow-to-elbow at the Martinique, shared a rare experience that March night. Now, join us as we follow the Hour Glass into the future of Southern music.

Epilogue

To spend time deep within the world of music, taking deliberate note of its complex gifts, is to acknowledge our place in that intricate and multidimensional system of life, notes, and universe. Howard Duane Allman vanished into the vastness of that system, and in doing so he became a fundamental component of it. Duane speaks to me when I walk into a concert and hear a talented guitarist testing his instrument or when I turn my car's ignition key and my favorite music magically bursts from my speakers, mysteriously beamed from outer space. So much of what has become part of me can be traced directly back to Duane Allman and the complex system of musicians and friends that included him, Gregg, Ringo, Pete, Paul, Johnny, Carl, Ralph, Kip, Scott, Mike, Ross, Tim, and so many others who have become part of my life circle. It is impossible to imagine that all of what this universe has laid at my feet can possibly be the end result of happenstance.

A deep sense of enduring gratitude exists in most of my old bandmates. This feeling of awe is commonplace in most of the musicians I knew from that time period who came of age in Central Florida...but especially those who came of age in Daytona Beach. I know that I will pass from this earth as unremarked as my footprints in the sand at low tide, and I am without regret, because there will be children who love this microcosm of music as I do, and they will carry these stories and notes with them forever...until it is time for them to sweep out the ashes.

Index

MUSIC AND THE AMERICAN SOUTH

TITLES IN THE SERIES

Jack† and Olivia Solomon†, *Honey in the Rock: The Ruby Pickens Tartt Collection of Religious Folk Songs from Sumter County, Alabama*

Zell Miller,† *They Heard Georgia Singing*

David Fillingim,† *Redneck Liberation: Country Music as Theology*

Willie Perkins, *No Saints, No Saviors: My Years with the Allman Brothers Band*

Anathalee G. Sandlin, *A Never-Ending Groove: Johnny Sandlin's Musical Odyssey*

Michael P. Graves and David Fillingim,† ed. *More Than Precious Memories: The Rhetoric of Southern Gospel Music*

Michael Buffalo Smith,† *Prisoner of Southern Rock: A Memoir*, with a Foreword by Billy Bob Thornton

Michael Buffalo Smith,† *Rebel Yell: An Oral History of Southern Rock*, with a Foreword by Alan Walden

Willie Perkins and Jack Weston, *The Allman Brothers Band Classic Memorabilia, 1969-1976*, with a Foreword by Galadrielle Allman

Michael Buffalo Smith,† *Capricorn Rising: Conversations in Southern Rock*, with a Foreword by Willie Perkins

Michael Buffalo Smith,† *From Macon to Jacksonville: More Conversations in Southern Rock*, with a Foreword by Charlie Starr

Michael Buffalo Smith,† *The Road Goes on Forever: Fifty Years of The Allman Brothers Band Music (1969–2019)*, with a Foreword Chuck Leavell

Doug Kershaw, *The Ragin' Cajun: Memoir of a Louisiana Man*, with Cathie Pelletier

Don Reid, *The Music of The Statler Brothers: An Anthology*, with a Foreword by Bill and Gloria Gaither

Paul Hornsby, *Fix it in the Mix: A Memoir*, with Michael Buffalo Smith†

Ben Wynne, *Something in the Water: A History of Music in Macon, Georgia, 1823-1980*

Willie Perkins, *Diary of a Rock-N-Roll Tour Manager: 2,190 Days and Nights with the South's Premier Rock Band*

Bill Thames, *Paper, Scissors, Rock-N-Roll: Ringo, Duane, & Me*